To Charron

Teach us, Forever Dead, there is no
Dream but Deed, there is no Deed but Memory.

The Autobiography of
W.E.B. Du Bois (1968)

Contents

Preface

The thesis of this book, simply put, is this: the import of the autobiographies of black people during the first century of the genre's existence in the United States is that they "tell a free story" as well as talk about freedom as a theme and goal of life. The history of Afro-American autobiography is one of increasingly free storytelling, signaled in the ways black narratives address their readers and reconstruct personal history, ways often at variance with literary conventions and social proprieties of discourse. Afro-American autobiography between 1760 and 1865 does not just record the process by which its protagonists became free of sin or slavery. During the evolution of this tradition, autobiographers demonstrate through a variety of rhetorical means that they regard the *writing* of autobiography as in some ways uniquely self-liberating, the final, climactic act in the drama of their lifelong quests for freedom. Such narratives provide important insights into the kinds of freedom their writers hoped to enact for themselves through their literary efforts. Given the uncertain status of Negroes, especially fugitive slaves, in the so-called free states of the antebellum United States, the definition of freedom for black people remained open. Autobiography became a very public way of declaring oneself free, of redefining freedom and then assigning it to oneself in defiance of one's bonds to the past or to the social, political, and sometimes even the moral exigencies of the present. This book does not contend, of course, that all early Afro-American autobiography tells its story in an equally free manner, only that free telling was the vital principle that pushed this tradition past its fetters and obstacles toward a perceptible literary emancipation by the middle of the nineteenth century. The problems of writing such autobiographical declarations of freedom and the meaning of success for narrative works with priorities such as these are the twin preoccupations of this book.

Many colleagues have helped me think through problems that the first century of Afro-American autobiography presents. I thank Jeffrey Steele for timely suggestions on theoretical avenues that needed to be explored and for reading two chapters of this book in manuscript. Susan Stanford Friedman and Elizabeth Hirsh gave me good advice on feminist literary criticism when I approached the question of interpreting *Incidents in the Life of a Slave Girl*. James Olney, Robert Stepto, and Henry Louis Gates, Jr., read this book in manuscript and gave me the kind of encouraging, knowledgeable audience that every scholar-critic wants and needs. Their advice has been most helpful. Nellie McKay's support has been sustaining and valuable to me, as always. I should also like to thank the professor who first introduced me to the subject of Afro-American autobiography some fifteen years ago, Blyden Jackson. Most of all, I am greatly obliged to my friend and colleague, Jay Clayton, for having invested so much of his time as a painstaking reader of draft after draft of this book, an incisive analyst of my thinking and writing, a wise and diplomatic critic, and a constant stimulant to my creativity (such as it is) in this book. Without his unflagging contribution, early on, to the process by which this book has taken shape, *To Tell a Free Story* would still be bound, I suspect, to many of the deficiencies of conception and execution that he saw in its first draft. Those deficiencies that remain are attributable to my short-sightedness alone.

I should also like to thank Helen McNutt of the Mifflin County, Pennsylvania, Historical Society, Krystine Dugas, Calvin Roso, and Michael Scherf for their aid in the bibliographical research for this book. The staff of the office of Interlibrary Loans at the Memorial Library of the University of Wisconsin has been unfailingly ingenious and patient in locating and retrieving rare books for my research. Betty M. Culpepper of the Moorland-Spingarn Research Center at Howard University has also been generous in her aid to my research. Kathy Dauck's considerable skills at the word processor, along with her sense of humor, have been a source of wonder and gratitude to me.

Preliminary research for this book began under a grant from the National Endowment for the Humanities. As a fellow of the Institute for Research in the Humanities at the University of Wisconsin–Madison, I continued my work. I am grateful to the Graduate School of the University of Wisconsin–Madison for salary support during two summers of research and writing on this book.

A preliminary version of Chapter 1 of this book was published as "The First Century of Afro-American Autobiography: Theory and Explication," in Joe Weixlmann and Chester J. Fontenot, eds., *Black American Prose Theory*, vol. 1 of *Studies in Black American Literature* (Greenwood, Fla.: Penkevill, 1984), pp. 4–42. Portions of Chapter 2 first appeared in "The First Fifty Years of the Slave Narrative, 1760–1810," in John Sekora and Darwin T. Turner, eds., *The Art of Slave Narrative* (Macomb: Western Illinois University Press, 1982), pp. 6–24.

Finally, I thank my wife Charron, who in some ways has always understood better than I have what this book is all about.

A widespread antislavery emblem, this design is taken from the seal of the English Committee for Affecting the Abolishment of the Slave Trade, first engraved in 1787. (Schomburg Center for Research in Black Culture, The New York Public Library, Astor, Lenox and Tilden Foundations)

1

The First Century of Afro-American Autobiography: Notes toward a Definition of a Genre

Whatever else it is, autobiography stems more often than not from a need to explain and justify the self. In his seminal article on "conditions and limits of autobiography," Georges Gusdorf says, "It is precisely in order to do away with misunderstandings, to restore an incomplete or deformed truth, that the autobiographer himself takes up the telling of his story." After all, "no one can better do justice to himself than the interested party." [1] It took "the interested party" of Afro-American autobiography almost fifty years after the initial appearance of the genre in 1760 to begin to prove that no one could do justice to himself better than himself. From these beginnings to the "year of Jubilo" in 1865 when full emancipation was proclaimed, black American autobiography evolved into a complex "oratorical" mode best exemplified in the narratives of ex-slaves who had become master rhetoricians on the antislavery lecture circuit. [2]

In the first 100 years of its existence, Afro-American autobiography was a genre chiefly distinguished by its rhetorical aims. During the first half of this century of evolution, most Afro-American autobiography addressed itself, directly or indirectly, to the proof of two propositions: (1) that the slave was, as the inscription of a famous antislavery medallion put it, "a man and a brother" to whites, especially to the white reader of slave narratives; and (2) that the black narrator was, despite all prejudice and propaganda, a truth-teller, a reliable transcriber of the experience and character of black folk. During the latter half of this century of evolution, the crucial themes of identity and veracity underwent much revision. Instead of defining the self according to traditional cultural models, greater and greater attention came to rest on those aspects of the self outside the margins of the normal, the acceptable, and the definable,

1

as conceived by the predominant culture. Selfhood became identified increasingly with individuality. Prevailing norms for judging propriety in behavior, speech, and writing came to be judged according to the personal standards of some narrative "other." This other was a good deal less solicitous of the white reader's empathy and trust than earlier black autobiographical personae had been. Instead of appealing to the reader's moral values and literary expectations, this other tried to alienate the reader from these kinds of supports, thus disorienting but also freeing him or her to participate in a new kind of social and psychological agenda for the reading of black autobiography. By the end of the first century of Afro-American autobiography, the genre had become the scene of a complex discursive encounter presided over by a self-determining narrator who makes free with text and reader in the name of truth *to* self, a standard that left both identity and veracity problematically intermeshed in their own mutual relativity.

Henry David Thoreau began his account of his experience at Walden Pond by declaring, "I, on my side, require of every writer, first or last, a simple and sincere account of his own life."[3] Thoreau did not bother to explain how one might prove one's sincerity. No doubt Thoreau would not have seen this as a problem, for white autobiographers could assume their readership would grant them the status of peer and would assume their sincerity unless they contradicted themselves or transgressed important moral norms in their narration. Because these conditions—the relationship of peers between autobiographer and audience and the assumption of trustworthiness between peers—existed as a matter of course in the white American autobiographical tradition, the white autobiographer's letter to the world has always had a social, cultural, and linguistic sanction, though not always success. When black autobiographers addressed the white world, however, they could assume no such sanction for their self-affirming literary acts. Many undoubtedly realized that they would have to defend or explain away the same literary egoism that in a white autobiographer might be praised as American pride and self-reliance at its best.[4] Knowing that they could not assume an equal relationship with the average white American reader, blacks set about writing life stories that would somehow prove that they qualified as the moral, spiritual, or intellectual peers of whites. White America was willing to suspend disbelief and assume the sincerity of an autobiographer whom it identified as a political peer and a racial equal. However, the knowledge that they could not predicate their life stories on this racially based trust forced black autobiographers to invent devices and strategies that would endow their stories with the appearance of authenticity. This was perhaps the greatest challenge to the imagination of the Afro-

American autobiographer. The reception of his narrative as truth depended on the degree to which his artfulness could hide his art.

As a class, no group of American autobiographers has been received with more skepticism and resistance than the ex-slave. Before the rise of the abolition movement, free blacks in the North as well as enslaved blacks in the South were seen as an alien population recognizably "depraved," "vicious," and, for the most part, incorrigible. Abolitionist defenders of the Negro would not deny that the ex-slave had been morally "degraded" by slavery; they insisted, nevertheless, that he could be elevated from his "inferior" condition.[5] But how could readers of slave narratives be assured that this moral rehabilitation had been completed, especially when a leader in the American Anti-Slavery Society warned the public about the fugitive slave in the North: "Simple-hearted and truthful, as these fugitives appeared to be, you must recollect that they are slaves —and that the slave, as a general thing, is a liar, as well as a drunkard and a thief."[6] Of course, there were those in the abolitionist movement who put the matter in a much more sympathetic and potentially clarifying light. As Samuel G. Howe, an interviewer of runaways in Canada observed: "The negro, like other men, naturally desires to live in the light of truth; but he hides in the shadow of falsehood, more or less deeply, according as his safety or welfare seems to require it. Other things being equal, the freer a people, the more truthful; and only the perfectly free and fearless are perfectly truthful."[7]

In this observation Howe tried to suggest that absolute "perfect" truth, a concept dear to evangelical abolitionism and nineteenth-century America in general, could not be used to measure the value of Afro-American autobiography since the demands of truthfulness and self-preservation were often at odds in the experience of blacks in America. Yet Howe was himself a prisoner of the semantic dichotomies of nineteenth-century moralizing; he could think of no label other than "falsehood" to apply to the words of a black narrator who could not see his way clear to "live in the light of truth." Today our sensitivity to the relativistic truth value of all autobiography and to the peculiar symbiosis of imperfect freedom and imperfect truth in the American autobiographical tradition makes it easier for us to regard the fictive elements of black autobiography as aspects of rhetorical and aesthetic strategy, not evidence of moral failure. To study early Afro-American autobiography in this context, rather than in the unrevealing light of nineteenth-century moral and epistemological categories, is one goal of this book.

Today every historian and analyst of the Afro-American autobiographical enterprise is faced with the problem of what Houston A. Baker has termed "the anthropology of art," the unearthing (or reconstruction) of the full context in which a genre originated, evolved, and took on cultural significance.[8] In the case of eighteenth- and nineteenth-century black American autobiography, this problem is compounded because of the unprecedented and largely unparalleled situation of black self-writers and their white audience. Nevertheless, there does exist a partial and instructive analogy to the way the Afro-American autobiographer negotiated with his skeptical, if not hostile white audience. Consider John Henry Newman's relationship to his British audience prior to the creation of the *Apologia Pro Vita Sua* (1864). Having left the Anglican clergy to become a Roman Catholic priest, Newman found himself under attack in 1864 for having preached, in the words of his accuser, Charles Kingsley, that "truth, for its own sake, had never been a virtue with the Roman clergy," that "it need not, and on the whole ought not to be."[9] A year later Newman published a pamphlet in which he reconstructed the process by which he decided to answer his attacker, via autobiography, rather than by some other mode of rhetorical defense.[10]

The priest knew there were many obstacles in the way of his being favorably heard. By virtue of his Catholicism he was regarded as "a member of a most un-English communion," an alien and a subversive "whose great aim is considered to be the extinction of Protestantism and the Protestant Church." In pursuit of this mission, a priest's chief weapons were "supposed to be unscrupulous cunning and deceit." The principal charge Kingsley had brought against him was plain and direct, Newman stated: "He called me a liar." Yet "how am I now to be trusted?" Newman wondered, when his greatest foe was not the arguments of Kingsley but "the bias of the court," the court of British public opinion. Newman's analysis of his position in the eyes of this biased court provides an insight into the problems that faced the Afro-American alien, the presumed subversive and guileful deceiver, when he attempted to prove that he was not a liar before the white American court of public opinion. Newman felt that it was "the state of the atmosphere" as much as any of Kingsley's charges that weighed so heavily against him. "It is that prepossession against me, which takes for granted that, when my reasoning is convincing it is only ingenious, and that when my statements are unanswerable, there is always something put out of sight or hidden in my sleeve; it is that plausible, but cruel conclusion to which men are so apt to jump, that when much is imputed, something must be true, and that it is more likely that one should be to blame, than that many should be mistaken in blaming him;—these are the real foes which I have to fight."

To "break through this barrier of prejudice against me," Newman decided that merely arguing Kingsley's charges would have little effect, no matter how well the arguments were made. "What I needed was a corre-

sponding antagonist unity in my defence," the beleaguered priest concluded. "I must, I said, give the true key to my whole life; I must show
what I am, that it may be seen what I am not, and that the phantom may
be extinguished which gibbers instead of me. I wish to be known as a
living man, and not as a scarecrow which is dressed up in my clothes."
Though he would answer the specific charges of Kingsley against his veracity and integrity, "such a work shall not be the scope nor the substance
of my reply." Instead, his greater theme would be to "draw out, as far as
may be, the history of my mind." A similar strategy incorporating the
same fundamental theme informs the major Afro-American autobiographies of the antebellum era.

For the Afro-American and his white sponsors, autobiography answered a felt need for a rhetorical mode that would conduct the battle
against racism and slavery on grounds other than those already occupied
by pro- and antislavery polemics. "Argument provokes argument," the
editor of the Boston *Chronotype* concluded about the abolitionist controversy in the 1840s; "reason is met by sophistry; but narratives of slaves
go right to the hearts of men."[11] Reaching "the hearts of men" was the
rhetorical aim of practically all black autobiography in the first century of
its existence, whether produced by an ex-slave or not. Afro-American literature of the late eighteenth and early nineteenth centuries is dominated by treatises, pamphlets, addresses, and appeals, all of which employ
expostulatory means to confront the problem of the black situation in
white America. Yet only black autobiography had a mass impact on the
conscience of antebellum Americans. Did early black narrators realize as
clearly as Newman did that this form of witnessing before a skeptical
public would earn more converts to the cause than any other mode of
address? Certainly experienced abolitionists recognized that first-person
narration, with its promise of intimate glimpses into the mind and heart
of a runaway slave, would be much more compelling to the uncommitted
mass of readers than the oratory and polemics of the antislavery press.[12]
Unlike Newman, however, early black autobiographers left behind very
little explicit comment about the strategies and intentions of their narratives. We are left to infer from their autobiographies how much and in
what ways these alien and suspect figures felt they had to prove themselves men instead of phantoms before anything else they said could be
received credibly.

Most slave narrators knew that the public did not read their stories primarily to find out what sorts of men these blacks were. Nineteenth-
century whites read slave narratives more to get a firsthand look at the
institution of slavery than to become acquainted with an individual slave.
Many ex-slaves were quite willing to accede to this expectation, espe-

cially when told by their abolitionist sponsors that their skeptical public would believe nothing but documentable facts in a slave narrative. From the standpoint of the advancement of the cause, abolitionists naturally felt that the most useful black autobiographies would be ones that forced the ugly facts of "the peculiar institution" to the forefront of a reader's attention and kept them there throughout the story. Moreover, American aesthetic standards of the time made a black narrative that exposed the institutional facts of slavery preferable to one that expressed the subjective views of an individual slave. As Ralph Waldo Emerson had written of all first-person writing in 1840, such literature could be judged according to "whether it leads us to nature, or to the person of the writer. The great always introduce us to facts; small men introduce us always to themselves." [13] Thus the most trustworthy of all slave narrators would be the one who effaced himself behind the universally applicable facts of slavery. The most reliable slave narrative would be one that seemed purely mimetic, in which the self is on the periphery instead of at the center of attention, looking outside not within, transcribing rather than interpreting a set of objective facts.

Obviously to follow this agenda was to alienate oneself from one's past and to banish oneself in the most fundamental ways from one's own autobiography. Yet speaking too revealingly of the individual self, particularly if this did not correspond to white notions of the facts of black experience or the nature of the Negro, risked alienating white sponsors and readers, too. Characteristically, the most significant black autobiographers refused this no-win choice between two alienating alternatives. Instead of either conforming to the rules of the literary game or refusing to play, they set about changing the rules by which the game was played even as they played along with it. White American readers believed that truth about slavery could be revealed through an objective recital of facts from an eyewitness, first-person narrator. Slave narratives often illustrate the contradictoriness of this objectivity based in subjectivity. Black narrators' prefaces and public pronouncements generally abide by the proposition that objective facts can be distinguished from subjective perception. However, their actual life stories frequently dispute, sometimes directly but more often covertly, the positivistic epistemology, dualistic morality, and diachronic framework in which antebellum America liked to evaluate autobiography as either history or falsehood. In this way, black autobiographers made their books something like Newman's "antagonist unity." They were antagonist works in two senses: (1) they functioned as ripostes against racist charges against black selfhood, and (2) they resisted the fragmenting nature of objective autobiography, which demanded that a black narrator achieve credence by objectifying himself and passivizing his voice.

The unity of black autobiography in the antebellum era is most apparent in the pervasive use of journey or quest motifs that symbolize multiple layers of spiritual evolution. In black spiritual autobiography the protagonist wishes to escape sinfulness and ignorance in order to achieve righteousness and a knowledge of the saving grace of God. In the slave narrative the quest is toward freedom from physical bondage and the enlightenment that literacy can offer to the restricted self- and social consciousness of the slave. Both the fugitive slave narrator and the black spiritual autobiographer trace their freedom back to an awakening of their awareness of their fundamental identity with and rightful participation in *logos*, whether understood as reason and its expression in speech or as divine spirit. The climax of the quests of both kinds of autobiographer usually comes when they seize the opportunity to proclaim what are clearly complementary gospels of freedom. Before the fugitive slave narrator could have success in restoring political and economic freedom to Afro-Americans, the black spiritual autobiographer had to lay the necessary intellectual groundwork by proving that black people were as much chosen by God for eternal salvation as whites. Without the black spiritual autobiography's reclamation of the Afro-American's spiritual birthright, the fugitive slave narrative could not have made such a cogent case for black civil rights in the crisis years between 1830 and 1865.

In a number of important black autobiographies of this era, however, a quest more psycholiterary than spiritual can be discerned. It is spurred by many motives, perhaps the most important of which is the need of an other to *declare* himself through various linguistic acts, thereby reifying his abstract unreality, his invisibility in the eyes of his readers, so that he can be recognized as someone to be reckoned with. Such declarative acts, as we shall see, include the reconstructing of one's past in a meaningful and instructive form, the appropriating of empowering myths and models of the self from any available resource, and the redefining of one's place in the scheme of things by redefining the language used to locate one in that scheme.

Reconstructing their past lives required many ex-slaves to undergo a disquieting psychic immersion into their former selves as slaves. During this journey backward and within, a freeperson was forced to relive the most psychically charged moments of his or her past and to be reminded of thoughts and deeds about which he or she had come to feel very ambivalent. Many male fugitives could not recall with pride their lonely

7

flight to Canada without acknowledging the residual guilt they felt about leaving their wives and children behind. The aggressive, self-regarding survival ethic that slaves and fugitives often had to live by did not harmonize easily with the image of rectitude and decorum that free blacks in the North needed to project to gain white sympathy. Some slave narrators, perhaps more politic than apologetic, professed conscientious regret for the violence, duplicity, and lack of Christian fortitude to which they fell prey during their time in slavery. Others—like Josiah Henson, lionized as the prototype for Harriet Beecher Stowe's Uncle Tom—who claimed to have fought the good fight against slavery's temptations had their earthly rewards in sizable sales of their narratives. A few ex-slaves, however, in seeming ignorance or defiance of the rhetorical risk, made much of their despair and unassuaged outrage, their transgressions of Christian morality, and their unheroic behavior. Nor did these narrators always apologize for these breaches or use them as pretexts for grand reversals of character at climactic moments in their lives. Ex-slaves who do not hide or apologize for the lingering evidence of the psychopathology of oppression in their writing present important problems for interpretations of the slave narrative as simply a mode of antislavery propaganda on the one hand or a means of self-advertisement for ambitious former bondmen on the other. When we find a gap in a slave narrator's objective reportage of the facts of slavery, or a lapse in his prepossessing self-image, we must pay special attention. These deviations may indicate either a momentary loss of narrative control or a deliberate effort by the narrator to grapple with aspects of his or her personality that have been repressed out of deference to or fear of the dominant culture.

One way of talking about these presumably inferior or negatively defined aspects of the personality is to use the Jungian term *the shadow*. Just as Jung believed that an understanding of "the dark side of the personality" was essential to full self-knowledge, so in the hands of major black autobiographers, the acknowledgment of the shadow within the self, not as projected in others (particularly women in the case of male autobiographers), constitutes a major step in the direction of self-declaration. Like spiritual autobiographers, slave narrators often incorporate into their stories some "dark night of the soul" when helplessness in the face of evil tempts them to despair, bitterness toward God, or rebellion against man. In conventional narratives this bleak night passes with the conquest of the "dark side" of the self by the ego, representing the narrator's better self, which insists on faith, patience, self-control, and, in general, repression of unconscious needs and fears. Some narratives, however, sound a different note by recording a continual upsurge of the shadow as the autobiographer, caught up in the creative retrieval of the past, no longer responds as readily to the mechanisms of repression. The danger for these black self-explorers is succumbing to the racist myth that the dark self within is the essence of their primitive, anarchic "black self" which must be subjugated by the ego, spokesman for the collective (white) consciousness, before they can become truly free. The triumph of these autobiographers comes when they see the shadow as both an index to the guilt and fears that white culture projected into black people and as an indicator of unconscious resources available to blacks who had learned to view them in an empowering light. When the unconscious finds vehicles of expression and engages the conscious mind in creative interaction, black autobiography begins to redefine freedom as the power to integrate the unknown and the known within the self, not just the black into the white in the broader social context.[14]

Writing autobiography involved Afro-Americans of the late eighteenth and early nineteenth centuries in yet another kind of journey, a search for language through which the unknown within the self and the unspeakable within slavery might be expressed. Many narratives reveal this to have been a frustrating, even anguishing mental and emotional struggle. Rare was the autobiographer who did not apologize for his lack of facility with words and his inability to portray what he experienced in or how he felt about slavery. Other blacks lamented the inadequacy of language itself to represent the horrors of slavery or the depth of their feelings as they reflected on their suffering. In some cases black narrators doubted their white readers' ability to translate the words necessary to a full rendering of their experience and feelings. On other occasions narrators questioned whether whites even wanted a thorough account of the truth of slavery. In the aggregate, these statements indicate that in their attempt to build a community of understanding between whites and blacks, Afro-American autobiographers were sensitive to the weaknesses of each link in the communication chain, from the writer through the linguistic medium to the audience.

Many narrators who said they were unequal to the task that writing put before them became eloquent in the admission of their supposed literary ineptitude. Their modest prefaces and apologies for their poverty of expression were a traditional rhetorical ploy, looking back to ancient judicial oratory in which such self-effacing talk was intended to dispose judges favorably.[15] The black autobiographer was similarly on trial and thus proposed, as a rule, to concentrate his supposedly feeble literary skills on a plain marshalling of the facts of his or her life. The promise of a straightforward rendition of facts allowed the black narrator to pose as an artless and unaffected person whose simple narrative manner bore the conviction of truth that white Protestants in America had traditionally invested in the plain style. Nevertheless, even the most natural of narratives can and ought to be analyzed for its rhetorical art, whether acknowledged or not. The structuring of one's experience in story form requires that one judge certain facts of one's life to be reportable, that is, significant beyond their merely factual content, worthy of display in a pattern that inevitably invites the reader's contemplation as well as his belief or disbelief. Even in the least apparently sophisticated first-person narratives, sociolinguists point out, there is enough "embedded evaluation" in various lexical, semantic, and syntactic features of the narrative to indicate the bases on which its narrator judged its reportability. If we can learn to find these evaluators in even the barest recitations of biographical facts, we should be able to speak more appreciatively of the coding mechanisms and the art of the supposedly nonliterary black autobiographer.[16]

As early as 1790, the black preacher John Marrant lamented in his *Journal* the failure of his "stammering tongue" and of language itself to signify his experience of divine love: "O where shall we find language sufficient to celebrate his praises?" In his *Narrative* of 1849, the fugitive Henry Bibb echoed Marrant on the inadequacy of language, although by this time the unspeakable hellishness of slavery, not the ineffable bliss of salvation, had become the text of most black autobiography. "Reader," Bibb wrote, "believe me when I say, that no tongue, nor pen ever has or can express the horrors of American slavery. Consequently I despair in finding language to express adequately the deep feelings of my soul, as I contemplate the past history of my life." The despair of autobiographers like Bibb manifests itself in literary silences similar to those that Tillie Olsen ascribes to an "unnatural thwarting of what struggles to come into being, but cannot."[17] A similar sense of frustration may have led other narrators to translate the pattern of their lives into the myths and images of the predominant culture's traditions, while silently omitting from consideration those elements of their experience that did not fit. However, as black autobiography developed into the nineteenth century, some narrators set out on intellectual quests for tropes through which they could embody in most provocative ways the previously unreportable in collective Afro-American experience.

What could not be reported explicitly in Afro-American experience had to be explored indirectly through metaphor. As Afro-American autobiography evolved, the institution of slavery and the individuality of the slave received increasingly metaphoric treatment as slave narrators realized the necessity of metaphor to their rhetorical mission. Black autobiography was as much a metaphor-making argument as poetry was, in Emerson's view, an argument metrically made. Current theorists of metaphor like Paul Ricoeur and Monroe Beardsley say that a metaphor is made when a word undergoes a turn or "twist" in its literal meaning occasioned by some sort of "semantic clash" between itself as the "principal subject" of a statement or expression and another word attributed to it as its "modifier." True metaphors reveal new and infinitely paraphraseable meanings of words in unexpected contexts, by introducing a tension, a "logical absurdity" in Beardsley's terms, between the significations of the "principal subject"—what we have come to call the "tenor" of the metaphor—and its "modifier," or again, more familiarly, its "vehicle." When we encounter an expression that generates a semantic clash between subject and modifier, we have the choice of either holding to the familiar significations of the subject and modifier, in which case we will simply dismiss the expression as absurd, or we may jump over the evident contradictoriness of the modifier as attributed to the subject and construe the modifier indirectly as significant because it contradicts our presuppositions about what may be attributed to the subject. When the reader discovers what connotations in the modifier enable it to be construed as a significant attribution of the subject, he also discovers some of the ways in which his presuppositions about the subject were limited. Ideally, then, metaphors do not simply adorn arguments for persuasive purposes. Metaphors *are* arguments. Their success depends greatly on the capacity of the reader to accept and explore the creative dialectic of the semantic clash until new meanings emerge from the debris of old presuppositions.[18]

There is little challenge to the reader's capacity for intellectual exploration in the "metaphors of self," to use James Olney's phrase, of very early black autobiography.[19] The central metaphor of the black spiritual autobiographer of the late eighteenth and early nineteenth centuries might be summarized as: "I am as Mr. Christian [in *Pilgrim's Progress*] was, a spiritual pilgrim in an unredeemed world." In this case we have what Ricoeur calls a metaphor of "simple substitution"; the modifier, Mr. Christian, may be easily substituted for the principal subject of the statement, the black narrator, by simply ignoring the superficial difference of skin color that separates subject and modifier. There is a spiritual identity between Mr. Christian and the narrator as pilgrims that makes it possible to accept the one as an attribute of the other without challenging our presuppositions about either. The metaphorical twist here functions as it does in allegory where apparent contradictions are reconciled once they are reviewed in an abstract or ideal perspective.

Consider, however, the basic metaphor of a later black spiritual autobiography, *The Confessions of Nat Turner* (1831). As far as the slave insurrectionist was concerned, the metaphor of his life seemed to be: "I am as Christ was, a Messiah in an apocalyptic world." Here we have a much

11

more problematic relationship between subject and modifier, which cannot be resolved simply by transferring the question to an abstract or ideal plane of consideration. If a slave insurrectionist has the attributes of Christ, either literally or spiritually, then something radical must be done with our preconceptions of both subject and modifier if we are to discover what Beardsley calls the "emergent meaning" of this metaphor. As we shall see later, Turner's immediate audience, his white amanuensis-editor Thomas Gray, rejected the "logical absurdity" of Turner's autobiographical metaphor. Nevertheless it is the purpose of such a metaphor of self to compel white readers to comprehend conceptual dichotomies as widely divergent as murderer and Messiah. Other polarities such as black-white, slave-free, past-present, truth-lie, and subject-object are placed in creative dialectic by the metaphoric experimentation of black autobiographers in the early nineteenth century. There was a great risk of alienating white readers through the daring absurdities of radical metaphorical arguments like Turner's. However, this willingness to work on the margins of discourse testifies to the Newmanesque antagonism of important early black autobiographers to inhibiting forms of categorical thinking about black experience and expression in white America.

The metaphor-making of the classic slave narrators of the 1840s and 1850s participates in the movement toward organic, nonlogical literary discourse as espoused by the classic nineteenth-century American Romantics. Eschewing the limitations of logical analogy, black and white I-narrators of the American renaissance used metaphors whose "emergent meaning" was not just a function of preexistent similarities between a subject and a modifier but was an organic outgrowth of the relationship of a subject and a modifier to "the whole which they create by their interaction." What Charles Feidelson says of the Romantic metaphor in *Symbolism and American Literature* applies no less to black autobiographers who explored this mode: from their metaphors emerge meanings that could not "fully exist" apart from the whole that only comes into existence itself as a result of the metaphors' having been created.[20] Through this circular logic of the metaphor, the great Afro-American autobiographies of the Romantic era communicate powerfully the paradoxes of the black existence in white America.

Afro-American autobiography did not start out offering an image of black selfhood that was either fully unified or notably antagonistic to popular white notions about who (or what) the Negro was. In his study of Euro-American autobiographical tradition, Karl Weintraub finds a basic contrast between writers who identify with "great personality ideals in which their culture tends to embody its values and objectives" and other writers who are convinced "that ultimately no general model can contain the specificity of the true self." [21] The history of Afro-American autobiography in its formative century reflects these contrasting views of the self in a creative dialectic. In some respects the image of the Negro evolves from models imported from the predominant culture to more individualized self-portraits in which idiosyncrasy and irony are displayed for a variety of reasons. It is also possible to see the genre evolving from what Olney has termed "autobiography simplex," in which a single dominant faculty or motif becomes the focus of attention instead of the complex, variegated self. [22] Or one might appropriate from Harold Bloom an idea that suggests another way of understanding the tradition of Afro-American autobiography in the nineteenth century.

The acquisition of literacy, the power to read books and discover one's place in the scheme of things, is treated in many slave narratives as a matter equal in importance to the achievement of physical freedom. In a famous passage in his *Narrative* of 1845, Frederick Douglass spoke of reading as the way he began to define himself via defiance of his master. For the boy Frederick to continue to study reading after being forbidden to do so by his Baltimore master, Hugh Auld, was to initiate a certain kind of "artistic Primal scene," as Bloom might term it, one emanating from an Oedipal "trespass of teaching." Douglass describes his subsequent resistance to his master as more than just intractableness. His behavior is founded on a deliberate "misreading" of everything Auld stands for and believes in. As Douglass put it, "What he most dreaded, that I most desired. What he most loved, that I most hated. That which to him was great evil, to be carefully shunned, was to me a great good, to be diligently sought." Douglass is rare among black autobiographers in picturing himself as such a radical misreader of the teachings of his master, but he is not alone among black writers of his era who qualify as Bloomian "strong readers" or, as one might just as accurately say, strong "misreaders." David Walker's *Appeal, in Four Articles; Together with a Preamble, to the Coloured Citizens of the World, but in Particular, and Very Expressly, to Those of the United States of America* (1829) represents a signal act of Afro-American misreading of a quasi-sacred American text, the U.S. Constitution. Martin R. Delany's novel, *Blake; or the Huts of America* (1859–62), contains strong misreadings of Old Testament history and New Testament theology, both sacred to the predominant culture.

The autobiographies of ex-slaves like Douglass and James W. C. Pennington indicate that the writing of their life stories could place slave narrators "in the dilemmas of the revisionist," Bloom's term for a reader "who wishes to find his own original relation to truth, whether in texts or in reality . . . but [who] also wishes to open received texts to his own

13

sufferings, or what he wants to call the sufferings of history." The "received texts," the tradition that Afro-American autobiography "wishes to open" and force the reader "to *esteem* and *estimate* differently" (Bloom's emphasis), are the culture-defining scriptures of nineteenth-century America, the Bible and the Declaration of Independence. The misreading of these texts in Afro-American autobiography is much more than an act of cultural commentary or moral criticism. It is often a fundamental part of the act of literary and self-creation, of "revisionary replacements" of scriptural ideas of the self with "a word one's own that is also one's act and one's veritable presence."[23] Thus as black autobiography necessarily establishes its relationship to the essential texts of oppressive American culture, it also becomes a revisionistic instrument in the hands of its greatest practitioners. It urges revision of the myths and ideals of America's culture-defining scriptures while it demands new sight of white readers to recognize the ways in which autobiography had become a mode of Afro-American scripture.

Next to the Bible itself, autobiography was the script—the sanctified record and the directing text—that the victims of the African diaspora in America needed most to sustain them during their tribulation and to explain to them the reasons for their suffering. Recent scholarship by Wilson J. Moses has identified a black jeremiad tradition in expository works like Maria Stewart's *Productions* (1835) and David Walker's *Appeal*. These writers mix analysis of and lamentation over the misery and humiliation of blacks in America. Their voices rise in constant warnings to whites to beware of the inevitable judgment of God for the sin of slavery. In this kind of jeremiad, blacks also revealed a concept of themselves as a chosen people whose covenant with God paralleled that between Jehovah and the Jews and whose history was also typified by that of the Israelites of the Old Testament. Black autobiographers in America were early participants in and developers of several motifs in the black jeremiad. African-born Olaudah Equiano, as we shall see, identified his people, the Ibo, with the Hebrews before they reached the promised land, thus establishing in the late eighteenth century a tradition on which many subsequent slave narrators drew. Ever direr and more explicit warnings of the wrath to be visited on southern white pharaohs appeared in slave narratives composed after the rise of evangelical Garrisonian abolitionism. Some autobiographers, like Leonard Black in 1847, prophesied obliquely: "The time is coming when the wrongs of the slave will be redressed. Yes, the time is coming when their blood will cry unto the Lord for deliverance." A more direct William Craft in 1860 promised in *Running a Thousand Miles for Freedom* that "a similar retribution to that

which destroyed Sodom is hanging over the slaveholders" unless they re-
pented their "reckless course of wickedness." [24]

Frederick Douglass's *My Bondage and My Freedom* (1855) exemplifies a third motif of the autobiography as jeremiad when he recalls a plantation "spectacle" whose "intensified degradation" ex-slave rhetoricians
regularly exploited—the auction of slaves and division of slave families.
The tragedy of families separated at auction drove home the humanity of
blacks at the hands of an inhumane system. What Douglass emphasized
even more in such a scene, however, was slavery's subversion of the
Great Chain of Being and the resultant denial of rank and distinction in
the order of things. "What an assemblage!" Douglass exclaims as he describes the valuation and division of the property of his deceased master,
Captain Aaron Anthony of Talbot County, Maryland, in October 1827.

> Men and women, young and old, married and single; moral and intellectual
> beings, in open contempt of their humanity, leveled at a blow with horses,
> sheep, horned cattle and swine! Horses and men—cattle and women—pigs
> and children—all holding the same rank in the scale of social existence; and
> all subjected to the same narrow inspection, to ascertain their value in gold
> and silver—the only standard of worth applied by slaveholders to slaves!
> How vividly, at that moment, did the brutalizing power of slavery flash be-
> fore me! Personality swallowed up in the sordid idea of property! Manhood
> lost in chattelhood!

This was the slave narrative's contribution to a time-tested *topos* of social
criticism as old as the Hebrew prophets and Greek and Latin satirists: the
idea of "the World Upsidedown." [25] In slavery, the black autobiographer
preached, in the words of Douglass, "the order of civilization is reversed."
Only a radical change in white American values could put right what had
been so radically "reversed." One reason why early black autobiography
deals as often as it does in melodramatic extremes and diametrical opposites is due to this perception of America as bereft of a sense of the
natural order of things and of the differences between things, so blinded
had whites become because of their bigotry, greed, and fear.

Regardless of how we speak of the developing motifs and traditions of
early black autobiography, we shall have difficulty in chronicling the evolution of the genre in patterns of steady progress. The tradition of black
autobiography is not layered in strata of ground-breaking predecessors
anticipating conscious successors. Some stages of development can be
marked in rough outline, but the route of the genre's historical evolution
is dotted with detours, deadends, half-blazed trails, and roads not taken.
How, then, can one address what Hayden White has termed "the problem
of change in literary history" as it is manifested in the first century of

Afro-American autobiography?[26] To do this, one must first posit a working definition of the genre in question, a definition general and inclusive enough to allow the tradition to reveal itself as a dialectic of continuity and change, not as simply a function of the parameters of the definition itself.

In defining autobiography for the purposes of this book I do not propose to establish an impregnable theoretical position but only a kind of staging area for further critical operations. Jean Starobinski states cogently the hesitancy that many critics feel when trying to characterize autobiography in a systematic way. "Autobiography is certainly not a genre with rigorous rules," he points out. "It only requires that certain possible conditions be realized, conditions that are mainly ideological (or cultural): that the personal experience be important, that it offer an opportunity for a sincere relation with someone else." In other words, to write autobiography one must take one's own life (or some major portion of it) seriously enough to find in it a significance that makes reconstructing that life valuable to another. In keeping with both the self- and other-directedness of autobiography, Starobinski's labeling of the genre as "discourse-history" seems a helpful kind of general description, though fraught with definitional difficulties that must be faced.[27]

The problem of the historicity of early Afro-American autobiography, and in particular the slave narrative, has been debated for decades. Led by Ulrich B. Phillips, the first historians of American slavery regarded slave narratives as merely an arm of abolitionist propaganda, strong in righteous indignation but weak in factual substance. In the 1960s and 1970s scholars like Eugene Genovese and John W. Blassingame denied that slavery could be fully understood apart from the perspective of its victims. This conviction led to the publication of a number of valuable studies of the institution based on the idea that many slave narratives are reliable historical documents.[28] Today no serious student of the slave narrative quarrels with Blassingame's contention that "most of the accounts written by the blacks themselves not only have the ring of truth, but they can usually be verified by independent sources."[29] However, the proven reliability of these narratives as sourcebooks of facts about slavery should not cause us to forget that as historical narratives they are subject to the same "poetic processes" of composition as any other works of that kind. Even the most objective and unrhetorical slave narrative is still a "fiction of factual representation," to use White's apt phrase. Slave narrators and abolitionist editors often tried to write autobiography in the manner of nineteenth-century positivist history, disclaiming fictive techniques or rhetorical aims as hindrances to the understanding of reality rather than as ways of apprehending it. But we must remember that in any slave narrative, no matter how verifiable in its particulars, "the facts do not speak for themselves." It is the narrator, the imputed eye-witness historian, who "speaks on their behalf, and fashions the fragments of the past into a whole whose integrity is—in its *re*presentation—a purely discursive one." [30]

What, then, does it mean to treat early black autobiography as discourse as well as history? In one respect, the discursive nature of black autobiography is simply a function of its rhetorical situation. As Lloyd F. Bitzer explains, all communication is conditioned and structured by its situation. When people, events, or relationships present a problem that can be affected or alleviated by the use of discourse to influence someone's thought or action, then a "rhetorical situation" comes into being. [31] Faced with the exigences of slavery and a mass refusal to see blacks as fully human or hear them as truth-tellers, black autobiographers naturally realized that theirs was a rhetorical situation. They could not think of their task simply as the objective reconstruction of an individual's past or a public demonstration of the qualities of selfhood or a private meditation on the meaning of a life of struggle. The writing of autobiography became an attempt to open an intercourse with the white world. Often the only context or tradition that black autobiographers had was their sense of the state of black-white discourse on the questions of slavery, black identity, and the capacity of blacks for reliable discourse in the first place. In some autobiographies we find a covert, often impromptu discourse on what the language of selfhood can mean when addressed to someone who doubts the selfhood of the addressor. At times this kind of reflectiveness and self-consciousness produces what might be called a running metadiscourse on the assumptions, conditions, and conventions necessary to discourse between black narrator and white reader. Regardless of the degree of sophistication, however, the early black autobiographer's discursive aims have much to do with the overwhelmingly "oratorical" character of the genre: its didactic intent, its treatment of life as representative or allegorical, its unifying sense of calling and vocation, and its stylistic sensitivity to the arts of persuasion. [32]

It is also useful to keep in mind what M. M. Bakhtin and White have posited about all discourse—that it is, in White's phrase, "quintessentially a mediative enterprise." Bakhtin emphasizes that discourse lives "on the boundary between its own context and another, alien, context." The successful speaker or writer "breaks through the alien conceptual horizon of the listener, constructs his own utterance on alien territory, against his, the listener's, apperceptive background." For Bakhtin, discourse always takes place in an environment of alienation. The words of a speaker or writer are always engaged in a "dialogic relationship" with alien words that a listener or reader might have chosen from his or her conceptual and linguistic horizon to express a same or similar thing. Noting the etymology of the word (*discurrere*, to run back and forth), White amplifies Bakhtin in stating that discourse "moves 'to and fro' between received encodations of experience and the clutter of phenomena which refuses incorporation into conventionalized notions of 'reality,' 'truth,' or 'possibility.'" One of my assumptions about Afro-American autobiography is that it is very much a mediative instrument not only between black narrator and white reader but also, in White's more general terms, between alternative ways of encoding reality, some of which are prescribed by tradition and others "of which may be idiolects of the author, the authority of which he is seeking to establish." [33]

Ultimately, the mode of black autobiographical discourse itself undertakes the task of validating its own claims to reality and its author's claims to an identity. Early black autobiographers seem preoccupied with authenticating their stories and themselves by documenting both according to their fidelity to the facts of human nature and experience that white Americans assumed to be true. We shall see, however, that as a discursive instead of a documentary mode, black autobiography is designed to establish the grounds on which one may decide what will count as fact in a narrative and what mode of interpretation is best suited to a full comprehension of that fact. As a rhetorical mode, black autobiography then employs various methods of persuading (or manipulating) the reader to make decisions about truth and significance in a narrative consonant with the aim of the autobiographer. Thus Afro-American autobiography mediates between historical, rhetorical, and tropological truth within the discursive framework of "narrative patterns of the recovered life" and "dramatic patterns of the evolving act of recovery." [34]

As is the case in discussions of other literary kinds, a generic definition of Afro-American autobiography is partly a function of the characteristics of the text that one selects as the beginnning of the tradition. In my scheme, the history of black American autobiography begins with the publication of the first discrete narrative text in which an Afro-American recounts a significant portion of his life: *A Narrative of the Uncommon Sufferings, and Surprizing Deliverance of Briton Hammon, A Negro Man* (1760). By 1760 black conversion to Christianity had started to assume noticeable proportions in the largest of the American colonies, a fact that figures prominently in the generation of early black autobiography from the tradition of the Protestant conversion narrative. [35] Approximately 100 years later black people in America reached the historical watershed of Emancipation, after which time they thought and wrote about themselves and their past in ways increasingly different from those that characterize antebellum autobiographies. Thus the period between

1760 and 1865 forms the chronicle of this book. Sixty years before Hammon's narrative there are records describing the efforts of one "Adam Negro" to win his freedom from his Boston master via petitions to the Superior Court of the colony. These materials, which have been lumped together under the title of "Adam Negro's Tryall," may be judged "a precursor of the slave narratives,"[36] but they cannot be treated as autobiography per se, because none emanates from the consciousness of the black man himself. Excepting the date of publication, the primary criterion for the inclusion of any work within the purview of this book is that it be written in the first-person singular. Unless scholarship can demonstrate the spurious authorship of a text,[37] I have considered potentially relevant to this study all the forms of first-person retrospective prose narrative that came from the mouths or pens of American blacks between 1760 and 1865.[38] This includes not only the well-known slave narrative genre but also Afro-American spiritual autobiographies, criminal confessions, captivity narratives, travel accounts, interviews, and memoirs. Although I have not made length of text a criterion for selection or rejection, I shall refer only rarely to black first-person narratives that were published in antislavery periodicals, annuals, or anthologies.[39] As Blassingame has stated, the number of interviews, dictated life sketches, and brief autobiographical narratives published in the abolitionist press is "staggering."[40] Anyone who wishes to examine a representative sampling of such material may consult Blassingame's *Slave Testimony*, an excellent compilation of first-person documents from English and American magazines of the nineteenth and early twentieth centuries. For my purposes, only separately published items between 1760 and 1865 qualify for extended comment. In addition, diaries, journals, and other private manuscripts that did not find their way into print until after 1865 are not treated in this book. I do not wish to confuse the public discourse of published autobiography with the private discourse of the diary or journal.[41]

One other case of generic confusion needs to be addressed. Problems of authenticity and interpretation inevitably arise when one considers the large number of dictated, edited, and ghostwritten narratives that appeared under the ostensible authorship of blacks during the period 1760 to 1865. Should an autobiography whose written composition was literally out of the hands of its black narrator be discussed on an equal footing with those autobiographies that were autonomously authored by the black subject himself or herself? Many so-called edited narratives of ex-slaves ought to be treated as ghostwritten accounts insofar as literary analysis is concerned, especially when these works were composed by their editors from "a statement of facts" provided by the black subject.[42] Blassingame has taken pains to show that the editors of several of the more famous antebellum slave narratives were people "noted for their integrity" and thus were unlikely to distort the facts given them by slave narrators.[43] From a literary standpoint, however, it is not the moral integrity of these editors that is at issue but the linguistic, structural, and tonal integrity of the narratives they produced. Even if an editor faithfully reproduced the facts of a black narrator's life, it was still the editor who decided what to make of these facts, how they should be emphasized, in what order they ought to be presented, and what was extraneous, or germane. It was the editor who controlled the manuscript and thus decided how a "statement of facts" became a "fiction of factual representation," a readable, convincing, and moving autobiography. Editors of early Afro-American autobiography assumed the right to do everything to a dictation from "improving" its grammar, style, and diction to selecting, arranging, and assigning significance to its factual substance.

Readers of black autobiography then and now have too readily accepted the presumption of these eighteenth- and nineteenth-century editors: namely, that the experiential facts recounted orally by a black person could be recorded and sorted by an amanuensis-editor, placed in various institutional contexts (aesthetic, philosophical, or moral, for instance), and then published with editorial prefaces, footnotes, and appended commentary—all without qualifying the validity of the narrative as a product of an Afro-American consciousness. Yet it is important to recognize, as speech-act theorists have pointed out, that even the simplest factual utterances depend on the rules and values of extralinguistic institutions for their meaning. Socioeconomic, moral, and aesthetic institutions bind many of the facts of our experience in complexly interwoven "systems of constitutive rules." If, as John Searle has argued, "every institutional fact is underlain by a [system of] rule[s] of the form 'X counts as Y in context C,'" then the crucial role of the editor in early black autobiography can be distinguished more clearly. It is the editor who decides what context C will be. It is the editor who contextualizes the essential facts of the narrator's dictation and thus has much to do with how they will be received as institutional facts by their white readers.[44]

Some collaborators with black oral narrators disclaimed all but the most minor editorial involvement in the autobiographies that they helped to create. George Thompson, a noted British abolitionist who served as the amanuensis for the *Narrative of the Life of Moses Grandy*, said that he had committed the story to paper "as nearly as possible in the language of Moses himself" without "casting a single reflection or animadversion of my own." Samuel A. Eliot described *The Life of Josiah Henson* as "written from the dictation of Josiah Henson. A portion of the story was told, which, when written, was read to him, that any errors of statement might be corrected. The substance of it, therefore, the facts, the reflections, and very often the words, are his; and little more than the structure of the sentences belongs to another." This was to assure his reader that the story of Henson was "not fiction but fact." David Wilson, the writer of Solomon Northup's widely selling story *Twelve Years a Slave*, believed he had been "faithful" and unbiased" in his "history of Solomon Northup's life, as he received it from his lips." After all, as amanuensis Wilson had "had an opportunity of detecting any contradiction or discrepancy" in what Northup said. But Northup had "invariably repeated the same story without deviating in the slightest particular, and [had] also carefully perused the manuscript, dictating an alteration wherever the most trivial inaccuracy has appeared." [45]

Transcribed narratives in which an editor delimits his role as explicitly as Eliot did undoubtedly may be regarded as more authentic and reflective of the narrator's thought in action than those edited works that flesh out a statement of facts in ways unaccounted for. Still it would be naive to accord dictated oral narratives the same discursive status as autobiographies composed and written by the subjects of the stories themselves. There is much that we do not know about the circumstances in which these oral narratives were dictated, for instance. Obviously the work was done in the context of a power relationship that gave the supposed passive amanuensis ultimate control over the fate of the manuscript and considerable influence over the immediate future of the narrator. Wilson helped make Northup a famous man. Thompson's name on Grandy's manuscript amounted to an endorsement that was worth much to the ex-slave when he solicited contributions in England to help him purchase his family in North Carolina. What effects would this sort of knowledge have on the kind of story an ex-slave might tell to his amanuensis? In his interviews with inner-city blacks, William Labov could never cancel out the inhibiting "interactive effect" that caused his informants to "monitor" their speech whenever they addressed "someone outside the immediate peer group of the speaker." [46] Would not ex-slaves have been inhibited similarly when talking to whites, particularly when the latter's confidence and favor were so necessary to a narrative's publication?

This seems very likely when we remember that analysis of the Works Progress Administration interviews with ex-slaves in the 1930s suggests that blacks often told their white interviewers what they seemed to want to hear. If it was sometimes impolitic for a former slave to tell all he knew and thought about his past to an interviewer in the 1930s, the same could be said of escaped slaves on the run in the antebellum era. The amanuensis was not automatically the narrator's sympathizer and advocate; he had to be won over, as in the case of Wilson and Northup, by a convincing performance and a consistent rendition of the facts. Dictated narratives, therefore, are speech acts of a distinct order even as they are literary texts of an indistinct origin. Lacking a way of distilling an authorial essence from the clouded stream of edited and dictated Afro-American autobiographies, I shall reserve close analytic readings for autonomously authored black texts. The collaborative texts will be discussed in accordance with the conditions that seem to have governed their literary character and function.[47]

Problems of origin, composition, editing, and control of manuscript complicate the study of early Afro-American autobiography and limit the conclusiveness of interpretive strategies that require a fully determinate text and identifiable "author-function."[48] Still, the silences in black autobiography that resist conclusiveness in some respects only heighten the need for heuristic principle that can initiate the kinds of discussion that the genre invites and allows.[49] To speak of Afro-American autobiography as a kind of rhetorical discourse is to posit one basic heuristic principle for the study of the genre. The rhetoric of Afro-American autobiography, however, ought to be understood in the comprehensive sense that Kenneth Burke has prescribed. All rhetorical action, he argues, arises from "the perception of generic divisiveness" among mankind. In its simplest forms, rhetoric, the art of persuasion, is designed to break down that divisiveness with discourse that reveals "consubstantiation" between speaker and audience. If the audience views itself or its interests as alien from the speaker or his interests, rhetoric becomes the means by which the latter attempts to identify with the former. A speaker may seek to affirm his identity with his audience by proving that he can talk their language "by speech, gesture, tonality, order, image, attitude, and idea." That some black autobiographers used this sort of rhetoric to establish identities in the minds of their white audience will be very apparent in later chapters of this book. When Burke states that successful rhetoricians know how "to display the appropriate 'signs' of character needed to earn the audience's good will," he points to another rhetorical feature of black autobiography in its first century of development. I will comment on the psychological import of character "signs" in black autobiography later in this chapter. All that need be said in this context is that displaying "appropriate 'signs' of character" is another way that black autobiographers pursued an implicit proof of their own humanity while simultaneously buttressing their arguments on slavery or religion with traditional rhetorical devices. If, in the largest sense, rhetoric embraces any use of language "as a symbolic means of inducing cooperation in beings that by nature respond to symbols," then all of the arts of language, including "purely *po-*

22

etic structures" according to Burke, qualify as potentially rhetorical in function. In seeking to combat "the perception of generic divisiveness," or what one might call "generic otherness" that whites applied to blacks in the eighteenth and nineteenth centuries in America, the art of black autobiography was inevitably put to the service of rhetoric. This did not entail a dismissal of the muse of personal history, however. It spurred experimentation in narrative modes, metaphors of self, and arts of address that challenged other "perceptions of generic divisiveness" between history (fact), literature (fiction), and propaganda (argument).[50]

Current debates about the nature and presence of the self, its expressibility in language, and its knowability by either its creator or its reader have had profound implications for a philosophical hermeneutics of autobiography. Like other modes of first-person discourse in the nineteenth century, black autobiography raises serious doubts about what William Spengemann has called "the assumption that a substantial soul or self precedes and governs individual experience and may be discerned through that experience" as recorded in an autobiography.[51] Because the ontology of autobiography is so problematic, it seems to me more fruitful to treat the form more as a complex of linguistic acts in a discursive field than as the verbal emblem of an essential self uniquely stamped on a historical narrative. This does not mean that historical or self-referentiality has no place in a discussion of the evolution of black American autobiography. It does mean that the assumptions of referentiality in autobiography that have usually informed our discussions of the genre can no longer claim privileged status. We must be more discerning in our thinking about the dynamics of signification in autobiography.

Speech-act theory explores the differences between various kinds of linguistic actions; it emphasizes that discourse has both a "constative" and a "performative" dimension. When we study the constative feature of speech, we consider the locutionary dimension of an utterance—that is, what a statement means, its sense and reference. When we study the performative dimension of speech, we consider the "illocutionary" aspect of an utterance—that is, what the speaker is doing in saying something, as opposed to what he means by the act of saying something. We are interested in the "illocutionary force" of an utterance in addition to its locutionary meaning. Moreover, if we are interested in the "consequential effects" of an utterance on the thoughts, feelings, or actions of its audience, we may study the "perlocutionary" dimension of that utterance. The examination of these three dimensions of speech in autobiographical discourse gives us a useful way of talking about the coding of referential meaning, rhetorical force, and potential effect in black autobiographical discourse.[52]

Speech-act theory insists on our remembering that "literary works, like all our communicative activities, are context-dependent." Thus, "as with any utterance, the way people produce and understand literary works depends enormously on unspoken, culturally-shared knowledge of the rules, conventions, and expectations that are in play when language is used" in literary contexts.[53] Some of the major rules applicable to any sort of speech action, in which something is not only stated but some sort of transaction between speaker and hearer also takes place, have been summarized by Wolfgang Iser in *The Act of Reading*, an important work of reader-response theory. Following the pioneering work of J. L. Austin, Iser outlines three basic conditions necessary to an utterance's becoming "operative." First, an utterance "must invoke a *convention* that is as valid for the recipient as for the speaker." For instance, in the antebellum South, a white man could invoke the convention of white supremacy over black chattel when he instructed his slave to work from dawn till dusk each day in the cotton fields. Should this same white man demand the same action from another white man, his statement would be rendered inoperative because the conventions underlying the speech transaction would not be operable. A second condition for effective speech-action is its following the "accepted procedures" whereby conventions of discourse take place. Were a slaveholder to announce to his slave, "You are free. You may leave this plantation at any time," the speech-act of freeing the slave would still not become operative, even though the master has the power and intention of manumission. This is because the convention of manumission requires a procedure entailing more than the speech-act of granting a slave his freedom. Without other kinds of speech and writing actions in a certain order of performance, the simple verbal announcement of freedom will fail to effect the transaction. The third condition that Iser points to as a desideratum for the accomplishment of a speech-act is this: "The willingness of the participants to engage in a linguistic action must be proportionate to the degree in which the situation or context of the action is defined."[54] This means that in additon to conventions and accepted procedures the context in which speech-acts are made and the disposition of speakers and hearers to accept that context are crucial factors in effecting a linguistic transaction.

Searle has identified four rules by which contexts are defined between speakers and hearers and dispositions are registered as well. These rules, which Searle calls the "appropriateness conditions" for speech-action, isolate the "propositional content" of a speech-act and other extra-linguistic conditions in the minds of speaker and hearer that must be met before an act can be said to have been performed. A master may promise to free his slave, thereby giving an utterance propositional content, which in turn gives it a certain force and encourages its hearer to respond to it in a certain manner. But if for some reason the slave does not wish to be freed, or if he knows he will be automatically freed at a certain time regardless of his master's verbal promise, then that promise does not meet the "preparatory rules" that Searle believes are necessary to make an utterance appropriate and hence potentially operative. Or if a master promises to free his slave with no intention of doing so, he has not abided by the "sincerity rule," which also must be in effect for the actualization of an utterance. Finally, if the master refuses to admit that promising to free his slave places him under the obligation to do what he promises, he violates Searle's "essential rule," which states that the essence of a speech-act like promising is the obligation to do what one promises.[55] All these appropriateness conditions, as well as the adherence to conventions, accepted procedures, and situation-demands that Austin identifies, must be met to insure that words do what they are empowered to do by the unspoken rules of a culture's institutions, both linguistic and extralinguistic.

Cogent arguments have been made for the analysis of English and American first-person writing as a kind of "autobiographical act." Speech-act theory can aid in the close reading of autobiography by calling our attention to the linguistic markers—pronoun usage, tense changes, modality, mood, use of direct or indirect discourse, to name a few—which help us define the context of the autobiographical act, particularly the relationship between writer and audience.[56] Of perhaps greater import to the study of Afro-American autobiography, however, is the research that has been done on ways that literary speech-action disrupts or dismantles the standard communication situation beween speakers and hearers, writers and audiences. Ordinarily communication situations become functional only when a speaker and an audience accept and play by the linguistic rules of the culture, i.e., when they pool their knowledge of the conventions, accepted procedures, and appropriateness conditions of speech action to effect verbal transactions of various kinds. However, literary language, especially that found in fictional texts, manipulates the conventions of speech action in a way that defies the rules of ordinary utterances. Fictional texts disrupt the hierarchy of values around which the conventions of ordinary speech action are structured; these texts do this by employing narrative techniques that place the conventions of speech action "in unexpected combinations, so that they begin to be stripped of their validity." The literary text may accept "the prevalent thought system or social system as its context, but does not reproduce the frame of reference which stabilizes these systems." Instead, the text creates a new frame in which the conventions, norms, and assumptions of existing thought and communication systems "are taken out of their social contexts, deprived of their regulating function, and so become subjects of scrutiny themselves." Having placed the conventions and norms of existing systems in abeyance, the literary text "almost invariably tends to take as its dominant 'meaning' those possibilities that have been neutralized or negated by that system." [57]

Though any autobiography may be treated as a fictional text in some sense, not all Afro-American autobiographies can be understood as disrupting or dismantling and realigning the conventions of literary discourse in the manner that Iser outlines. Many black narrators, however, had to reckon with the fact that the same appropriateness conditions for white autobiographical acts did not apply to blacks engaged in the same literary enterprise. Fugitive slaves, for instance, could not recount the horrors of their southern captivity secure in the knowledge that whites would accept their sincerity or rely on the accuracy of their memories. Slave narratives usually required a variety of authenticating devices, such as character references and reports of investigations into the narrator's slave past (almost always written by whites), so that the slave's story might become operative as a linguistic act.[58] On the other hand, narratives written by whites about their captivities among hostile Indians rarely required such documentation to fulfill the preparatory and sincerity conditions of autobiographical discourse by and for whites.

Many slave narrators were aware of the racist and nationalistic biases that made the average northern reader suspect any black person who characterized southern whites as barbarous and inhuman. This caused some slave narrators to declare openly the paradoxical preparatory condition of much antebellum slave autobiography: white acceptance of a slave narrative as truth depended on how judiciously the slave had censored the facts of his life into something other than the whole truth. Thus the first sentences of Harriet Jacobs's preface to *Incidents in the Life of a Slave Girl* (1861) state: "Reader, be assured this narrative is no fiction. I am aware that some of my adventures may seem incredible; but they are nevertheless, strictly true." Having brought up the problem of how a white person could believe in a seemingly "incredible" black narrative, Jacobs blandly announces the basis on which her story can be taken as "strictly true": "I have not exaggerated the wrongs inflicted by Slavery; on the contrary, my descriptions fall far short of the facts." In other words, the white reader could have confidence in Jacobs's sincerity because she had promised to be sufficiently insincere, to fall sufficiently far short of the facts, to prove that she had written no fiction. This is only a sample of the ways in which early Afro-American autobiography fictionalized itself to adapt to the contradictory and perverse social system and communication situation that white culture enforced over the genre and the people who wrote in it. That Jacobs would not adapt to the paradox of her literary situation without exposing it with such ingenuous irony is a tribute to her truth-telling in the midst of her bold assertion that she had not told the truth.

In its most sophisticated forms early Afro-American autobiography works like any literary text in separating the conventions, norms, and patterns of discourse of an existing genre from their standard context. Thus deprived of their regulating function in a narrative, they "become objects of scrutiny themselves." An examination of the opening paragraphs of a typical white American autobiography of the early nineteenth century will reveal that it was conventional to cite one's birthdate, one's place of birth, and one's family background in considerable detail as a way of introducing oneself to the reader. To locate oneself at a particular point in the temporal continuum gave the autobiographer a uniqueness and a degree of self-knowledge that can only augment his status in the eyes of the reader. To speak of where one comes from is to imply where one belongs, which is further to imply that one belongs somewhere. And if one's connectedness to the land helps to establish one's identity as part of something larger, the citing of family names and family history simply reinforces this impression of connectedness. One is literally related to some part of the human family; to bear the same name as another is a sign of a mutual identity. We might speculate that many American autobiographers engaged in this ritual of personal documentation at the opening of their narratives because they felt a need to stake out a fixed point for themselves on the mental grids of their readers. Without precise temporal, spatial, and familial coordinates, an autobiographer remained in some sense unidentified and unidentifiable to American readers.

The handicap for slave narrators in trying to initiate a discourse with whites according to these conventions and procedures is obvious in the beginning paragraph of William Wells Brown's *Narrative* of 1847.

> I was born in Lexington, Ky. The man who stole me as soon as I was born, recorded the births of all the infants which he claimed to be born his property, in a book which he kept for that purpose. My mother's name was Elizabeth. She had seven children, viz.: Solomon, Leander, Benjamin, Joseph, Millford, Elizabeth, and myself. No two of us were children of the same father. My father's name, as I learned from my mother, was George Higgins. He was a white man, a relative of my master, and connected with some of the first families in Kentucky.

Brown's awareness of the conventions of personal documentation for an autobiographer is obvious. "I was born in Lexington, Ky." puts his reader on familiar ground and invites the expectation of information on the narrator's birthdate and family antecedents. Abruptly a stranger intrudes into the narrative, as he did into Brown's life. The appearance of the shadowy "man who stole me" disrupts the narrative, frustrating the reader's expectations and subjecting him to a kind of dislocation in the act of reading analogous to what Brown attributes to himself in the act of reconstructing his past. Like Brown, the reader has been robbed of the information he wants to know. Parodying conventional white practice of keeping family histories in family Bibles, Brown notes that his birth was secreted away in someone's property book. This is his telling metaphor of the chattel principle: the facts of his life do not belong to the slave. How then, by implication, can he give his white reader that most believable of documents, a factual autobiography? Brown tries, but the incompleteness of the rest of his personal documentation in the paragraph drives home the impossibility of his writing his life story according to the conventions and accepted procedures of white autobiographical discourse. His mother has no family name; his siblings have no common father; he knows only his father's name, and that only from a secondary source. When he cites his connections to "some of the first families in Kentucky," the remark is ironic, for his mixed blood and bastardy delegitimate him and any conventional claim he may make on the reader's interest and admiration.

The tone of Brown's prose offers no apologies for his "lower" status or for the partial invisibility of his self-portrait as a child. This is because the ordering and emphasis of information in the paragraph are designed to deny the reader his normal responses and judgments just as they frustrate his expectations. Instead of passively assimilating Brown's name, birthdate and place, and family situation, the reader is compelled to consider actively such questions as: What is the narrator's name, and how did he get it? What does it mean not to know one's birthdate? What sort of woman was the narrator's mother—immoral? indifferent? helpless? victimized? Does the word *family* apply to the situation in which the narrator grew up? What sort of priority should "the first families in Kentucky" receive in light of the actions of George Higgins?

These questions represent the sort of scrutinizing of the thought system and discursive conventions of a given genre that Iser says is a primary activity of literary texts. Brown's opening paragraph exemplifies the manner in which the most rhetorically sophisticated antebellum black autobiographers like to "change the joke and slip the yoke" (to use Ralph Ellison's phrase), in this case, the yoke of a cultural system that valued a person according to what he possessed. From the beginning Brown's narrative attempts to pry apart the yoking of intrinsic merit with extrinsic possessions by asking to what extent the conventional "properties" of a self—a name, birthdate, a father, a homeplace—had become the determinants of personhood in white America. The paragraph launches the reader on a journey of reconstruction with Brown. While the narrator is presumably engaged in reconstructing his life, he is also at work structuring a set of conditions in which the reader will find it appropriate to reexamine his concept of identity and personal value.

The emphasis on reader response in this discussion of Brown is intended to point toward an aspect of rhetorical strategy in Afro-American autobiography that subsequent chapters of this book will investigate, namely, the handling of fictive and implied readers. With Wayne Booth, I believe that many an author creates, along with an image of himself or herself in a text, an image of, and implied model for, the reader. A "successful reading" of a text is thus dependent on the degree to which "the created selves, author and reader, can find agreement." [59] Black autobiographers of the antebellum era were profoundly concerned with being successfully read. Like many writers, they introduced into their works implicit or explicit models by which their readers might be guided or measure themselves. When these reader models are addressed and characterized within a text, I will term them "characterized" or "fictive readers." [60] They appear often in slave narratives as embodiments of official white moral standards. A fugitive slave may project into a fictive reader his or her own anxieties about the justifiability of the means he or she used to flee slavery. Many slave narrators devote much art and energy to proving that their motives and actions, when viewed in the proper perspective, were consistent with white cultural ideals of justice. Before the crisis decades of the antislavery movement (the 1840s and 1850s), black autobiographers seem to have been most concerned with identifying themselves (in a Burkeian sense) with the characterized fictive reader, the symbol of the court of public opinion that presumably only needed to be correctly informed before it would acquit the Negro of guilt and alienation.

In the 1840s, however, black autobiographers began to declare their independence from the characterized fictive reader as a model of moral judgment. Instead of trying to prove his consubstantiality with the fictive reader, the autobiographer often addressed this figure as a negative foil, as someone who needed to be enlightened, not a moral or cultural arbiter. Instead of flattering his audience with a favorable image of itself in the fictive reader, the autobiographer challenged his audience to liberate itself from the wrongheadedness and moral myopia of this rhetorical straw man. In his 1849 *Narrative*, Henry Bibb admitted that he had stolen a horse as a means of escaping from slavery. He thought some would find fault with his action, but since he could not imagine anyone censuring a white man in the same situation, Bibb asked no pardon from his captious fictive reader. "I have nothing to regret," he insisted, "for I have done nothing more than any other reasonable person would have done under the same circumstances." Bibb's explicit demand in this passage is to be judged by a standard of "reason," not hair-splitting morality. He does not take time to explain what this alternative to abstract Victorian morality is. Instead he dismisses the fictive reader as unreasonable and implicitly calls for a reader who can interpret his actions according to the standards that emerge dramatically and pragmatically in the narrative itself. In this sense Bibb structures into his autobiography an implied reader, someone who can read his story and judge him according to a set of norms, both moral and aesthetic, that text and author—not the predominant culture—require. The rhetorical aim of autobiographers like Bibb is to create implied readers, not placate fictive ones. Such writers try to make the implied reader an intermediary between themselves and the world of the conventional-minded fictive reader. The act of reading autobiographies like Bibb's involves the reader in a decision about his own identity and his own position vis-à-vis the black and white categories of any socio-moral system of thought. Careful study of the implied reader as ideal interpreter of the text of the author's life is perhaps our most reliable guide behind the public persona and into the consciousness and purposes of writers like Bibb, Brown, Douglass, and Jacobs.

Scholarly study of Afro-American autobiography has accelerated ever since the civil rights movement in the United States challenged, indeed compelled, intellectuals to recognize and respond to black consciousness and black culture. The pioneering work of Marion Wilson Starling and Margaret Young Jackson identified the slave narrative as a literary genre and proved that it had to be taken seriously as a force in America's cultural history. Extending the argument for the significance of Afro-American autobiography, Charles H. Nichols's *Many Thousand Gone: The Ex-Slaves' Account of Their Bondage and Freedom* (1963), Sidonie Smith's *Where I'm Bound: Patterns of Slavery and Freedom in Black American Autobiography* (1974), Stephen Butterfield's *Black Autobiography in America* (1974), and Frances Smith Foster's *Witnessing Slavery: The Development of Ante-bellum Slave Narratives* (1978) approached the genre as the vital, continuing story that a distinctive culture in America had written about itself.[61] These critics have proven amply that black autobiography in America offers special access to the myths, norms, ideals, and self-perception of the culture that it embodies. These books from the 1960s and 1970s speak for and to the social and intellectual needs of black and white students of Afro-American literature at that time. Nevertheless, their capacity to answer the kinds of questions that I have posed in this essay is necessarily limited, for in some cases they were not concerned with such questions, and in other cases they conceived of the questions primarily in terms of their historical and sociopolitical ramifications. Much of literature's "lost ground" needs to be recovered still in the study of black American narrative,[62] particularly in its first century of development. My hope is that this book will map out a few exploratory routes that might be taken.

CHAPTER

2

Voices of the First Fifty Years, 1760–1810

The opening statement of black autobiography in America is addressed "To The Reader" of *A Narrative of the Uncommon Sufferings, and Surprizing Deliverance of Briton Hammon, A Negro man,—Servant to General Winslow of Marshfield, in New-England* (1760):

> As my Capacities and Condition of Life are very low, it cannot be expected that I should make those Remarks on the Sufferings I have met with, or the kind Providence of a good GOD for my Preservation, as one in a higher Station; but shall leave that to the Reader as he goes along, and so I shall only relate Matters of Fact as they occur to my Mind—

What follows thereafter is a fourteen-page account of Hammon's thirteen-year separation from his master, during which time he was shipwrecked, was captured by Florida Indians, was imprisoned by the Spanish in Havana, and worked as a cook aboard an English man o' war before being fortuitously and joyfully reunited with General Winslow in London. The exact authorship of this narrative is a matter of dispute,[1] but the sphere of responsibility claimed by the black subject and ostensible narrator of the story is explicitly defined. The persona states in his preliminary address to the reader that he will limit himself to relating "Matters of Fact as they occur to my Mind." The persona's sense of the difference—his reduced "Capacities" and his low "Condition of Life"—between himself and the white reader requires that he defer to that reader as his caste superior. This deference structures the role the reader must play in the discourse, that of assigning reference and value to the black man's spontaneously related "Matters of Fact." Thus from the outset of black autobiography in America the presupposition reigns that a black narrator needs a white reader to complete his text, to build a hierarchy of abstract significance on the mere matter of his facts, to supply a presence where there was only "Negro," only a dark absence. Appropriately, after the narrative's title neither its events nor its point of view call attention to Hammon as a black man. Blackness does not work to characterize Hammon as a subject; it serves a structural function only. Blackness is the difference that keeps him from becoming differentiated as a character in his own autobiography.

The division of literary labor explicitly stated in Hammon's "To The Reader" pervades Afro-American autobiography during the first fifty years of its existence. It was assumed that the black first-person narrator was a shallow intellectual vessel whose capacity would be strained by more than the oral relation of simple facts about his life. Before the early nineteenth century, only one black autobiographer, Olaudah Equiano, seems to have had the power of the pen to turn his life's facts into a meaning-making argument. Much more typical of the genre was *A Narrative of the Most Remarkable Particulars in the Life of James Albert Ukawsaw Gronniosaw, An African Prince* (1770), which was "related by himself" but "committed to paper by the elegant pen of a young lady of the town of Leominster, for *her own* private satisfaction" (emphasis mine). Similarly, the *Narrative of the Lord's Wonderful Dealings with John Marrant, A Black* (1785) was "taken down from [Marrant's] own relation" and then "arranged, corrected, and published" by an English Nonconformist minister. The anonymous amanuensis-editor of *A Narrative of the Life and Adventures of Venture a Native of Africa* (1798) pledges that he had added "nothing in substance to what [Smith] related himself." However, he acknowledges that he had "omitted" "many other interesting and curious passages of his life" because of considerations of space and size in the printing of the autobiography. The largest group of slave narratives published during this time, the confessions of condemned black felons, were all dictated to amanuenses who did not need to be told the moral, political, or financial ramifications of their writing. In the lurid *Dying Confession of Pomp, A Negro Man* (1795), broadside publisher Jonathan Plummer promised that he had "endeavored to preserve the ideas" of the criminal while taking "liberty to arrange the matter in my own way, to word his thoughts more elegantly . . . than he was able to express them." [2]

One may reconstruct from these statements what appears to have been a fairly standard procedure for the composition and publication of Afro-American autobiography during its earliest decades. The subject of the autobiography, the narrator himself, reported the basic "who-what-and-where" of his past experience. An amanuensis-editor took down these facts and later created a narrative by (1) selecting from the oral report

33

A former slave dictating the story of his life. (From Charles H. Wesley's *In Freedom's Footsteps* [1967])

those elements that seemed most significant, (2) arranging and "improving" their style and wording, and (3) often prefacing the final text with a statement placing the narrative in an intellectual context and interpretive perspective. One is left, therefore, with a black narrative severely enclosed by the transcribing, editorial, and prefacing practices of white litterateurs. To open such a narrative to discussion, one must first recognize, in order to discount, the white influence informing and enforcing the putative meaning and purpose of that narrative. This, however, is next to impossible since the very language of much early Afro-American autobiography is of indeterminate origin. Who decided to flavor James Gronniosaw's conversion story and travel narrative with unconscious ironies in the mode of Oliver Goldsmith's "Citizen of the World" letters— the "lady of Leominster" or the African himself? What is to be made of a condemned black rapist who pronounces himself astonished at "the indulgence" and "the lenity of the court" that sentenced him to hang? Are these the words of Joseph Mountain or Judge David Daggett, who tried and convicted Mountain, recorded his confession, and saw to the publication of his story in the popular form of a rogue's autobiography?[5] It is difficult to be sure when we are hearing an authentic black voice instead of witnessing an act of literary ventriloquism. Because the diction, style, and tone of oral speech in many early narratives have been filtered through their amanuensis-editors' moral and literary sensibilities, we must question their psycholinguistic credibility.

Even as autobiography seemed to admit Afro-Americans to a discourse with the world, it screened them off. In early black autobiography to preface is to prejudice, if not predetermine, the way a white reader would interpret a black narrative. Walter Shirley's preface to Gronniosaw's narrative characterizes the former slave as one whose "call was very extraordinary" and whose "deliverance" came because "his faith did not fail him." Having indirectly prepared the reader to interpret Gronniosaw's kidnapping from Africa as his call to Christianity, Shirley goes on to insist that "though born in an exalted station of life, and now under the pressure of various afflicting providences, I am persuaded (for I know the man) that he would rather embrace the dunghill, having Christ in his heart, than give up his spiritual possessions and enjoyment to fill the throne of princes." This character endorsement serves to foreclose the possibility of reading Gronniosaw as a man who should have had more options in life than the extremes of embracing dunghills in the white world or occupying a throne in Africa. Shirley's preface prepares readers in advance to see in Gronniosaw only a modern-day Job, afflicted by "providences," not by his fellow man.

The earliest black American autobiographies are almost always a variant of what James Olney has called "autobiography simplex," a narrative dominated by a single metaphor, faculty, or function. The question is, did the metaphor emanate from the black narrator's perception of his own life, or was it applied to that life, like a kind of overlay, by amanuensis-editors and/or preface writers? One may feel confident that the dominant metaphor of black criminal confessions—the black outlaw as recreant and rebel against white paternal authority[4]—did not occur spontaneously to a condemned black felon. But in cases like Hammon's or Gronniosaw's, editors probably solicited these stories because they conformed or were conformable to cultural myths and literary traditions with an already established audience appeal, such as Indian captivity or evangelical conversion narratives. The African boyhood and initiation into the West that Gronniosaw and Smith could recall gave each man's account a romance and exoticism certain to attract the attention of admirers of the "noble savage." But these features are incidental to the basic themes of both narratives, the "trials and calamities" of the Afro-American man of faith and fortitude, a variation on *Pilgrim's Progress* in which a heathen but noble African is shown in quest of religious salvation (Gronniosaw) and secular success (Smith) in the Vanity Fair of the West. When editors recognized affinities between black narrators and Western archetypes like Mr. Christian or the biblical Joseph or Job, they stressed these parallels in their prefaces and gave them precedence in their characterizations of the black subjects themselves.

Reading the first fifty years of Afro-American autobiography is thus something of an exercise in creative hearing. There are so many silences in these narratives, so little individualized expression or ethnic perspective divergent from the structures of discourse that the Judeo-Christian literary and cultural tradition valorized. The result is that pioneers like Hammon and John Marrant become the first invisible men in black American first-person narrative. They can hardly be seen as black men in their stories, although (and perhaps because) they possessed a perspective on oppression and alienation that could have rendered the terms of the captivity genre truly "tellable" in their special cases.[5] Hammon and Marrant were in a peculiar position to compare Indian and white forms of captivity. Instead of leaving us what one critic has called a "colorless" recitation of clichéd facts,[6] they might have produced a black autobiographical act, "tellable"—worthy of display—because it represented something extraordinary and problematic, a dual perspective on the significance of captivity in America. The repression of this perspective in Hammon's and Marrant's stories and its restriction in other early black autobiographies require the critic to call attention to the ways that autobiographical discourse at that time ruled out black tellability as an appropriateness condition for writing about the lives of blacks. One must also pay special regard to seams or cuts in these enclosed narratives when facts are revealed—made tellable—in a way subversive to the text, when the presence of colorless white screens is deconstructed long enough for the absence to call attention to itself and demand a creative hearing for the silences in the text.[7]

In an illustrative anecdote, Gronniosaw recounts an episode that happened early in his American experience as a house slave to a New York gentleman.

> My chief business was to wait at table and tea, and clean knives, and I had a very easy place; but the servants used to curse and swear surprisingly, which I learned faster than anything; indeed, it was almost the first English I could speak. If any of them affronted me, I was sure to call upon God to damn them immediately; but I was broken off it all at once, occasioned by the correction of an old black servant that lived in the family. One day I had just cleaned the knives for dinner, when one of the maids took one to cut bread and butter with; at which I was very angry, and immediately called upon God to damn her, when this old black man told me that I must not say so. I asked him why? He replied that there was a wicked man called the devil, who lived in hell, and would take all who said these words, and put them into the fire, and burn them. This terrified me greatly and I was entirely broken off swearing. Soon after this, as I was placing the china for tea, my mistress came into the room just as the maid had been cleaning it, and the girl had unfortunately sprinkled the wainscot with the mop, at which my mistress was very angry. The girl very foolishly answered her again, which made her worse, and she [the mistress] called upon God to damn her. I was vastly concerned to hear this, as she was a fine young lady, and was very good to me, insomuch that I could not help speaking to her; "Madam," said I, "you must not say so." "Why?" said she. "Because there is a black man called the devil, that lives in hell, and he will put you into the fire and burn you, and I shall be very sorry for that." "Who told you this?" replied my lady. "Old Ned," said I. "Very well," was all her answer; but she told my master of it, and he ordered that old Ned should be tied up and whipped, and he was never suffered to come into the kitchen with the rest of the servants afterwards. My mistress was not angry with me, but rather diverted with my simplicity, and by way of talk, she repeated what I had said to many of her acquaintances. (Gronniosaw's *Narrative*, 8–9)

Gronniosaw apparently recounted this anecdote to show how he had been broken of taking the Lord's name in vain early in his spiritual evolution as a Christian. Although his innocent correction of his mistress brought her wrath down on a fellow slave, the persona draws an ingenuous conclusion from the episode: his "simplicity" of speech "diverted" his mistress so that she "was not angry with me." In fact, as the narrative goes on to reveal, her retelling of the story brought Gronniosaw's name to the attention of the minister who eventually bought and freed him. Thus while Old Ned received a cruel punishment for doing his Christian duty by the ignorant young African, James himself emerged from his violation of slave code (correction of his white mistress) with the woman's favor. One obvious silence in the text is why it was that Old Ned should be punished for young James's actions. All we are given is an unprobed narrative fact: James's words to his mistress signified the opposite of what Ned's message to James conveyed. No effort is made in the narrative to render this the tellable feature of the episode. And yet the very absence of interpretation in this vein, the implicit insistence on a simple reading of the episode, might give one pause. It was such simplicity that saved James from his mistress's anger, that allowed him to correct her while diverting her punishment. Could this be an anecdote that calls attention to its own simplicity as a *rhetorical* diversion, as a strategy adaptable to autobiography whereby a white reader's resistance to correction might also be diverted? In Afro-American writing, subterfuge and diversion have traditionally played a deconstructive role vis-à-vis conventional white literary modes and messages. Gronniosaw's "simplicity" suggests a rhetorical technique open to black narrators of white-controlled texts—narrative diversion as a way of making an injustice tellable even when it is not correctable.

Most early Afro-American autobiographies seem intended by their editors and publishers to celebrate the acculturation of blacks into the established categories of the white social and literary order. Silences of the kind noted in Gronniosaw's story made it possible for the amanuensis-editors of early black autobiography to accommodate these narratives to the organizing principles and cultural values of popular white autobiographical genres, in particular, the captivity narrative, the conversion account, the criminal confession, the spiritual autobiography, and the journal of ministerial labors. Within the boundaries of these genres, black self-portraits were cropped and framed according to the standards of an alienating culture. It would be a mistake, however, to think that the culture-endorsing purposes of these narratives turned their black subjects into objects, even though in the early decades of the genre they lacked the power to oversee what was written in their names. The process of acculturation did not divest the black narrator's experience of its specialness, though that narrator might not have had the liberty to comment—directly—on its significance. Nor did acculturation efface from the narrator's mind those special semantic fields in Afro-American culture that allowed certain words and concepts—Africa, black, freedom, human, and evil, for instance—to "reflect a specifically black segmentation and classification of experience."[8] Thus, while early black autobiographers usually celebrate the acculturation process, the process itself does not go uncritically examined. Some white-controlled narratives imply that acculturation changed black outsiders into insiders, but a few early black autobiographies resist this easy conclusion. In these latter works the acculturation process leaves the narrator with a dual perspective, that of the insider who remains outside in some crucial sense. It is this "double-consciousness," as W. E. B. Du Bois would term it much later, a sense of the "unreconciled strivings" involved in being both black and American, that emerges as the most telling revelation of early black autobiography.[9]

In the beginning black autobiography conceived of life as a difficult journey toward some sort of ultimate blessedness. Hammon's ordeal of repeated capture and fortuitous deliverance; Gronniosaw's conversion and faithful endurance of tribulations; Venture Smith's gritty struggle for freedom and independence in the white world were all adaptable to the trials-of-the-spirit autobiographical mode that bridged narratives of spiritual and secular adventure during that era.[10] Black criminal confessions also paralleled structurally and didactically many of the white rogue autobiographies of England and New England. In the shadow of the gallows most black criminals claimed to have found peace and hope through conversion. Their stories teach many of the same moral lessons that the spiritual autobiography urges, but by negative object lesson.

One of the fundamental moral issues treated in any autobiography is the proper relationship between the individual and the world. In the popular white autobiographical exempla of the late eighteenth century, the Christian individual was instructed that he or she must live in the world but must not be of the world. In America, living within the settled world was considered a desideratum for survival and a modicum of the amenities of a frontier society. As the Indian captivity narrative proved, the settlement was a realm of order and security, an outpost of moral values in a land of savagery. Outside the white man's sunny clearings lay darkness, chaos, and destruction, to be warded off only by the merciful hand of Providence. This did not mean, of course, that fallen human nature could not find much to tempt it within the gates of the civilized world. In evangelical conversion narratives from England and America, the narrator characterizes his or her unregenerate past as a time of self-indulgence, sensuousness, or irresponsibility, oftentimes exacerbated by the corruptness of society. After conversion these narrators generally feel called to redeem the world through their individual example. Keeping their moral distance from the carnality of the world, spiritual autobiographers count their suffering and alienation from the world as a blessing; their missionary individualism gains strength and self-confidence as it refuses to compromise with the world. However, as the criminal confessions indicate, an excessively uncompromising self, which became a law unto itself in both a secular and spiritual sense, needed to be restrained and punished by the world. One could not spurn some worldly institutions, such as the home, the church, or the state, without casting oneself in the role of subversive or rebel. To step outside the divinely sanctioned institutions of the world was, once again, to plunge into the chaos of the unbridled self and savagery. Even the more left-wing Christian individualists like the Methodists recognized that the redeemed self remained liable to err without a method to guide its devotional life. Purified institutions and rigorous self-discipline were necessary as structures and boundaries by which the heavenward soul could measure its progress.

Most early slave narratives are structured around these same assumptions about the relationship of the individual soul and the world. In Hammon's narrative the world outside the control of his benevolent master is extremely precarious and oppressive. Once the slave is separated from his master's care and influence, he is rendered defenseless and directionless in the great world. Only God can resurrect him from the Spanish dungeon in Jamaica: only "Divine Goodness" is strong enough to restore the black man, "like one arose from the Dead," to his patron. Let the slave stray outside the known world of stratified white-over-black relationships, Hammon's narrative implies, and he will risk a life in limbo. He will become a type of the lost soul, disconnected from civilization's preserving institutions, sustained solely by the survival instinct.

Gronniosaw's narrative draws more explicitly on the presumed pathos of the Negro as a lost soul in the sinful world while also giving its readers one of the first portraits of the ex-slave as wretched freeman. Whether enslaved or free, Gronniosaw is a man in search of a refuge from the world. Ever the alien, even in his African boyhood, young James finds upon conversion to Christianity an initial sense of self-sufficiency. "I felt an unwillingness in myself to have anything more to do with the world, or to mix with society again." Nor would he have had to, but his master, Mr. Freelandhouse, dies not long after James's conversion, leaving him free and patronless. He readily attaches himself to Mrs. Freelandhouse and other members of her family, but they all die soon thereafter, forcing Gronniosaw to decide once again what to do with himself. Emigrating to England, he seeks "some Christian friends, with whom I hoped to enjoy a little sweet and comfortable society" safe from the wickedness of the world. Adversity far outweighs charity for a black man in Britain, yet Gronniosaw professes to be undismayed. For now, he is "willing, and even desirous to be counted as nothing, a stranger in the world," so that one day he might be welcomed into "the everlasting glories of the world to come." To be a nullity in this world is not something just to be accepted but to be desired. The less worldly identification he claims, the greater heavenly identity he may anticipate.

In the black criminal confession, the majority of which concern slave-born men, the narrator's first and greatest mistake is his rejection of parental advice and/or his master's supervision in favor of a bid for self-sufficiency in the world. Virtually all these slaves characterize their relationships with their masters as lenient and often morally instructive. Joseph Mountain, criminal extraordinaire, grew up as a house slave in Philadelphia, where he learned reading, writing, and "the sentiments of virtue." But he "neglected" his training, shipped to England (for unstated reasons), and soon went "in quest of amusements" in London. The remainder of his narrative lists in detail the various "species of debauchery" he took up after falling in with a band of gamblers and highwaymen. Twenty-one-year-old Arthur also enjoyed many privileges as a slave growing up in Massachusetts, but for no clear reason he ran away and immediately descended into a life of thievery and sexual crime. Facing the gallows, he warned blacks "as they regard their own souls, to avoid desertion from their masters, drunkenness, and lewdness."[11]

The average black criminal narrative is the story of a young man whose break with the authority figures in his life is presented as a symbol of his willful contempt for all systems of ordering and restraining the self. What a twentieth-century school of psychology would interpret as a violently expressed but natural "striving for power" and "superiority" over the impinging world, the eighteenth-century black criminal narrative viewed as a manifestation of the inherently anarchic self at war with instituted controls over it. The classic conflict between natural and civil liberty, first outlined by John Winthrop, is dramatized repeatedly in the slave's rejection of all the "ordinances of God" and reversion to the state of a "wild beast" run amuck.[12] In the nineteenth century the fugitive slave narrative would be used to justify a slave's rejection of his society's moral code and his forcible flight from its ethical as well as physical bonds. But in the eighteenth century the fugitive slave had no such champion in the slave narrative. The anarchic careers of escaped slaves like Arthur, Edmund Fortis, and Stephen Smith proved the necessity of maintaining the status quo in the social hierarchy and hinted strongly that the Negro who fled outside it would find himself lost in the chaos of his own selfish appetites.[13]

Black narratives based on the captivity, conversion, and criminal confession models invited a pitying or retributive response from the white reader, depending on whether the Afro-American was depicted as impo-

41

tent or wayward when placed on his own in the world. The pathetic element in the stories of Gronniosaw or Venture Smith is accentuated in such a way as to celebrate these men for endurance, not active heroism. Although Smith reminds his sympathetic amanuensis-editor of "a Franklin or a Washington . . . in a state of slavery," the white man is most impressed by an absence of what "might have been," not by what Smith actually was. He "might have been a man of high respectability and usefulness"; he "might have been an ornament and an honor to human nature." Smith's failure to live up to these arbitrary, culture-bound standards is attributed to his enslavement, which, according to his amanuensis-editor, left him "wholly uncultivated, enfeebled, and depressed." Yet a reading of his narrative suggests, if nothing else, what "might have been" made of this ex-slave's adventures had his prefacer been able to see him as more than a victim.[14]

The restless, rootless lives and ignominious deaths of men like Arthur and Mountain provided testimony for the widespread colonial belief that the average Afro-American needed supervision, if not rigorous control, on his life's journey between the Scylla of an innately savage self and the Charybdis of the perverted world.[15] Most narratives climax in either (1) rituals of reintegration and domestication for homeless blacks adrift in the world, or (2) professions of black reconciliation to the white sociomoral order. In either case the individual discovers that his felicity coincides with his fate within the instituted structures that white society has erected for him as a bulwark against the world. At the conclusion of the large majority of black autobiographies between 1760 and 1810, there is an attempt to turn the tragedy of the lost Negro into a sort of Christian comedy by showing the wandering protagonist being led providentially home to the protective authority of his master, the state, or his Heavenly Father.

To make black narratives fit this pattern of separation yielding to integration, many concepts crucial to an evaluation of the significance of a Negro's life in America had to be defined in limited, if not grotesque, ways. The ideas of captivity and deliverance, freedom and necessity, ignorance and enlightenment, salvation and damnation—the thematic substructure of most early black narratives—are generally defined according to the semantic fields and constitutive rules of white institutions and discourse. As a result, much early black autobiography traffics in ignorance about the actual choices black people had in America and about the meaning of those choices from a black perspective. In the white Indian captivity narrative escape from the savages meant deliverance from bondage into freedom and community among one's fellows. But when Briton Hammon was released from the Florida Indians who held him, he was not restored to a community. He was subjected to worse savagery by the Spanish authorities in Jamaica, who ransomed him only to reimprison him for four more years. White people are not Hammon's fellows; they are with rare exception part of the indifferent and cruel world. At the end of his story the persona declares that he has been "freed from a long and dreadful Captivity," that he has been "return'd to my own Native Land," and that the Lord is to be praised for his deliverance. Such ritualized statements are standard stuff in ordinary captivity narratives, but they sound peculiar and contradictory coming from a man of Hammon's race and caste. In what sense was he freed if the experience led to his being restored to a previous slavemaster? In what sense might a black slave speak of New England as his "Native Land"? Did Hammon include in his period of "dreadful Captivity" the eight months he spent as an independent, wage-earning seaman in England before his reunion with his master and return to Massachusetts? The dualistic worldview and racist semantic fields that underlie the genre of the captivity narrative do not admit the sorts of specialized questions one might wish to pose to the earliest Afro-American autobiographers.

These kinds of questions proliferate upon reading a typical black criminal confession. Drawn up according to the formula of the time, these accounts never answer satisfactorily the question of why a slave ran away or why a black man became a criminal in the first place. One simply has to assume that these narrators were guilty of the charges brought against them. Some blamed "lewd women" for their troubles, others strong drink and Sabbath-breaking, and one admitted that he had always been "naturally too much inclined to vice" to live virtuously.[16] But none traced his sociopathic behavior back to his alien condition in American society or his prior treatment as a slave. The implication of almost all black criminal narratives is that the slave youth was at home in bondage; he became an ingrate when he alienated himself from that familial institution. The attempt of the amanuensis-editors of these narratives is to mold the condemned man's story into an exemplum of the prodigal son. Thus, standing on the edge of eternity, the typical criminal narrator professes to have found peace and hope at the end of his miserable career. Mouthing grave warnings about the wages of sin, he asks forgiveness from all he has injured. He thanks the jailor for his kindness and the priest for his concern for a willful soul's salvation. The punishment handed down by his white surrogate father, the judge in his trial, seems to him fair and necessary as a just "forfeiture" of life to "the injured laws of his country." The hangman offers him one last chance to expiate his sins.[17]

Inasmuch as the black criminal confession was usually narrated by escaped slaves or rebellious ex-slaves, it is an obvious literary ancestor of

43

the fugitive slave narratives of the mid-nineteenth century. However, nothing in the literature of antislavery in America better illustrates the revolution in social attitudes toward the slave than the thematic polarities between the eighteenth- and nineteenth-century fugitive slave narratives. One of the more important rhetorical achievements of the slave narrative from 1830 to 1865 was its identification of the fugitive with romanticized culture heroes like Moses, Patrick Henry, or even Spartacus. But in the eighteenth century the rebellious slave is treated as a skulker from duty, not a seeker of liberty. The interrogators and amanuenses of these condemned men were agents, not reformers, of church and state, and the narratives they published were aimed at justifying the ways of God and the state to the black man. Even the Reverend Richard Allen, who remembered his youth in slavery as "a bitter pill" and who vigorously defended blacks from criminal slander in broadly social contexts, could find nothing to mitigate the awful guilt of John Joyce, murderer of a white woman. In Allen's eyes the causes of Joyce's deed stemmed from the fact that he, like too many other black Philadelphians, had been a "slave of Sin." In two or three decades abolitionists and fugitive slaves would indict slavery itself as a cause of black transgressions against morality and law. In the first fifty years of the slave narrative, however, the slavery of sin received much more condemnation than the sin of slavery.[18]

James Gronniosaw's narrative bears out this contention. After the adolescent slave undergoes the spiritual tortures familiar to readers of conversion accounts, he receives grace, which liberates him from the only kind of bondage he fears—enslavement to his "corrupt nature" as a sinner. For this brand of salvation Gronniosaw is profoundly thankful. The providential removal of his earthly master, emancipating the young slave, only makes Gronniosaw feel "distressed." He speaks of freedom as a blessing solely in spiritual terms. The death of Freelandhouse sets Gronniosaw free in the world, where he could see only temptations and tribulations, as the conversion narrative model prescribed. Not surprisingly for a man raised in dependency, freedom does not connote secular opportunity but trials of the spirit. Gronniosaw's editor-amanuensis interpreted his fear of the world and his ceaseless search for "some Christian friends" in conventional evangelical terms, as a manifestation of his righteousness, not as a sign of his unpreparedness for life in the world.

The idea of freedom in spiritual autobiography is relative, depending on the protagonist's saved or unsaved status. The meaning of freedom is summed up in the Pauline paradox: to place oneself under the mastery of Christ is to liberate oneself from the bondage of sin.[19] Nevertheless, one does not deliberately select Christ's saving yoke; one cannot liberate oneself from sin. A slave to sin from birth, the unregenerate man has neither the power nor the freedom to extricate himself from guilt unless Christ, through grace unmerited by the sinner, extends moral strength to him. Thus in the conventional conversion narrative, which is a kind of slave narrative in spiritual terms, the hero-liberator is always Christ, never the convert. The convert's role is limited for the most part to recording the action of Providence that rescued him or her from enslavement to sin and death.

This concept of freedom in white spiritual autobiography further diminished the independent agency of blacks in first-person narratives that concentrated on conversion as the central fact in a black person's life. The title of a widely known Afro-American conversion and captivity narrative is very illustrative: *Narrative of the Lord's Wonderful Dealings with John Marrant, A Black*. Marrant's racial identity in this work is almost totally subsumed under his generic identity as Christian pilgrim who accepts his fate with these submissive words to his Lord: "I will thank thee for what is passed, and trust thee for what is to come."[20] The epigraph placed on the title page of Gronniosaw's narrative similarly identifies the protagonist of this story as the object, not the subject, of the action: "I will bring the blind by a way that they know not; I will lead them in paths that they have not known; I will make darkness light before them, and crooked things straight. These will I do unto them, and not forsake them" (Isaiah 42:16). God is given the responsibility for leading the slave to a point where his "darkness" is enlightened and "crooked things" are straightened out. Thus, as his story develops, Gronniosaw does not analyze his adversities to find out how the world works. He thinks his job as narrator is to recall how his experiences "have all been sanctified to me." Consequently, in remembering one desperate winter in Colchester, England, Gronniosaw never ponders the reasons why he was jobless and had to depend on the charity of four carrots from a gentleman's gardener to keep himself and his family alive. He never speculates on what lay behind the "envious and ill natured" reaction of "the inferior people" of Norwich when they saw him and his white wife prospering in their town. He simply states that these "inferior" whites "worked under price on purpose to get my business from me; and they succeeded so well that I could scarcely get anything to do, and we became again unfortunate."[21]

Calling this an injustice, not to mention condemning its apparently racist origins, would be inconsistent with Gronniosaw's role as a spiritual pilgrim with his eye on how everything had been sanctified to him. Still, Gronniosaw's un-Christian judgment of his rivals as "the inferior people" raises tantalizing questions. At this point, did Gronniosaw's resentment of caste prejudice against him betray his pious persona? Is this snag in the narrative, when the pathos of Gronniosaw's tone is punctured, an indication of the black narrator's momentary usurpation of God's (or the white reader's) role as judge and interpreter of the dark and crooked things in his life? Or did the word "inferior" come from the pen of the lady of Leominster and thus reflect her sympathy for Gronniosaw against unfair competition? It is impossible to be certain about such matters in a dictated narrative such as this.

Some things we can be sure of, however. The structures whereby the captivity and conversion genres organized and interpreted Afro-American experience proved a mixed blessing to early black autobiography. On the positive side, the Bible, the main source of ideology and metaphor for eighteenth-century personal literature in America, spoke profoundly of the telos of life as liberation from bondage. If early Afro-American culture engendered a "pregeneric myth" whose theme was the quest for freedom and literacy,[22] then the captivity and conversion genres offered models that could express and justify that quest in spiritual terms which did not seem to threaten white institutions. Moreover, the publication of conversion narratives about blacks supported humanitarian arguments that far from being a subhuman brute, the African had a soul as worthy of salvation in God's eyes as the Caucasian's. In addition, if the conversion narrative, with its attention to the spiritual affairs of ordinary people, spurred the democratization of English and American literature, then by embracing lowly blacks, it admitted Afro-American spiritual experience into literature on a footing apparently equal to that of whites.

Nevertheless, there were serious liabilities in the spiritual autobiography's concept of liberation when it was applied to the experience of blacks. As Sacvan Bercovitch has stressed, the personal literature of the Puritans, from which the conversion and captivity narratives evolved, teaches that "self-examination serves not to liberate but to constrict; selfhood appears as a state to be overcome, obliterated."[23] Thus the conversion model offered the slave narrator an ideal of freedom *from* the self, not *for* the self. In this way the conversion narrative sanctioned and encouraged self-hatred and the rejection of one's past—attitudes that later black autobiographers have identified as special nemeses of black people in search of authentic selfhood. The conversion narrative's view of the origins and Christian response to the evils of the world also handicapped the early Afro-American autobiographer. Implicitly or explicitly, the narratives of Hammon, Gronniosaw, and Marrant echo George White's faith that despite "adversity, pain, and sickness" the Christian must "rejoice in the wisdom of God, as ordering all events." The miseries of this world will "turn to his advantage," White assured his reader, since "whom the

Lord loveth he chasteneth" (Proverbs 3:12).[24] As a result of this conviction, none of the early black narratives of deliverance and conversion questions or, more importantly, analyzes reversals and suffering, whether of natural (sickness and accidents) or human (deceptions, fraud, or violence) origin.

Rather than temporal causation, the reader of these early narratives is offered the indefinite design of Providence in what now might be called the "metaphysics of presence" of early black autobiography. This presence, we have seen thus far, exerted a repressive influence on the potential of the new genre to inscribe a competing presence of its own onto black autobiography. What we discover, however, as we pursue the genre into the early nineteenth century, is a growing tension between two models of presence in black autobiography, the one providential and inexplicable except by faith, the other historical and understandable (to some important extent, at least) by experience, particularly of the situation of blacks in the white world. This tension is mirrored in other kinds of double consciousness in these early narratives, such as that which pits an ahistorical view of the Negro as Christian Everyman, symbol of every pilgrim soul, against a counter-realization of the Negro as historical and cultural individual, whose enforced alienation from Every(white)man furnishes a commentary on the Christian culture. This tension is not resolved in those early black autobiographies that feature it. It becomes instead the intellectual field in which the viability of an ahistorical versus a historical conception of presence is tested. The few narratives that do insist on a more historical conception do not resolve the problems that arise from this new way of contextualizing, and thus inevitably enclosing, selfhood in a new frame. But from a rhetorical standpoint, adopting a historical framework in which to conduct discourse about a black self made it possible for autobiographers to probe discrepancies between their temporal experience and the providential rationale for it. For the first time black narrators had a basis from which to call the trouble they had seen an injustice to their humanity that must be resisted, not a trial for their faith to be endured. When early black autobiographers started assigning causation and culpability to *men* for the evils *they* brought on their peers, the genre could begin to distinguish itself as an Afro-American form of discourse.

The first steps in this direction appear in the narratives of four onetime slaves: a murderer named Pomp, executed in 1795, the African-born Venture Smith, and two preachers, George White and John Jea. None of these men goes so far as to espouse abolitionism in his story, but all testify against "the peculiar institution" as an instrument of oppression, and all feel justified in seizing their chances to escape it. White was born a slave in Virginia in 1764. At the age of five he was separated from his mother, whom he never saw again. He does not detail the "cruel bondage" that was his for the next twenty-one years, but he censures the "vice and immorality" that arose from the "abject slavery" he witnessed in the Old Dominion. Freed in his master's will, White emigrated to the North, where all but the opening pages of his *Brief Account* is set. Still, in the first two pages of this narrative, he delivered the most unrelenting attack on slavery as a social system that had yet appeared in Afro-American autobiography. One should note that White was the first slave narrator to compose and write down his life on his own.

Almost simultaneously with the publication of White's narrative appeared *The Life, History, and Unparalleled Sufferings of John Jea, the African Preacher* (c. 1811).[25] In the opening pages of Jea's dictated story, the generalities that White used to characterize a monstrous regime receive detailed documentation for the first time in Afro-American autobiography. Anticipating the kind of exposé-writing that would make the slave narrative in the nineteenth century so popular, Jea wasted no time in seizing his reader's attention via a recitation of ugly facts from his past. In the first paragraph of narration Jea described the ration allotted him by his New York master: "Indian corn pounded, or bruised and boiled with water, the same way burgo is made, and about a quart of sour butter-milk poured on it; for one person two quarts of this mixture, and about three ounces of dark bread, per day, the bread was darker than that usually allowed to convicts, and greased over with very indifferent hog's lard." In his second paragraph he recalled his master's mode of "correcting" his slaves: "We were corrected with a weapon an inch-and-a-half thick, and that without mercy, striking us in the most tender parts, and if we complained of this usage, they then took four large poles, placed them in the ground, tied us up to them, and flogged us in a mannner too dreadful to behold." Noting these outrages at the beginning of his story enabled Jea to use his life as a text from which he could preach against hypocritical Christians such as his former master. In the latter two-thirds of his life, during which he was a free-lance evangelist in America, England, France, and Holland, Jea met with resistance and exploitation of various kinds, which he complains of but does not denounce as racially motivated. Instead, like a much more conventional preacher, he uses his trials to illustrate homilies on faith, repentance, fear of the Lord, and sinless living, which increasingly crowd out the narrative portions of his autobiography. In the same way the conventional image of the pilgrim for Christ usurps the persona of the righteously indignant African who launches the narrative.

Venture Smith and Pomp also commented explicitly on the abuses that they suffered as slaves and freemen, but this feature of their narratives is not what most deserves our attention here. The most remarkable thing about both of their stories is the impingement of the irrational on the structures of order and meaning that the notion of providential presence enforced in most black autobiographies. In Pomp's *Dying Confession*, the irrationality of a slaveowner's arbitrary power supplants providential design as the causal agent in a slave's life. This irrational agent spawns a unique persona in this narrative—a derationalizing other, an antagonist to the white amanuensis-editor's power to rationalize and thus explain away a slave's violation of social and moral norms.

Pomp was a Massachusetts slave who was hanged in 1795 for the premeditated murder of his master, Captain Furbush. From his early youth in Andover, his narrative suggests, Pomp felt himself the object of forces beyond his control. When he first learned in his teens that he could not leave the master to whom he had been bound, the young slave was stricken with "convulsion fits which continued to oppress me at times ever after, to the fatal night that I murdered Capt. Furbush." Under Furbush's rule, Pomp suffers from constant harassment and cruelty, the unreasonableness of which is underlined by the fact that the slave has managed his master's farm to financial success. Furbush's crazy behavior, which includes turning his own horses loose in a cornfield from which Pomp expected a fine harvest, drives his slave to desperate attempts to run away. When captured, Pomp is beaten and humiliated; meanwhile he is "frequently troubled with convulsion fits and [is thought?] crazy" by Furbush, who locks him in his quarters each night. On the day of the murder Pomp rises "considerably disordered, having a great singing noise in the ears, and something whispering strange things to me." After being "seized with a fit" and hearing voices urging him "now is your time! kill him now! now or never! now! now!" Pomp enters Furbush's bedroom, decapitates him with an axe while he sleeps next to his wife, and then docilely allows Mrs. Furbush to call the sheriff. In jail he reports to his amanuensis, Jonathan Plummer, that he no longer suffers from "fits and lunacy." Having prayed for and achieved the "new heart" that his ministers have prescribed for him, he now sees himself as fast becoming "a very extraordinary priest." In fact, "now I have scarcely a drop of black blood left in me, my blood having so faded into the blood of a Minister, that I am [becoming] as white as a Mulatto." [26]

Plummer could not let such comments as these stand as a conclusion for Pomp's confession without having the last word. By attaching to Pomp's story a guide to correct interpretation, the white man asserted his editorial prerogative to decide the referentiality of a black man's words.

To Plummer, Pomp's story was significant in that it showed the necessity of the moral education of slaves, especially when they seemed as industriously inclined and as long-suffering as Pomp. Plummer was very disturbed by evidence that Pomp seemed untroubled by the enormity of his deed. Because he displayed "no idea of the calm, but irreversible ire, the deliberate but vindictive, vengeance of offended Justice and of Heaven" toward his crime, Plummer decided that the slave had no perception of the difference between good and evil or of the dire consequences of breaking the law. The moral to the story of "poor Pomp," Plummer concluded, was the Negro's tragic lack of moral discrimination and restraint unless compensated for by white instruction and restraint. As for Pomp's exculpatory references to "something telling him to kill," this was merely "a falsehood," Plummer asserted, a fiction "contrived by [Pomp] to excuse his crime."

Pomp's *Dying Confession* pits two explanations of black criminal behavior against each other for the first time in Afro-American autobiography. Plummer's argument is based on the notion of the Negro as absence. His lack of remorse for murder shows that he has no moral sense, and in justifying his crime with the "whispering" voices, he proves that he lacks truthfulness. Pomp's narrative, on the other hand, insists that there was something at work in the black man's psyche, a dynamic whose manifestations in the actions and language of Pomp resisted Furbush's methods of control and Plummer's system of reference. The symbols of this dynamic—the whispering voices before the killing of Furbush, the "new heart" and whitening skin after it—have psychological reference for today's reader, who may translate Pomp's sense of whitening as a metaphor of his belief that through his ritual of violent purification, he had earned the right to assimilate into the white world. Plummer could not read Pomp in this way because to the white man, black consciousness was a dark tabula rasa, either imprinted by whites and thus decodable by them, or left blank and void. Pomp's personal metaphors of purgation and deliverance, together with his inversion of light-dark imagery, were not explainable according to Plummer's grammar of symbols. This did not suggest to Plummer the inadequacy of his interpretation but the perversity of Pomp's. The slave had "contrived" something other than truth, which Plummer could name only as "falsehood."

Today we may still be unable to say what Pomp's tropes and symbols mean. Rather than attempting to assign them definite psychological meanings, however, I think that we should take note of the arbitrariness and culture-defying perversity of Pomp's figurative language. The very indeterminateness of Pomp's symbology has its own rhetorical force. On Pomp's tabula of consciousness, the symbols of the "new heart" and the "whitening" self have been inscribed and then placed "under erasure," in Martin Heidegger's and Jacques Derrida's terms,[27] so that the concepts cannot be read in Pomp's narrative without our realizing what is *not* there—a recognizable presence investing "new heart" and "whitening" with determinable meaning. Some indeterminate other whispers through Pomp's symbols as untraceably as the strange voices that led the black man to kill his master. Just as arbitrarily as the symbols of "new heart" and "whitening" could be made to signify repentance, so does Pomp's use of them signify the opposite. This derationalizing of Christian signs into arbitrary and indeterminate symbols constitutes as profound an assault on the white man's intellectual order as the killing of Furbush was on the white social order. Like many in the nineteenth century whose ontological and semiological assumptions were contradicted by slave narrators, Plummer preserved his world view by denying Pomp's. For reasons such as this, the myth of the slave narrator as a teller of "falsehoods" contrived to "excuse his crimes" spread widely.

Disillusionment with the myth of black acculturation into white society is the explicit theme of Venture Smith's dictated autobiography. After life in slavery subjects him to white treachery and meanness, life as a freeman, Smith discovers, offers him little recompense. He tries to deserve white respect by purchasing his freedom (instead of running away) and by adopting middle-class values. Advising his reader on the way to wealth, Smith recalls, "I bought nothing which I did not absolutely want. All fine clothes I despised in comparison with . . . a decent homespun dress, a good supply of money and prudence. Expensive gatherings of my mates I commonly shunned, and all kinds of luxuries I was perfectly a stranger to." Such Franklinesque self-denial helped Smith accumulate the money with which to buy his enslaved family. It also made him prosperous enough to avoid expulsion from Long Island during an antiblack purge. But if Smith thought the acquisition of real estate, sailing vessels, and capital would win him power and respect among whites, he admits at the end of his narrative how mistaken he was. After years of being deceived and cheated by whites (and some blacks), he concludes that slave or free, the black man is little more than a "defenceless stranger" in the white world. Institutions like the courts have little to do with "reason or justice," Smith states after learning the futility of resisting a rich white man's suit against him. "Such a proceeding as this, Smith concludes, "whatever it may be called in a Christian land, would in my native country have been branded as a crime equal to highway robbery. But Captain Hart was a *white gentleman*, and I a *poor African*, therefore it was *all right, and good enough for the black dog*."[28]

This is the climax of Smith's narrative, this assertion of an idealized African point of reference for defining morality in the face of the arbitrariness of American standards. In this culminating instance of betrayal, the former slave demonstrates a lesson in American sociolinguistics, namely, that all reference is in the service of racism. The italics emphasize the key factor in his suit with Captain Hart. This was not a contest between equals but rather between a privileged white and his caste inferior. The translation of "poor African" into "black dog" illustrates graphically a basic rule of American discourse—that any word, when used by whites, means "whatever it may be called in this Christian land." This lack of a fixed core of meaning and value in America leads Smith to declare at the end of his story, "Vanity of vanities, all is vanity."

The first in a long line of black bourgeois autobiographers,[29] Smith dedicated himself to the quest for assimilation via material success, only to end up condemning the society that rejected him. Although his narrative totals up his losses in one betrayal after another, this is not the autobiography of a loser. Standing at the end of his life's quest, without power, community, or religious faith to assuage his sense of alienation, Smith could yet draw consolation from his love for his wife, his conviction of his own integrity, and, above all, his freedom. By recognizing these quasi-existential resources, not the glimmering promises of the American dream, as the sine qua non for the black pilgrimage in America, Smith posited a certain stoic pride in his own uncompromised and alien self as a secular standard for heroism in black autobiography.

Like Venture Smith, George White was also an ambitious man to whom freedom from slavery was merely the first stage in an extended quest for status and power in the white world. There were important differences between the two men's strategies and careers, however. Smith hoped to succeed as a black rugged individualist in the rough-and-tumble of American economic life. White opted for status in a white institution as his ticket to the kind of independence and power he desired. Smith's is a story of constant reversals of fortune leading to a largely embittered conclusion. White's *Brief Account* recalls a string of triumphs over considerable odds. After his emancipation from twenty-six years of slavery, White recounts his ecstatic conversion to Christianity and the evolution of his conviction of having been called to the ministry. He applies for an exhorter's license in the New York Methodist Conference, overcoming illiteracy and platform phobia to qualify for it. Convinced later that "God required me to preach his gospel in a more direct manner, than my license as an exhorter permitted me to attempt," White petitions for a preaching license and endures repeated refusals by his white examiners to admit him to full ministerial status in the Methodist church. Eventually, however, he wins the presiding elder's approval and ordination as a full-fledged preacher in the predominantly white church. The lesson of his experience defies the disillusionment of Venture Smith: "By putting my trust in God," White states, "and obeying his will, under all these trials, infinite goodness has caused all events to turn to my account at last" (33).

The image that White assumed, that of the patient man of faith enduring trials under the guidance of the Lord, is consistent with the formula of the other narratives of Christian pilgrimage that were published in the names of blacks during this time. White is singular, however, in the direction that his pilgrimage took—toward a specific position within a white institution. White claims that God called him to aspire to the exhorter's and then the preacher's role. Regardless of whether we read this as an explanation of or a justification for his ambition, his example demands attention. White is the first organization man in Afro-American autobiography. White's successors in the genre include the many black ministers and educators, epitomized by men like Bishop Daniel Payne and Booker T. Washington,[30] whose autobiographies define the self largely in terms of the institution with which the autobiographer most identified. Like their white counterparts in the nineteenth century, many black organization men portrayed their institutional careers as exercises in sublimation, whereby devotion to the mission of the institution disciplined the individual in self-denial and altruism. This unselfish orientation reinforced the tendency in early black autobiography to absent the individual self from narrative attention and to put in its stead some institution—the church or the state most often—to represent the narrator's "better self," to which he ought to conform. White, however, reveals something about the psychological and social negotiations that lay behind a black man's assumption of an institutional identity. In his *Brief Account* we recognize the sociopolitical significance of White's institutional aspirations and the price his individuality had to pay, in "real life" and in his narrative recounting of it, to be institutionalized in the white world.

White's negotiations with a white institution began when he applied for a license to exhort in the Methodist church. His "brethren," as he termed them, willingly acceded to his request. The early Methodist church in America did not specify exactly what an exhorter's duty was, but it is clear that he occupied the lowest standing in the church's hierarchy, beneath bishop, elder, deacon, and preacher. Exhorters had to have permission to preach before the individual societies of the church. It appears that the role was limited to para-ministerial duties, such as the leading of Sabbath school classes, prayer meetings, and other informal evangelistic gatherings.[31] A vision from God only a few months after becoming an exhorter heightens White's sense of calling beyond this level of service. His sermon to a licensing committee does not move the members, however, nor do his second and third performances in subsequent months. He declares that he accepted these "trials" in "the spirit of Christian fortitude" until his fifth petition for a preaching license in the winter of 1807. Then, when the committee again tells him he ought to remain an exhorter, he replies that he cannot be satisfied without "greater liberty than I now enjoy." When asked what sort of "liberty" he feels is denied him as an exhorter, he answers, "Liberty to speak from a text." At this point a member of the committee who White thought was a friend informs him that "it was the devil who was pushing me on to preach" (pp. 24–25). Although hurt by this impugning of his motives, White shows no further resentment of this sort of intimidation, nor does he speculate on its cause. Instead, he says that he put the matter into God's hands and, eventually, saw it work out to his vindication and triumph.

George White's life is presented as a continuing quest for "greater liberty." Freedom from chattel slavery in the South was not sufficient liberty, nor was the opportunity to serve in the lowest echelon of white institutional life in the North. Having gained the liberty to speak before church gatherings, he soon demanded the profounder liberty of speaking from, that is, interpreting, the institution's sacred text, its raison d' être, the Bible. The sanction to speak *from* Christianity's talismanic text to the white, as well as black, people of God would identify this "African" in a radically new way, as both White and the licensing committee knew. Inscribed in the Western literary tradition, first through the narrative of James Gronniosaw and later through the much more widely known story of the Anglo-African Olaudah Equiano, was the striking image of the Negro's discovery of the Bible as a sealed and silent text that refused to speak to him.[32] Initially unacknowledged by the Bible in this manner, the Negro in the West set out in quest of the power of literacy in the white man's tongue in order to open up a saving intercourse with the Book of Books. The knowledge of reading would make the book of white magic "talk to" a black; but much more important was the freedom to elaborate the words of the white text in a black voice through a black perspective. This kind of power would place the black reader-speaker in a crucial *mediative* position between God's text and His audience. With this liberty a Negro like White could move beyond both the heathen African's alienation from the Bible and the Afro-American exhorter's parasitic dependency on the white man's version of the Word. White could become a facilitator of discourse in his own right.

Three years after attaining the crucial power to "speak from a text" in the Bible, White took the next logical step in his campaign for freedom of expression. He spoke from his own text by composing his autobiography in 1810. The subtitle of White's *Brief Account—Written By Himself—*

proclaims a "greater liberty" than the genre had had previously. The salvation story of White lent itself to the unself-conscious manner of a Marrant or Gronniosaw, but his career as an orator led him to write in the "oratorical mode" of autobiography, to use William Howarth's terms.[33] Stressing, as such autobiographers usually do, the idea of evolving vocation, White compels our special attention because his story embodies the archetypal stages of evolution that appear again and again in nineteenth-century black autobiography. Physical liberty from bondage leads inevitably to the struggle to free the mind and empower the self via the arts of language: speaking, reading, and writing. White's conception of his vocation within a semantic field whose parameters are "liberty," "speak," "text," and "written by himself" anticipates the black autobiographer in his primary nineteenth-century role—as wordsmith. The fear that White's desire for linguistic liberty instilled in his "white brethren" forecasts the resistance that black speech action often aroused, as books like Frederick Douglass's *My Bondage and My Freedom* (1855) attest. Taking liberties with the sacred texts of white institutions would be justified by writers like Douglass as a Promethean rather than simply a Luciferian act.

If George White was aware of what hindsight suggests is the social and literary import of his autobiographical act, he gave no inkling of it in the *Brief Account*. As he recounts his humiliations and frustrations at the hands of the white Methodists, he seeks no more significance in these "trials" of his faith than did the conventional spiritual autobiographer. However, this refusal to impute ulterior motives to others gave him one advantage: he did not have to acknowledge and plumb the same inner dimension in himself. This strategy allowed him to approach his reader in much the same pose as he employed before the hearers of his petitions to preach. Despite the fact that he was clearly a man of great aspiration and will, he won over the suspicious Methodists by displaying an uncomplaining, undesigning manner. These are the salient attributes of the persona that White employs in his probationary effort as autobiographer, too. The year 1810 was too early for a black autobiographer to start taking whites into his confidence, particularly about such "institutional facts" (to use John Searle's term) as the significance of a black preacher in a white episcopacy. Moreover, White would have risked much of what he had gained had he used his insider's perspective to its fullest advantage in his narrative. If he had written his autobiography a decade later, after he had withdrawn from white Methodism to help found the African Methodist Episcopal Zion church in New York,[34] White might have left a more revealing account of his "trials" seen from the outsider's perspective. As it is, the *Brief Account* keeps the reader so far outside the realm of the narrative consciousness that one feels almost as screened off from the private White as one does from Marrant or Gronniosaw in their dictated stories.

Nevertheless, the example of George White is impressive. Next to Marrant's and Gronniosaw's stories, the *Brief Account* suggests what White's pen could do that the Reverend Aldridge's or the lady of Leominster's could not. It could place words like "liberty," "speak," and "text" in relationship to each other and to the structure of a narrative so that one senses a door being opened into an Afro-American semantic field. White's persona, however, closes this opening into significance by creating a gap between the linguistic sign and its *black* cultural significance, which only a historical awareness of the development of black discourse can fill. By inhibiting the interpretation of these key signs in a bicultural perspective, the persona invites the reader to understand White's career in the familiar, one-way linear pattern of acculturation, from outsider to insider. Later in the nineteenth century, as black autobiography becomes a more dialectical form of discourse, the double consciousness of the African-American's interstitial and mediative situation in the United States challenges the monomyth of acculturation. But in the first fifty years of black autobiography, we must look outside the American tradition to find this sort of critical perspective of marginality. We must look, in other words, to the autobiography of Olaudah Equiano.

The most famous and influential black autobiography of its time, *The Interesting Narrative of the Life of Olaudah Equiano, or Gustavus Vassa, the African*, was first published in London in 1789. Despite the fact that Equiano was a British citizen who addressed his autobiography to the English Parliament as part of a campaign to end the slave trade in the Empire, the *Narrative* has often been claimed for Afro-American letters. Yet a reading of Equiano's story will reveal he apparently spent no more than two years in the North American colonies during his entire life. In 1756 at the age of eleven this son of Ibo nobility arrived in Virginia to work on a plantation, but he was purchased soon thereafter by a British naval officer who kept him abroad during the next few years. Working in the 1760s as an itinerant seaman and trader in the Caribbean, Equiano witnessed the horrors of slavery in the British West Indies. It was this model of slavery that spurred him to become the first black autobiographer in English to indite a detailed analysis and powerful denunciation of slavery. Business compelled Equiano to visit seaports like Charleston and Savannah relatively often in the mid-1760s, but the injustices he encountered there as a black freeman meant that he tarried in these places no longer than he had to. England, as he says in his narrative, was the land "where my heart had always been."[35] America he visited only rarely and briefly during the last thirty years of his life. After 1786 he devoted himself to black colonization and antislavery work in England, where he died and was buried in 1797. In light of these facts alone, it seems more sensible to view Equiano as an Anglo-African writer whose compatriots were figures like Ignatius Sancho and Ottabah Cugoano than to discuss him as one of the early voices of the Afro-American autobiographical tradition.[36]

Equiano's narrative is different in kind as well as degree from the more schematized Afro-American autobiographies of the late eighteenth and early nineteenth centuries. In a history of Afro-American autobiography it serves best as a comparative example, indicative of literary possibilities inherent in the Westernized African's marginal, bicultural perspective, although such possibilities would not be fully realized in Afro-American autobiography until the 1840s. More than quadruple the size of any other slave narrative of its era, the *Interesting Narrative* is an elaborate spiritual autobiography that exploits the idea common to evangelicals and romantics that all of life's incidents become meaningful and valuable when viewed from an enlightened perspective. With no editor to channel the reconstruction of his past through a monolithic point of view, Equiano had greater liberty to explore his life through the multiple perspectives that he had gained from his cosmopolitan experience. He brought to the writing of autobiography the memory (improved by research) of an African pastoral way of life that he pictured as the moral superior of the West in virtually every respect except in religion.

At the same time, Equiano was no facile romancer of noble savagery. Having been initiated into the wonders and terrors of the Euro-Christian world order, he could not blink away the material and technological advancement of that civilization over the one from which he had been kidnapped. Unwilling to deny his affinities with either civilization, Equiano designed an autobiographical persona that embraced both. Unwilling to hymn a testimonial to the blessings of acculturation, he paid special attention to the processes of acculturation, noting what was gained and lost as the African outsider took up a new role within the Western world order. Most important, Equiano structured the development of his own bicultural perspective in his narrative so as to conduct his white reader along the same path of psychic evolution. The result was an oratorical autobiography whose vocation was as much the creation of an implied reader as the education of the narrator. This implied reader was to be converted from his monocultural errors by experiencing repeatedly the gap between Western materialism and Western idealism. To recognize the gap, Equiano's reader is obliged to undergo a de-culturation process through which he divests himself of his insider's cultural myopia and accepts the complementary value of the African outsider's perspective. With both perspectives balancing and complementing each other, the reader is recreated in the image of Equiano instead of the other way around, as is the standard case in Afro-American autobiography of this era.

In a history of Afro-American autobiography, one cannot discuss at length the rhetorical art of a signal achievement of the Anglo-African literary tradition. I must limit myself to brief comments on the de-culturation process in Equiano's narrative and its significance in light of the Afro-American autobiographical tradition. This process begins in the first chapter of the book as Equiano lovingly reminisces about the Ibos' way of life. The simplicity of their manners and institutions, the justice of their moral values, and the harmony of their society make for a strong, though often not directly insisted on, contrast to the European world. The concept of whiteness is examined from the Ibo perspective to reveal the arbitrariness of Western white-over-black symbology: "I remember while in Africa to have seen three Negro children who were tawny, and another quite white, who were universally regarded by myself, and the natives in general, as far as related to their complexions, as deformed" (1:21 – 22). Equiano consistently unites himself with the Ibo people through the use of the first-person plural pronoun. With obvious pride he cites Western scholars to back his claim that a "strong analogy" exists between "the manners and customs of my countrymen and those of the Jews, before they reached the land of promise." By arguing that his people live like "the patriarchs while they were yet in that pastoral state which is described in Genesis," Equiano removes the African from the status of other and places him in a much more complex relationship to the Euro-Christian scheme of things. If Africans are like the Jews, then they both partake of and stand apart from the Western Christian tradition. They are a chosen people who still await their "land of promise," whose spatial and moral relationship to the West is marginal and unresolved. Equiano's people are in a liminal phase of a collective cultural rite of passage. Will their encounter with the West prove only another period of postponement and affliction, or will it bring about the fulfillment of their destiny? [37]

Equiano presents himself as a type of these "descendants of Abraham" seeking their "land of promise." At the beginning of his quest, the narrator pictures his first encounter with whites through the innocent eye. To the African boy-prince, the white slave traders are marvelous and terrible "spirits" who "looked and acted, as I thought, in so savage a manner" that he believed them cannibals. The de-culturating irony here is reinforced by the ingenuous outrage that poses the following question to the reader at the end of Chapter II: "O, ye nominal Christians! might not an African ask you, learned you this from your God, who says unto you, Do unto all men as you would men should do unto you?" (1:87). From the vantage point of the African pastoral ideal, the reader's Christian identity seems only nominal, a mere name, a sign that signifies nothing, a cultural mask to be stripped away by true innocence. More extensively than Venture Smith, Equiano use the status of the uncorrupted outsider to conduct a kind of semiotic critique of Western discourse, so that signs may once again be attached to their true significance. Even as he recounts the stages of his own acculturation, he is determined to place these autographical facts in a special context, not one casting credit on himself (à la Franklin, the white culture-hero) but one that calls attention to the contrast between himself as fortunate insider and his fellow blacks in the West Indies who remain outside the boundaries of humane treatment.

After reviewing atrocities on West Indian plantations, Equiano cites several laws enacted by the Assembly of Barbados to free whites from prosecution for the murder of blacks. He concludes: "Is not this one of the many acts of the islands which call loudly for redress? And do not the assembly which enacted it deserve the appellation of savages and brutes rather than of Christians and men? It is an act at once unmerciful, unjust, and unwise; which for cruelty would disgrace an assembly of those who are called barbarians; and for its injustice and *insanity* would shock the morality and common sense of a Samaide or a Hottentot" (1:218–19). Here again, the African is engaged in his critique of moral signifiers in English culture. His effort is to detach falsely applied appellations of otherness—savagery and brutishness—from outsiders like the Samaide[38] and the Hottentot and reassign to the white "barbarians" that name which they truly "deserve." Living up to his own name of Olaudah—"one favoured, and having a loud voice and well spoken" (1:31)—the African "calls loudly" on the Christian reader to learn to call things (and people) by their right names. As the de-culturation process alienates the reader from the "savage brutes" who govern the West Indies, it also seeks to engender in him or her an ambivalence, a double consciousness regarding signs of privilege like "white," "Christian," and "men." As the double consciousness matches the privileging sign with what it supposedly signifies, it may discover disparities between them that check the easy assumptions of the insider and make possible new outside readings.

Equiano's Afro-American contemporaries in autobiography do not attempt to create such readers for their narratives. They had to accept the readership that their editors and amanuenses created for them. In Equiano's story we find an optimistic conviction that African and English cultural values and semantic fields could be made to intersect in a complementary fashion. The white-edited narratives of African-born James Gronniosaw and Venture Smith suggest the irreconcilability of African and American cultural values and perspectives. Gronniosaw's story invites a reading of acculturation as a sign of salvation; in Smith's account ac-culturation signifies exploitation. By implication, the Afro-American has two mutually exclusive options in the Western world: he may imitate Gronniosaw and seek transcendence of the world, or he may imitate Smith and retreat from the unjust world into his own alienated selfhood. Both readings posit the ineffectuality of black self-affirmation within the Western world. Equiano, on the other hand, did not see his options in such diametric terms. By defining himself as a marginal man between two cultures, he found the means to imagine his relationship to the world in terms that did not require his becoming either totally coopted by or to-tally alienated from the Western sociocultural order. Perhaps because Equiano had grown up outside America's system of black conditioning and acculturation, he escaped the categorical, self-constricting thinking of men like Gronniosaw and Smith.

The causes of Equiano's intellectual independence are much less easy to trace, however, than their effects; this man was able to create a per-sona independent of both extremes of his contemporaries' images of the Westernized African. He was not the innocent African as sacrificial lamb (Gronniosaw), nor was he the outraged African as shorn and dishonored lion (Smith). He was both—and he was neither. He was outsider and in-sider and somewhere on the margin in between, with the self-appointed freedom to move from pole to pole on the axis of African-Western con-cepts of self. It was this intellectual and aesthetic freedom of the imagina-tion that was Equiano's special triumph as an ex-slave narrator. Equiano's autobiography affirms the power of the narrating persona to create a sub-jective world than can, in turn, effect change in the discursive realm be-tween text and reader, wherein the white reader could become em-powered to read signs outside of himself, i.e., biculturally. Thus Equiano's represents a new kind of black conversion narrative, less simply *about* the narrator than *for* the white reader who needs to learn to read the world redemptively, that is, doubly, inside-out and outside-in. Equiano's is also a new kind of black captivity narrative. The book is not designed to reinforce the predominant culture but to liberate the captive reader from it. Now inscribed by the text and implied in it, the reader is thrust into an unfamiliar but potentially clarifying interpretive situation in some re-spects outside his or her previously accepted cultural norms. It was this exploration of first-person writing as the grounds on which discourse be-tween two cultures could take place that made Equiano the prophet, if not the father, of Afro-American autobiography.

CHAPTER

3

Experiments in Two Modes, 1810–40

Between George White's seminal autobiography of 1810 and the classic narratives of Frederick Douglass, William Wells Brown, and Henry Bibb in the 1840s, Afro-American autobiography underwent a period of experimentation during which time two modes of reading and writing about personal history were explored. One group of narrators read the past, we might say, deductively. Their aim was to create a narrative rhetoric that would cause the reader to infer the significance of their personal experience from its applicability to strategically selected biblical passages and themes. This mode of autobiographical argument is anticipated in eighteenth-century black spiritual autobiographies. There the white reader is asked to deduce from the major premise that all Christians should love one another, and from the minor premise that a James Gronniosaw or a John Marrant is a Christian, the conclusion that these black men should be regarded as the reader's brothers in Christ. Black spiritual autobiographies of the early nineteenth century do not depart from this syllogistic mode of persuasion. However, because the careers of narrators like Jarena Lee, the female evangelist, and Nat Turner, the slave insurrectionist, extended well beyond the boundaries of spiritual experience posited in earlier black spiritual autobiography, the genre adopted an increasingly metaphorical, or tropological, reading of scriptural language. The tropological turn that this kind of reading entailed was not essentially different from that required by another form of antebellum black spiritual autobiography, that is, the sacred song of the slave community, the spiritual. Just as the spiritual "Didn't My Lord Deliver Daniel?" invited a reading of biblical precedent in terms specific to the secular aspirations of American slaves, so spiritual autobiographers like Lee and Turner projected their lives as secular figurations of scriptural *mythoi*.[1] Their readers are left with the task of figuring out the import of their lives according to the extent to which their careers can be subsumed under particular myths, prophecies, or other gnomic statements in the Bible. As we shall see, however, the effort of these autobiographers is not simply to make their lives fit the Scriptures—as is the case in most of the dictated spiritual autobiographies of the eighteenth century—but to appropriate scriptural texts in such a way as to "potentialise," in the words of Paul Ricoeur, the depicted black life.

During the same decades that black spiritual autobiography took on a more expansive tropological reading of experience, a countermovement in black autobiography urged a more restrictively empirical, or mimetic, narrative orientation. This countermovement was epitomized in the slave narratives of the 1830s and the early 1840s. The autobiographies of Charles Ball (1836), Moses Roper (1837), and James Williams (1838) represent the beginnings of the classic fugitive slave narrative genre in the United States. The genre developed in response to a well-publicized desire on the part of abolitionists, white and black, to marshall the most forceful evidence available in the battle against slavery, the testimony of eyewitnesses. The sponsors and sometime editors of the early fugitive slave narratives were abolitionists who had learned from experience on the antislavery lecture that an ex-slave's oral narration of life under the lash was a powerful way to galvanize sentiment for the cause. Antislavery agitators also knew that while their words against slavery might be regarded skeptically by many in the North, the facts of slavery as detailed by a fugitive himself would be much more readily believed. Theodore Dwight Weld, a lecturer and secretary of the American Anti-Slavery Society, was convinced that "the north is so blinded it will not *believe* what we [abolitionists] say about slavery." But he was equally certain that "facts and testimony as to the actual condition of the Slaves" would "thrill the land with Horror" and confound many of the skeptics.[2] Weld proved his contention with the publication of *American Slavery as It Is* (1839), a best-selling compendium of atrocities and other documentary evidence against slavery drawn exclusively from southern newspapers.[3] Likeminded editors determined to "give facts a voice" sought out black testimony as another way to document the hideous truths of slavery.

In his preface to the *Narrative of James Williams*, John Greenleaf Whittier, Williams's amanuensis and a colleague of Weld's, advanced this narrative as an important supplement to the testimony that had already emerged against slavery. Much could be learned, Whittier admitted, from the advertisements for human property and runaways that appeared daily in southern newspapers. "But for a full revelation of the secrets of the prison-house, we must look to the slave himself." [4] Thus, for Whittier at least, a fugitive slave's story was an excellent resource for anyone desiring a thorough exposé of the peculiar institution. Williams's "simple and unvarnished story" is recommended because the man's "situation" gave him special "advantages for accurate observation of the practical workings of the system." This comment indicates Williams's basic function in his narrative. He is not the subject of his autobiography; slavery is. Williams is the medium through whom, as Whittier promises the reader, "the scenes of the plantation rise before us, with a distinctness which approaches reality." The slave narrator reveals plantation scenes like a window from which the shade has finally been drawn. For his story to be taken seriously as something approaching reality, he must become transparent, unsubstantial. Reality is measured by the "distinctness" with which the object, the plantation world, is transmitted through the narrator without impediment or distortion.

By implication the truth of a slave narrative is proportionate to the degree of objectification achieved by the narrator. The more distance he can place between himself as perceiving ego and as receiving, transmitting eye, the more his story will be assumed to approach reality. Thus Isaac Fisher, the ostensible editor of *Slavery in the United States: A Narrative of the Life and Adventures of Charles Ball*, solicited his reader's confidence in the truth of Ball's story by promising that subjective elements of the Negro's narration had been "carefully suppressed" in the final written form of the autobiography. For example, Ball's "sentiments upon the subject of slavery" had been "cautiously omitted" from the book on the basis of their "being of no value to the reader." What is valuable are "the facts" of Ball's life, which Fisher uses to "exhibit, not to [the reader's] imagination, but to his very eyes" a "faithful portrait of the manners, usages, and customs of the southern people" insofar as they came under "the observations of a common negro slave." [5] Here, as in Whittier's preface, the traditional association of mimesis with painting necessarily rules out the slave narrator as part of the picture on exhibit. [6] For how can the observing eye mirror objective facts distinctly if it discovers itself in the mirror and thus becomes self-reflective? This is the reason for Fisher's banishing of Ball's "sentiments" and "opinions" from his narrative: consciousness contaminates facts, rendering them less fit for the reader's "eye" than for his "imagination." To make a slave narrative qualify as a positivistic mode of truth-telling, the editors of the slave narrative felt they needed to disengage the reader's imaginative response to black experience. At the same time, black spiritual autobiographers sought ways to elicit such empathetic, subjective engagement.

Black spiritual autobiographers of the early nineteenth century faced their greatest challenges when they set about appropriating biblical texts to their own view of themselves and the world. By appropriation I mean the kind of heremeneutical activity that Ricoeur believes is central to the process of understanding—the act of overcoming cultural distance and/ or historical alienation to make one's own what was initially alien. When Ricoeur says that "interpretation brings together, equalises, renders contemporary and similar,"[7] he suggests in general terms the sociopolitical as well as literary significance of early black spiritual autobiographers' use of hermeneutics in their own texts. Early black religious leaders like Richard Allen and Jarena Lee approached the Bible from a vast distance created not only by their personal sense of moral unworthiness (a conventional admission in spiritual autobiographies) but also by a culturally imposed view of the Negro as a "Canaanite, a man devoid of Logos," whose servitude was "a punishment resulting from sin or from a natural defect of soul."[8] After conversion, when Allen and Lee turned to autobiographical narration, they recorded both the process by which they were saved from sin and the subsequent empowering effect that the appropriation of the Logos had on them when they became preachers. Such spiritual autobiographies are, therefore, much more than conversion narratives. They serve as preacherly texts, as models of the act and impact of biblical appropriation on the consciousness of the black narrator as bearer of the Word.

According to Ricoeur, when a reader appropriates a literary text, he or she does not merely reduce the text to personal egoistic needs or translate the text into a set of signifiers corresponding to present reality. The experience of interpretation and understanding of texts allows the reader to discover something new about the possibilities of what Heidegger called *Dasein*, "being-in-the-world." The phrase does not apply to the reader's normal notions about being or the world, however. Rather, in appropriating the text, the reader discovers in the text "a *proposed world* which I could inhabit and wherein I could project one of my ownmost possibilities." Also revealed in the act of appropriation is "an enlarged self" that the text has "potentialised" for the reader. In the process of making the text his own, the text makes the reader its own by "metamorphosing" the ego of the reader and revealing "new capacities for knowing himself." The appropriating reader is "broadened in his capacity to project himself by receiving a new mode of being from the text itself." Appropriation thus occasions a dispossession of the ego and a discovery of a new self that emerges from the understanding of the text.[9] For the black spiritual autobiographer, the discovery of this new self demands a personal narration that is mimetic in a way very different from that of the contemporaneous fugitive slave narrative. The spiritual autobiographer reviews the past through the eyes of the metamorphosed, empowered self and appropriates from the past a myth of the true self beneath the accidents of race, gender, and caste. The slave narrator, by contrast, is expected to concentrate on race, gender, and caste, institutionalized in chattel slavery, as ends in themselves. The one justifies the imaginative leap from empirical to a presumed essence because the real subject of imitation is the "potentialised" self. The other restricts such imaginative projection because its priority is to expose an institution's power to destroy, not celebrate an individual's potential to preserve, the essential self.

Instead of appropriation, the fugitive slave narrative up to the time of Douglass partakes of an opposite characteristic of discourse—what Ricoeur has called (borrowing from Hans-Georg Gadamer) "distanciation." [10] In touting the narratives of Williams and Ball as documents of empirical fact, abolitionist editors of slave narratives tried to give the genre a certain positivistic, quasi-scientific status. What sustains the genre's pretenses in this direction is its subordination of subject to object, its attempt to make the slave narrator an eyewitness, not an I-witness. The danger of such objectification is "distanciation" of the perceiving self from what Gadamer describes as a sense of primordial "belongingness," in the case of the slave narrator, a sense of belonging to and participating in his own past. [11] The fugitive needed to distance himself physically from slavery in order to save his body and free his mind. But the slave narrative required another brand of denial, a psychic distancing of the fugitive from slavery as a point of *self*-reference that would always belong to him even after he had ceased to belong to it.

The fugitive slave needed an autobiographical form that would allow him to recognize, in all the term suggests, what slavery meant as a condition of existence, as the locus of his past, as the crucible of his identity, and as a kind of heuristic tool, a text that helps him realize his potential in ways similar to those noted in connection with contemporaneous black spiritual autobiographers. What the fugitive slave needed, furthermore, was a mode of autobiographical discourse that subtly reoriented a reader's response to his text away from a distanced perspective and toward one that authorized appropriation. Through such a mode of discourse, a revolution in hermeneutical priorities could begin in black autobiography. In Ricoeur's terms, understanding, that is, the transference of the reader into the psychic life of the narrator, could be facilitated in texts that had once been read only for explanation, i.e., the empirical verification, description, and analysis of some feature of objective reality (like slavery). [12] The early slave narrative shows us the first steps toward this kind of autobiographical text. The significance of the early slave narrative as autobiography lies in its strategies of resistance to the distancing that the form encouraged between the narrator and his past, and by implication, himself in the past. How the slave narrator resisted self-repression and made possible a discourse of understanding will be the chief theme of the latter half of this chapter.

Tropological readings of the past in early nineteenth-century black spiritual autobiography range from the more traditional to the radical. It is helpful to begin with a traditional example of this mode, *A Narrative of Some Remarkable Incidents in the Life of Solomon Bayley, Formerly a Slave* (1825). Bayley's narrative is divided into three parts: an opening section recounting his attempted escape from slavery in 1799, a second section highlighted by his complete dedication of his life to Christ and his subsequent purchase of his wife and son, and a final miscellany of letters between Bayley and his editor, an English preacher named Robert Hurnard.[13] Only the opening section of this autobiography is relevant to our present purposes. Here under the pretense of praising God for His care during the slave's flight from his Delaware master, Bayley engages in a subtle but noteworthy act of self-justifying autobiographical rhetoric.

The beginning fifteen pages of Bayley's narrative contain the most sustained and suspenseful account of a fugitive slave's flight to freedom that had yet appeared in Afro-American autobiography. Yet, unlike the fugitive slave narratives of Roper or Williams, there is no attempt in Bayley's story to capitalize on this for political purposes. Bayley does state that according to Delaware law he had been made a freeman automatically when his master took him from Camden to Virginia in 1799. The slave sued his master for his freedom in Delaware courts but was kidnapped and taken to Richmond, where he was jailed for safekeeping before his removal to the Virginia back country. While sitting in a wagon awaiting transport westward, Bayley decides that he is "'past all hope'" of securing his freedom through either God's providence or man's laws, so he jumps from the wagon and runs into the woods. During the rest of his narration of his flight, the significance of his actions is drawn from the spiritual context in which Bayley reads them; the political significance of his rebellion against his master is left undeveloped.

Beginning with his decision to run, Bayley reconstructs this crucial event in his life so that it will be read as a spiritual test, not as a sociopolitical act. In the midst of his deepest despair, he tries to take comfort from the scriptural promise that "'they that trust in the Lord, shall never be confounded'" (3). But "I thought I was not fit to lay hold of the promise," and "I did not know to what bounds his mercy would extend." Thus he alights from the wagon and flees only to find himself calling on God for protection along the route back to Delaware. God hears his prayers consistently, which convinces Bayley at the end of his journey that "I had come through difficulties and troubles, in order that my faith and confidence might be tried; and that I might be made strong in the faith that so high and holy an one . . . would hereafter help so poor an object as me, out of his great mercy and condescension, and that I might be afraid again to sin against his majesty" (14–15).

Bayley thus asks his audience to read his ordeal in a familiar way, as an illustration of the way in which God tries the faithful to prove "his loving-kindness and mercy." Bayley presents himself as a type of the Christian pilgrim, "a monument of mercy, thrown up and down on life's tempestuous sea," but traveling on "in hopes of overcoming at my last combat." Terms like overcoming through combat could be applied literally to the specific case of this fugitive from slavery, but Bayley takes some pains to encourage his audience to read such terms tropologically, as having only spiritual, not sociopolitical import. This maneuver is also evidenced in the self-descriptive language the narrator uses. At the height of his ordeal, when some slavecatchers fail to discover him in a thicket, Bayley is overwhelmed by this proof of God's "gracious readiness to help the stranger in distress: though he is high, yet hath he respect unto the lowly" (13). That moment of deliverance convinced Bayley that "the power of God has overthrown the power of darkness for me a sinner."

It is significant that the narrator identifies himself as a "sinner," not a slave, as a "stranger in distress," not a fugitive hiding out from Virginia authorities. To read his story metaphorically as a spiritual adventure is to acquiesce in the fundamental rhetorical turn on which this narrative must pivot if it is to accomplish its object. By turning the individual slave into the generic sinner, by figuring the fugitive on the run as the stranger in distress, the narrator makes an implicit argument about how the fugitive slave should be seen. The reader is being asked to look beyond the facts of the slave's individual identity in order to discover his greater significance as a metaphor of everyone's spiritual struggle. To present the slave in this light is to "potentialise" his image profoundly in the eyes of the white reader. His enslavement and his lonely and desperate flight are converted from signs of degradation and alienation into "consubstantiating" metaphors that link his plight with that of the white reader on the spiritual level of interpretation. Moreover, by subsuming the fugitive slave under the general classification of the poor, the lowly, the helpless, and the stranger in distress, Bayley argues implicitly that the escaped slave has the same claim on God's deliverance as "all them that call on him." Besides helping to legitimize the fugitive's actions, this kind of argument makes it possible for one to deduce the fugitive's sociopolitical salvation from the same principles that promised the white reader spiritual salvation.

The Life, Experience and Gospel Labors of the Rt. Reverend Richard Allen (1833) attempts in a way similar to Bayley's narrative to recount a unique event—the birth of the first black religious denomination in America, the African Methodist Episcopal church—so as to subsume and legitimize it within the larger traditions of Protestant church history. Although Allen's story begins with his conversion and traces his evolving preaching career, this is primarily a work of church history. Allen is the first historian of and apologist for a black power movement in the Afro-American autobiographical tradition. He places little emphasis on how he as an individual overcame the bondage into which he had been born in 1760; he is much more concerned with the triumph of the black community of believers over the "spiritual despotism" of white Methodism.[14] Allen bought his freedom from his Philadelphia master sometime in the waning years of the Revolutionary War. Thereafter, his own gradual self-emancipation from dependence on white spiritual authorities foreshadows and symbolizes the liberation of black community consciousness from the idea that spiritual authority must be conferred from without rather than emanating from within. In this way the narrator deliberately treats himself as a trope, points his reader from Richard Allen the specific man to Richard Allen the spokesman, and makes his the story of the "potentialising" of a people. Although the central scene in the autobiography is a moment of personal humiliation—Allen's forcible expulsion from a white Methodist church for praying in the wrong pew—the episode is presented only in terms of its communal significance. It is as though Allen the powerless black petitioner dies at this moment in the story, to be resurrected as the new institutional man in the remainder of the narrative. Simultaneously, the story becomes no longer his but that of the new church whose raison d'etre it is Allen's charge to recreate and defend.

Allen appropriates from Scripture and the Protestant tradition a privileged language that, when applied to the new black institution, encourages one to read the founding of the A.M.E. church as a metaphor of the historic purification of Christianity through dissent. Lest whites misread his movement as an aberration, Allen is careful to picture the alien status of the black Methodists as a mark of their nonconforming piety in the face of "persecution" by the established Methodist church. Through Allen, the black church takes its stand for pure Methodism, "the plain doctrine," which the white church with its preachers who "act to please their own fancy" has forsaken. Like a jeremiad, Allen's autobiography judges white Methodism according to its failure to live up to its own standards. "It is awfully to be feared," Allen pronounces like a biblical prophet, "that the simplicity of the Gospel that was among them fifty years ago, and that they conform more to the world and the fashions thereof, they would fare very little better than the people of the world. The discipline is altered considerably from what it was. We would ask for the good old way, and desire to walk therein" (30).

In such terms Allen privileges himself, the original African Methodist, with the moral authority to reclaim "the good old way" from those who have perverted it, namely, the present-day white Methodists. By endowing himself with this authority, Allen also privileges that which he symbolizes, African Methodism. He turns an apparent syncretism—the linking of African (traditionally connoting paganism and darkness) with Methodism (suggesting Christian enlightenment to the white reader)— into a sign in which the term African is necessary to the validation and intensification of Methodism. *African*, in Allen's story, is not handled as a modifier but as an identifier of Methodism, as an indicator of the real thing. This is why, when the white Methodist elders threaten to read the Allenites out of the church, the blacks reply undismayed, "If you deny us your name, you cannot seal up the scriptures from us, and deny us a name in heaven" (27). From this point to the climax of the story, when the blacks denominate themselves officially as African Methodists, Allen the historian shows us nothing that will allow us to deny the African Methodists their name, the sign of their morally empowered bicultural identity. Nor will the reader learn anything to contradict the idea that self-denomination is the right of blacks in an abstract as well as this specific sense. Allen's autobiography offers, therefore, an early commentary on the import of self-naming in Afro-American culture, a theme that would be rendered more dramatically and explosively in the great slave narratives of the 1840s and 1850s.

Moving from the narratives of Bayley and Allen to *The Life and Religious Experience of Jarena Lee, A Coloured Lady* (1836) reveals black spiritual autobiography's increasingly radical challenge to traditional systems of naming. Bayley and Allen identify and name themselves as fugitive slave and African Methodist respectively, embracing their special otherness through the act of narrating their life stories. Both are intent on turning the alienating implications of their names to their own rhetorical advantage. Bayley argues implicitly that the fugitive slave participates in the Christian pilgrim's spiritual drama and is thus the same except in name. In Allen's case we see that the African Methodist demonstrates more claim to the name of Methodism than white Methodists who lack the essence of "the good old way" in their religious practice. Lee extends this tradition of rehabilitating alien names into the area of gender, as well as social and racial, signs. Her autobiography claims beneath the other-denoting identity of her title—*A Coloured Lady*—a spiritual essence that abolishes the privileging power of male over female and qualifies her for the androgynous identity she adopts at the end of her narrative. This identity she signifies by appropriating to herself from Romans 8:14 the empowering concept of "'sons of God,'" which can be applied to any who "'are led by the *Spirit* of God.'" [15]

The first half of Lee's story recounts the stages of a conventional conversion experience. However, after having undergone what John Wesley would call sanctification by God, she gradually comes to the conviction that it is her duty to preach the gospel. Like George White, Lee informs Richard Allen, her minister, of her sense of divine appointment. He gently puts her off: "He said that our Discipline knew nothing at all about it—that it did not call for women preachers." Accepting Allen's demurral, Lee sublimates her sense of mission by marrying a minister when she is barred from becoming one herself. But in looking back on her life, she knows that her acquiescence to Allen allowed "that holy energy which burned within me as a fire . . . to be smothered." Such repression leads to her "falling into a general state of debility" as a wife, from which she recovers only by holding fast to her hope one day to preach. When her husband dies, leaving her two infant children and no means of support, she successfully wins from Allen a license to exhort. What she calls a "supernatural impulse" spurs her on to greater self-assertion one Sunday morning in the A.M.E. Bethel Church in Philadelphia. Springing to her feet during an ordained minister's uninspired sermon, she supplants him, in effect, by exhorting the congregation with a discourse from the man's own selected text. Announcing "that I was like Jonah," Lee identifies herself tropologically, converting her example from a genetic reference—the uncontrolled woman—to a generic one—the preacher who, having rejected God's control, now determines to do His will. Having appropriated from Scripture an identity to justify her past actions and empower her future aims, Lee concludes this episode with Allen's endorsement of her preacherly qualifications.

The remainder of Lee's narrative offers further proof of her right to the name of preacher, regardless of sexual identity. She confronts her fictive male reader with a vigorous and sustained argument from analogy and biblical precedent supporting the right of any woman, appropriately inspired, to preach. "Why should it be thought impossible, heterodox, or improper for a woman to preach," she asks, "seeing the Saviour died for the woman as well as the man?" Successful evangelistic forays among "lawyers, doctors, and magistrates," climaxing in a victorious dispute with a slaveholding Deist over the issue of whether black people have souls, show her at home in the male sphere of her society, indeed, tri-

From the *Religious Experience and Journal of Mrs. Jarena Lee* (1849).

umphant over those presumed by gender and race to be her superiors. Lee's most arresting testimonial to a "new mode of being" derived from her sense of scriptural empowerment appears in her choice of mission over what would have been viewed as her maternal obligations. "Just as Saul of Tarsus was sent to Jerusalem," Lee believes that God intends her to carry the Word to distant towns, though this requires "breaking up housekeeping" and leaving her sickly son with another during her travels. The proof that the Lord favors this desertion of the traditional maternal role lies in the fact that during her first week of absence "not a thought of my little son came into my mind; it was hid from me, lest I should have been diverted from the work I had to do." Thus Lee caps her incipiently feminist argument for a woman's right to pursue her self-declared work, though it take her outside the home and the family. Her justification for such radical action rests on an appeal to the priority of the private conscience, the inner light, and the sense of sacred promptings within, which traditionally in Western culture has been the nonconformist's ultimate sanction. It is intriguing to wonder to what extent this claim to religious sanction served as Lee's metaphor for an equally inviolable, but unclaimable sense of the secular self's right to its own sanction, apart from what class, race, or gender could accrue to or take away from it.

In *The Confessions of Nat Turner* (1831), we find the most audacious tropological reading of Scripture in nineteenth-century black autobiography.[16] The narrative describes the making of a prophet-rebel through acts of appropriation that empowered this slave from Southampton, Virginia, to lead a kind of holy war against white people, whom he seems to have regarded as the enemies of Christ. The title of the work, however, provides the first of several signals that this is a text divided against itself, in which there is a fundamental competition between two opposing wills for the power that comes from the act of appropriation, the power to endow and legitimate a self with mythic significance. A confession can emanate from two radically different kinds of men, a man of great piety and spiritual insight, like St. Augustine, or someone judged guilty of the worst transgressions and inner corruption, like Pomp, whose eighteenth-century criminal autobiography we have already examined. Nat Turner evidently wanted his confession to be read as a spiritual testament of his faithfulness to his mission in life. Thomas Gray, his court-appointed attorney and amanuensis, was determined that the narrative be read as a terrible tale of religious dementia, somewhat in the tradition of Pomp's *Dying Confession* of 1795. Ironically, the result of this diametric collaboration is a text in which the two men's myths of Nat Turner exist in a relationship of *différance* because of the traces of signification that link

Turner's image of himself as avenging "prophet" with Gray's imposed image of Turner as "gloomy fanatic." [17]

The conditions under which Turner's narrative was spoken, composed, and published raise unanswerable questions about the origin and authenticity of the language ascribed to the convicted insurrectionist. We cannot know why Turner gave the deposition. Since he pleaded "not guilty" at his arraignment, "saying to his counsel, that he did not feel so," it does not appear that he would have dictated his story to Gray in order to clear his conscience in the manner typical of his predecessors in gallows confessions. At the beginning of his narrative, Turner uses the word "enthusiasm" to signify the motivating force behind a career "which has terminated so fatally to many, both white and black, and for which I am about to atone at the gallows." But it is very unlikely that a slave preacher would have identified himself as an enthusiast in need of atonement. "Enthusiasm" was a class-conscious word, used pejoratively by high-church conservatives to denigrate evangelical fervor as little more than an anarchical excess of the imagination. The word probably belonged to the aging slaveholder Gray, who felt confident in his diagnosis of Turner's mental condition and who did not mind prejudicing his reader from the outset of the slave's narrative.

If Turner's reasons for telling his story are unclear, Gray's purposes in publishing it are not. "Public curiosity has been on the stretch to understand the origin and progress of this dreadful conspiracy, and the motives which influence its diabolical actors," Gray wrote in his prefatory remarks to Turner's statement. To satisfy this curiosity, the Virginia lawyer interviewed the manacled rebel in the Jerusalem, Virginia, jail and in the presence of witnesses secured his endorsement of the written record Gray made of that interview. Then the lawyer hurried to the District of Columbia, where he had his transcript of the interview copyrighted while the condemned man awaited hanging in Southampton County. The printing of as many as 50,000 copies of *The Confessions of Nat Turner* by Gray implies that capitalizing on public curiosity as much as satisfying it was a prime motive behind his soliciting and publishing of the rebel's story.[18]

Following precedent in the criminal confession genre, Gray takes control of the narrative from the outset by presenting Turner to the white reader in imagery carefully designed to restrict the slave's access to the empowering text, the Bible. Turner is "a gloomy fanatic" who led a "fiendish band" in "schemes of indiscriminate massacre to the whites" for "hellish purposes" known only to "his own dark, bewildered, and overwrought mind." Lest antislavery people conclude that the black man had

73

been driven to the rebellion because of outrage over enslavement, Gray scotches this unwelcome charge at the beginning of the narrative. The Negro's motives were not "revenge or sudden anger"; they were "the off-spring of gloomy fanaticism." By picturing Turner in this light, no doubt Gray hoped to convince paranoid slaveholders throughout the South that there was more madness than method in this uprising and that it was not the product of a more widespread slave conspiracy ready to explode in violence at the appointed hour. This was not the only reason for stressing Turner as a religious fanatic. Gray knew that in Turner's own deposition he would explain and justify his actions on the basis of scriptural prece-dent, divine revelation, and conscientious adherence to his perception of the will of God. Before Turner could occupy that sacred ground rhetori-cally, Gray tried to deny him a tropological avenue by introducing a countertrope that would turn the reader's thinking about the slave's sig-nificance in a direction opposite from that in which Turner would try to take it. Thus we find from the beginning the prejudicing metaphors of Satanic influence pervading Turner's undertaking. Not only does Turner lead a "fiendish band" for "hellish purposes"; he is also an exemplar of Satan's besetting sin—pride, in particular the pride that John Milton's Satan instills in man, an ambition that "excites" the mind "with more de-sire to know."[19] Thus Turner's story, Gray emphasizes, teaches "a useful lesson, as to the operations of a mind like his, endeavoring to grapple with things beyond its reach." Having indirectly analogized the black rebel to Christ's adversary, the Arch-Conspirator who refused to serve his heavenly master, Gray's prefatory remarks end.

The first half of Turner's narrative is the crucial section because it re-counts the evolution of his sense of mission up to the night of August 21, 1831, when the rebellion began. The rationale for Gray's linkage of Tur-ner and Satan becomes apparent as we encounter in the slave's retelling of his life repeated parallels between himself and Christ. From childhood, blacks who knew him believed "I surely would be a prophet, as the Lord had shewn me things that had happened before my birth." Even his mas-ter "who belonged to the church, and other religious persons who visited the house" noted that his "uncommon intelligence" did not fit him to be a slave. Religion became the chief object of his thought, and he grew up living an austere, rather set apart life. Contemplation of the scriptural promise "'Seek ye the kingdom of Heaven and all things shall be added unto you'" confirmed in him a sense of having been "ordained for some great purpose." Once a runaway, he is tempted to seek earthly freedom, but "the Spirit" directs him back to his master, "'for he who knoweth his Master's will, and doeth it not, shall be beaten with many stripes, and thus have I chastened you.'"[20] This citation from the gospel of Luke was a favorite text of slaveowners who used it to justify whipping uncooperative slaves. Turner's appropriation of it reflects his equation of "Master" with God and his conviction that all he did and was to do was in keeping with his heavenly Master's will.

In his mid-twenties, Turner's sense of Christological mission grows with every increasingly apocalyptic vision that he sees. "I sought more than ever to obtain true holiness before the great day of judgment should appear." Once he is "made perfect" under the tutelage of "the Holy Ghost," bloody portents in the fields and forest make it "plain to me that the Savior was about to lay down the yoke for the sins of men." After baptizing himself and a small band of disciples "as the Savior had been baptized," Turner learns from the Spirit that "the Serpent was loosened, and Christ had laid down the yoke he had borne for the sins of men." His mission, dictated from heaven, is to take on Christ's yoke and "fight against the Serpent, for the time was fast approaching when the first should be last and the last should be first." At this point, Gray interrupts the rising action to urge Turner to recant: "Do you not find yourself mistaken now?" The messianic murderer insists, blasphemously, on a typological link between himself and the Savior: "Was not Christ crucified?" The slave's audacity here at the climax of his narrative turns Christ into a type, a historical prefiguration, of himself, the ultimate bearer of the responsibility for the eschaton in which whites will be judged and blacks redeemed. His impending execution at the hands of men like Gray also serves to validate instead of disprove to Turner his conviction of his own sacrificial Christhood. We might conclude, therefore, that the "emergent meaning" (to borrow Monroe Beardsley's phrase again) of Turner's mounting metaphorical association of himself with Christ is the merging of the two identities into one. In doing this, Turner relegated the New Testament to the status of a figurative text roughly parallel to that which the Old Testament occupied in the eyes of conventional Protestant American typologists. As his narrative fulfilled the prophecy of the white man's Scriptures, it sought to displace them, just as the New Testament displaced and even annulled the authority of the Old Testament in Christian thought.[21] In this respect Turner tried to make his story something more than a metaphorical vehicle of a scriptural precedent. It was to serve as a book of revelations, in its own way, of the true tenor and outcome of Christian history.

Lacking control over the text, Turner had to yield closure in the *Confessions* to his antagonist Gray, who did his best to undermine the slave's Christological pretensions by leaving the reader with a final Luciferian image of the rebel: "The calm, deliberate composure with which he spoke of his late deeds and intentions, the expression of his fiend-like face when excited by enthusiasm, still bearing the stains of the blood of help-less innocence about him; clothed with rags and covered with chains; yet daring to raise his manacled hands to heaven, with a spirit soaring above the attributes of man; I looked on him and my blood curdled in my veins." The image provides additional grounds for Gray's belief that the rebellion underlined the absolute necessity "of our laws in restraint of this class of the population." The Virginia state legislature agreed, passing new laws in February 1832 to restrict black religious assemblage and abolish for all intents and purposes slave preachers.[22] This was, no doubt, the easiest way that the slavocracy could see to control access to the Bible, whose ideology, when appropriated and tropologically applied to the condition of black people, could inspire other messianic figures like Nat Turner. But after the fact, *The Confessions of Nat Turner* was needed as much to draw the right conclusions about Turner's larger significance as it was to provide the correct details of his case. Interestingly, Gray does not deny that Turner has a kind of tropological significance based on the mythology of Scripture. The lawyer simply tries to counter Turner's view of himself as Savior with an opposing estimate of him as satanically inspired. This in itself constitutes a rhetorical victory for Turner. The force of his claims for himself, taken as they are from Scripture, compels Gray to oppose him, not dismiss him as Jonathan Plummer does with Pomp's psychologically grounded self-justifications in 1795. To oppose Turner in Gray's manner is to engage in a discourse with him that as much defers to him as differs with him. In fact, in this antagonistic collab-oration, the act of differing could not take place without the act of defer-ring. Without the opposing yet supplementary other, furthermore, nei-ther narrator could exist in the text in his chosen role or claim the privilege of troping as extravagantly as he does on his opposite.

Turner needs Gray as much as Gray needs Turner, in the sense that Milton needs Satan as much as he needs Christ, or rather, in order that he may identify Christ as he does in his narrative poem. Unless Turner ar-gues his mythic identity as a type of Christ, Gray has no precedent for his troping in an equally mythic manner on Turner as a Satanic influence. Without Turner's notion of a black slave Messiah, Gray has no standard by which to define a black spiritual leader of equal though opposite propor-tions. Unless Gray participates in (and thus lends credence to) Turner's appropriation of an extraordinary identity, the latter's claim to Christo-logical significance will lack the foregrounding and authentication that slave narratives needed in order to be taken seriously by whites. Thus this act of literary antagonism becomes collaborative through the play of *différance*, which turns Gray and Turner into inadvertent collabora-tionists, whose defense against the other ironically leads each into a treasonable cooperation with the other. For each one's definition of Nat Turner carries with it and inevitably depends upon the trace of the other that is supposedly being denied and replaced. Perhaps it is this play of the text that has rendered it in so many ways problematic and indeterminate, as the lingering controversy over William Styron's "meditation" on Turner's example illustrates.[23]

The distinguishing mark of the original *Confessions* is its refusal to let its reader understand or explain (in Ricoeur's sense of these two verbs) Nat Turner as a discrete entity, as either Gray's or Turner's opposing selves. Instead of triumphing over or canceling out each other, these two versions of Turner supplement and "potentialise" each other, to create finally the closest thing to Roland Barthes's "writerly text" that we have in early black spiritual autobiography. As such, the *Confessions* fulfills few of our expectations of finality and closure. The meaning of Nat Turner is perpetually postponed and relative, a function of the innumerable alignments of the two Nat Turners produced by a text that always keeps one partially eclipsed by the other. Although he cannot be recuperated as a historical presence from this writerly text, the *Confessions* does give us a chance to ponder its protagonist as a manifestation of the play of *différance* itself. In this sense we should not think of Nat Turner as a historical personage or as a character created by Gray or Turner, but as a product of the dynamics of the text itself. "Nat Turner" is not a sign of what either Gray or Turner intended to signify. He figures as a sort of textual tar baby. Efforts either to affirm or deny an opposite view of Turner get stuck in and are incapacitated by the ironic functioning of "Nat Turner" in the *Confessions*. Still this play of *différance* can have an enabling effect on the reading of the *Confessions*. One can see how the cultural perspective of racism, in which the marginalizing of black as absence and the maintaining of white as a prior and present plenitude are attempted, is powerfully deconstructed by the play of "Nat Turner" in the *Confessions*. Such a recognition of Turner in the most useful context in which we can conceive of him now—within this text—may do more justice to the significance of the *Confessions* than has been done by anyone who claims to have recuperated the real Nat Turner from history.

Before abolitionists in the late 1830s realized the propagandistic potential in the narratives of ex-slaves, a runaway from Georgia named William Grimes, unaided and undirected by whites, published the first fugitive slave narrative in America. The longest autobiography yet written by an Afro-American, the *Life of William Grimes, the Runaway Slave* appeared in New York, in 1825, designed explicitly to raise money for its author, who had been recently rendered penniless after having been forced to purchase his freedom from his former master. Having been a slave in four southern states for some thirty years and having known "the hard treatment, ill-usage and horrid abuse the poor slave experiences while groaning under the yoke of bondage," Grimes told a story of almost unrelieved anguish and outrage. He was the first black autobiographer in America to picture the South in what would become a standardized image in abolitionist propaganda: the plantation as rural chamber of horrors, a nightmare world presided over by near-demonic whites as capricious as they were sadistic. Unlike the former slaves George White and Solomon Bayley, Grimes refused to conclude his story on a comic upswing despite his eventual attainment of freedom. Like Venture Smith, he candidly admitted that "the sweets of liberty," as he ironically termed them in his introduction to his autobiography, had been "embittered" through the misfortune and unjust treatment he had suffered while trying to make a place for himself and his family in Connecticut.[24] Autobiography became for Grimes a means of venting his outrage and baring the bitterness that he had accumulated during forty years of life in "a land boasting its freedom."

The *Life* reads like a list of grievances against America, South *and* North, with Grimes picturing himself almost as much a class as a caste victim in this country. This was a risky step, one that few slave narrators would take. The preponderant ideology of the antislavery movement did not favor studying the slave in the light of class oppression, as proslavery apologists like George Fitzhugh did when he compared the Negro slave to the free white working class in England and New England, to the moral detriment of capitalists on both sides of the ocean.[25] The fugitive slave narratives that abolitionists popularized demanded radical socioeconomic reform in the South, not in the North. Romantic, nationalistic ideals, epitomized in the fugitive as symbol of individualism triumphant over corrupt institutions, were the stock-in-trade of the famous slave narratives of the 1830s and 1840s. Because Grimes did not subscribe to these myths, it is not surprising that he had to publish his story on his own and that the antislavery movement ignored it both when it first appeared and in 1855, when Grimes reprinted a somewhat expanded new edition.[26]

Ontological "distanciation," suggested at the opening of this chapter as a special problem for the fact-oriented fugitive slave narrator, does not alienate the Grimes persona from his past in this text. Instead of screening the self behind a mask of objective presentation of the facts of slavery, Grimes suffuses his narrative with a subjectivity that leaves its signature in the tone, structure, diction, and themes of the *Life*. The final injunction of his opening message "To The Public" is: "Let any one imagine this [his betrayed liberty in Connecticut], and think what I have felt." "What I have felt" is insisted upon throughout the subsequent narrative as the reader is led through a sometimes maundering, often dizzying succession of violent, unexpected, and irrational situations that Grimes claims to have been his perpetual lot in life. Grimes's feelings of injury and outrage lend a certain emotional coherence to a text that otherwise reads like a free-associative act of memory. The *Life* is not so much a representation of Grimes's past as it is the record of his psyche in the act of reviving and revenging itself on its past. To open Grimes's book is to open the wounds of the ex-slave's body and mind, for the book is the man's psychic body manifested in language. The violation of many literary proprieties in the *Life* testifies to the violation of the act of recall by unrepressed affects associated with the memories of his life. Most later slave narratives would keep these affects suppressed behind the objective facts of slavery. A few narrators, as we shall see, devised subtle strategies to permit the controlled violation of literary and cultural proprieties for rhetorical purposes. Yet even in these cases shocking psychological revelations that might alienate a white audience were often displaced.

William Grimes, however, seems to have been unable to navigate such a sensitive course through the psychological minefield of his own memories, on the one hand, and white sensibilities, on the other. The closer he got to the full subjective signifying power of his memories, the more explosive and self-destructive the text becomes and the more threatening it must have appeared to the white reader of its era. Recalling a flogging he received after having beaten corn into unsatisfactory hominy for his exacting mistress, Grimes concludes: "It seems as though I should not forget this flogging when I die; it grieved my soul beyond the power of time to cure" (15). Of another cruel mistress, the slave comments in the same tone of rankling bitterness, "She is dead, thank God, and if I ever meet her again, I hope I shall know her" (8). We will not see again in the classic slave narrative such outright defiance of the Christian commandment of forgiveness. What we will see is considerable evidence, sedulously distributed throughout abolitionist-sponsored slave narratives, testifying to the compassionate feelings of fugitives toward their former cruel owners.

Grimes insists on some occasions that he has been a man of prayer and faith; he advises his reader that "if we trust in God, we need have no fear of the greatest trials," for "under the consolation of religion, my fortitude never left me" (29). His actual narrative, however, is filled with evidence to the contrary, when Grimes's fortitude did desert him and alcohol became his solace, when he resorted to every mode of deception he could think of in order to survive, when he consulted his wits in preference to

God's will. Slavery, the persona maintains on one occasion, is so totalitarian a state of oppression that "we must submit to our fate, and bear up, as well as we can, under the cruel treatment of our despotic tyrants" (30). Yet we see Grimes beating a slave driver with his own stick once, and we hear him announce another time, "I had too much sense and feeling to be a slave; too much of the blood of my father [a white man], whose spirit feared nothing" (20). Grimes's fears, however, are legion throughout the narrative, as well they might have been given the duress under which he lived as a slave. Yet he does not denounce slavery as an institution from which all blacks ought to be delivered. "Those slaves who have kind masters are, perhaps, as happy as the generality of mankind. They are not aware that their condition can be better, and I don't know as it can: indeed it cannot, except by their own exertions. I would advise no slave to leave his master." Why contradict his own example of a slave justified in leaving his master? Grimes's experience in Connecticut has proven to him that runaways are sure to be recaptured, and if they are not, the exploitation and injustice that he has encountered as a free black in New England stand as sufficient proof that "there is no inducement for a slave to leave his master and be set free in the Northern States" (67).

The many contradictions in Grimes's narrative, leading up to his final advice to slaves that contradicts the purpose of his whole life, subvert the consubstantiating relationship that he claims to seek with his fictive reader—one of trust, understanding, and sympathy. At the same time that these conventions of the autobiographer's pact with his reader are being defied, we are pushed into the role of implied reader with the task of considering the significance of these deviations. Regardless of its lack of ostensible literary merit, Grimes's *Life* does function as a literary text, according to Iser's conception. That is, the *Life* "takes the prevalent thought system or social system as its context, but does not reproduce the frame of reference which stabilizes these systems." Instead, as a literary text it "tends to take as its dominant 'meaning' those possibilities that have been neutralized or negated by that system."[27] In one sense Grimes's text signifies the possibility that the black self could not be recovered in the slave narrative without revealing a complex of disturbing psychological affects that the social system, including the antislavery movement, would have preferred to be neutralized or negated in and by autobiography. In a more profound sense, Grimes's text signifies the possibility that the black self—as a unitive, knowable essence, as the locus of a usable past for its creators and sponsors—could not be recovered at all in the slave narrative. For if, as one theorist of autobiography has argued, we must ultimately choose in autobiography between a strictly historical truth, unmediated by art, and a deeper truth, revealed through literary design,[28] then we must reject Grimes's narrative on both grounds. It fails to give us either truth or design with consistency; it frustrates facile choices between history and art. Small wonder, therefore, that this pioneering text has stimulated so little comment from literary or social historians of Afro-American autobiography.

Instead, the *Life* has stood as a loaded gun, a "death weapon," as Roger Rosenblatt has termed modern black autobiography,[29] as much a threat to the literary system of autobiography as to the social system of slavery. The final sentences of the *Life* deliver Grimes's parting shot at both systems: "I am now entirely destitute of property; where and how I shall live I don't know; where and how I shall die I don't know; but I hope I may be prepared. If it were not for the stripes on my back which were made while I was a slave, I would in my will leave my skin as a legacy to the government, desiring that it might be taken off and made into parchment, and then bind the constitution of glorious, happy, and *free* America. Let the skin of an American slave bind the charter of American liberty!" (68). Grimes's macabre offer of his own skin as binding for the Constitution, the text that bound him to slavery even after he had escaped to Connecticut, is open to multiple interpretations. Ordinarily binding serves the physical text by covering, protecting, and holding it together. On the other hand, binding also encloses a text physically and intellectually; the title on the spine has much to say about what is contained within. Grimes knows that to enclose and entitle the Constitution with a slave's skin, particularly that of a mulatto fugitive persecuted in the "glorious, happy, *free* America," would demonstrate major contradictions in the myth of America, the contradictions, for instance, of the white Negro (Grimes himself), the unfree freeman, and the false truths of the Bill of Rights. Grimes also knows, however, that his skin will never make good parchment since it has already been marred by the whips of his former owners. Yet if these stripes signify his former binding in slavery, they also delineate him as a text inscribed by the whip (slavery's perverse pen) and thus empowered to bleed meaning once the wounds are opened. The purpose of Grimes's narrative, as I have said, is to open and display those wounds, to make a text in which, as Ralph Waldo Emerson said of Montaigne's personal essays, "the marrow of the man reaches into his sentences" so that, were we to "cut his words," "they would bleed."[30] Later abolitionist-sponsored slave narratives would put the physical wounds of the slave on display, but in a much more objectifying narrative context, the more to keep bandaged and bound the psychic wounds that the *Life of William Grimes* uncovers.

More than a decade later Isaac Fisher, the amanuensis-editor of *Slavery in the United States: A Narrative of the Life and Adventures of Charles*

Ball, faced some of the same problems found in Grimes's *Life*—the problem of how much to reveal of the slave in the course of the narration of his experience, the problem of what kinds of facts should be included and excluded in order to make a slave narrative both convincing and acceptable to white readers. Charles Ball had been a bondman for some fifty years; he had traveled widely in the Southeast; he had known comparatively kind masters and ruthless ones; he had seen the coffles, the jails, the miserable slave quarters, and the mansions of the master class; he had known firsthand the sufferings of the hungry, the insufficiently clothed, the cruelly beaten, and the falsely punished slave; and he had seen even worse cruelty inflicted on other blacks before escaping from Georgia in 1812. Like Grimes he had been recaptured in freedom and, having no money to purchase himself, was sold back to slavery in Georgia in 1830. Before he could effect his second escape, his wife and children in Baltimore were seized and sold into slavery, so that upon his return home in 1832, the fugitive found his triumph enveloped in tragedy. To the end of his narrative he remained "fearful, at this day, . . . that as an article of property, I am of sufficient value to be worth pursuing in my old age" (517).

To Fisher it was natural "that a man who had passed through so many scenes of adversity, and had suffered so many wrongs at the hands of his fellow-man, would feel much of the bitterness of heart that is engendered by a remembrance of unatoned injuries." Nevertheless, he assured the reader in his preface, "every sentiment of this kind has been carefully excluded from the following pages." Thus Fisher established quite explicitly for his reader a "preparatory condition" (to use John Searle's phrase) for discourse in the slave narrative. He would censor and thereby repress the psychological affects "engendered by a remembrance of unatoned injuries" so that the reader might proceed into the narrative secure in the knowledge of what the rules of the speech situation were. The narrative would contain a full but "unadorned detail of acts." The reactions of the slave would be presented in a psychological vacuum so as to insulate the reader from the natural but distressing "bitterness" generated in the narrator by the reliving of his "unatoned injuries."

The implications of this decision of Fisher's ought not to be underestimated. Hailed by many in the antislavery movement, Ball's narrative was reprinted often in the decades following its initial publication; it directly influenced the manner and matter of later fugitive slave narratives.[31] Fisher established important precedents for the slave narrative tradition, not the least of which was to define the discursive status of the fugitive slave narrative according to a particular class of speech act that Searle has termed the *assertives*. Assertives are designations of a speaker's commitment to the truth of an expressed proposition. When speaking (or writing) an assertive, one is engaged in making one's words (or, more exactly, the propositional content of those words) signify, conform to, or "fit the world." One way that Searle distinguishes between assertives and other kinds of speech acts is by identifying the "direction of fit" between linguistic signs and that which they signify outside the code of signifiers itself. A writer like Fisher prepares his audience for a new form of discourse, a fugitive slave narrative, by assuring them that the direction of fit in this "unadorned detail of acts" will be, in Searle's phrase, "word-to-world." Such an assurance structures the reading of Ball's narrative in accordance with two assumptions: that words can and will fit the world and, conversely, that the world, even the unfamiliar world of slavery, can be known by decoding the denotations of words assigned to that world. Offering the fugitive slave narrative to whites as an assertive speech act was tantamount, therefore, to issuing one-way tickets to the understanding of slavery. Decoding would be conducted in one direction, from the signifier to its presupposed signified in the world of slavery. In no other way would language be allowed to sidetrack the reader.

For rhetorical purposes, the direction of fit in more polemical narratives might be reversed at times. In these cases instead of words fitting the world, the corrupt world of the South or the unenlightened world of the northern reader's mind might be called upon to fit, to adjust to, the words of a slave narrator calling for some kind of reform. Such world-to-word speech acts can be labeled *directives* in Searle's terminology, because the intention of such statements is to get some other to do something desired by the speaker.[32] Fisher made Ball's narrative predominantly assertive, however, almost never overtly directive. This was, perhaps, a necessarily politic decision, given Fisher's unabolitionized readership in 1837. Still, it was a decision that severely restricted the discursive potential of this prototypical narrative.

We should recognize, however, that even if directives became the slave narrator's alternative mode to assertives, the slave narrator was still boxed into a "prison-house of language." For whether the slave's words served as assertive representations *of* the world or as directive models *for* the world, they remained bound *to* the world, to an alien ("distanciating") locus of reference and signification. This assumed and expected linkage of words to world in either or both directions was, of course, arbitrary and culturally determined. But how was the slave narrator to be liberated from such assumptions and expectations?

The answer is that the limitations of the assertive-directive mode of black autobiographical act had to be discovered before new ideas of signification could be explored. This process of discovery could not begin so long as (1) whites controlled slave narratives as either ghostwriters (Fisher for Ball) or amanuensis-editors (Whittier for Williams) and (2) the direction of fit between words and the world remained the overriding concern in the black autobiographical speech act. It may be that men like Fisher and Whittier took up the ghostwriting and editing of early slave narratives as much to insure that these works would have a discernible and conventional fit with the world as to help illiterate slaves send a letter to the world. The first New York publisher of Ball's narrative disclosed that Fisher had told him "in a private communication, that many of the anecdotes in the book illustrative of southern society, were not obtained from Ball, but from other and creditable sources."[33] These unspecified sources—probably Fisher himself in many cases[34]—lard Ball's account with lengthy passages of southern local color that inform the reader about the dimensions and ecology of the magnolia tree, the techniques of combating the tobacco worm, the inner workings of a cotton gin, and popular pastimes and games in southern taverns. Was this fit material to inject into the narrative of an ex-slave? From the standpoint of word-to-world fitness, it was; these materials give a documentary, encyclopedic weight and breadth to a volume ambitiously titled *Slavery in the United States*. From the standpoint of autobiographical authenticity, however, Fisher's concern only with word-to-world fitness seriously compromised the potential of his book as discourse, as a means of mediation between its reader and its (ostensible) black narrator. The word-to-world direction of fit, augmented by the indistinct sources of the narrative, frustrates the reader's attempt to recreate the implied author of this book or in other ways to resist the response programmed by Fisher's assertives.

The assertive mode of speech action used in this pioneering fugitive slave narrative ought to be understood, therefore, as a way of channeling and controlling a reader's response. The mode also served to enclose the new autobiographical form within a world circumscribed by language used in a deliberately restricted, univocal way, in a one-to-one relationship of signs to facts. Facts were that which was representable through this restricted, non-tropological use of language. Thus the world in which the slave narrative developed was a closed world of signifiers arbitrarily linked to facts that were themselves delimited by an arbitrary restriction on the power of language to signify at all. In part such restrictions might be attributed to the desires of the sponsors of the early slave narrative to propitiate its audience, but one ought not to ignore the fact that such restrictions also bound the slave narrator to a predictable set of speech-act options, which doubtless made the management of this new genre less problematic for its sponsors.

Had the bitterness of a Charles Ball been allowed to emerge in a slave narrative, the program of reading reinforced by the assertive mode would have been modified and in some important ways redirected. To express or imply bitterness about something is to undertake a third kind of speech act, one that we may call an *expressive* (again, borrowing from Searle's taxonomy). This kind of speech act is designed to express one's psychological state with respect to the propositional content of a given utterance. Unlike both assertives and directives, expressives are exempt from considerations of fitness with the world. Searle's paradigmatic expressive verbs—thanking, apologizing, deploring—*presuppose* the truth of the propositon being stated, so that neither the assertion of the statement's validity nor the directing of the world's acceptance of that validity is at issue anymore.[35] Thus an expressive is based on a presupposition, a presumption, that changes the rules of the discursive situation, with crucial consequences in the case of the slave narrative. Every time the slave narrator utters an expressive, he engages in an act of presumption. He presumes upon his reader's expectations of fitness. He begins to pay special attention to the psychological foregrounding of his statements. Expressives mark the beginning of more inwardly reflective than outwardly directed modes of speech action in the slave narrative. Stating or implying that "I feel resentful or bitter" about something becomes an especially powerful form of foregrounding when used by the slave narrator. Such foregrounding amounts to an act of double presumption. First, the narrator presumes the truth of what he is about to state without resorting to the conventions of assertives or directives. Second, he makes his propositions about the world grammatically dependent on—and by implication epistemologically relative to—his psychological disposition as stated in the initial clause of his expressive speech act. When that psychological disposition is one of bitterness, additional conventions of moral fitness, we might say, are also put in abeyance, as the slave autobiographer refuses to forgive what his antislavery sponsor and reader do not want him to forget. Expressives, therefore, could subvert the conventions of speech action and reader response that defined and legitimized the early slave narrative in the 1830s.

Fisher's resistance to black expressives, particularly of bitterness, was such that he could not be satisfied with merely censoring Ball. He had the persona of *Slavery in the United States*, supposedly a much-abused fugitive slave, assert his mistrust of the outcome of universal emancipation because of the slave's propensity to bitterness and vengefulness. According to Ball the slave is "an ignorant man" who "cannot reason logically." Thus the slave fails to realize that he would "always remain in poverty, without the judgment of [the whites] in directing labour to a definite and profitable result" (299–300). Instead of embracing the idea of the Christian heaven where "all distinctions of colour, and of condition, will be abolished, and they shall sit down in the same paradise, with their masters, mistresses, and even with the overseer," the "gross and carnal minds" of the southern slaves demand retribution. "Heaven will be no heaven to him [the slave], if he is not to be avenged of his enemies" (220–21). "Christianity cannot be, with propriety, called the religion of these people" (165), not when the "crown" of the slave's "highest ambition" is to supplant his master and take possession of "his young and beautiful [white] mistress" (222). Thus the persona of Ball's narrative hedges on the wisdom of emancipating such people. The black man wants liberty as much as the white would if he were deprived of it, but "it is not for me to say that the one is as well qualified for the enjoyment of liberty as the other. Low ignorance, moral degradation of character, and mental depravity, are inseparable companions; and in the breast of an ignorant man, the passions of envy and revenge hold unbridled dominion" (379). Statements like these point to Fisher as the voiceover in *Slavery in the United States* while they also indicate one way that the slave narrative could be used as a weapon against blacks who expressed instead of repressed the pain and outrage of slavery.

Given the indifference that Grimes's narrative of outrage encountered and the resistance that Fisher displayed toward Ball's bitterness, it is not surprising to find the abolitionist press in the 1830s endorsing and promoting narrative by fugitives of an especially self-effacing disposition. Self-effacement meant not only more opportunity for the facts of slavery to come to the fore. It also meant that the slave could be used as an effective dramatic foil to the rapacious, mercurial, self-indulgent slaveholder of abolitionist typecasting. A fugitive's failure to be expressive gave him a certain moral as well as dramatic distinction, too. The less a slave narrator had to say of himself, the more he could be idealized as self-abnegating. The more he espoused or demonstrated the selfless virtues of trust, forgiveness, and love, the less he might be distrusted as a social alien or economic competitor in the North. Did William Grimes steal pigs and geese from his master when he could get the chance for a decent meal? Of course. "Why, I have been so hungry for meat that I could have eat my mother." The deliberate exaggeration here, despite the readiness of whites to think of blacks as potential cannibals, indicates Grimes's determination to show how slavery could make survival, the animal law of self-preservation, take priority over even the most sacred of social taboos. By contrast, James Curry, a fugitive whose story the *Liberator* printed in January 1840, refused to steal from his master even though the white man had wrongfully taken a pig from him. "My mother had taught me not to steal," Curry explains. In the early abolitionist-sponsored slave narrative, the idealized fugitive remains in possession of his good angel, his selfless self, one might term it, symbolized by Curry's scrupulously moral mother. In Grimes's vision of slavery, the self, representative of the humanity of the slave, may be as readily consumed by survival's desperate instincts as Grimes's mother might be consumed by her own starving son.[36]

The controversy surrounding the *Narrative of James Williams*, the first fugitive slave narrative to be published and promoted by the American Anti-Slavery Society, helps to crystallize the literary politics of publishing black autobiographies in the 1830s. John Greenleaf Whittier tried to anticipate challenges to Williams's reliability by citing the slave's "evident candor," his large supply of factual knowledge of slavery, his consistency under cross-examination, and his concessions to the South of "every thing of a mitigating character which fell under his observation." The narrative was buttressed with an appendix in which white witnesses to slavery testified in corroboration of Williams's story. Enthusiastically received, it went through three printings in the first six months after its publication.[37] A one-time house servant to Virginia aristocrats, Williams said that he had been sold to Greene County, Alabama, in 1833, where he became a slave driver on a cotton plantation overseen by an alcoholic sadist named Huckstep. The atrocities occasioned by Huckstep's reign of terror over the slaves gave Williams's facts of slavery a gruesome appeal.

Two months after the appearance of Williams's narrative, J. B. Rittenhouse, editor of the Greensborough, Alabama, *Beacon*, published the first of several attacks he would level against the factual accuracy of the new autobiography. A native of Greene County, Rittenhouse disputed the existence of anyone named Huckstep and of other slaveholders named by Williams as residents of the county. Williams's dating of events in his Alabama experience was questionable; so were the distances the fugitive claimed to have traveled during his escape. Subsequent inquiries by the executive committee of the American Anti-Slavery Society unearthed other irregularities in the fugitive's account of his boyhood among the Larrimores of Powhatan County, Virginia. The committee decided that it could not refute Rittenhouse, but it would not concede that the book was an out-and-out fraud, either. The abolitionists trusted the general outline of the characters and events in the narrative. How could an illiterate slave make up such a story out of whole cloth, replete with such specificity, such powerful episodes, and such convincing characterizations? Williams had impressed them as much as he had Whittier, his amanuensis-editor. They remembered this dignified man with his "expressive countenance shadowing forth 'sorrow' rather than 'anger'—a symmetrical figure, graceful in its movements—an intelligence that seemed to be the result of acquaintance with the style and usages of the best society in the South. He gave way to no denunciatory language—no resentful expressions against his master who had deceived, nor against the monster Huckstep who had degraded and *abused* him." This sort of man, the committee deduced, could be trusted. "*His* story he must have known needed no exaggeration—but rather a reduction from its realities, to secure for it the fullest confidence of those who were not intimately conversant with the horrors of Southern slavery."[38] This character witnessing for Williams did not prevent the narrative from being withdrawn from circulation by the Anti-Slavery Society in November 1838, however. In the absence of Williams himself, who had taken passage to safety and freedom in England several months earlier, no way could be found to validate those facts in his narrative that had been impugned.[39] No one ever *proved* the narrative false in any of its particulars; no one ever went to Greene County to review the evidence raised against the book. Yet the *Narrative of James Williams* is generally remembered as an untrustworthy document whose facts were "proved unreliable" by its southern critics.[40]

In actuality, what "proved unreliable" was the abolitionists' faith in the image that Williams had projected as he told them his story in the first place. The executive committee's defense of Williams's narrative reveals how important the "performative" feature of a slave's narrative was to its securing the credence of its original and most crucial audience, the abolitionists who would decide whether to underwrite it for publication. Whittier and the other abolitionists could not test the validity of Williams's facts; they could only test the man himself as a believable narrator of those facts. Their endorsement of his narrative rested as much on their response to the man who presented those facts as on the facts themselves. The abolitionists were probably more convinced by the "illocutionary force" of what Williams said—that is, by their perception of what he intended in telling his story as he did—than by the locutionary content of what he said. The committee's description of Williams's behavior as he told his story and the committee's ascription to him of intentions seemingly evidenced in his act of narrating help to clarify the discursive situation in which the slave's autobiographical act took place. Williams recalled his past without using "denunciatory language" or "resentful expressions" against anyone who had used him badly. In other words, he had not used what we might term negatively expressive speech action, the "anger" which the committee was happy not to find in his "expressive countenance." Instead, as a reading of his narrative reveals, Williams stayed within the boundaries of the assertive and occasional positively expressive speech acts, so that he seemed a Christ-like man of "sorrow," not outrage. In so doing, the fugitive met a crucial "preparatory condition" for a discourse with his white audience. To the executive committee, the "illocutionary force" of a black negative expressive translated into "exaggeration," i.e., a fictionalizing of the facts. Never mind that there was no intrinsic reason to suppose that expressing one's own negative psychological response to an autobiographical fact necessitated the distortion of the fact itself.

As an interpretive entity, the executive committee, well meaning as it appeared to be, was a creature of its own guilty fear of slave runaways, its own assumptions about the proprieties of black-white discourse, and its own sense of how black subjectivity could undermine that discourse. If the committee regarded black negative expressives as signs of exaggeration, it would naturally believe someone like Williams who spoke in an opposite manner, who followed "the style and usages of the best society," who identified himself as brother, not other, by observing the social and linguistic etiquette of genteel white America. Through his emotional restraint, reticence about personal feelings and judgments, and apparent propensity to forgive and pity, Williams either played to or, through lucky coincidence, conformed to his audience's expectations of the fugitive slave as autobiographer. The "illocutionary force" of his narration—what he seemed to be doing in telling his story—not only convinced his hearers that he was not exaggerating or fictionalizing; it also convinced them that he could be trusted to "reduce" the unpleasant "realities" of his story in exchange for "the fullest confidence of those who were not intimately conversant with the horrors of Southern slavery."

The case of Williams reveals, therefore, that we must think of slave narratives not just as performatives but as performances. They could not have been otherwise as long as their narrators had to depend on whites to publish and promote their autobiographies. Williams's case also suggests that from the inception of the slave narrative, white publishers of the genre did not object at all to the fictionalizing of a slave's autobiography, as long as that process aimed at "reducing the realities" of the slave's life to a level tolerable to white sensibilities. The pressure on the slave narrator might be twofold; to censor the past and/or to reduce the multidimensional realities of autobiography as a discourse of present *with* the past. Such a reduction of discursive possibilities between the past and the present would constitute another form of "distanciation" of narrating consciousness from the facts of the narrator's past.

If the Williams case indicates a kind of fictionalizing that the slave narrator might feel obliged to undertake, however, it also suggests what the limits of fictionalizing were in the minds of early slave narrative publishers. One could fictionalize by playing down the horrors of slavery.

One could not fictionalize by playing them up. Hence the assertive mode of speech action became predominant. One might risk playing up the self by using expressives to augment the psychological realism of one's narrative, regardless of how much the factual horrors of slavery might need to be reduced. But here again, negative expressives, revealing the horrors within the psyche—outrage, vengefulness, bitterness—could very well cause the facts of a narrative to be dismissed as exaggerated. Reduction and repression of past and present realities seemed to be the price one paid for being read as a realist in the early slave narrative, therefore—until the slave as *writer*-narrator could find ways to aggrandize the autobiographical act that were beyond the potential of the slave as oral narrator.

In the *Narrative of the Adventures and Escape of Moses Roper* (1837), the first fugitive slave narrative since Grimes's to be composed and written by the slave himself, the "ontological distanciation" that we have found in the Ball and Williams narratives is readily evident. Epitomizing the inductive mode of black autobiography in the 1830s, Roper introduces his story by stating that it "did not arise from any desire to make myself conspicuous, but with the view of exposing the cruel system of slavery."[41] Later he remarks, "I have never read nor heard of any thing connected with slavery so cruel as what I have myself witnessed" (20), which leads him to punctuate his story with descriptions of man's inhumanity to man unparalleled in any slave narrative up to that time. Yet in recounting these multiple incidents of sadism and mayhem suffered by himself and other blacks, Roper keeps rigidly to the assertive mode, maintaining a dispassionate tone and an undeviating attention to the plain facts of the matter. Here are his diagram of and accompanying commentary on one kind of torture he underwent after running away from Mr. Gooch, the most monstrous of Roper's masters.

Roper then provides the following analysis of his diagram: "This is a machine used for packing and pressing cotton. By it he [Mr. Gooch] hung me up by the hands at letter *a*, a horse, and at times, a man moving round the screw *e*, and carrying it up and down, and pressing the block *c* into the box *d*, into which the cotton is put. At this time he hung me up for a quarter of an hour. I was carried up ten feet from the ground when Mr. Gooch asked me if I was tired? He then let me rest for five minutes, then carried me round again, after which, he let me down and put me in the box *d*, and shut me in it for about ten minutes. After this torture, I stayed with him several months, and did my work very well" (53).

Except for the word "torture," the entire passage sounds almost textbookish in its absence of emotional response or identification of the narrator as subject with himself as the object of this brutality. This kind of

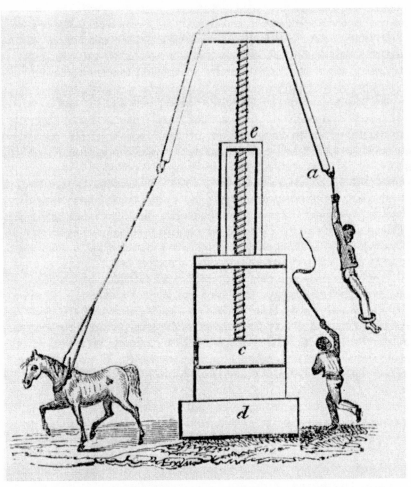

From *A Narrative of the Adventures and Escape of Moses Roper* (1838).

objectification and lack of emotional context in which to understand these facts has led Charles T. Davis to criticize Roper's narrative as incoherent and artless. Without "an effective principle of order and a center of feeling or consciousness" in the narrative, we are prevented, in Davis's view, from engaging the ugly facts of Roper's story as a meaningful unity, an artistic whole. "Instead of development and unity" in the narrative, "there are repetition and disjunction," which keep Roper's story from being either convincing or moving in Davis's estimation. Roper's greatest violation of effective rhetorical art occurs at the conclusion of his story, when the ex-slave living in England reflects on his feelings about his native land. In spite of the fact that he was victimized as a slave in the South and virtually terrorized in the North while a fugitive, Roper will speak no evil of God or man. Like James Gronniosaw and the other spiritual pilgrims of eighteenth-century black autobiography, he resigns himself (and his family still in bondage) to the will of God. Should the Lord "see fit to keep them still in suffering and bondage, it is a mercy to know, that he orders all things well" (107). Of America, "I am unwilling to speak in any but respectful terms." As for the slaveholders who did him so many wrongs, "I bear them no enmity . . . but regret their delusions." Thus, in Davis's view, "extraordinary horror is succeeded by even more extraordinary Christian compassion" in this autobiography, nullifying its power to move us either emotionally or aesthetically.[42]

However much one may question Davis's formalist prescriptions for art, it is hard to disagree with him that Roper's narrative is in certain respects an alienating text. Regardless of our estimate of the book as a factual exposé of slavery, the reading of the story as autobiography, as a narrative record of a self, what Davis calls "a center of feeling or consciousness" in the text, is likely to prove frustrating. The narrative seems almost deliberately to resist the attempt of even as sensitive a reader as Davis to understand (in Ricoeur's sense of the word) Moses Roper, the presumed center of the autobiography. Assuming that Roper had the power to determine how this text would work as a speech act,[43] we must also conclude that the alienating, decentered, disjunctive qualities of his autobiography are not the product of white editorial meddling but are attributable to Roper, either through conscious intention or unconscious omission. The question thus becomes, why did Roper allow his story to violate traditional notions of rhetorical art, to estrange his reader from all but the simple facts of a slave's experience, and to leave that reader unprepared for the disjunctive effects of the pious conclusion of the narrative? Was Roper a naive narrator, as artless as Davis reads him? Or is his an artful strategy of autobiography?

The *Narrative* shows that during Roper's several attempts to escape from slavery, he was regularly stopped and required to give an account of himself to suspicious whites. On these autobiographical occasions, Roper learned how to invent an identity and a past for himself that were close enough to the facts so that he could sustain cross-examination yet were free enough with the facts to let him manipulate whites into thinking he was someone to help and sympathize with. Because he was the light-skinned son of a white man and a woman of African and Indian ancestry, Roper could pass himself off as a runaway indentured servant, a cross-breed of white and Indian, not white and black, blood. On other occasions, he admitted he was a slave separated from his master, but he insisted that he was not running away, only trying to return to his owner from whom he had become lost. Through the adroit handling of these half-truths, Roper proves that he was not ignorant of the art of autobiographical persuasion in dealing with whites. Moreover, knowing that his readers will find his looseness with the truth disconcerting in a man who now asks for their trust and credence, Roper starts out his narrative by "deploring" all such behavior in his past. His only defense, he states in his introduction, was his ignorance, because of the benighting effect of slavery, of a person's "moral duty" to tell the truth (xii). The more difficult question of *how much* of the truth a slave owes his white audience is not broached in Roper's narrative. Nor is the problem of how to evaluate the slave as a hero, an object of admiration and support, according to his adherence to truthfulness or freedom as a moral priority. The resolution of these kinds of tensions would tax the art of black rhetoricians more skillful than Roper in the 1840s. Roper shows us that even the most apparently artless of slave narrators were schooled by slavery in the survival art of self-invention. Such training taught slaves that in the white world, making free with the facts of one's identity was a primary empowering step toward making oneself free.

As is the case in black spiritual autobiography of the 1830s, Roper's narrative also makes free with biblical precedent in order to aggrandize his self-image and teach his white audience how to read him. Roper's account of an escape attempt that he made from South Carolina in 1831 when he was about sixteen years old includes his joyful reunion with his mother and sister, whom he had not seen for ten years since being sold away by his mother's owner. In the region of Caswell Courthouse, North Carolina, Roper tries to locate his mother while in flight to the North, but he knows the chances of finding her are very slight. Nevertheless, he makes guarded inquiries to a slave girl whom he meets by chance on the road, discovering to his surprise that she is his sister, though she does not recognize him. Following her home, he comes face to face with his mother who, like his sister, does not immediately identify him. Instead of revealing himself, however, he quizzes his mother with tantalizing questions and oblique answers until she finally realizes who this stranger is. At this joyous moment Roper's narrative states that nothing could represent his feelings as well as the "42nd, 43rd, 44th, and 45th chapters of Genesis"—the story of Joseph's reunion in Egypt with his brothers and father. Fleshing out the parallels between himself and Joseph, Roper quotes from Genesis 42:7–8, "'And Joseph saw his brethren, and he knew them, but made himself strange to them. And Joseph knew his brethren, but they knew not him'" (34).[44] Roper notes "how applicable" Genesis 45:1–3 was to his experience of reunion with his mother: "'Then Joseph could not refrain himself before all them that stood by him, and he wept aloud, and said unto his brethren, I am Joseph, doth my father still live.'" A quotation from chapter 45 (verse 15) emphasizes further the family jubilation occasioned by the return of the long-lost son.

The ostensible reason for this appropriation of Scripture stems from Roper's profession of his inability to describe the emotions that he felt when he was united with his family. The biblical parallel seems to be the artless black narrator's only recourse when faced with the problem of how to justify the revelation of inner feelings in a factual narrative. Then, too, any white reader who could not understand the slave's need to recover his family might be enlightened by realizing the metaphorical relationship between Jacob's ancient family and the contemporary Afro-American family. Both had been ravaged and fragmented by slavery, and both are reunited by the irrefrangible love of a formerly enslaved son. But let the white reader consider further the emerging meaning of this metaphorical relationship. He will find it hard to escape the implicating power of this text to assign *him* a role in the metaphor, a role that helps to explain why this text functions as it does.

While there is a clear analogy between Roper and Joseph as lost sons reunited with their families, the parallel between Joseph's brethren and Roper's family is limited and unclear until we realize the direction in which the trope turns. In the Genesis story Joseph's brothers betrayed him and sold him into slavery because of jealousy. Roper's family, of course, was guilty of no such crime. That is, the *black* side of his family have no role in this metaphor. The white side, the family of Roper's white father, on the other hand, correspond aptly to the role of the betraying brethren who sell one of their own into slavery. The white wife of Roper's father, for instance, tries to murder the infant in a fit of jealousy and rage. Throughout the narrative whites in the South and the North betray the man whom they initially mistake as their racial brother, once they discover that he is Moses Roper, runaway slave. Not surprisingly, then, whenever whites asked Roper for an explanation of himself, he told a lie; he concealed his true identity; he "made himself strange" to these doubtful brethren in order to avoid discovery and betrayal.

In the Genesis story Joseph made himself strange to his brothers when they came to him in Egypt to ask for grain to preserve them and their families during a prolonged famine. The former slave who had risen to the place of Pharaoh's favorite concealed his identity from his former betrayers until he had put them through a series of tests. Exploiting his power over them, Joseph devised several stratagems that allowed him to determine whether they had learned penitence for their former crime against the family and whether they could demonstrate a renewed fidelity to brotherly bonds. When his brothers passed these tests, Joseph revealed himself, forgave them, and sent for his extended family to be reunited with him in Egypt.

Like the Genesis account Roper's narrative begins with the act of betrayal and enslavement, and it ends with the act of forgiveness of those who betrayed their brother. In the course of his story Roper estranges himself from his reader in a way similar to the way Joseph made himself strange to his brothers—as a means of forcing the reader to recognize himself in a role analogous to that of the false brothers in the biblical story. In this sense the text promotes what Ricoeur calls the reader's self-understanding "in front of the text." As a result of exposing himself to the text, the reader is exposed *by* the text; he is implicated by and in the text. The text implicates him morally in the role of the indifferent or estranging brother; it implies metaphorically a standard of true brotherhood that can be appropriated by the reader. Thus the white reader can discover "an enlarged self" in front of the text, the understanding of which is perhaps more important than what might be hypothesized about Roper's masked self behind the text.[45]

The priority of the reader's self-understanding before the narrator's self-revelation suggests that before the estranged other can be known as brother, those who have done the estranging must recognize their complicity in this alienating discourse. The act of cultural alienation, perpetrated by whites upon blacks, precedes the reaction of aesthetic "distanciation" in black autobiography. Roper's distancing from his reader and his own text serves to reveal to the white reader the discursive grounds and cultural foregrounds of alienated and alienating autobiographical acts. Given these constitutive rules underlying black autobiographical discourse at this time, it seems more important that the reader understand himself on the text's terms than that he understand the text on his own terms. Only by doing so can he discover the emergent meaning of the metaphors of brotherhood and estrangement in Roper's narrative that are crucial to the process of hermeneutical understanding in the first place.

Roper's narrative was the first popularly successful Afro-American autobiography to explore the rhetorical possibilities of combining the inductive and tropological modes of writing autobiography. It was the first narrative to place its reader's responses in a kind of strategic tension. As an inductive narrative, the facts of Roper's story distance the reader. They allow him or her to react as a spectator, to indulge in the voyeuristic pleasure of observing without being touched physically or emotionally. Additionally, inductive narratives have a fragmenting and decentering effect on autobiography. The effort to keep the expressive mode of speech action out of the narrative's repertoire decontextualizes scenes and actions from the past. They retain a superficial temporal context but their power to generate psychological resonance is inhibited. They are, as a result, brutalized linguistically. That is, they become a series of "brute facts" instead of taking on signifying power as "institutional facts," facts instituted by the rules of autobiographical discourse. In contrast, tropological narratives compel the reader to become a participant in the making of metaphorical meaning. The reader has the task of figuring out the full relationship between the narrative subject and its biblical modifier. As the vehicle of the basic metaphors in tropological narratives, Scripture does not become the center of these texts, however, because oftentimes, the application of biblical precedent to Afro-American experience is so unsettling that the reader's assumptions about that precedent will become themselves decentered. Since the narrator does not provide full explanations of the purpose or significance of these metaphors, the reader is left to pursue these significances on his own. The reader's consciousness becomes a kind of center-seeking principle in a text like Roper's, where the distanciation of the inductive mode pulls against the invitation to appropriation offered by the tropological mode. In the 1840s the placing of these two modes in a dialectical relationship, with similarly conflicting messages to the reader, would become the standard rhetorical premise from which all the great slave narrators proceed.

The Performance of Slave Narrative
in the 1840s

In July 1849, after a decade in which the publication of American slave autobiographies created a growing international literary sensation, Ephraim Peabody, a Boston Unitarian minister and moderate abolitionist, wrote the first review of what he called this "new department" in "the literature of civilization" whose appearance it was America's "mournful honor" to claim. In "Narratives of Fugitive Slaves," Peabody listed five notable autobiographies for discussion: *Narrative of Henry Watson, a Fugitive Slave* (1848); *Narrative of the Sufferings of Lewis and Milton Clarke* (1846); *Narrative of William W. Brown, a Fugitive Slave* (1847); *Narrative of the Life of Frederick Douglass, an American Slave* (1845); and *The Life of Josiah Henson, Formerly a Slave, Now an Inhabitant of Canada* (1849). The reviewer reserved his comments, however, for only three texts: Douglass's, Brown's, and Henson's. Peabody stressed the impact that this new Afro-American literary genre had made on public opinion in the 1840s. Fugitive slave narratives had achieved an "immense circulation" throughout "the whole of the North." Douglass's book, the first of the best-selling ex-slave autobiographies of the decade, "has in this country alone passed through seven editions, and is, we are told, now out of print." "Of Brown's Narrative, first published in 1847, not less than eight thousand copies have already sold."[1] Peabody might have added that although these were the two most prominently mentioned slave narratives in the 1840s, their popularity was by no means unusual. Henson's *Life* sold 6,000 copies in its first three years of existence, before the association of his name with Harriet Beecher Stowe's Uncle Tom made him and later editions of his autobiography internationally famous in the 1850s. The *Narrative of the Life and Adventures of Henry Bibb* (1849) and *The Fugitive Blacksmith; or Events in the History of James W. C. Pennington* (1849), two works that will figure prominently in this chapter along with the narratives of Douglass and Brown, also sold widely in multiple editions in the English-speaking world.[2]

Peabody accounted for the popularity of the fugitive slave narrative by noting its superiority to much conventional fiction of the day. Beside those "who have sufficient force of mind and heart to enable them to struggle up from hopeless bondage," the "ordinary characters" of literature seemed "dull and tame." There was something epic about the careers of men like Douglass and Brown. "We know not where one who wished to write a modern Odyssey could find a better subject than in the adventures of a fugitive slave." In an era charged with revolutionary romanticism over "the freedom and wrongs of Greece and Poland and Ireland," "the slave who endeavours to recover his freedom is associating with himself no small part of the romance of the time." Peabody was not alone in this conclusion. The transcendentalist clergyman and activist Theodore Parker considered slave narratives the only indigenous American literary form; "all the original romance of Americans is in them, not in the white man's novel." To both men, the slave narrative partook of and gave expression to a romantic concept of the human spirit, the cultivation and preservation of which had been America's raison d'être. Peabody summarized the central theme of the slave narrative as "the irrepressible desire to be free," the "secret, ever-urging instinct of [the] soul" that the bondman, like all mankind, "must obey." The testimony of the slave narrator confirmed Peabody's romantic faith in "the force and working of the native love of freedom in the individual mind." Thus, with Parker, Margaret Fuller, and many other liberals of the day, the Unitarian minister embraced and celebrated the fugitive slave as a kind of culture-hero who exemplified the American romance of the unconquerable "individual mind" steadily advancing toward freedom and independence.[3]

Echoing the editors and publicizers of slave narratives in previous decades, Peabody recommended the books in his review to anyone who wanted to take an inside look at the "peculiar institution" and "the mixed character of American civilization." But it was the intimate disclosure of the character of the fugitive, as much as the shocking exposure of the conditions of the chattel system, that seems to have impressed Peabody. No doubt a great many other readers in the 1840s were won over by what Peabody called "the force of character" emanating from a narrative like Douglass's. As fugitives like Douglass, Brown, Bibb, and Pennington stepped forward to indite their own life stories, they infused into their writing a quality that the dictated Afro-American narratives of earlier decades rarely communicated—a sense of an individual authorial personality, the sound of a distinctive authorizing voice. These qualities, along with the ideological import of the narratives of Douglass, Henson, and others, made possible for the first time in the 1840s the widespread recognition and acceptance of black autobiography as a uniquely American literary form. No longer did Afro-Americans seem on the margin of discourse in their own country or in the Western world.

Several factors help to explain this striking change in the fortunes of the Afro-American autobiographer in the 1840s. To begin with, this was a decade in which for the first time in American literary history both educational preparation and ideological justification for black autobiography existed on a scale sufficient for the needs of a minority genre trying to make a place for itself in the literary mainstream. A hard-earned literacy freed men like Douglass, Bibb, Brown, and Pennington from second-class citizenship in the world of letters and a secondhand role in the composition of their own life stories. Yet without the moral rationale and international audience that the antislavery movement provided the slave narrator, the most accomplished writer among this new group of literary lions might never have put pen to paper. A fugitive from slavery would not acknowledge himself as such—unless he was convinced that his gesture would redound favorably on himself and his people. Douglass recalled that before his appearance on the antislavery lecture circuit in 1841, "a colored man was deemed a fool who confessed himself a runaway slave, not only because of the danger to which he exposed himself of being retaken, but because it was a confesssion of a very *low* origin!"[4] Abolitionist propaganda removed the invidious class associations surrounding the fugitive slave by recasting him in the 1840s as precisely the kind of hero that Peabody and Parker celebrated.

The abolitionist crusade also endowed slave narratives with a moral justification similar to that which evangelicals from earlier decades had applied to the spiritual autobiographies of James Gronniosaw, John Marrant, or Solomon Bayley. In keeping with the new evangelicalism of radical abolitionism under the leadership of William Lloyd Garrison,[5] the new slave autobiography had an important mission as a conversion narrative. In the traditional spiritual autobiography, the emphasis had been on the challenges to the faith and fortitude of the soul in its perpetual resistance to the claims of the secular world and its perpetual quest for salvation. Black autobiography in the 1840s secularized the Christian soul into the spirit of American individualism and reoriented the concepts of testing and salvation to the contemporary sociopolitical scene. Abolitionists were happy to shift the question of the need for conversion from the black subject to the white reader of the slave narrative. In his preface to the *Narrative of Henry Box Brown* (1849), Charles Stearns exhorted his reader to let the ex-slave's story find an avenue to "the citadel of your soul, and there dwell in all its life-giving power, expelling the whole brotherhood of pro-slavery errors" so that the reader could be "aroused from 'the death of the sin' of slavery, and cleansed from the pollutions thereof." Joseph C. Hathaway's preface to the *Narrative of William W. Brown* hurries to its proselytizing peroration: "Reader, are you an abolitionist? What have you done for the slave? What are you doing in his behalf? What do you purpose to do? There is a great work before us! Who will be an idler now?"[6]

In their role as preachers from the antislavery pulpit, slave narrators gained valuable training for their literary careers. That the major slave narratives of the 1840s were produced by seasoned veterans of the abolitionist lecture circuit, not by lonely fugitives like James Williams newly arrived from the South, had much to do with their appeal to white audiences. Frederick Douglass spent more than four years on the abolitionist platform under the auspices of Garrison's American Anti-Slavery Society before that organization published his narrative in 1845. Williams Wells Brown had been employed as a lecturing agent for the Western New York Anti-Slavery Society for four years before he ventured to write his autobiography. Henry Bibb served an even longer apprenticeship in the Midwest and Middle Atlantic states before he saw his narrative into print in 1849. As these famous fugitives repeated their life stories to curious white audiences from Maine to Michigan, they had numerous chances to polish their narrative and rhetorical skills.[7] Lionized in one town and reviled in the next, they were well schooled in the ways that their self-presentation, their modes of address, their idiom, and their tones of voice would affect whites. This preparation as oral self-historians on the abolitionist platform instilled in them a rhetorical sophistication and audience-consciousness unprecedented in the history of Afro-American autobiography.

The degree of egocentrism in black autobiography of the 1840s, when compared to the self-effacement instanced in so much of the genre before that decade, could not have appeared or have met with such public sympathy without the support and sanction of the antislavery movement. Antebellum America had never been receptive to black autobiography as an expressive mode unless it could be packaged and recommended by whites as something else—e.g., in the case of the criminal confession up through Nat Turner's work, as a warning *against* black introspection and trust in the arrogant, deluding intuition. The besetting sin in the eyes of evangelical reformers in the 1830s and 1840s was self-gratification,[8] a charge that could easily be leveled against anyone who engaged in the egotistical act of autobiography. Yet the slave narrative of the 1840s largely escaped this censure, except from southern critics offended by notices of the celebrity of runaways among the aristocrats of Europe. Abolitionism conducted a very successful campaign of identifying the slaveholder as criminal selfishness personified, next to which the slave narrator's mere literary egoism shrank into insignificance.

Most slave narrators made the conventional modest apologies for their awkwardness and lack of personal relish or preparation for the literary task that their consciences required of them. But even when an ex-slave gloried in his triumph over his master or voiced his personal criticism of American institutions, his rebellion against authority was applauded as a demonstration of Negro nobility and his censure of the republic was welcomed as a sign of the Negro's powers of analysis and argument. Thus the abolition movement acquiesced in the self-aggrandizement that a popular slave narrative could offer its author as long as the image promulgated by the narrative did not contradict the propaganda about the essential character of the Afro-American. Although Douglass's speaking and writing sometimes led to accusations of "egotism" and "conceit,"[9] radical abolitionists in the 1840s usually defended the ex-slave's temerity as unquestionable proof of their own arguments about the natural dignity of the Negro and his unfitness for anything less than immediate freedom and citizenship. Garrison himself had taken an uncompromising stand on the question of freedom of self-expression in the denunciation of slavery. Should "the convictions of an honest soul" regarding human bondage be "gentle, and carefully selected, and cautiously expressed?" he asked the critics of his impolitic manner. "Away with such counsel," he replied; "call things by their right names and let the indignant spirit find free utterance."[10]

As "romantic reformer" and peripheral transcendentalist, Garrison was not the only person in the antislavery movement to tap the new literary ideals of Romanticism for justification for letting the "spirit find free utterance."[11] Slave narrators could also thank Romantic thinkers in the 1830s and 1840s for helping to prepare New England to discover value in the first-person writing of black outsiders from the South. In 1837, Ralph Waldo Emerson had informed the Phi Beta Kappa Society at Harvard that a cultural revolution, a democratization of literature, was underway; now "instead of the sublime and beautiful," "the near, the common" were to be explored. Among the new "topics of the time" was "the literature of the poor," which Emerson embraced as revelatory of "the highest spiritual cause" and law. With such a conviction he and Margaret Fuller launched *The Dial* in 1840, determined "to report life" based on resources that were "not so much the pens of practiced writers, as the discourse of the living."[12]

101

One of the barriers that Emerson and his intellectual compatriots wanted most to transcend was that which separated life from the merely literary, living experience from dead, ossified language. The best of the slave narratives, as Peabody and Parker observed, broke through these barriers and helped to restore political and literary discourse on the subject of slavery to first considerations—the tangible experience and direct perceptions of the individual. In its absence of conventional art, its rejection of elegance and classic form, its apparently spontaneous rhythms of consciousness, and its dependence on plain speech and empirical facts, the slave narrative exemplified many qualities of "living discourse" that transcendentalists believed were the grounds of true eloquence. The convergence of spiritual self-examination, romantic self-consciousness, and democratic individualism in transcendentalist writing made the self, its nature and its potential, an inescapable "topic of the time."[13] Such an intellectual climate fostered an increasing preoccupation with selfhood and identity in the slave narrative and an expanding search for the rhetorical means by which to give them voice.

In the *Narrative of Frederick Douglass*, we see some of the first fruits of the emancipation of the black autobiographer under the influence of the cultural forces just discussed. In his preface to the *Narrative*, Garrison praised Douglass for having "very properly chosen to write his own Narrative, in his own style, . . . rather than to employ some one else."[14] Douglass's style, the signature of his individuality more than the recitation of the facts of his past, was the most telling aspect of the ex-slave's narrative. The "most thrilling" incident in the story was not, in Garrison's view, the famous battle between the sixteen-year-old Douglass and the slave-breaker, Edward Covey. It was instead "the description DOUGLASS gives of his feelings, as he stood soliloquizing respecting his fate, and the chances of his one day being a freeman, on the banks of the Chesapeake Bay" a few months before the crucial fight with Covey. In contrast to the editor of Charles Ball's story ten years earlier, Garrison urges his reader to pay special heed to what the ex-slave reveals of himself, of his own psychological state, as he contemplated his desperate status and his ideal of freedom. Garrison directs his reader toward what Isaac Fisher shielded his reader from—a slave narrator's use of the expressive mode of speech action. Douglass's narrative is freely laced with both positive and negative expressives, utterances through which Douglass not only asserts a proposition about something but also conditions his reader's response to that assertion by couching it in an expression of his psychological state as he makes the assertion. Before the ascendency of Garrisonian radicalism, slave narratives, when they ranged beyond the assertive mode (as in the case of Moses Roper), were, in Garrison's words, "gentle" and "cautiously expressed." Douglass was the first Afro-American autobiographer to risk the negative expressive for rhetorical purposes that involved more than simply "letting the indignant spirit find free utterance." For Douglass and those who followed him, the expressive was a way to recontextualize baldly factual assertives about the past so that the reader could be shown not just the incident or what the incident signified but how to *feel* about the incident. The extensive use of the expressive in the 1840s represents an important stage in the authorizing of the narrative voice in the slave autobiography.

Douglass's *Narrative* instances an even more radical stage in the process of self-authorization that distinguished black autobiography in the 1840s. At the end of the fifth chapter of his narrative, Douglass pauses to reflect on a turning point in his life when, at the age of seven or eight, his Eastern Shore master sent him to live in Baltimore with Hugh and Sophia Auld. "Going to live at Baltimore laid the foundation, and opened the gateway, to all my subsequent prosperity," he remarks. "I have ever regarded it as the first plain manifestation of that kind providence which has ever since attended me, and marked my life with so many favors." Regarding oneself as chosen by Providence for a special destiny was not, of course, unusual among black spiritual autobiographers before Douglass. However, Douglass's special providence was not to become a minister but a rebel and later a fugitive from the law. He acknowledges his white reader's likely skepticism at his presumptuousness: "I may be deemed superstitious, and even egotistical, in regarding this event as a special interposition of divine Providence in my favor. But I should be false to the earliest sentiments of my soul, if I suppressed the opinion. I prefer to be true to myself, even at the hazard of incurring the ridicule of others, rather than to be false, and incur my own abhorrence" (75). This is a crucial declaration in the history of black autobiography. For the first time, the black writer announces that truth to the self takes priority over what the white reader may think is either probable or politic to introduce into discourse.

What is the authority that justifies this declaration of independence in a black man's interpretation of his own life? He does not appeal to divine inspiration, nor does he appropriate from Scripture in order to empower himself with moral or prophetic authority. Instead, his authority comes from (1) the act of having claimed it; (2) his allegiance to the self rather than to the other, the reader; and (3) his definition of truth and falsehood as that which is consistent with intuitive perception and needs, not as absolute standards. In language like this Douglass and his important successors in the slave narrative implied that the writing of autobiography was itself to be understood as an act of self-liberation, part of the continuum of events narrated in the text. Instead of existing as the theme of the text, that which the slave narrative is *about*, freedom becomes the crucial property and quality *of* a text—not just *what* it refers to, but *how* it signifies. This kind of textual freedom may be read as apparent testimony to the extent to which the creator of the text has liberated himself from the authority of extratextual assumptions and conventions. Or it may be read as an index to the play of the text itself, independent of the intention of its author.[15]

These important changes in the nature and source of authority in black autobiography point to the appearance, in a self-conscious way, of a fourth and final mode of speech action in the major slave narratives of the 1840s. John Searle's term *declaration* will serve our needs for a label for this class of speech acts in which "one brings a state of affairs into existence by declaring it to exist." In declarative acts, "saying makes it so." [16] Assertives and directives are concerned with the relationship of language to the world that it proposes to describe (in the case of assertives) or instruct (in the case of directives). I have noted in a previous chapter the restricting authority that the world assumes over a text when the former becomes either the epistemological locus for assertive or the didactic telos for directive speech action. Because expressives report the psychological condition in which a speech act is made, they are free from considerations of fitness with the world. They may be used to influence the world indirectly, but their primary reference is to the speaker, whom we might also call the self. Through expressives the self begins to recontextualize discourse through a kind of psychological foregrounding. The objectivity of a slave narrative becomes deliberately qualified and compromised when expressives begin to punctuate its address to the reader.

Nevertheless, the use of the expressive requires an autobiographer to relativize the objective authority of recalled facts in only a limited sense. Consider this expressive in Douglass's *Narrative*: "My blood boils as I think of the bloody manner in which Messrs. Wright Fairbanks and Garrison West, both class-leaders [in a white Methodist church], in connection with many others, rushed in upon us [slaves] with sticks and stones, and broke up our virtuous little Sabbath school, at St. Michael's—all calling themselves Christians!" (120). In this case, Douglass makes his first concern, literally, the subject of this statement, his psychological reaction to his memory of what Fairbanks and West did. But this priority of subjectivity does not displace or undermine the objective status of the predicated assertive about Fairbanks and West. Indeed, the expressive seems designed to underline the fact of the white men's bloody deed by noting the response of Douglass's blood pressure to it.

A declarative speech act, on the other hand, unites the subject and predicate of a proposition in subjectivity, in the authority of the ego. In making declaratives, a slave narrator becomes a godlike authority over the world of his text and seeks to extend his authority to the world outside his text by abrogating his responsibility to the rules that govern and validate normal discourse. The particular realm of declarative action in slave narratives is that of definition and denomination, a realm in which extralinguistic conventions are no longer required. Like Emerson's Poet, the great slave narrators are "namers" who realize that "words are also actions, and actions are a kind of words." Douglass, for instance, is an Adamic autobiographer determined to rename the world of the corrupted Garden of the South so that men and animals can be rightly distinguished.[17] In the *Narrative*, Edward Covey is dubbed "the snake," while Douglass uses himself as a paradigm of manhood regained from brutehood. William Wells Brown succinctly summarizes the importance of declarative action when he says of his first days in freedom: "So I was not only hunting for my liberty, but also hunting for a name" (98). The new name is both a key to and an index of liberty. The assumption of the autobiographer's prerogative to define himself empowers the slave narrator to redefine the rest of the world of the past according to that egoistic standard. How he manipulates this power, and what freedom he makes of it, can reveal important things about the potential of the text to redefine the discursive relationship of narrator and reader in Afro-American autobiography.

Our discussion thus far has emphasized the positive impact of the "romantic reformers," both sociopolitical and cultural, on the slave narrative. Yet it would be a mistake not to recognize that the cultural and political forces that helped to forge new modes of slave narrative in the 1840s did so by contraries. While Romantic reform helped create a propitious political and intellectual climate in which slave narratives could be read, these reformers often established a very different set of conditions in which slave narrators could think and write about themselves. The self-authorizing strategies in ex-slave autobiography may have arisen as much of necessity as of choice, therefore. The enlistment of the self, through the autobiographical act, in the antislavery movement required, subtly and simultaneously, literary acts of resistance *to* the antislavery movement in order to preserve the text as autobiography and the narrator as an independent entity, something more than a coopted organization man. Tensions, disjunctions, and silences can serve as an index to a struggle going on in a narrative between its role as the work of a movement, identified by its consistency with the ideology of the movement, and its role as the text of an other, identified by its inconsistency, its un- resolved relationship within and without the movement.

Historical scholarship on the role of blacks in the antislavery move- ment confirms the tense, often suppressed conflicts between ex-slaves and white reformers over authority and priorities.[18] The writing of slave narratives was informed by and in some ways reflects these tensions. The literary autonomy of men like Douglass, Brown, and Bibb, though greater than that of most black autobiographers before them, was nevertheless restricted by those who seemed to encourage them most in their literary efforts. The antislavery movement did not provide them a forum for their speaking and writing just so that they could express themselves. Slave narratives were solicited and published to promote the great social aim of abolitionism, not the personal needs of an individual. Slave narrators were not always free creative agents who could make what they wished of the facts of their lives. As public men and professional fugitives these men were the creatures of abolitionism. They knew that the autobiogra- phies they wrote were in a crucial sense not their own. They were shared property with the antislavery movement on whose platform and in whose press they had taken form and significance. Thus the movement itself formed the slave narrator's first and probably most critical audience. Its priorities and expectations had to be reckoned with and converted to narrative account if the slave narrator hoped to gain a wider hearing for his story.

Henry Bibb's situation is a case in point. After hearing Bibb lecture in Michigan in 1845, James G. Birney, former corresponding secretary of the American Anti-Slavery Society, threatened to expose the ex-slave as an imposter if he did not document his oral narrative to Birney's satisfaction. Careful not to offend this influential man, Bibb wrote a mollifying reply in which he flattered Birney as just the sort of "friend of high Standing" that he had long been seeking. Bibb then promised "to collect some facts to prove the reality of my Narrative."[19] In the spring of 1845, he submitted himself to a committee appointed by the Detroit Liberty Association, which rigorously interrogated him and wrote letters of inquiry to several Kentuckians, among them two whom Bibb had claimed as former own- ers, regarding the facts of his case. After reading the replies to its letters and evaluating its gathered evidence, the committee endorsed both Bibb's statements about himself and his character. Four years later, when Bibb put his life story into print, he capitalized on the committee's inves- tigation by having it featured prominently in the introduction to his *Nar- rative* as an authenticating document. Thus Bibb tried to turn abolitionist suspicion to his rhetorical advantage even as he acquiesced in the power of white men like Birney and the Detroit committee to decide whether he would be heard at all.

Douglass learned early that abolitionists had an old-fashioned prejudice against letting an ex-slave comment freely on the significance of his experience as he narrated the facts of his life. Douglass's fellow speakers on the antislavery lecture circuit in the early 1840s wanted him to keep to a "simple narrative," he recalled. "'Give us the facts,'" they urged him. "'We will take care of the philosophy.'" This was the traditional division of labor in Afro-American autobiography, looking back as far as Briton Hammon's narrative, in which the Negro supplies the raw materials, the "brute facts" of a life, and the white man manufactures and packages them for public consumption. Abolitionists were sensitive to the way slave narrators conducted themselves in the American marketplace of images as well as ideas. In 1855 Douglass revealed the behind-the-scenes coaching that he had received from his antislavery co-workers as to the proper image that he should present to the public. Although his self-education was making him an increasingly bold and trenchant rhetorician, his colleagues worried that people would no longer believe that he had ever been a slave. Thus, while all the time reminding him to "'be yourself'" and "'tell your story,'" they also pressed him to mask himself by keeping "'a *little* of the plantation manner of speech'" and thus not seeming to be too articulate or "'too learned.'" The question naturally arises, as it must have for Douglass and others like him, what kind of self did the Garrisonians want him to be? To what extent was the former slave being asked to sell himself in a rhetorical sense from the antislavery platform in order to profit new patrons who, as Douglas became convinced in the 1850s, had a master complex all their own?[20]

Second only to Douglass among slave narrators of national fame in the 1840s, William Wells Brown seems to have been particularly mindful of the need to cultivate his abolitionist audience, whose approval was the first step to the literary recognition he would later seek in the 1850s and 1860s. Knowing that he would be inevitably compared to Douglass, Brown used his autobiography partly as a means of helping him to emerge from Douglass's shadow. Before his book went to press, Brown revealed his "anxiety of influence" in his wish, confided to a white reader of his manuscript, that his autobiography could be given a title different from that of Douglass. Failing that, Brown made sure that both the matter and the manner of his story would be favorably distinguished from Douglass's narrative by reformers in need of an effective propaganda instrument. Douglass's firsthand knowledge of slavery was limited to Maryland's Eastern Shore and Baltimore. Because Brown had traveled from New Orleans to St. Louis as a slave of Mississippi River merchants, he could make more sweeping statements about slavery as an institution, and he did. This convinced his manuscript reader, Edmund Quincy, a member of Garrison's inner circle, that Brown's was "a much more striking story than Douglass's," yet told with "great propriety & delicacy." These qualities of Brown's literary manner contributed to the personal impression that he made on Quincy, namely, that he was "of a much higher cast of character" than Douglass. As Quincy opined to a white friend after reading the Brown narrative in manuscript, this new black spokesman, unlike the proud, prickly Marylander, evidenced "no meanness, no littleness, no envy or suspiciousness about him." "He never seems [to] (& says he never does) think uncomfortably about his being a black man." A politic Negro like this, who never made whites uncomfortable by talking about his own sense of alienation in their midst, would naturally please them with his "propriety and delicacy." Small wonder, then, that Brown was regarded as in many respects "more valuable" to the Garrisonians than Douglass, the eventual apostate. Never breaking with the Garrisonians, Brown maintained much the same politic persona throughout his antislavery literary career, while Douglass's changed. An abolitionist like Joseph C. Hathaway took the "simplicity and ingenuousness" of Brown's narrative manner as assurance of his "truthfulness." But Samuel J. May, a Boston minister of many causes, knew something more lay behind the mask. May told an English reformer that Brown, though "a good fellow," was a man to be watched, for "he likes to make popular and taking speeches, and keeps a careful eye upon his own benefit." [21]

Keeping an eye on his own interest was necessary for the fugitive slave, given the fact that all the white world was, in truth, a stage and his narrative a public act in a play of national proportions. Under these circumstances, slave narrators had to look out for their own benefit, though they could not afford to seem to be doing so. More than a few slave autobiographies were published as fund-raisers for their narrators, and most were labeled so. The narratives of Lunsford Lane (1842) and Henry Watson (1848) were inspired at least in part by the two men's practical need for money with which to support their families. Moses Grandy's amanuensis recommended his narrative to anyone who wished to help the ex-slave achieve "the object which engages so entirely [his] mind . . . namely, the redemption of those who are in bonds belonging to his family." [22] As long as moral and political profits accrued to the antislavery cause, abolitionists did not object to the financial gain an ex-slave might reap from his narrative. In a society as hostile to blacks as the North was in the 1840s,[23] an ex-slave who hoped for a good sale of his narrative was not likely to embarrass his white sponsors or contradict his audience's expectations by talking about slavery or himself in an unsanctioned manner.

While the more radical abolitionists of the 1840s permitted a more expressive mode of slave narration, moderates in the movement tried to encourage, if not enforce, self-restraint in persons like Douglass who seemed likely to damage the movement by speaking out too freely. Although he admired Douglass and his *Narrative* Ephraim Peabody took the occasion of his review to chide the ex-slave for a "fault" in his "mode of address" as both a speaker and a writer. If Douglass wanted "to accomplish any practical end" for the movement, he needed to stop "indulging himself" in "vehemence of tone or expression," "violent and unqualified statements," and "sweeping denunciations." These could only "create in his hearers a secret distrust of his real earnestness,—a vague feeling that after all he is thinking more of his speech than of the end for which he professes to make it." Peabody recommended that Douglass take a lesson from the commercial side of American life. A merchant truly dedicated to the success of "some enterprise" could be known by the "moderated accuracy . . . of his statements." "Extravagance and passion and rhetorical flourishes" were just the sorts of "trifling" that no man "serious" about his dealings with others would engage in. These were the earmarks of "the personated passion of the theatre." Success in the socioliterary marketplace, as in the business world, depended on "a few sober words from a calm, wise, discriminating mind." Such a mind, Peabody strongly implied, belonged to Josiah Henson.

In the 1840s Henson was best known as an ex-slave who had helped to found and raise funds for a manual labor school and an accompanying settlement for blacks in Dawn, Canada, near the Detroit River. Peabody thought Henson's dictated *Life* "simple, straightforward, and to the point, as the character which it describes." On the public platform, this "large-hearted, large-minded man" showed himself to be "tolerant, calm, benevolent, and wise." "We believe that our readers will be interested in the efforts of one who, without noise or pretension, without bitterness towards the whites, without extravagant claims in behalf of the blacks, has patiently, wisely, and devotedly given himself to the improvement of the large body of his wretched countrymen amongst whom his lot has been cast." Henson's altruistic, uncontroversial manner inspired faith where Douglass's combative style raised doubts. Moreover, Henson's dedication to "the idea of improvement," a word that Peabody repeats in his characterization of Henson, struck a responsive chord in the Unitarian minister. The man from Canada had a businesslike approach to expression and reform that Douglass seemed to lack. Henson's "native good sense and benevolent heart" had instilled in "the sluggish minds of his brethren" at Dawn a practical knowledge of principles espoused by Adam Smith and John Stuart Mill. Henson was molding a God-fearing, hard-working, land-owning class of black farmers in Canada, Peabody concluded from reading the *Life*, and, like white readers of *Up from Slavery* fifty years later, he was much taken with this application of the traditional American work ethic to racial uplift.[24]

It could be argued, of course, that Douglass was practicing a kind of literary and rhetorical self-reliance, too, but Peabody could not praise it so unreservedly because Douglass seemed to be "indulging himself" while Henson seemed to be concerned only with "improving" others. Douglass was guilty of self-gratification whenever he gave himself up to "extravagance and passion and rhetorical flourishes" to make his unsettlingly "violent" arguments. The signs of this transgression against propriety lay in his "passionate" utterance (in other words, his use of the expressive), his frequent stabs of "sarcasm" instead of direct and "sober" words, and his use of rhetoric in general, particularly his *self-conscious* employment of the tricks of the orator's trade.

Peabody realized that Douglass was taking the discourse of the slave narrator away from the reportorial, objective, fact-oriented mode and into a new relationship to the self and language. At times Douglass seemed to be deliberately defying the appropriateness conditions of black-white discourse that Henson so exemplarily abided by. Douglass was making "his speech," his expression, his rhetoric—himself as wordsmith, not the program of abolitionism—the focal point of attention. Douglass was turning the slave narrative into a metaphor of self. In the press and on the platform he was beginning to engage in the politics of literary gesture, to demonstrate what Richard Poirier has called in contemporary literature "the performing self."[25] Through narrative acts of "self-discovering, self-watching," and "self-pleasuring" (the latter upsetting Peabody the most), Douglass was starting to remove the scene of black-white discourse from the merchant's counting room, where Peabody wanted to keep it, to the theater. It is not surprising that Peabody's Yankee sensibilities were discomposed. The traditional inductive slave narrative traded in quantifiable facts that summed up the truth about slavery in an efficient, detached manner. It was a fixed commodity of information whose face value was plain: it meant what it said and said only what it meant. Douglass's brand of discourse, on the other hand, with its vexing marks of theatricality and self-consciousness, was neither fixed nor commodifiable. Its face value might mask its truth value. How then could one be sure what was "personated passion" and what was the genuine article? Peabody wanted to believe in Douglass's "real earnestness," but the kind of play arising from his "loose, extravagant, and violent declarations" contradicted the white man's assumptions about how credibility was signified and truth encoded. For the first time, the performative nature of slave narration and the concomitant interplay of power and credibility between narrator and audience were becoming themselves topics of black autobiographical discourse.

Frederick Douglass's liberties with his expression and his audience can be best discerned against the background of the implicit compact of understanding and trust between slave narrator and northern reader that abolitionism tried to invoke in its black autobiographical publishing efforts in the 1840s. This compact is reflected in the narratives of Lunsford Lane, Moses Grandy, and Josiah Henson, all of which were dictated to or edited by abolitionists who further aided their publication and promoted their sale.[26] Both Lane and Grandy were North Carolina–born slaves who had achieved their freedom in the legal way, through hiring their time and husbanding their savings until the day they could purchase themselves. A former house servant to a Raleigh planter, Lane proved himself an enterprising tobacconist in that city and managed to raise $1,000 with which to buy himself in 1835. In the process of purchasing his wife and six children on a $2,500 installment plan, he was expelled from the state in 1841 for being an illegal free black immigrant. The charge was based on his having gone to New York with his master six years earlier to be manumitted after North Carolina authorities had judged his master's petition for his emancipation unmerited. Lane spent about a year in the North speaking before abolition and church groups and soliciting money for his family's purchase. When he returned to Raleigh in April 1842 with the requisite sum, he was arrested as an abolitionist lecturer, mobbed, and tarred and feathered, but was then allowed to leave the state with his family. He returned to Massachusetts to continue working in the antislavery cause.

Grandy also underwent many trials on his way toward the purchase of his freedom. As a bargeman in the Dismal Swamp region, he worked tirelessly for his manumission money, only to have three different masters break their verbal contracts with him and pocket a total of more than $1,400 that he had saved for his freedom. Only on his fourth attempt at self-purchase could Grandy find a white man who would not cheat him out of the additional $650 that he earned for his manumission. Moving to Boston, he eventually bought his wife and a son. If his narrative and other activities on the abolitionist circuit were well received, he hoped to amass another $500 for a daughter's freedom.

Like Lane and Grandy, Henson distinguished himself in slavery as an industrious and profitable worker, so much so that his Maryland master made him manager of his plantation before Henson was twenty years old. In his late teens Henson also was converted to Christianity and became a slave preacher of some reputation. So reliable was he that his master entrusted him with conducting eighteen slaves, in addition to Henson's own family, from Maryland to a plantation in Kentucky, where Henson was to go to work for his master's brother. Faithful to his charge, Henson suppressed the temptation to escape to freedom across the Ohio River and delivered himself and his fellow slaves to their new master. Only after being cheated in one attempt to buy his freedom and learning later that he was intended for sale in New Orleans did he flee with his family to Canada in 1830, when he was forty-one. His *Life* goes on to recount the founding of the Dawn community in 1842 and his efforts as a fund-raiser for the manual labor school established in the settlement.

The strategy of each of these three narratives is to present the ex-slave as an exemplar of the traditional Protestant work ethic, worthy of the admiration and sympathy of northern middle-class America. The successes of all three men in making and saving money allied them to the entrepreneurial spirit of expansionist America in the 1830s and 1840s which struck De Tocqueville so forcefully. There was not a little of the self-made man in each of these blacks, and their narratives, especially those of Lane and Henson, made much of it by stressing their talents for invention and managerial skills, their shrewdness, their self-regulating habits, their responsibility and loyalty to family—and to their masters, up to a point. Like any self-respecting American, these men had dedicated themselves to rising above their low conditions, but they had tried to do so in a conventional, proper manner. Each had patiently worked to earn his freedom according to the laws of his society; each had seen the quid pro quo between slave and master exploited and nullified at the master's whim. Each rested his case for freedom not on abstract sociopolitical rights but on the inviolability of economic contract, the cornerstone on which nineteenth-century bourgeois society considered itself to be built. Each of these narrators demonstrated that, while still a slave, he had proved himself worthy of a freeman's role in a true society, that is, one based on the law of contractual obligation. The South, by implication, was not in a real sense a society at all but rather a kind of Hobbesian state of nature in which only power and self-preservation obtained.[27]

Grandy, Lane, and Henson were all highly sensitive to the class consciousness of the bourgeoisie, which they exploited to their own rhetorical advantage. Anecdotes and factual observations in their narratives seem quietly and indirectly intended to alienate the northern reader from his assumed kinship with the white southerner. At the same time, the black narrator is engaged in promoting himself ahead of the southerner into a consubstantial relationship with the fictive reader. Calling slaveholders "proprietors," Grandy's narrative generalizes about their prospects in the following disparaging way: "The proprietors, though they live in luxury, generally die in debt; their negroes are so hardly treated that no profit is made by their labor. Many of them are great gamblers. At the death of a proprietor, it commonly happens that his colored people are sold towards paying his debts. So it must and will be with the masters while slavery continues: when freedom is established, I believe they will begin to prosper greatly" (41). Henson helped to popularize the stereotype of the slaveholder as idlers, wastrels, and business incompetents: "My master's habits were such as were common enough among the dissipated planters of the neighborhood; and one of their frequent practices was to assemble on Saturday or Sunday, which were their holidays, and gamble, run horses, or fight game-cocks, discuss politics, and drink whiskey, and brandy and water, all day long." [28] It was logical that such a man would need his sober and industrious slave to oversee the daily management of the plantation. In the 1840s the southerner as bumpkin became one of the prime targets of the upwardly mobile fugitive's ridicule. As Lewis Clarke told it, "In Kentucky, if you should feed your horse only when you come to a schoolhouse, he would starve to death." [29]

Neither Grandy nor Lane was guilty of making the sort of sweeping denunciations of southerners that Peabody criticized in Douglass. Lane stressed that it was "the rabble" of Raleigh that persecuted him when he returned to buy his family. "The first men and the more wealthy were my friends: and they did everything in their power to protect me" (42). Grandy's narrative also mentions a handful of southerners who sympathized with the justice of his claim to freedom, including both "gentlemen" and an overseer "who was never known to speak in favor of a colored person." Having such persons speak in their favor in their narratives, embedded in the recitation of the facts of their lives, let Grandy and Lane integrate into their stories "objective" character endorsements from compelling sources. Integrated letters and comments from "the more wealthy" and thus respectable element in the South enhanced the character of the ex-slaves without the narrators' having to resort to more direct modes of self-promotion. In the quoted responses of "the first men" of the South, there is an implicit cue to the northern reader as to how he might measure his own response to an ex-slave trying to improve his lot in the white world. Surely this reader could be as supportive as the best people of a region dominated by the worst.

When Grandy first went to the North in 1832 at the age of forty-six, he recalled, segregation in churches, streetcars, and steamboats (where regardless of weather blacks were not allowed below decks) was widespread. Because "the abolitionists boldly stood up for us," however, much progress had been made on this front. Now "we begin to feel that we are really on the same footing as our fellow-citizens. They see we can and do conduct ourselves with propriety, and they are now admitting us, in many cases, to the same standing with themselves" (42). The key here is the emphasis on blacks' conducting themselves "with propriety" as the means of gaining admittance to white institutions. The idea of "proper" conduct, i.e., behavior in accordance with white middle-class mores, as the ticket to racial advancement was almost a cliché at this time among black leaders.[30] What is important to remember, however, is that in the 1840s slave narratives like Grandy's became one of the most visible demonstrations of the black man's ability to conduct himself "with propriety" in the North, despite his background in slavery. The conduct of his life in the South proved the allegiance of Grandy (or Lane or Henson) to middle-class values. Moreover, the conduct of their narratives, the manner in which they recited the facts and addressed their readers, was designed to qualify them as proper men fit for admission "to the same standing" with whites.

There is an implicit deference in Grandy's plain, assertive mode of speech action, in the absence of directives or expressives in his retelling of a story of great injustice, in his eschewal of irony, and in his optimistic "before-and-after" image of a progressive North purging itself of racial discrimination. In effect this mode of autobiography proposes its own literary contract of confidence between narrator and reader based on Grandy's ability to perform certain speech acts "with propriety," according to implied conventions that Grandy had learned through a lifetime spent in a racist society. Could he describe, for instance, the sale of his brother without risking the transaction of credit in credibility that he had undertaken with his white reader? Here is the account of the sale:

> I looked into the store, and saw my brother lying on his back on the floor, and Mr. Williams, who had bought him, driving staples over his wrists and ankles; an iron bar was afterwards put across his breast, which was also held down by staples. I asked what he had been doing, and was told that he had done nothing amiss, but that his master had failed, and he was sold towards paying the debts. He lay in that state all that night; next day he was taken to jail, and I never saw him again. This is the usual treatment under such circumstances. I had to go by mother's next morning, but I feared to tell her what had happened to my brother. I got a boy to go and tell her. She was blind and very old, and was living in a little hut, in the woods, after the usual

manner of old, worn-out slaves; she was unable to go to my brother before
he was taken away, and grieved after him greatly. (10)

If, as George Thompson claimed, he wrote this anecdote "as nearly as
possible in the language of Moses himself" without "a single reflection or
animadversion of my own" (iv), then these few sentences represent an
impressive act of concentration on the narrative business at hand. The
facts of the brother's fate lead Grandy to conclude simply that this was
"the usual treatment"; his mother's banishment was also "the usual" response to old age and infirmity in a slave. This business-as-usual approach
to inhumanity furnishes a rhetorically viable context in which to indict
slavery, to be sure. It does so, however, at the expense of an effort to indi-
vidualize the case, to rescue it from the routine, chattelizing discourse of
the slave system and restore it to the ex-slave so that he might declare its
human cost and consequences. The expected grief of the mother *is* duly
noted, but the impact of it all on Grandy, then and especially at the time
of recall, is omitted. Did Grandy silence himself in this respect because of
doubts about how much outrage, bitterness, or despair a man in his position could afford to acknowledge? Could black "tellability" and white
propriety coexist in a discursive situation such as the one that Grandy,
Lane, and Henson worked in?

The *Narrative of Lunsford Lane* comments cryptically on this problem
without trying to resolve it. In his preface Lane states that he will dwell
"as little as possible upon the dark side" of slavery, choosing "rather to
come short of giving the full picture" than to "overstate." The sentence
that follows offers up a "dark" innuendo from the narrator who has just
promised to keep to the "bright side" of his story: "And yet I would not
venture to say that this publication does not contain a single period
which might be twisted to convey an idea more than should be expressed." The convoluted, doubly negating structure of the sentence may
have been designed to lose the unwary reader. Only one who knows how
to twist the language will get at that supplemental meaning outside and
beyond what should be expressed in a discursive role such as Lane was
playing. Yet there is no clear indication of the way this twisting should be
done or what it should be applied to. All we know is that while Lane plays
the role of politic narrator who defers to his reader by never overstating
his case, he simultaneously invites—perhaps needs—another kind of
"misreader" (in Harold Bloom's sense) to reconstruct what he says to his
reader and recuperate it from the repression he admits to have engaged
in. In other words, Lane seems to address two kinds of readers: a fictive
reader representative of the class that he, Grandy, and Henson wished to
ingratiate on the bright side of his text, where one said what one meant,

and another kind of reader, an implied misreader created out of the oblique enlightenment that might come from twisting the darker side of a text into significance. To speak so openly of a dual audience was rare among slave narrators, but in Lane's experience duality, if not duplicity, had always been a basic condition of discourse anyway.

Lane's preface goes on to comment on the characterization of Benjamin Smith who, as the *Narrative* shows, treated his slaves (among them Lane's wife and children) with a niggardly meanness that contradicted his high reputation among white Methodists in Raleigh. Some of his conduct "will doubtless seem strange to the reader," Lane warned, but in that event "they should remember that men, like other things, have 'two sides,' and often a top and a bottom in addition." The generalization could be aptly applied to Lane as well. In the South Lane reveals himself to have been a Franklinesque role player whose success was due as much to his shrewd manipulation of appearances as to his industry, frugality, and perseverance. He elaborates his technique for his reader:

> Ever after I entertained the first idea of being free, I had endeavored so to conduct myself as not to become obnoxious to the white inhabitants, knowing as I did their power, and their hostility to the colored people. The two points necessary in such a case I had kept constantly in mind. First, I had made no display of the little property or money I possessed, but in every way I wore as much as possible the aspect of poverty. Second I had never appeared to be even so intelligent as I really was. This all colored people at the south, free and slaves, find it peculiarly necessary to their own comfort and safety to observe. (31)

This is the politic, pragmatic Lane, ever conscious of himself on stage, ever calculating his advantages behind a deceiving display. This, Lane assures his northern reader, was only the role he played in the South. Who, then, was the real Lunsford Lane, now liberated from the necessity of masking himself? The *Narrative*'s persona provides few clues. When he offers his reader a glimpse inside himself, the view is obscured by the misty sentiment and pious clichés that regularly invade the picture. How did it feel to become free? We are given the bright side: it was like passing from "spiritual death to life," like having one's sins forgiven, like being "in heaven" (17). And what of his prospects in the North as a freeman? Lane concludes his story with an expression of gratitude to "my kind friends in Massachusetts." Then this wish gushes forth: "To be rocked in their cradle of Liberty,—Oh, how unlike being stretched on the pillory of slavery! May that cradle rock forever; may many a poor care-worn child of sorrow, many a spirit-bruised (worse than lash-mangled) victim of oppression, there sweetly sleep to the lullaby of Freedom, sung by Massachusetts sons and daughters" (52).

Thus Lane infantilizes himself (and other ex-slaves in the North) in his parting impression for the northern reader. In the process he evokes an image of the Negro in vogue among romantic racialists of the time in the North as well as the South. He participates in the stereotype of blacks as childlike, sweet-tempered, docile, and in need of the protection of whites.[31] The metaphor of Lane as black "child of sorrow" safely deposited in the endlessly rocking cradle of white love and support in the North is so inconsistent with the previous image of him as wily adult in the South that several twists of the metaphor may be required to get at its purpose. Its purpose for the northern fictive reader seems to be this: Lane has been reborn in the North, restored to his family, and blessed by the nurture of maternal Massachusetts, which represents the ex-slave's extended family in freedom. This is reading the metaphor on "the bright side" as the comic climax to Lane's story. He has finally been integrated into a new home in the interracial family of man in the free state of Massachusetts. There is arguably some sort of wish fulfillment at work here, but for whose benefit— the narrator's or the northern fictive reader's?

Misreading the metaphor—considering not what it seems to signify but what it may be designed to conceal and defend against—will let us probe the "dark side" of this metaphor. Now we may consider the location of the metaphor in the text with respect to Lane's strategy of closure as well as climax. Coming on the last page of the narrative, the metaphor forecloses as well as encloses. It forecloses narrative pursuit of the practical question facing Lane at the end of his story—how will he provide for a ten-member family dependent on him in a strange land? Simultaneously, the metaphor encloses the reader as well as the text in a sentimental fantasy of lost children restored to their cradles, of outcasts returned home, of tranquil resolution to the problems of the freeman, soothed of his fear and care by "the lullaby of Freedom." Such sentimentality may help to lull the fictive reader to the "sweet sleep" of the romantic racialist oblivious to the complex problems attendant to the integration of ex-slaves into northern society. However, the clash between this sentimentality and Lane's earlier pragmatism may also jar more wary "misreaders" into remembering what he said at the beginning about the inherent duplicity of men. With this in mind one can see that the tactics of guile and gamesmanship that Lane learned in the South he did not repudiate or forget in the North. He just reapplied them to narrative art after considerable experience in the dramatic arts of his own social role-playing. Lane knew northern readers would enjoy watching a slave practice his masking craft on slaveholders and the white rabble of the South. But a freeman in the North who wanted to gain the confidence of whites would have to dissociate himself from that duplicitous conduct, leaving it in the past, in the South, in the other self that slavery had forced him to be.

Autobiography furnished the freeman a rare chance to acknowledge and even celebrate the artfulness of that other side of himself. As yet another kind of performance, however, slave narrative required him to distance himself from the arts of the other and declare himself a new man, a freeman, an American. As such, he received the opportunity extended to all American autobiographers—to reinvent himself as Benjamin Franklin, *pater familias*, had shown them how to do. For the slave narrator, this opportunity came as a peculiar obligation and responsibility, a qualification for acceptance into the white social unit. Lane responded to this form of contract in the way he had learned in slavery; he adopted the new mask that awaited him in the new world of the North. Thus he feigned the self-declarative act, or perhaps more accurately, he declared himself *through* the act of feigning as a man of masks, as a self-made (up) man in both a literary and a theatrical sense. This kind of covert self-declaration lies on the underside of Lane's invitation to his fictive reader to view what he had made of himself in primarily economic terms.

Grandy and Lane were both engaged in self-declarative autobiographical acts predicated on the silencing or sublimation of the other self from the slave past. Grandy has virtually nothing to say about himself that contradicts his cultivated self-image as *Homo economicus* and a man of propriety. The internal struggles that may have arisen from his aspirations to freedom are kept outside the narrative. This is the story of a steady individual against a shifty world. Slaveholders change as their whims and their perceptions of their own interest dictate; Grandy remains constant and single-focused. Lane admits that he was a two-sided man in slavery, but he maintains that only his exterior was subject to change, and that for purposes of socioeconomic necessity alone. Thus at the end of his story Lane seems to dismiss as simply role-playing anything in his past other than the image with which he wished to leave his reader. This image is that of the persevering freeman, in the South and North, who had always known his goal and had never swerved from it. The drama of his story, as is the case in Grandy's, too, stems from the conflict between this essentially self-possessed man and the exterior forces that buffet him as he seeks the vindication of his worth through freedom. The inner self, apparently fixed and unitary, seems untouched, inviolable, by this exterior turmoil.

Josiah Henson added a deeper level of dramatic conflict to his success story that helps at least partly to explain why his narrative of a self-made black man outsold Grandy's or Lane's. As part of a psychologizing trend in the slave narrative after 1845, Henson's *Life* emphasizes the internal as well as external struggles that faced a self-respecting black man of "pride and ambition" (8) caught in the yoke of slavery. Henson's external struggles were with conniving, deceitful masters, as Grandy's and Lane's had been. His Kentucky master had so often broken faith with him, rewarding his honesty and charity with lies and greed, that he eventually felt "absolved from all obligation . . . to pay him any more, or to continue in a position which exposed me to his machinations" (48). Yet the slaveholder's broken contracts and abrogated responsibilities were not Henson's primary justification for taking the radical step of stealing himself and his family away to Canada. His defense rests on the reconstruction of his life in slavery as a kind of morality play in which the best and worst sides of him were pitted against each other for control of his character and destiny. Henson's was an updated version of the trials-of-the-spirit autobiography, only now the purpose of the text was to show why escape from slavery, not the patient endurance of it, was a Christian's moral obligation.

The central characters in Henson's autobiography are two conflicting sides of himself, or, more particularly, the dual potential that lay within him, indeed, within everyone. This is the message that emerges from the first episode recounted in his *Life*. When he was three or four years old, he recalls that his father was whipped and mutilated after fighting with an overseer who had assaulted Henson's mother. "Furious at such treatment, my father became a different man, and was so morose, disobedient, and intractable" that his master had to sell him to Alabama. Before this the slave had been "a man of amiable temperament" and "considerable energy of character," but afterward he was "essentially changed" by the injustice done him. Slavery had subverted an "amiable" Negro workman into a menacing black rebel. About a year later, Henson's mother was sold away from him in a heart-rending scene. The trauma of the experience, "one of my earliest observations of men," gave rise to a "bitterness" in the boy "dark enough to overshadow the whole after-life with something blacker than a funeral pall" (4). Fortunately for young Josiah, however, he was restored to his mother soon thereafter. Had he not been, these outrages might have converted the parentless boy into the same kind of desperate, embittered, and intransigent fellow as his father had become.

Black people were subject to the same laws of human nature that many white Americans subscribed to, Henson implies throughout his story. In 1842 the educational reformer Horace Mann had proclaimed that "human nature occupies the vast intermediate space between the angels and the demon. It may ascend to the one; it may fall to the other."[32] Slavery,

Henson argues, precipitates this fall into "the other." Christianity and the hope of freedom (in that order) buoy the soul upward and inspire it to the improvement of its condition, something Henson stresses as his aim throughout his life. Whether in Kentucky or Canada, the slave leader had "labored to improve myself and those around me." He lived by the gospel of work before he preached the gospel of Jesus. After conversion, he dedicated himself to both, so that by "strenuous and persevering efforts" he could attain, in spite of his enslavement, moral distinction—"the perception of my own strength of character, the feeling of integrity, the sentiment of high honor" (25).

"Strenuous and persevering efforts" were required to resist the demoralizing counterforce that slavery persistently applied to the aspiring self. The accumulated outrages of life in bondage could break a man, in the sense that Henson's father had been broken. What slavery broke in his father was the improving spirit in man as expressed through the willingness to work, the acceptance of authority, and a hopeful view of the future. Henson's father's lapse from this standard made him an other, a threat to harmony and progress as both a northern and a southern reader might think of them. This man's downfall, however, was not a special case. Within even as exemplary a Christian as Henson himself, there lay a "shadow" (as Jungians might term it), or a "wild man" (as conceived more generally in Western thought), which incorporated some of the most destructive impulses of the self and which had to be controlled lest it plunge the self into utter accursedness.

For centuries in the West, the figure of the wild man represented humankind in its most desolate state, "released from social control," regressive to the point of amoral animality, motivated by gross desires and violent passions. Perhaps the Reverend Henson knew when he evoked this image of the quintessential terrible other that throughout the Judeo-Christian heritage, the wild man had been marked by blackness since his procreation by Ham, Noah's cursed son.[33] At any rate, Henson seems to have deliberately and dramatically elaborated this supposed black wildness within himself as a way of endowing his life story with a melodramatic power guaranteed to galvanize his white readership.

The morality play of Henson's life in slavery climaxes in a decisive struggle between the Christian conscience and the wild man within. In the spring of 1830, Henson was sent with his master's son, Amos Riley, to New Orleans, ostensibly as the youth's attendant, but in reality to be sold in the city's great slave market. Reflecting on all his service to the Riley brothers and "their utter inattention to my claims upon them . . . turned my blood to gall and wormwood, and changed me from a lively, and I will say, a pleasant-tempered fellow, into a savage, morose, dangerous slave"

(40–41). "Blinded by passion," agitated with an almost uncontrollable fury, and "stung to madness," Henson seizes an ax one dark, rainy night within a few days of New Orleans, and, in a scene reminiscent of Pomp's murder of Furbush in 1795, prepares for his revenge. At the moment of delivering the blow to the sleeping Amos, however, Henson hears another sort of whisper from that which Pomp claimed to have prompted him. It is the voice of conscience: "'What! commit *murder*! and you a Christian?'" "I was about to lose the fruit of all my efforts at self-improvement, the character I had acquired, and the peace of mind which had never deserted me." Freedom at such a moral cost must be a bad bargain, Henson decides. He chooses instead "my self-control and serenity" and resigns himself to the will of God. Providence delivers him when Amos contracts malaria and becomes dependent on Henson for his life and safe return to Kentucky. Only after he sees that the Rileys have no intention of changing their plans for his ultimate sale does Henson feel justified in taking flight to Canada with his family.

Henson's *Life* testifies in an effectively melodramatic way to one black man's victory over the wildness within, the shadowy "dark side," the savage and passionate impulses, whose restraint, defenders of slavery had attested, was a major justification for the peculiar institution. Henson grants his reader the belief in the potential beast within the black man and then shows how slavery engenders it and exacerbates the problem of its control. It was slavery that transformed Henson the "pleasant-tempered fellow" into the would-be murderer. A black man free to pursue his "efforts at self-improvement" would not be tempted to such regression. Overcoming the wild man within while still in slavery doubly qualified Henson for his white audience's approval. He exemplifies a kind of heroism that they would find especially comforting in a Negro of admitted "pride and ambition." He first triumphs over himself—that is, over all the perturbing connotations of black selfhood, such as aggression, passion, and bitterness and vengefulness when wronged. *Then* he extricates himself, nonviolently, from slavery. A Negro who could emerge from all of this with his "self-control and serenity" intact, as the *Life* confidently stated, further underlined his trustworthiness by dedicating himself to "the rescue and elevation of those who were suffering the same evils I had endured" (66). By noting how he was engaged in promoting this elevation of other fugitives—"It was precisely the Yankee spirit which I wished to instil [*sic*] into my fellow-slaves"—Henson cemented a bond of consubstantiality between himself and his middle-class reader.

Ephraim Peabody thought the importance of Henson's *Life* lay not so much in its portrayal of slavery as in its Franklinesque portrait of the leader of the Dawn community. Peabody recommended Henson as a man who "possesses the wisdom to conceive, and the practical talent and energy to carry out, large and far-reaching schemes for the improvement of his brethren." Four years later, when Harriet Beecher Stowe sought documentation with which to answer skeptical critics of *Uncle Tom's Cabin*, she cited Henson's "invulnerable Christian principle" as a real-life parallel to Uncle Tom's unshakeable righteousness.[34] No other slave narrator before Booker T. Washington would prove so adept at conflating Yankee pragmatism and Christian piety in the myth of his life and in his persona. Both Henson and Washington were masters of self-promotion via autobiographies that seemed to celebrate just the opposite in both men. Peabody read Henson as the personification of benevolence and altruism whose schemes were all devoted to the improvement of his fellow blacks. Stowe was enthralled by the episode in the *Life* in which young Henson delivered the slaves in his charge to his Kentucky master rather than break his word and skulk off to freedom. This decision, which even Henson admitted had caused him "painful doubts" ever since, was nothing less than a "most sublime act of self-renunciation" to Stowe. Modestly, Henson would only say that his "consoling reflection" had been "that I acted as I thought at the time was best" (25). Nonetheless, this remark seizes the maximum rhetorical advantage that could be gained from retelling the episode. Conservative readers could admire Henson the slave for having kept his promise to authority despite the blandishments of self-interest, while liberals could be assured from Henson the freemen that he would no longer be bound by any such compact with slavery.

Thus it is not surprising that Stowe should have made a special point of this episode when she inadvertently launched Henson to fame through her praise in *The Key to Uncle Tom's Cabin*.[35] Stowe had found in Henson's "act of self-renunciation" first, the proof of her romantic idealizations of the African character,[36] and, second, a demonstration of Henson's qualifications as a truth-teller, a completely reliable slave narrator. Henson's faithfulness to his promise to his master proved in a singular way that this ex-slave's word was his bond. He had placed a verbal contract with a slaveowner above the claims of self. As a narrator he could be relied upon not to play false to his contract with his reader, either. Having established himself, therefore, as mindful only of principle, not of self, nothing stood between Henson and the accrual to himself of all the benefits of self-abnegating benevolence, all the advantages of a man who espoused only the advancement of others. Picturing himself bound to his word even in slavery helped keep people like Peabody and Stowe from asking whether a man of admitted "pride and ambition" might later make free with his words, especially if his pact with his white reader seemed yet another enslaving verbal contract.

We cannot know how much of Henson's narrative was liberated from the less self-serving facts of his life when he dictated it to Samuel Eliot in 1849. Nineteen years had passed since he had made his escape from Kentucky, ample time for a man's recall of events and the image of himself to sift, settle, and harden into a personal myth. Moreover, his years of fundraising for Dawn in Canada, England, and America probably heightened his "other-perception," his sense of how whites saw him and, more importantly, how they wanted to see him in order to invest belief and money in that which he represented.[37] Perhaps, however, slavery itself trained Henson first and most crucially for his success in the craft of black autobiography. He had grown up, he claimed, with the consuming desire to "surpass" his black peers in any activity that might "obtain, if possible, the favorable regard of the petty despot who ruled over us." "I was guided in it more by what I supposed would be effectual, than by a nice judgment of the propriety of the means I used" (8). Did the same strategy apply in securing the favor of the white reader, the petty despot who ruled over the slave narrative? When we consider how effectually Henson manipulated the proprieties of his contract with that reader, first exploiting his racist phobias about black wildness and then pandering to his romantic fantasies about black self-denial, we have as much of the answer as we are likely to extract from this consummately artful autobiographical performance.

When he wrote his *Narrative* in 1845, Frederick Douglass was not indifferent to the ideological consensus that the narratives of black "men of propriety" like Grandy, Lane, and Henson tried to establish with the white middle-class reader of the North. In his own unprecedented way, Douglass participated in and appealed to this consensus by fashioning his autobiography into a kind of American jeremiad. This genre differs from that which Wilson J. Moses has labeled the black jeremiad in one crucial sense: while the latter was preoccupied with America's impending doom because of its racial injustices, the American jeremiad foretold America's future hopefully, sustained by the conviction of the nation's divinely appointed mission. The practitioners of both literary traditions tended to see themselves as outcasts, prophets crying in the wilderness of their own alienation from prevailing error and perversity. While the white Jeremiahs decry America's deviation from its original sacred mission in the New World, they usually celebrate the national dream in the process of lamenting its decline. The American jeremiad affirms and sustains a middle-class consensus about America by both excoriating lapses from it and rhetorically coopting potential challenges (such as those offered by Frederick Douglass) to it.[38]

With Herman Melville and Henry David Thoreau, contemporary Jeremiahs who also addressed the national sin of slavery, Douglass confronted America with profoundly polarized emotions that produced in him a classic case of Du Boisian double consciousness. As a fugitive slave orator in the early 1840s, he denounced the institutionalized racism that pervaded America and perverted its much-heralded blend of liberty, democracy, and Christianity. Following the Garrisonian line, his speeches poured contempt on the Constitution of the United States as a compact with slavery and condemned northern as well as southern Christians for being the slave's tyrants, "our enslavers." [39] The *Narrative*, however, goes to no such political or religious extremes. In that book, Douglass deploys the rhetoric of the jeremiad to distinguish between true and false Americanism and Christianity. He celebrates the national dream by concluding his story with a contrast between the thriving seacoast town of New Bedford, Massachusetts—where he was "surrounded with the strongest proofs of wealth" (148)—and the run-down Eastern Shore of Maryland, where "dilapidated houses, with poverty-stricken inmates," "half-naked children," and "barefooted women" testified to an unprogressive polity. Appended to Douglass's story is an apparent apology for his narrative's "tone and manner, respecting religion," but this quickly gives way to a final jeremiad against the pharisaical "hypocrites" of "the *slaveholding religion* of this land" (153). "I love the pure, peaceable, and impartial Christianity of Christ," Douglass proclaimed. All the more reason, therefore, for him to appropriate the language of Jeremiah 6:29 for his ultimate warning to corrupters of the faith: " 'Shall I not visit for these things? saith the Lord. Shall not my soul be avenged on such a nation as this?' " (157). The *Narrative* builds a convincing case for Douglass's literary calling and his ultimate self-appointment as America's black Jeremiah.

Douglass's account of his rise from slavery to freedom fulfills certain features of the jeremiad's cultural myth of America. The *Narrative* dramatizes a "ritual of socialization" that Sacvan Bercovitch finds often in late eighteenth- and early nineteenth-century jeremiads: the rebellion of a fractious individual against instituted authority is translated into a heroic act of self-reliance, a reenactment of the national myth of regeneration and progress through revolution. The great rhetorical task of the jeremiad is to divest self-determinative individualism of its threatening associations with anarchy and antinomianism, the excesses of the unbridled self. In America the jeremiad made much of the distinction between rebellion and revolution. The rebel disobeys out of self-interest and defiance of the good of the community and the laws of Providence. His act parallels Lucifer's primal act of disobedience, which produced only discord and a (temporary) thwarting of the divine plan. The revolutionary, on the other

124

hand, promotes in the secular sphere the same sort of upward spiral toward perfection that God demanded of each individual soul in its private progress toward redemption. The American jeremiad obviated the distinction betweeen secular and sacred revolution in order to endow the former with the sanction of the latter, the better to authorize the national myth of the American Revolution. America was a truly revolutionary society in the sense and to the extent that its people—that is to say, those who had been accorded the status of personhood in the Constitution—remained faithful to God's plan for the progressive conversion of their land into a new order. Americans were therefore called to be revolutionaries, but revolutionaries in the service of an evolving divine order within which Americans could achieve corporate self-realization as God's chosen people.

As several critics have noted, Douglass's *Narrative* seems to have been consciously drawn up along structural and metaphorical lines familiar to readers of spiritual autobiographies.[46] The young Frederick is initiated into a knowledge of the depravity of man when he witnesses the hideous flogging of his aunt Hester. "It was the blood-stained gate, the entrance to the hell of slavery, through which I was about to pass" (51). Though seemingly damned to this southern hell, the eight-year-old boy is delivered by "a special interposition of divine Providence in my favor" from the plantation of Edward Lloyd in Talbot County to the Baltimore home of Hugh Auld. From that time forward, the boy is convinced that freedom—"this living word of faith and spirit of hope" (75)—would be his someday. The thought "remained like ministering angels to cheer me through the gloom." Douglass's faith in this intuitively felt heavenly promise of liberation undergoes a series of trials in his boyhood and early teens, when he is first led out of his "mental darkness" by Sophia Auld, who teaches him his letters, and then is thrust back into "the horrible pit" of enforced ignorance by her husband, who fears a mentally enlightened slave.

The middle chapters of the *Narrative* recount the slave youth's growing temptations to despair of deliverance from bondage. Returned to the rural region where he was born, Douglass discovers the hypocrisy of Christian slaveholders whose pretentions to piety mask their cruelty and licentiousness. He reaches a dark night of the soul in 1833, when the harsh regime of Edward Covey, "the snake," breaks him "in body, soul, and spirit." And yet, he undergoes "a glorious resurrection, from the tomb of slavery, to the heaven of freedom" (113) by violently resisting Covey's attempt to apprehend him, one August morning, for another infraction of the rules. Thus, "resurrected," the sixteen-year-old youth, "a slave in form" but no longer "a slave in fact," begins to put his revived faith in freedom and his "self-confidence" into practice. Hired out in 1834 to William Freeland, he starts a "Sabbath school" in which to teach slaves how to read the Bible and "to imbue their minds with thoughts of freedom" (122). "My tendency was upward," states Douglass, firmly committed to following the road to freedom analogized in the *Narrative* in imagery reminiscent of *Pilgrim's Progress.* The first escape attempt, appropriately timed for Easter, is foiled, but his second, in September 1838, succeeds.

The last pages of the *Narrative* describe the new freeman's call to witness for the gospel of freedom that had preserved, regenerated, and pointed him northward. A subscription to the *Liberator* sets his "soul" on fire for "the cause" of abolitionism. At an antislavery meeting in Nantucket in August 1841, "I felt strongly moved to speak," but Douglass is restrained by a sense of unworthiness before white people. Still the promptings of the spirit cannot be resisted, even though it is "a severe cross" for the new convert to take up. "I spoke but a few moments, when I felt a degree of freedom, and said what I desired with considerable ease." This liberation of the tongues climaxes the life-long quest of Frederick Douglass toward his divinely appointed destiny in the antislavery ministry. The special plan of Providence is now fully revealed at the end of the *Narrative.* Frederick Douglass is a chosen man as well as a freeman. His trials of the spirit have been a test and a preparation for his ultimate mission as a black Jeremiah to a corrupt white Israel. This autobiography, as Robert G. O'Meally has emphasized, is a text meant to be preached.[41]

Like all American jeremiads, the *Narrative* is a political sermon. Douglass's self-realization as a freeman and a chosen man takes place via a process of outward and sometimes violent revolution as well as inner evolution of consciousness. The strategy of Douglass's jeremiad is to depict this revolution as a "process of Americanization," to use once again a key phrase in Bercovitch's analysis of the genre. As Bercovitch notes, the jeremiad was responsible for rationalizing and channeling the revolutionary individualistic impulse in America so as to reconcile it with the myth of America's corporate destiny as a chosen people. This meant distinguishing firmly between the truly American revolutionary individualism and the rebellious, un-American individualism of the alien and seditious Indian, Negro, or feminist. Those marked by racial heritage as other had to *prove* that they were of "the people," the American chosen, by demonstrating in their own lives the rituals of Americanization that had converted them from non-persons, as it were, into members of the middle-class majority. "Blacks and Indians . . . could learn to be True Americans, when in the fullness of time they would adopt the tenets of black and red capitalism."[42] Along with Lane and Henson, Douglass pledges allegiance to the economic tenets of the republic in his autobiography, entitled, appropriately enough, the narrative of "*An American Slave*." Douglass goes beyond either Lane or Henson, however, in using this orthodoxy to justify his revolution against slavery and its perverse, un-American profit motive.

John Seelye has pointed out some of the affinities between Douglass's *Narrative* and the cultural myth of America as dramatized in Franklin's memoir. Douglass is "Ben Franklin's specific shade," argues Seelye, though the ex-slave's story is "not a record of essays to do good but attempts to be bad, Douglass like Milton's Satan inventing virtue from an evil necessity."[43] It is no small part of Douglass's rhetorical art, however, to translate his badness into revolutionary necessity of a kind his white reader could identify with. Douglass's life, like Franklin's, describes a rising arc from country to city; then it follows a downward curve of expectations when the town slave is returned to the plantation; but it revolves upward once more, after the fight with Covey, carrying the black youth from Talbot County to Baltimore and finally to New York and New Bedford. When given the opportunity for self-improvement in the city, young Fred is every bit as enterprising as Father Ben. As a boy he overcomes adversity to learn reading and writing on his own. Discovery of an eloquence handbook entitled *The Columbian Orator* foreshadows the day when he will become one. But first he must become a man. The battle with Covey halts his regression into the slave's "beast-like stupor" and "revived within me a sense of my own manhood." "Bold defiance" replaces "cowardice"; significantly, the spheres of this defiance are intellectual and economic. As a Sabbath school teacher at Freeland's, Douglass uses as his text the Bible, and his aim is consistent with America's middle-class civil religion. He encourages his slave pupils to behave "like intellectual, moral, and accountable beings" rather than "spending the Sabbath in wrestling, boxing, and drinking whisky" (120). Douglass domesticates a greater gesture of defiance, his first escape attempt, by analogizing it to the hallowed decision of Patrick Henry (ironically, a slaveholder) for liberty or death. "We did more than Patrick Henry," the fugitive advances of himself and his fellow runaways, because their liberty was more dubious and their deaths more certain if they failed. By implication, then, these dauntless blacks were more heroically American in their struggle for independence than was one of the most prominent delegates of the convention of 1776.

After Douglass's return to Baltimore in the spring of 1835 to be hired out in various employments, the *Narrative* concentrates increasingly on the economic humiliations of an upwardly aspiring "slave in form but not in fact." While apprenticed as a ship's carpenter, the slave is attacked and beaten by four white workers who felt it "degrading to them to work with me." Manfully, Douglass returns the blows in kind despite the adverse odds. Taught the calking trade, he "was able to command the highest wages given to the most experienced calkers," $1.50 a day. The money "was rightfully my own," Douglass argues. "I contracted for it; I earned it; it was paid to me." Yet every week Hugh Auld took it. "And why? Not because he earned it,—not because he had any hand in earning it,—not because I owed it to him,—nor because he possessed the slightest shadow of a right to it; but solely because he had the power to compel me to give it up" (135). With Grandy, Lane, and Henson, Douglass appeals to his reader's respect for contract and resentment of arbitrary power as a way of preparing his case for the final break with slavery. The right at issue here is pragmatic and economic, not abstract or romantic. Douglass analogizes Auld to a "grim-visaged pirate" and a "robber"— an outlaw, in other words—to banish him from a consubstantial relationship with the northern reader. Meanwhile, Douglass qualifies himself for acceptance as an economic revolutionary in the best American tradition. He works his way up the economic ladder in the South from country slave to city apprentice to the quasi-free status of one who "hired his time" (the situation of Grandy, Lane, and Henson before they extricated themselves from slavery).

Hiring his time required Douglass to meet all his living expenses out of the income that he could make for himself, while still paying his master a fixed return of $3 per week. This was "a hard bargain," but still "a step toward freedom to be allowed to bear the responsibilities of a freeman" (140). Here again, Douglass stresses how he qualified himself, step by step, for freedom and its "responsibilities" as well as its "rights." "I bent myself to the work of making money," adds Douglass, by way of proving his dedication to the quintessential responsibilities of an American free man. "I was ready to work at night as well as day, and by the most untiring perseverance and industry, I made enough to meet my expenses, and lay up a little money every week" (140). The savings were used, presumably, to help Douglass in his flight to freedom, for less than a month after Auld halted the slave's hiring out (fearing that too much freedom would go to the black man's head), Douglass retaliated by taking the ultimate "step toward freedom."

One of the most unconventional features of the *Narrative* was Douglass's refusal to end his story with the stock-in-trade climax of the slave narrative. Watching the panting fugitive seize his freedom just ahead of snapping bloodhounds and clutching slavecatchers left white readers with a vicarious sense of the thrill of the chase as well as the relief of the successful escape. In the slave narrative a generation of readers found a factual parallel to the capture-flight-and-pursuit plots of their favorite romances by James Fenimore Cooper, William Gilmore Simms, and Robert Montgomery Bird. Yet Douglass left only a hiatus in his story where the customary climax should have been, insisting, quite plausibly, that to recount his mode of escape would alert slaveholders to it and thus close it to others. The conclusion he chose for his *Narrative* indicates that in his mind the high point of a fugitive slave's career was not his arrival in the free states but his assumption of a new identity as a free man and his integration into the American mainstream.

Douglass notes graphically the initial terrors of the isolated fugitive in a strange and often hostile land, but his emphasis is on how quickly and happily he assimilated. He marries within two weeks of his arrival in New York. He and his wife Anna move immediately to New Bedford, where the morning after his arrival he receives from his Negro host a new name to denote his new identity in freedom. Two days later, he takes his first job stowing a sloop with a load of oil. "It was the first work, the reward of which was to be entirely my own." "It was to me the starting-point of a new existence" (150). Everything falls into place for Douglass in New Bedford, where the American dream of "a new existence" is always possible for every man, black or white. New Bedford fulfills the ex-slave's socioeconomic quest; here every man pursues his work "with a sober, yet cheerful earnestness, which betokened the deep interest which he felt in what he was doing, as well as a sense of his own dignity as a man." Most marvelous of all, the black population of this paragon of industrial capitalism lives in "finer houses" and enjoys "more of the comforts of life, than the average of slaveholders in Maryland." True, Douglass admits, "prejudice against color" along the docks of New Bedford kept him from resuming his former trade as a calker. But a note to the text removes even this blemish from the image of the town as the epitome of progress and justice: "I am told that colored persons can now get employment at calking in New Bedford—a result of anti-slavery effort." Perhaps this is the reason for the mild manner and the absence of irony or bitterness with which Douglass brings up this lone instance of racism in the North. The refusal of New Bedford's calkers to work with him moves the narrator to none of the moral outrage that accompanies his recall of the same kind of treatment that he received from Baltimore's calkers. Now Douglass is more thick-skinned and matter-of-fact; his narrative business is not to complain about the barriers to his progress but to show how he, like his adopted city, overcame them. Now is the time for understatement: "Finding my trade of no immediate benefit, I threw off my calking habiliments, and prepared myself to do any kind of work I could get to do" (150).

For the next three years, Douglass had to support his family via whatever manual labor jobs he could find, including sawing wood, shoveling coal, sweeping chimneys, and rolling casks in an oil refinery. Yet the *Narrative* stresses only the bright side of this experience—Douglass's American ingenuity and industry—not the ugly side—New Bedford's economic repression of a trained black tradesman. Only in 1881, in his *Life and Times*, when Douglass no longer had the same rhetorical stake in a dramatic contrast between North and South, would he call the whole humiliating episode "the test of the real civilization of the community" of New Bedford, which the town plainly failed.[44] In 1845 New Bedford had to serve as Douglass's standard of "real civilization," of true Americanism, so that he as a jeremiad writer could have something by which to measure the South's fall from national grace.

Like earlier popular literary genres from which Afro-American autobiography sought authentication and other rhetorical advantages, the American jeremiad provided a structure for Douglass's vision of America that was both empowering and limiting at the same time. The jeremiad gave the ex-slave literary license to excoriate the South pretty much as he pleased so long as the ideals and values by which he judged that region's transgressions remained American. Thus while bitterly evoking the nightmare of slavery, Douglass's example invoked just as reverently the dream of America as a land of freedom and opportunity. In a letter to Douglass several weeks before the *Narrative* was published, Wendell Phillips, one of the most forthright abolitionist critics of racism in the North as well as slavery in the South, urged the autobiographer to include a comparison of the status of blacks in both sections of the country. "Tell us whether, after all, the half-free colored man of Massachusetts is worse off than the pampered slave of the rice swamps!" (45), Phillips requested, with his usual penchant for irony. In Douglass's jeremiad, however, such a topic was not tellable. In the spiritual autobiography and the success story, of which Douglass's *Narrative* is an amalgam, doubts about the achievement or significance of salvation and success are clear evidence that they have not been attained. Douglass's story, by contrast, is determined to declare New Bedford as more than one slave's attainable secular salvation in America. Such a declarative act brought into being New Bedford as Douglass needed it to be—a symbol of his belief in America as a free, prosperous, and progressive social order that thrived without caste distinctions or the exploitation of labor. For the sake of this symbol in his vision of America, Douglass could make his own exploitation in the New Bedford labor market seem like a useful lesson in the school of hard knocks, the sort of adversity that self-made men generally glory in. For the symbol's sake, Douglass would censor himself and say nothing of more humiliating Jim Crow experiences that he had been subjected to in the North, although he had been recounting such incidents from the abolitionist platform for the past three years.[45]

The American jeremiad structured Douglass into a fixed bipolar set of alternatives with which to define the experience and aspirations of "an American slave." As a revealed truth represented symbolically, America in the jeremiad could be understood only in terms of "alternatives generated by the symbol itself." That which was not American was conceived of as an absence, un-Americanism, false Americanism. America was constantly being analyzed and measured against its opposite, which was only the negative function of the interpretive possibilities of the symbol.[46] To get outside this self-enclosed heuristic dualism, one had to liberate oneself from the symbol of America as a self-valorizing plenitude and from the binary oppositions that maintained the symbol within a field of meanings of its own making. Henry Louis Gates, Jr., has argued convincingly that in the first chapter of the *Narrative*, the binary oppositions that inform and enforce the culture of the slavocracy are "mediated" by the narrator so as to "reverse the relations of the opposition" and reveal that "the oppositions, all along, were only arbitrary, not fixed."[47] For instance, as both the son and slave of his father-master, the mulatto Douglass deconstructs the fundamental opposition between white people and black animals on which much of the rationale for slavery was based. That separation between white and black cannot hold because it is culturally, not naturally, determined. By the time we finish the last chapter of the *Narrative*, however, it becomes evident that Douglass is not bent on the same kind of critique of the binary oppositions that govern and validate the symbol of America. The *Narrative* turns, structurally and thematically, on such dualities as southern slavery versus northern freedom, "slaveholding religion" versus "Christianity proper," Baltimore versus New Bedford, compulsion versus contract, stagnation versus progress, deprivation versus wealth, violence versus order, community versus caste system. And very little mediation takes place between these fixed, shall we say "black-and-white," antitheses.[48] Indeed, Douglass suggests that the gap between these poles of true and false Americanism is growing wider, as New Bedford's progress against racial discrimination seems to testify.

Thus as an American jeremiad, Douglass's *Narrative* deconstructs binary oppositions that uphold slavery in the South while reconstructing the pattern of his life around other sets of oppositions whose support of the myth of America he might as readily have questioned, too. In 1845, however, Douglass was still exploring the heuristic and rhetorical possibilities of binary oppositions as a means of establishing his own identity relative to America, South and North. It is through his own experiments with rhetoric that we see Douglass's particular brand of "opposing self" at work. As a jeremiadic autobiographer, he has more than his own story to tell. He must preach in such a way as to discredit the false oppositions and hierarchies of value that have arisen as a consequence of slavery's perversions of the true oppositions between good and evil, the natural and the unnatural. This is the major reason for Douglass's self-conscious introduction of traditional tropes of rhetoric into the slave narrative.

Douglass followed the figural convention of earlier tropological black autobiographers when he appropriated from Christian theology the metaphors of spiritual *revolutio* that let him convert his violent resistance to Covey into a "glorious resurrection, from the tomb of slavery." But analogical argument could not help the ex-slave expose the stark inconsistencies between southern practice and the American promise or the inversions of nature and value that slavery forced. Hence his regular use of paradox, hyperbole, chiasmus, and other varieties of antithetical clausal constructions.[49] Captain Thomas Auld "was a slaveholder without the ability to hold slaves" (97). Slaves "sing the most pathetic sentiment in the most rapturous tone, and the most rapturous sentiment in the most pathetic tone" (57). The overseer Austin Gore "dealt sparingly with his words, and bountifully with his whip" (66). Once "the fatal poison of irresponsible power" was put in Sophia Auld's hands, "that cheerful eye, under the influence of slavery, soon became red with rage; that voice, made all of sweet accord, changed to one of harsh and horrid discord; and that angelic face gave place to that of a demon" (77–78). Covey was such a harsh taskmaster that "the longest days were too short for him, and the shortest nights too long for him" (105).

Had Douglass confined himself to these tropes for the reinforcement of his criticism of an inverted and perverted culture, he might not have troubled a man like Ephraim Peabody very much. But Douglass's tropological action is much more diverse and includes theatrical and other "playful" effects that are only loosely bound to the service of fact and theme. Repetition is Douglass's favorite rhetorical technique for experimentation. In the first chapter he uses it within a structure of antitheses to impress upon his reader the immitigable, metronomic rhythm of a whipping.

> I have often been awakened at the dawn of day by the most heart-rending shrieks of an own aunt of mine, whom he [Captain Anthony, young Fred's first master] used to tie up to a joist, and whip upon her naked back till she was literally covered with blood. No words, no tears, no prayers, from his gory victim, seemed to move his iron heart from its bloody purpose. The louder she screamed, the harder he whipped; and where the blood ran fast-

est, there he whipped longest. He would whip her to make her scream, and whip her to make her hush; and not until overcome by fatigue, would he cease to swing the blood-clotted cowskin. (51)

Here Douglass repeatedly "whips" his reader with a word in order to induce in that reader a response to a literary figure that will be in some slight sense analogous to his aunt's experience of being beaten. This is rhetoric used for a traditional purpose in the slave narrative: to put the reader in the place of someone with whom he or she ought to sympathize. Whipping is a fact of slavery of which the white reader must have empathic as well as objective knowledge.

Consider, by contrast, Douglass's later repetitious use of the same word in characterizing the Reverend Rigby Hopkins of Talbot County.

> Mr. Hopkins could always find some excuse for whipping a slave. It would astonish one, unaccustomed to a slaveholding life, to see with what wonderful ease a slaveholder can find things, of which to make occasion to whip a slave. A mere look, word, or motion,—a mistake, accident, or want of power, —are all matters for which a slave may be whipped at any time. Does a slave look satisfied? It is said, he has the devil in him, and it must be whipped out. Does he speak loudly when spoken to by his master? Then he is getting high-minded, and should be taken down a button-hole lower. Does he forget to pull off his hat at the approach of a white person? Then he is wanting in reverence, and should be whipped for it. Does he ever venture to vindicate his conduct, when censured for it? Then he is guilty of impudence,—one of the greatest crimes of which a slave can be guilty. Does he ever venture to suggest a different mode of doing things from that pointed out by his master? He is indeed presumptuous, and getting above himself; and nothing less than a flogging will do for him. Does he, while ploughing, break a plough,— or, while hoeing, break a hoe? It is owing to his carelessness, and for it a slave must always be whipped. (118–19)

In this passage Douglass harps on the word "whip" in order to sting Hopkins and his ilk with their own cruel consistency. The narrator's mockery depends on several levels of repetition: linguistic, syntactic (the "Does he . . .? Then he . . . ." construction), and thematic (everything the slave does supposedly signifies the same thing and must receive the same response). Douglass's genius lies in the stage management of these effects so that they will do their maximum moral damage to the slaveholders while accruing literary benefits to the slave narrator as satirist.

Douglass begins with a come-on, the promise of something "astonishing," and then states his sweeping thesis—that virtually anything the slave does can be used as an excuse for a beating. Instead of listing the possible occasions for the whip in a plain and factual manner, however, Douglass sets up a dramatic structure in which he impersonates both

133

sides of an imaginary dialogue, or question-and-answer session. As questioner Douglass plays the role of an objective observer of phenomena who inquires innocently about their meaning, somewhat as the curious white reader of the North might do. As respondent Douglass, now the southern white authority for the northern innocent, answers in such a repetitive and compulsive way that his explanatory authority is swept away by his reductive cant. Douglass surveys the vernacular and official modes of explaining slave behavior,[50] from "he has the devil in him" to "he is indeed presumptuous," but the more inflated the terms become, the more the pretense of it all is exposed by its automatic translation into the same gross and brutal consequence, the whipping. The outcome of the satire is reductio ad absurdum. The slaveholder's reductive reading of his slave is ironically reversed to reduce *him* to the level of a comic grotesque.

In both the Anthony and the Hopkins passages, Douglass takes a "brute fact" (linguistically and morally) like the whipping of slaves and experiments with rhetorical contexts in which to turn that fact to his own expressive account. Simple assertions about the method, incidence, or justifications of whipping are insufficent to this slave narrator's purposes. Nor is he satisfied to couch the fact of whipping in a standard expressive speech act that will convey his own psychological response in the hope of prompting his reader to similar feelings. Instead, Douglass makes a crucial decision: to present the fact of whipping to the reader in two deliberately stylized, plainly rhetorical, recognizably artificial contexts. There is nothing masked about this presentation. On the contrary, Douglass's choice of repetition as his chief rhetorical effect in both passages leaves his mark unmistakably on the text in bold strokes that constitute his stylistic signature.

In passages like these, Douglass calls attention to himself as an unabashed artificer, a maker of forms and effects that recontextualize brute facts according to requirements of self. The freeman requires the freedom to demonstrate the potency of his own inventiveness and the sheer potentiality of language itself for rhetorical manipulation. As Douglass develops his style, he gains literary mastery over the brute facts of the slave past. As he deliberately exhibits that style, he repossesses autobiography as a self-expressive, not simply a fact-assertive, act. This does not mean of course that the style of autobiography provides the key to Douglass's essential self. What is expressed through the style of the Anthony and Hopkins passages is Douglass's performing self, plainly and exuberantly engaged in performing rhetorical operations on brute facts and consciously aware of itself in the process as a player of roles, a maker of effects, and a manipulator of readers.

William Lloyd Garrison's preface to the *Narrative* promises its reader that Douglass had been "essentially true in all [his] statements; that nothing has been set down in malice, nothing exaggerated, nothing drawn from the imagination" (38). In Garrison's sense of the word, the imagination was the wellspring of fabrications and exaggerations, and hence not to be acknowledged as part of a slave narrator's intellectual resources. Today, questions about whether Douglass imagined or exaggerated matters in the *Narrative* continue to be researched by historians.[51] What is more to our purpose is Douglass's employment of his imagination, his ability to portray images in language and thereby evoke sensations in his reader, as a means of influencing his reader's perceptions of and response to him and his world. The Anthony passage exemplifies in the *Narrative* what Philip Wheelwright has termed the "confrontive imagination." The aim of Douglass's style in that instance is to confront the reader with particular details of a specific whipping, not the general idea of whipping. Through an imaginative use of rhetoric, Douglass attempts "to intensify the immediate experience itself," to bring it home to the reader, as it were. By contrast, in the Hopkins quotation, Douglass is engaged in the "imaginative distancing" of his reader from the subject at hand. Douglass's style is disassociative in that his humor reduces and removes Hopkins from the normal relationship of respect that he would have with the white reader. Douglass's satiric humor carries the reader away from its object while the tragic seriousness of the confrontative style draws the reader to its object.[52]

Douglass's rhetoric, aided by these two modes of imagining, is concerned, therefore, with moving its reader not just emotionally but also spatially with respect to the text. Traditionally, I have argued, black autobiography tried to move its white reader in one direction, from an alien to a consubstantial relationship with the text and the black self presumably represented by the text. Douglass's rhetoric ran the risk, according to Ephraim Peabody, of reversing that momentum toward empathetic identification. This, in turn, could only realienate white readers fearful of manipulation and suspicious of rhetoric as the mask of an uncandid man. The adoption of the American jeremiad as the structure within which he would undertake his rhetorical experiments helped Douglass ensure a fundamental ideological consubstantiation with his white reader despite the occasional shifting designs of his rhetoric. The jeremiad identifies Douglass in a formal way; it situates him in a conventionalized relationship to his subject and his audience; its bipolar system of opposing values provides a set of standards whereby narrator and reader can negotiate their differences and achieve rapprochement. The push-pull of Douglass's rhetorical imagination, however, suspends this rapprochement at times, leaving the relationships of reader and narrator undefined, unstable, and fluid. At these key moments in the text, Douglass declares new rules and conditions whereby the white reader may approach his text and reach an understanding of and with it.

One such crucial rhetorical moment in the *Narrative* occurs as Douglass tries to describe his state of mind upon arrival in the free states. Usually this was a climactic moment in the slave narrative, something to be glorified and sentimentalized. But Douglass stresses the terror of betrayal.

> The motto which I adopted when I started from slavery was this—'Trust no man!' I saw in every white man an enemy, and in almost every colored man cause for distrust. It was a most painful situation; and, to understand it, one must needs experience it, or imagine himself in similar circumstances. Let him be a fugitive slave in a strange land—a land given up to be the hunting-ground for slaveholders—whose inhabitants are legalized kidnappers—where he is every moment subjected to the terrible liability of being seized upon by his fellow-men, as the hideous crocodile seizes upon his prey!—I say, let him place himself in my situation—without home or friends —without money or credit—wanting shelter, and no one to give it—wanting bread, and no money to buy it,—and at the same time let him feel that he is pursued by merciless men-hunters, and in total darkness as to what to do, where to go, or where to stay,—perfectly helpless both as to the means of defence and means of escape,—in the midst of plenty, yet suffering the terrible gnawings of hunger, —in the midst of houses, yet having no home,—among fellow-men, yet feeling as if in the midst of wild beasts, whose greediness to swallow up the trembling and half-famished fugitive is only equalled by that with which the monsters of the deep swallow up the helpless fish upon which they subsist,—I say, let him be placed in this most trying situation,—the situation in which I was placed,—then, and not till then, will he fully appreciate the hardships of, and know how to sympathize with, the toil-worn and whip-scarred fugitive slave. (144)

This cumulative sentence, with its showcase of rhetorical effects, climaxes Douglass's *Narrative* in a defiant yet directive way. Its fundamental purposes are to reclaim the concept of climax from conventional expectations and to declare the conditions under which a white reader could actually understand and appreciate the climax of a fugitive slave narrative. Douglass was aware that for many readers the point of highest interest in a slave narrative came when they finally knew how the fugitive escaped and what it felt like finally to be free. These were the ultimate facts that whites wanted to learn from such narratives; to "deprive . . . the curious of the gratification" that they expected from the revelation of such facts might jeopardize the discursive relationship that Douglass had been building with his reader. Yet Douglass did not want that relationship predicated on the assumption that whites could read slave narratives from the standpoint of the distanced, uncommitted, merely curious collector of facts and still expect to know what and who they were about. Douglass did not want to indulge his reader in a servile way; he wanted his reader to learn something about his or her responsibility to the text. For there to be a significant climax to the text, the white reader had to understand—in Ricoeur's sense of hermeneutical understanding—the ironies of Douglass's initially "painful situation" in the North. For the white reader to have the greatest possible emotional response to this moment in the text, he had to "experience it, or imagine himself in similar circumstances." Since the reader could not have the actual experience, the understanding of it was up to his or her capacity to imagine it.

In this statement Douglass, for the first time in Afro-American autobiography, declared a new and crucial role for the imagination as a mode of mediation, not distortion and deception, in black-white discourse. He was pointing toward an unprecedented answer to the central rhetorical problem of the slave narrative—how to build a bridge of sympathetic identification between the diametrical points of view of the northern white reader and the southern black fugitive. In the passage under consideration here, Douglass implies that such a bridge could not be extended from the pilings of fact set down by the black narrator. It had to be suspended from imaginative supports that connected each opposing shore of the discourse. That is, Douglass was calling for a genuine discursive relationship of equals in the slave narrative, one based on an active, flexible engagement of the white reader with the black text free from preconceived roles, instituted agendas, and programmed responses. As long as the black narrator played the suppliant role of purveyor of facts for the consumption of the preeminent reader, full appreciation and understanding of the slave narrative could not be attained. Imaginative self-projection of the reader into the text had to be the basic preparatory condition for the kind of understanding that Douglass wanted whites to derive from his story, the understanding of the individual emotional significance of the facts of a fugitive's life.

Thus Douglass repeatedly insisted of the white reader, "let him place himself in my situation" if he wished to appreciate and "know how to sympathize with" the struggle of the fugitive. This seems to have been the kind of knowledge with which Douglass hoped his *Narrative* would climax for his reader. Equally climactic is Douglass's declaration that whites had to learn how to sympathize with the fugitive slave. What accounted for their lack of the knowledge of how to do this? Perhaps Douglass was suggesting that the kind of knowledge traditionally sought from slave narratives fed only the dominant race's appetite for curious, exciting, or pathetic details of the life of the subjugated race. Such knowledge might

137

stimulate the sentimental reflexes of the comfortable and secure toward unfortunates below them. But real sympathy, Douglass implies, could only come through an imaginative leap into the total situation of the fugitive and the world of the text.

Douglass does not talk about how the white reader could be prepared and guided in his imaginative leap into sympathetic understanding of the black narrative. His emphasis is on the reader's disposition to make that effort, and on its necessity ("then, and not till then") before real understanding could result. As we have seen, Douglass obviously understood some of the rhetorical means by which readers might be moved imaginatively to confront or distance themselves from the text. Yet he would not speak openly of the role of the black autobiographer's creative imagination in activating the white reader's sympathetic imagination. To do so would have contradicted his leader's prefatory promise that Douglass's *Narrative* contained "nothing drawn from the imagination." At this point in his literary career, Douglass, still in many ways Garrison's man, would not authorize himself at Garrison's expense. Nor would he try to authorize the slave narrative as an imaginative act at a time when its factuality and supposed eschewal of the arts of rhetoric and invention were still its greatest selling point. Nevertheless, what Douglass did declare with regard to the centrality of the imagination in the Afro-American autobiographical enterprise helped to open up the rhetorical options of black autobiographers as they had never been explored before. For if the activation of the imagination were the sine qua non for the understanding of the slave narrator's situation, then by unstated but plain logic, any rhetorical means, based more or less in fact, could be justified in an autobiography as long as it enhanced the reader's sympathetic imagination and thus his comprehension of the facts in question. Douglass set the example by appointing himself the country's black Jeremiah so as to rekindle the flame of his reader's nationalistic imagination and fan the fires of sectional division in America. After Douglass, many black autobiographers felt empowered to try out even bolder strategies of enlisting the sympathetic imagination of American readers in the cause of freedom.

The *Narrative* of Frederick Douglass was the great enabling text of the first century of Afro-American autobiogaphy. Its sales—4,500 copies in the first five months of its existence—prompted repeated reissues in America and, in the next two years, English, Irish, and French editions.[53] Popular demand for the literature of fugitive slaves surged. Published simultaneously with Douglass's, the *Narrative of the Sufferings of Lewis Clarke*, a very light-skinned fugitive from Kentucky, matched the Maryland fugitive's barbed wit and surpassed him in the adaptation of the arts of the comic raconteur to the purposes of antislavery propaganda. What Richard Bridgman has called "the colloquial style" in American prose, characterized by the intrusion of regional dialect, either in the form of words or rhythms of vernacular speech, into more "serious" discourse, makes a notable early appearance in Clarke's narrative.[54] The salty flavor of this narrative's anecdotal satire is present in sentences like these describing "the Algerines of Kentucky." "Some of the slaveholders may have a *wide* house; but one of the *cat-handed*, snake-eyed, brawling women, which slavery produces, can fill it from cellar to garret. I have heard every place I could get into any way ring with their screech-owl voices. Of all the animals on the face of this earth, I am most afraid of a real mad, passionate, raving, slaveholding woman." Through the bestializing imagery, the broad exaggerations, and the lists of homely hyphenated adjectives, the passage gets about as close as a slave narrator safely could to the no-holds-barred freedom of native American profanity. The droll self-depreciation of the native humorist was also part of Clarke's bag of rhetorical tricks. "Some people are very much afraid all the slaves will run up north, if they are ever free. But I can assure them that they will run *back* again, if they do. If I could have been assured of my freedom in Kentucky, then, I would have given anything in the world for the prospect of spending my life among my old acquaintances, where I first saw the sky, and the sun rise and go down. It was a long time before I could make the sun work right at all. It would rise in the wrong place, and go down wrong; and, finally, it behaved so bad, I thought it could not be the same sun."[55] Playing the simpleton, an old ploy in the oral humor of the black and white cultures of the South,[56] was an effective way of laughing off northern fears of a tidal wave of black immigrants following forced emancipation.

Clarke's *Narrative* joined Douglass's in trying out stylistic and tonal experiments that could broaden the slave narrative's rhetorical range and emotional appeal while also personalizing the voice of the narrator himself. Unfortunately, comparison of the two narratives is hampered by the fact that Clarke's is a collaborative work, written from the fugitive's dictation by a Boston abolitionist minister, Joseph C. Lovejoy. Lovejoy's preface is typically ambiguous about his role as Clarke's amanuensis-editor. "In all material points every word is true," the minister assured his reader, and "much of it [the *Narrative*] is in his own language." But we shall never know how much of the peculiar distinction of this text, its vernacular humor, directly reproduces Clarke's oral style and how much is Lovejoy's imitation of that style. What we can be certain of is that Clarke learned early on the antislavery platform that "the uncouth awkwardness of his language had a sort of charm" to northern whites,[57] and with Lovejoy's aid he exploited that vernacular uncouthness self-consciously and with rhetorical success in his dictated autobiography.

There is much less to praise in some of the other slave narratives that appeared in the wake of Douglass's and Clarke's successes. Both William Hayden and Leonard Black believed that they like Douglass had been chosen by God while in slavery for special missions in freedom, but neither man possessed the rhetorical or storytelling skills to distinguish himself as a writer. Slightly better known was the *Narrative of Henry Watson, a Fugitive Slave* (1848), the product of a professional abolitionist lecturer whose work was endorsed by Garrison himself in the *Liberator*. Watson's brief, impersonal, fact-oriented story added very little to the matter or manner of the slave narrative, except in its description of the instruction that the prospective fugitive received from an abolitionist in how to lie to white people during his northward flight. Psychological causes and effects, which Douglass made central themes of the slave narrative, are absent from Watson's little book. His silences have left his autobiographical message largely unheard.[58]

Autobiographical writing by free blacks as well as former slaves received an impetus from Douglass's *Narrative*.[59] Pennsylvania-born Zilpha Elaw, an itinerant evangelist in England at the time of Douglass's triumphant speaking tour of the British Isles in late 1845 and 1846, may have been emboldened to publish her *Memoirs* (1846) as a consequence of the strong interest that England was showing in the famous slave's autobiography. Elaw's account of her conversion, call, and ministry continues the incipiently feminist tradition in black autobiography that Jarena Lee began in 1836 and reasserted in 1849 in the enlarged *Religious Experience and Journal of Mrs. Jarena Lee*. Lee's *Journal* adds to the 1836 *Religious Experience* a record of her ministerial activities up to her fiftieth birthday. From the *Journal* one also learns that Lee met Elaw while both were proselytizing in western Pennsylvania, and that as a temporary preaching team they enjoyed success. Unfortunately, because the *Journal* reads much like a log of distances travelled, scriptural texts expounded, places visited, and numbers of people converted, the new material in Lee's 1849 autobiography adds little of a personal nature to the self-portrait painted in the 1836 *Life and Religious Experience*. Elaw's *Memoirs*, on the other hand, is considerably longer than that of her sister in the spirit and more revealing of what its author called "the lineaments of my inward man" (iv).

Like the ministerial journals of John Marrant, Daniel Coker, and Jarena Lee,[60] Elaw's *Memoirs* treats her life as a "pilgrim course" from which her readers may draw inspiration and edification. Usually the inspiration stems from seeing the gospel preached diligently and effectively against great obstacles. The edification derives from moments when the episodic narration slows long enough to let the autobiographer expatiate on the moral significance of some trial or triumph. Much of Elaw's story is given over to inspiring and edifying in conventional ways about topics of standard concern to evangelical ministers, black or white. At times in her book, however, she speaks more forthrightly than any of the black ministerial autobiographers before her about the need for a social gospel that would inspire righteousness on the racial front.

Perhaps the example of Douglass in England witnessing against the evils of slavery encouraged Elaw to enter into her autobiography yet another denunciation of the peculiar institution for the further edification of the British. At any rate, while narrating an account of her travels in the slave states in 1828, preaching unattended despite the threat of being arrested and possibly sold into bondage, Elaw left no doubt where she stood regarding the chattel principle. "Oh, the abominations of slavery! though Philemon be the proprietor, and Onesimus the slave, yet every case of slavery, however lenient its inflictions, and mitigated its atrocities, indicates an oppressor, the oppressed, and the oppression" (73). Here Elaw comes very close to contradicting the Apostle Paul himself, whose letter returning Onesimus the slave to his master Philemon, a Greek Christian, was widely used by slaveholders to justify the restoration of runaways to their owners. Elaw was not simply another attacker of slavery via autobiography, however. She went to the heart of the race problem in the United States while recounting her experience as a teacher in a segregated school in Burlington, Vermont. "The pride of a white skin is a bauble of great value with many in some parts of the United States, who readily sacrifice their intelligence to their prejudices, and possess more knowledge than wisdom. The Almighty accounts not the black races of man either in the order or nature or spiritual capacity as inferior to the white," she maintained (52).

English racism did not escape her censure either. While describing a revival among the blacks of Salem, Massachusetts, she paused to analyze the moral conditions and obligations of whites and blacks as she had observed them on both sides of the ocean. "I hope to be forgiven by my English brethren, in saying, that it is not an uncommon thing for white Christians to reprobate the morals of their sable brethren, without an adequate occasion. . . . The illiterate colored Christian is competent to, and ought, practically, to carry out the precepts of the Christian religion to the utmost extent his circumstances admit of; but Christian charity will not rashly judge him, for an imperfect conformity to the politer standard of morals and tasteful delicacy, which have been superadded to the

Christian precept, by the supererogative pride of high-toned sensibility and civilization." As Elaw warmed to her topic, she bluntly contrasted black immoralities, which "are easily visited and purged by the discipline of the church," with the "covetousness and worldly pride" that hid behind "the whited exterior, the artificial delicacy and current respectability or pride of life of much of the present-day Christianity" (103–4). Her double consciousness as outsider (black and female) and insider (Christian preacher) fostered in her a cultural relativism that sometimes questioned the moral hierarchies and social categorizing of genteel civilization. Thus, when a mother of five who had been "cohabiting with" a man in Flushing, New York, was refused membership in the local Methodist church, Elaw hedged on the justifiability of this form of moral discrimination. The marriage customs and laws set forth in the Bible seemed to her "so widely opposite from those of civilized nations in modern times" that it was "not easy to determine what course ought to be pursued by a Christian communion" faced with the Flushing case (134).

Elaw's Bible contained exceptions to almost every rule that white patriarchal civilization erected to preserve its status quo. She would grant that "in the ordinary course of Church arrangement and order," Paul's rule forbidding women to speak in church ought to be followed. However, "the Scriptures make it evident that this rule was not intended to limit the extraordinary directions of the Holy Ghost, in reference to female Evangelists, or oracular sisters; nor to be rigidly observed in peculiar circumstances" (114). Without saying so explicitly, this black woman reserved to herself the right to decide when these circumstances and "the extraordinary directions of the Holy Ghost," which she alone could monitor, required that the rules not obtain so rigidly. This subversion of patriarchal rules in the name of a higher Ruler let Elaw recast her self-will into "obedience to His sovereign will." The more men opposed her preaching mission, the more plainly she declared her mission in opposition to patriarchal prerogative. Her most outspoken declarative act occurs as she recalls the "pride and arrogancy" of the men on the board of a London antislavery society that challenged her divine appointment to preach in their midst. "As a servant of Jesus," she announces to her reader, "I am required to bear testimony in his name, who was meek and lowly, against the lofty looks of man, and the assumptions of such lordly authority and self-importance" (141). In other words Elaw felt that her mission as writer and preacher required her to dispute the lordship and authority of man in the name of the Lord Jesus within, into whose image, she was convinced, she was becoming "increasingly assimilated." Elaw's is another black narrative of liberation from bondage, therefore, involving this time the self-emancipation of a woman of the Word from the "authority" of man. More than a record of conversion and ministerial labors, her autobiography is a quiet but firm apology for her resistance to patriarchal authorities and a testimony to what she called her "power in weakness."

The warm reception of Douglass's *Narrative* created a literary climate favorable to the growth of a "heroic fugitive school of American literature."[61] By the end of the decade three former fugitives—William Wells Brown, Henry Bibb, and James W. C. Pennington—had published narratives that rivalled Douglass's in their distinctiveness of voice, their facility of style, and their effectiveness in combining thrilling, pathetic, and factual details of slave life into an absorbing story. Yet what makes these men important in the evolution of black autobiography is not that they turned their pasts into real-life romances of fugitive heroism or that they made themselves famous in doing so. Nor is the most arresting feature of their contribution to the slave narrative genre the fact that they viewed slavery from a different angle of vision than that employed by Douglass.[62] From the standpoint of the rhetorical problems that these narrators posed for themselves in the retrieval and revelation of the past, the most noteworthy feature of their autobiographies is the amount of attention that each one pays to the *non*heroic dimension of his slave past. This does not mean that their narratives fail to establish rhetorical conditions in which the actions of a slave resister or fugitive could be interpreted by whites as heroic. Brown, Bibb, and Pennington dramatized their lives as a series of heightening conflicts with various personifications of the dehumanizing power of slavery to break a man, as Covey sought to break Douglass's heroic spirit. What makes the work of Brown, Bibb, and Pennington so compelling is the expanded dramatic role of the nonheroic in their autobiographies and its consequent impact on psychological and narrative resolution.

As epitomized in Douglass's *Narrative*, the heroic fugitive is the rugged individual whose struggle against repression culminates in his successful escape from it. The heroic fugitive is he who severs the links that chain him to the past and lives instead for the future. Single-mindedly, he dedicates himself to freedom, which he achieves despite all obstacles by maintaining his indomitable will to overcome. As Douglass pictured him, the heroic fugitive was a man with a mission which, when discovered, radically transformed his sense of self with a fervor not unlike evangelical conversion. *Before* that transformation, Douglass was only a "brute," i.e., an absence of self, a non-man; *afterward*, he was a man "revived" and "inspired" with an iron resolution to resist unto death all attempts to convert him back into the no-self of slavery. In his brutalized state the slave undergoes oscillating moments of hope and despair, as evidenced in the

143

famous apostrophe to the sloops on the Chesapeake Bay delivered by Douglass while under the Covey regime.[63] But in the state of revived manhood, implicitly defined as heroic resistance to oppression, Douglass suffers no dark nights of the soul, no wavering in his commitment to freedom and self-fulfillment. He may try to include others in his plans for freedom, but ultimately he will take his chances alone if necessary.

Brown, Bibb, and Pennington do not subscribe to this romanticized, before-and-after scheme of psychological conversion of the self to heroism. They differ from Douglass in that throughout their autobiographical self-portraits there is a consistent mediation between the bipolar opposites of heroic and nonheroic behavior that Douglass was at some pains to schematize and separate. They risk their reader's ambivalence toward them as heroes by acknowledging that they did things that conventional heroes were not supposed to do. Douglass does not appear to have been hampered by the conflicts that these men acknowledge within themselves. Their bondage is complicated by psychological and moral factors that have no place in or do not fit into Douglass's scheme. Their autobiographies reveal them to be still grappling with elements of the intractable "shadow" of the slave past in the hope of making the struggles of the personality with itself an acceptable subject of black-white discourse. In the process they subtly alter the appropriateness conditions of slave narrative discourse as practiced by black men of propriety, including the heroic Douglass himself.

One of the features of William Wells Brown's autobiography that made it so popular—its reportage of exterior facts of slavery, not interior facets of the slave narrator's character—makes it difficult to compare to a work like Douglass's. This may very well have been Brown's intention. No mere imitator of his famed predecessor, Brown does not make the evolution of his self-consciousness the center of his *Narrative*. His is not a *Bildungsroman*. He does not identify himself according to Douglass's myth of the heroic resister; indeed, from the outset of Brown's story, we see the inevitable fall of admirable black men who aspire to dignity in slavery through forcible resistance to ruthless masters. Against such overwhelming physical odds, the slaves in Brown's recollection have to protect by guile and deception what they cannot preserve through more direct, conventional means. Brown was also a trickster, a very accomplished one in fact, and he recounts with some pleasure his ruses and manipulations of whites, even though doing so might have risked his audience's respect for him. Sometimes the deception could be justified because of the extraordinary conditions of slavery. The wife of Brown's final owner, Captain Enoch Price of St. Louis, forced Brown to lie to her about his love for a slave woman named Eliza to whom Mrs. Price wanted to marry him. Brown interpreted Mrs. Price's purchase of Eliza, an apparently kindly act, as a "trap laid . . . to make me satisfied with my new home, by getting me a wife" (88). A prospective fugitive's best hope for success lay in remaining single, yet Brown also knew that to refuse his mistress's offer would incur her distrust and lessen his chances for freedom. Consequently he had to play false to both Mrs. Price and Eliza in order to hold true to his own higher aim of self-emancipation. Brown had the same justification for subsequent lies to Captain Price about his disaffection from the free states. That he never tries to justify his deceptions of white slaveholders suggests that he believed that self-preservation and the aim of freedom absolved a tricky slave from the blame of an overly nice reader. In this Brown had the support of other slave narrators of his time.[64] On the other hand, Brown could not have expected the sympathy of either whites or blacks for the cruel, self-serving trick he played on an innocent freeman in Vicksburg in 1832. And yet, instead of recounting the incident so as to focus on his moral failure, Brown accords the retelling of that incident, not the moralizing over it, the full attention of his imagination and his art. The manner in which he tells this story that he claims to be so shameful tempts his implied reader to respond with comic approbation and respect for a Negro antihero who defies all the norms of respectability which the fictive reader would presumably hold dear.

As personal servant to James Walker, a slave trader on the Mississippi River, Brown once angered his master during a hotel meeting with some prospective buyers. While serving wine, the slave "accidentally" filled some of the glasses too full, which resulted in some dampened shirts and vests among the white gentlemen and some embarrassment to Walker. The next day the trader gave his slave a note to take to the town jailer along with a dollar to give to him when Brown arrived. Mistrusting his master's intentions, Brown gets a sailor to read the note to him. " 'They are going to give you hell,' " the sailor informs Brown. " 'This is a note to have you whipped, and says that you have a dollar to pay for it.' " (53– 54). "Determined not to be whipped," the slave calmly ponders his alternatives until he spies another black man about his size on the scene. Then Brown describes how he set up his victim. First he asks to whom this stranger belonged. When he learns that this is a freeman new to town, not someone's slave whose injury would be investigated by white authorities, he proceeds with his ingenious bit of dupery. "I told him I had a note to go into the jail and get a trunk to carry to one of the steamboats; but was so busily engaged that I could not do it, although I had a dollar to pay for it." The trustful freeman takes the bait: "He asked me if I would not give him the job. I handed him the note and the dollar, and off he started for the jail" (54).

Having baited his reader also, Brown plays out the narrative line leisurely and skillfully, building up suspense instead of simply stating the
factual outcome of the incident. After making sure that the hapless freeman went into the jail, Brown slyly hides himself around the corner, "intending to see how my friend looked when he came out." He soon overhears a brief conversation between two other blacks, which, instead of
summarizing, Brown as narrator imaginatively reconstructs.

> "They are giving a nigger scissors in the jail." "What for?" said the other. The
> man continued, "A nigger came into the jail, and asked for the jailer. The
> jailer came out, and he handed him a note, and said he wanted to get a trunk.
> The jailer told him to go with him, and he would give him the trunk. So he
> took him into the room, and told the nigger to give up the dollar. He said a
> man had given him the dollar to pay for getting the trunk. But that lie would
> not answer. So they made him strip himself, and then they tied him down,
> and are now whipping him." (55)

The narration of the events in the jail through the perspective and colloquial language of the anonymous black observer was an artful decision
by Brown. It let him satisfy his reader's curiosity about what happened in
the jail, something he himself supposedly could not know. At the same
time, letting the observer recount the events added a layer of unconscious irony to the other cruel but comic reversals revealed in the course
of his narration. Even the black observer, not to mention the freeman and
the jailer, is taken in by the trickster's scheme. This constitutes a hefty
tribute to the power of the trickster's art, when even an ordinary black
man on the street does not sympathize with a brother being beaten.
Through it all the white reader remains in his position of smug privilege,
the only observer to know whose lie set all this rascality in motion.

The story does not end with Brown's successful escape from the beating. Instead of putting as much distance between himself and his victim
as possible, the trickster waits around for the reappearance of the man
ironically tagged in the narrative now as "my customer." When the freeman emerges from the jail "complaining bitterly, saying that I had played
a trick upon him," Brown plays dumb. "I denied any knowledge of what
the note contained, and asked him what they had done to him." This ruse
elicits from the freeman corroboration of the story Brown had already
heard. "He had received twenty lashes on his bare back, with the negro-
whip," plus a note, which the quick-witted Brown immediately purchases
from the freeman for fifty cents. At this point, the reader can begin to
understand why the trickster waited for his victim; there was something
more for him to take from his gull.

Returning to Walker's hotel, the slave selects "a stranger whom I had not seen before" to read the jailer's note to him. Once again Brown lingers over narrative developments when he might have pressed on to the outcome of the episode. The note could have been summarized in a simple phrase, but Brown enters it into the story "as near as I can recollect it" for the clear but unacknowledged purpose of enhancing the reader's enjoyment of the ironies of the situation. The jailer writes: "Dear Sir:—By your direction, I have given your boy twenty lashes. He is a very saucy boy, and tried to make me believe that he did not belong to you, and I put it on to him well for lying to me. I remain, Your obedient servant." This is testimony to the jailer's complete deception by the trickster, whose power is confirmed more insistently, as a result. Yet it is not enough. The game has one more inning, the wily slave has one more fool to make, and the narrator has one more scene to play with for his own and the reader's delight. Brown could have stated simply that he returned the note to his master without the latter's ever having suspected what actually happened. Instead, he dramatizes the scene, imaginatively reconstructing the verbal interchange between the slave and his master. "Before I went in where Mr. Walker was, I wet my cheeks a little, as though I had been crying. He looked at me, and inquired what was the matter. I told him that I had never had such a whipping in my life, and handed him the note. He looked at it and laughed;—'and so you told him that you did not belong to me.' 'Yes sir,' said I. 'I did not know that there was any harm in that.' He told me I must behave myself, if I did not want to be whipped again" (57).

The discrepancies here between the way things looked to Walker and the way they actually were encourage the reader to pause and reflect on the double meanings in the passage. For instance, the trickster speaks more truly than Walker understands when he says that he "had never had such a whipping in my life." There is also consummate irony in the last statement of the passage, for clearly, as the whole episode has demonstrated, the best way for the slave to keep from being whipped again is to *mis*behave himself in the manner that Brown has revealed to the reader. What, then, is the reader to conclude from the whole episode? Good behavior obviously would have impelled Brown to the whipping Walker intended for him; bad behavior rescued him from his master's unjust punishment. Given the fact that forcible resistance is impossible in Brown's world, which was the right course—to accept squarely the beating with a kind of heroic fortitude or to avoid it by a selfish, unheroic deception?

This is the moral dilemma to which the episode inevitably leads, but only implicitly. As narrator, Brown retreats to a safer, more familiar didactic conclusion—an explicit condemnation of slavery. "This incident shows how it is that slavery makes its victims lying and mean." He adds, "I have often, since my escape, deeply regretted the deception I practised upon this fellow"; he hopes that someday he can make amends to the freeman for "his vicarious sufferings in my behalf" (57–58). These remarks offer a pseudo-resolution to the moral problem posed implicitly in the episode: William Wells Brown the freeman deplores William Wells Brown the slave trickster. In the second edition of the *Narrative* (1848), Brown underlined his conviction that "had I entertained the same views of right and wrong which I now do," he would not have stooped to deceive and exploit "that poor fellow." [65] These comments are designed to relegate the unheroic, self-serving trickster to Brown's slave past. They identify the trickster with some other that the freeman has disowned and risen above. This was not an unusual rhetorical strategy in the slave narrative, as we have seen. It let the ex-slave speak openly of a shadow within that whites needed to be cognizant of, despite their fear and rejection of it. At the same time, by embracing the American and evangelical myths of the changed man, the slave narrator could sever his ties with the shadow self, declare it a thing made by slavery, and thus turn its transgressions to propagandistic account.

Brown made sure that his *Narrative* dramatized his repudiation of the shadow of the "lying and mean" trickster. While still on the journey through Ohio, after escaping from Enoch Price's Mississippi riverboat on New Year's Day, 1834, Brown informs us that he was preoccupied with naming himself anew. He discards his slave name of Sandford, which he always despised because it had been forced on him by his master in his boyhood, and reclaims his original name, William, given him by his mother. What this implies about Brown's rebirth into a new identity is made more explicit when he later accepts the name of Wells Brown, the benevolent Quaker who, along with his wife, fed, clothed, and nursed the fugitive "as if I had been one of their own children." The transition from Sandford to William Wells Brown signifies the transformation of the narrator from a man of deceitful appearances, denoted by the false name he had to wear as a slave, into a radically changed man, symbolized by the amalgamated name that he gladly receives from the two best influences in his life, his mother in bondage and his surrogate father in freedom. "Base indeed should I be," Brown intones in his *Narrative*'s dedication to Wells Brown, if he ever did anything "to disgrace that honored name." The *Narrative*, of course, gives no evidence to suggest that William Wells Brown ever returned to Sandford's lies or that he used his wits again to advance himself at the expense of his fellow blacks.

And yet, William Wells Brown did return in his autobiography to the scene of Sandford's most shameless deception, and not simply to deliver his mea culpa to the reader. Had that been his purpose, he would not have recounted the incident of the dodged whipping in such a way as to call attention to its comic reversals, dramatic ironies, and, most importantly, the success of the trickster in manipulating people and determining events supposedly beyond his power. The antislavery moralist may be sorry for what Sandford did, but the self-celebrating autobiographer cannot, will not, recall it without a measure of pride. Brown lets the antislavery moralist have the last word,[66] but only after he has created interpretive dilemmas and elicited responses from his reader that the moralist will not be able to resolve or satisfy. This undermining of the kind of closure that antislavery propagandists would have preferred leaves the text open to questions about the identity and purpose of this self-sabotaging narrator.

In the main, the narrator of this autobiography speaks through the voice of William Wells Brown, a man of mixed blood whose name symbolizes, as we have noted, an amalgamation of the best influences of the black matriarchy in the South and the white patriarchy in the North. Brown depicts himself as ever loyal to this name. In slavery, William is shown to be self-sacrificial and family-oriented. From his youth he pledges not to desert his mother and sister in slavery, though they urge him to place his own interests above theirs. After his sister is sold away from the family, William makes a break for Canada, but not without his mother. Their apprehension several days after leaving St. Louis causes Elizabeth Brown's master to have her sold down the river to New Orleans. During their last moments together, Brown pictures her praising him as a dutiful son and pleading with him to think of himself now that he can do nothing more for the family. After his flight to freedom, Brown outlines the ways in which he continued to devote himself to the welfare of black people, spurred on by the altruistic example of Wells Brown. He worked on the underground railroad in Cleveland, preached temperance to his fellow freemen, and, after 1843, "devoted [his] time to the cause of [his] enslaved countrymen."[67] Brown, therefore, portrays himself modestly but emphatically as a rising champion of the unfortunate and oppressed, motivated not by selfish motives but by a deep sense of filial duty to others.

Nevertheless, on a few occasions in Brown's *Narrative* another voice breaks into the text, the voice of the subversive Sandford. Sandford functions as a commentator on the autobiographical performance of William W. Brown. Indeed, if we distinguish between the persona and author of the *Narrative*—calling the former William W. Brown, as he is identified on the title page, and the latter William Wells Brown—then William W. Brown and Sandford may be read as two of William Wells Brown's performing selves. The priority of these personae is much more difficult to pin down than the occasions and the effect of their interpenetrations in the text. When Sandford's voice interrupts William W. Brown's narrative performance, it is generally to remind the reader that he or she has been witnessing an ongoing declarative act through which someone has been trying to name himself credibly in the eyes of his audience. One of Sandford's reminders comes as William W. Brown recalls his visit to a black St. Louis soothsayer shortly before he escaped from Enoch Price. Brown notes that Uncle Frank was a busy consultant, one whom many people, white as well as black, believed could foresee the future. At this point, the narrative flow is interrupted by a single wry observation: "Whether true or not, he had the *name*, and that is about half of what one needs in this gullible age" (92).

The remark helps to remind the reader that people do not just receive names, they acquire them in the form of reputations that the "gullible" all too readily accept. Autobiography is one of the arts of credible reputation-making, of living up to a name one wishes to acquire. Thus, as we read William W. Brown's story, we must not forget that the prevailing narrative voice is at pains to make his reconstructed history fit his acquired name. When Sandford breaks into the text, we see a resisting and a sabotaging of this reconstruction of personal history according to the demands of the acquired name. William W. Brown generally presides over the narrative, posing as its exclusive namer, but Sandford's subversion of the reputation of Brown prevents the latter's ever taking full and sole possession of the narrative that bears his name. Sandford in this sense is the liberator of this narrative. He prevents it from becoming the literary chattel of William W. Brown.

This is perhaps the major significance of the incident involving the dodged whipping. For more than a brief moment, Sandford liberates the narrative from William W. Brown's moral control and proceeds to celebrate himself as a trickster instead of a truth-teller. The appropriateness conditions upon which William W. Brown built his relationship to the reader suddenly shift as the narrator turns shifty and teasing. The voice that savors Sandford's misbehavior cannot be that of a man of propriety; this voice is too crafty, too well versed in the art of manipulating readers into enjoying and approving what they should not. This narrator does not say all that he thinks; his discourse often takes the tone of double entendre. He masks piquant ironies behind the bland assertive mode that he adopts from William W. Brown. As a consequence of these tricks, the role of the implied reader in the text is transformed, too. Suddenly one is enabled to read this narrative as a celebration of roguery, not conventional heroism, wherein self-serving acts become the norm in a world in which the ideal of service to others has been perverted by slavery. Sandford inducts his reader into the vernacular world of blacks in the South, where

tales of the exploits of John the slave trickster and Brer Rabbit, John's analogue in the animal world, served as outlets for repressed feelings and as
a means of inculcating a survival ethic. Sandford survives despite the repression of his literal master, Walker, and his literary monitor, William W.
Brown, because he practices what tricksters and rogues of his region,
white and black, knew: in the words of Simon Suggs, "It is good to be
shifty in a new country." [68]

In the "new country" of the slave narrative, Sandford proves that "it is
good to be shifty;" it is good for the narrative voice to shift out of con-
stricting poses, to be self-seeking in both a positive and negative sense,
not self-satisfied. By the same token, the reader must shift with Sandford
to be liberated from the unsatisfying narrative perspective of William W.
Brown. Through Sandford one learns to appreciate an agile and adaptive
hero of grit and motherwit, a master of mental invention who translates
weakness into strength through the power of his words. Sandford's duplicity, his "lying" according to William W. Brown, empowers and requires his reader to learn to listen for ironic doubleness in his voice and
to appropriate from him a mode of double consciousness suitable to the
interpretive demands of his text. Because of Sandford, we can hear more
creatively the sub rosa voices in the texts of other black men of propriety
whose words, as Lunsford Lane cryptically hinted, "might be twisted to
convey an idea more than should be expressed."

Amid Henry Bibb's detailed revelations of that most exciting stage in a
fugitive's career, life on the road to freedom, readers could find even
more Sandford-like behavior than William Wells Brown had acknowledged. More candidly than any slave narrator before him, Bibb discussed
what he called "my manner of living on the road," [69] leaving the facts of
life on the plantation much less space in his autobiography. This decision
was not due to any lack of acquaintance with the peculiar institution.
Bibb had been in bondage in Kentucky and Louisiana and was one of the
few ex-slaves to characterize from firsthand experience the practice of
involuntary servitude in the Indian Territory. He had occupied the highest and lowest rungs on the slave's social ladder, having been a whipped
fieldhand on a cotton plantation and the personal valet to itinerant
"Southern sportsmen" who sold him to a Cherokee half-blood, whom
Bibb judged to have been his most humane master. Nevertheless, what
Bibb knew best was "the art of running away." From the time he was
twenty years old, he had "made a regular business of it," he claims in the
opening pages of his *Life and Adventures*. Through a repeated pattern of
flight and pursuit, capture and escape, played out five different times between 1837 and 1841, Bibb's narrative becomes a kind of "road narrative," [70] in which we confront the moral problem of how freely a fugitive

from injustice could sidestep traditional laws and mores to gain his own advantage.

The resolution of such a problem could strongly influence a reader's sense of the narrator's character both past and present. Bibb's avowal and vigorous defense of his transgressions of conventional morality while on the road leave little doubt of his conviction that the ends justified the means by which one made one's escape from slavery. He recounts numerous occasions when he lied to potential purchasers about his past, faked sorrow over the death of a master while plotting to run away, passed as a bibulous white man to trick a group of Irishmen into buying him a steamboat ticket to freedom, stole various articles, including a mule and a Bowie knife, from his Kentucky master, and robbed strangers of horses to speed him on his getaways. Bibb prepares his reader for these revelations by stressing in his opening chapter that "the only weapon of self defence that I could use successfully, was that of deception" (17), resistance being useless and generally fatal in the world of Bibb's recollection, as it was in William Wells Brown's. The fugitive was aware of the likelihood that some would censure his horse thievery, but he replied, "If a white man had been captured by the Cherokee Indians and carried away from his family for life into slavery . . . would it be a crime for the poor fugitive, whose life, liberty, and future happiness were all at stake, to mount any man's horse by the way side, and ride him without asking any questions, to effect his escape?" (163). Anyone familiar with the mythology of Indian captivity narratives, which in Bibb's time were undergoing an unparalleled revival of interest in America,[71] could empathize with such a mode of self-liberation, especially when couched in the famous phrases of the Declaration of Independence. Bibb followed up this appeal with an even more pointed rhetorical question: "who would not do the same thing to rescue a wife, child, father, or mother?" He had married and fathered slaves whose hope of liberty depended on his freeing himself the most expeditious way he could in order to deliver them from bondage, too. This, even more than "self defence" or the abstract right to "life, liberty, and future happiness" was Bibb's justification for his morally dubious conduct as a fugitive.

As a family man in slavery, Bibb's quest for individual liberty was complicated psychologically and morally in ways that neither Douglass nor Brown had to consider. Douglass, the heroic individualist par excellence, gave no indication that he had been responsible to or for anyone but himself when he set out alone for his freedom in the fall of 1838.[72] Brown made it plain that his mother and sister had released him from his filial obligations to them before he ran away. He also avoided entangling attachments to an enslaved woman to whom he was attracted, knowing an

Henry Bibb (circa 1849), from an engraving by Patrick Henry Reason. (Schomburg Center for Research in Black Culture, The New York Public Library, Astor, Lenox and Tilden Foundations)

emotional commitment to another might be his undoing as a fugitive. But Bibb had neither the foresight nor the restraint of these two men. Like them, he had experienced brutal treatment, which "kindled a fire of liberty within my breast which has never yet been quenched." Bibb followed Douglass in tracing his "longing desire to be free" back to romantic promptings from intuition and Nature. The "fire of liberty within" was "a part of my nature; it was first revealed to me by the inevitable laws of nature's God" (17). At eighteen he pledged himself to the achievement of the ideal of personal liberty, but "strong temptations" from the "bright and sparkling eye" of Malinda, a beautiful and talented mulatto slave, "gradually diverted [his] attention" from his great aim (35).

"To think that after I had determined to carry out the great idea which is so universally and practically acknowledged among all the civilized nations of the earth, that I would be free or die, I suffered myself to be turned aside by the fascinating charms of a female, who gradually won my attention from an object so high as that of liberty; and an object which I held paramount to all others" (33). The thought is a matter of both shame and remorse for the narrator, of which he cannot acquit himself except through an autobiographical act that begins in confession and develops through a narration of the trials that Bibb underwent in attempting to rectify his original fecklessness. Although Bibb's trials were more desperate and terrible than those Douglass faced, he does not try to qualify for the heroic status of his predecessor. Douglass's narrative shows us a slave transmuted by the revolutionary idea of liberty into a superior man, a leader whose singleness of purpose commands our admiration, if not awe. Bibb, by contrast, presents himself as a hero of what Northrop Frye would call "low mimetic or domestic tragedy," in which a reader's response to the hero as pathetic is invited. Like Frye's pathetic hero, Bibb is "isolated by a weakness which appeals to our sympathy because it is on our own level of experience." Bibb's is "the story of how someone recognizably like ourselves is broken by a conflict between the inner and outer world."[73] We are introduced to the slave as a youthful idealist of sorts, aspiring to the "high object" of liberty. Soon, however, he is dragged down by a pathetic flaw of the flesh, susceptibility to the "charms of a female." Bibb plays on both misogynist fears of the tempting female and on more genuine sympathy for a man "deeply in love" with a woman "equalled by few." Malinda is clearly a prize, but she is not *the* prize, not the sine qua non of life. Misled by the passionate side of his nature, Bibb deviates from his aim and falls into the world of social responsibility. He compromises himself first by making Malinda his wife in slavery and then by fathering a daughter, Mary Frances, by her.

As narrator, Bibb looks back on his commitment to Malinda as the great tragedy of his life. "If ever there was any one act of my life while a slave, that I have to lament over, it is that of being a father and a husband of slaves" (44). Guilt over this (and all that transpired from it), not over what he did on the road, gives Bibb's voice a plangent quality rarely heard in the heroic fugitive school of male slave narrators. Despite the fact that "Malinda was to me an affectionate wife" who stood by him "in trial and persecution," Bibb was tormented by the fact that in her greatest persecution, he could only stand by impotently. He had to be "eye witness to her insults, scourgings and abuses, such as are commonly inflicted upon slaves" without raising a hand to stop them. This was "more than I could bear." What was worse, because the pain continued to haunt Bibb every time he told his life story, was the guilt of having been "the father of a slave, a word too obnoxious to be spoken by a fugitive slave" (44). Mary Frances "is bone of my bone, flesh of my flesh; poor unfortunate child." Bibb could never name himself a completely free man as long as this issue of his identity was called "slave." The ever-present knowledge that "my only child is still there, destined to bear the fate of all" the calamities her mother faced, was "too much to bear." Bibb's confessional narrative reiterates the obnoxious words that the fugitive would like to repress in order to try to unburden himself of his guilty responsibility for the fate of his child. The writing of his autobiography reenacts once more the pattern of his life depicted therein—the return of the fugitive to the South, to the land of his love and shame, in the hope of restoring the past to himself so that he could be released to the future.

Bibb's first successful flight to the North occurred during the Christmas season of 1837. He left his family in Bedford, Kentucky, on the plantation of William Gatewood, and took passage alone aboard a steamboat to Cincinnati. He did not inform his wife or child of where he was headed or if he planned to return for them. Malinda was an impediment to "the fulfilling of my pledge" to freedom: "Had [she] known my intention at that time, it would not have been possible for me to have got away, and I might have this day been a slave" (47). Despite the "voice of liberty . . . thundering in my very soul," Bibb felt bound to his situation by many "strong attachments to friends and relatives" that "twined about my heart and were hard to break away from." Malinda, of course, represented the strongest of these emotional attachments. The bond that chained him to her required more "moral courage" to break than any that held him to Gatewood because "the love of home and birth-place" is "so natural among the human family" (47).

For a family man, then, Bibb's flight for freedom seemed very unnatural, yet he argued that the idea of freedom had first been revealed to him "by the inevitable laws of nature's God." This paradox turned Bibb's "bolt for Liberty" in 1837 into "one of the most self-denying acts of my whole life." In other words, for Bibb to attain liberty he had to cut himself off from himself, from "the centre and object of all my affections." Running away was not a selfish act of escape, therefore, though it probably appeared so to family men and women in Bibb's readership who were likely to be troubled by his admission that he had deserted his family without even telling them of his plans. From a psychological standpoint freedom required the slave father to abandon the only sustaining identity he had received in bondage, a heartfelt sense of self defined in terms of emotional ties to wife and child. There was no escape from the dilemma that slavery forced upon Henry Bibb: "I must forsake friends and neighbors, wife and child, or consent to live and die a slave." Initially, he chose life without his wife and child, but within six months of the time he crossed the Ohio River to freedom he was back in Kentucky seeking to give his new life the emotional focus of his past. During the next eight years of a fugitive life, he would search for a psychological orientation in relation to the past that would let him become a truly free man.

Bibb jeopardized himself repeatedly for the family that "never expected to see [him] again" after he departed in 1837. In June 1838 he held a clandestine reunion with his wife on Gatewood's plantation, where he gave her money for steamboat passage to Cincinnati in the expectation of meeting her there a week later. Before that meeting could take place, however, Bibb was betrayed and apprehended by Gatewood and conveyed out of Ohio to Louisville. Daringly Bibb broke away from his guards and made his way back to his wife in Bedford, despite the risk of discovery. They planned to wait until the excitement died down and then rendezvous at an appointed place in Ohio two months hence. When Malinda did not come, Bibb reimmersed himself in danger, feeling it "my duty, as a husband and a father, to make one more effort" to rescue his family (83). Returning to Bedford in July 1839, he was again betrayed, jailed, and transported, this time with his family, to the Louisville slave market. After a miserable stay in the workhouse of the city, the Bibbs were bought by a slave trader who took them to Vicksburg, Mississippi, to be sold as a threesome. There Bibb was allowed to seek out a prospective purchaser of himself and his family. When he met Francis Whitfield, a cotton planter in southeastern Louisiana who "looked like a saint" and "talked like the best slave holding Christians," Bibb thought he had found a likely owner. But at home the Baptist deacon turned out to be a hypocritical tyrant, from whom Bibb tried twice to escape, once with his family. Failure resulted in his being sold away from his loved ones in December 1840. Briefly owned by a band of southern gamblers and a Cherokee half-blood, Bibb managed yet another escape in the spring of

1841 that took him across the Indian Territory and Missouri to St. Louis. There he devised an ingeniously simple bit of imposture that let him gain a berth on a steamboat headed up the Mississippi to Ohio. Working his way to Detroit, Bibb hoped to find a way to get an education, but he discovered that people were "not disposed to show me any great favors." The new year found him safe and free but still without a solution to the great problem of his life. "I was not settled in mind about the condition of my bereaved family for several years, and could not settle myself down at any permanent business" (174). Ironically, his heroic efforts on his family's behalf had only removed him farther from them and cut him off from the knowledge he needed the most in order to decide what to do with himself in freedom.

Joining the abolitionist movement is pictured in Douglass's narrative as the culmination of his steady progress toward self-realization and integration into the world of freedom. Bibb's description of his work on the anti-slavery lecture circuit in Michigan and Ohio during the mid-1840s reads more like another phase of his life on the road. Relating "the sad story of my wrongs" may have been one of the few routes of action left to a man whose unresolved past left him perpetually unsettled. His co-workers raised money to finance inquiries into the South, but when nothing came of this, Bibb went to Madison, Indiana, in the winter of 1845 where he could get the news from Gatewood's plantation on the other side of the Ohio River. He soon learned that for the past three years his wife had been living as the concubine of a man to whom Whitfield had sold her after the family break-up in 1840. Mary Frances remained with her, but Malinda "had finally given me up" (189).

This is the turning point in Henry Bibb's story. The knowledge that Malinda had given him up allows Bibb to relinquish his responsibility to her. "I gave her up into the hands of an all-wise Providence" (189). Thus renounced, "she has ever since been regarded as theoretically and practically dead to me as a wife, for she was living in a state of adultery, according to the law of God and man" (189). This severs Bibb's binding link to the past and makes it possible for him to become, for the first time in his life, a completely free man. Malinda's release, however, constitutes only a partial resolution of Bibb's problem of psychological fulfillment in freedom. He remained, as he says, "isolated in this peculiarly unnatural state"—presumably, the paradoxical status of a freeman not fully unmarried from his slave spouse—and spent 1846 back on the road as an abolitionist lecturer. Full "settlement" of his life does not come until two years later, when he marries Mary E. Miles of Boston, "a lady" noted "for her activity and devotion to the anti-slavery cause, as well as her talents and learning, and benevolence in the cause of reforms, generally." This replacement of the slave woman by the antislavery lady completes Henry Bibb's psychological reorientation in the world of freedom. The good wife delivers him from the pathos of the "unnatural state" in which his unfaithful wife had left him. Henry Bibb's autobiography turns out to be a domestic tragicomedy in which Malinda can be finally given up. The other woman in Bibb's story, it seems, is as disposable as the other self in the slave past of narrators like Josiah Henson.

There is much to learn from Henry Bibb's *Narrative* about the psychological dynamics of the making of a freeman. As we have noted, Douglass's rhetorical strategy was to separate slavery and freedom into binary oppositions, the better to dramatize them in before-and-after contrasts (the brute become the man) and appearance-versus-reality distinctions (the slave in form but not in fact). Henry Bibb could not categorize so neatly the joint mediation of slavery and freedom, freedom and slavery. During the crucial years of his life, from 1837–46, his freedom had always been compromised by the slavery of his bond to Malinda. Thus marriage became Bibb's metaphor of the inescapable presence of the past and of the claims of slavery on the psychic well-being of the freeman. One cannot read Bibb's autobiography without wondering if he were not the more representative man than Douglass. Douglass's *Narrative* gives one the impression of a man who shucked off his past like his slave name and never again looked back once he arrived in New Bedford, "the starting point of a new existence." By contrast, when Henry Bibb reached Ohio he could not reject, cast off, and forget the past; he was in fundamental ways "married" to it and identified with it. He could not become free by denial of the slave past unless he intended to deny part of himself as well, i.e., all that he had invested of himself in his union with Malinda and his fatherhood of Mary Frances. Bibb's story shows us a man who could not accept the consequences of such a radically "self-denying" act either as a fugitive or as an autobiographer. His narrative is designed to complete the process of freeing him from the hold of the past, without abrogating his responsibilities to it, or, more acutely, to himself in it.

As an autobiographer, Bibb lives up to his responsibilities to the past by acknowledging, via the confessions at the beginning of his story, his tragic flaws and his complicity in the guilt of slavery. To be the husband of a slave was to bind oneself emotionally to an exquisite form of misery. To father a slave was to be, in a strictly conscientious sense, a slave maker. Mary Frances was "the first and shall be the last slave that I will father, for chains and slavery on this earth," Bibb assured his reader. But the knowledge that his union with Malinda had produced a daughter perhaps destined for her mother's unhappy fate weighed heavily on Bibb's conscience even as he wrote his narrative. Confession did not free him from his guilt. It did intensify the pathos of his condition, which in turn induces in the implied reader a strong desire for some sort of resolution of Bibb's "peculiarly unnatural state." The more Bibb's heroic efforts fail to redeem his past, the more frustrated the desire for climax and resolution becomes. In this way Bibb prepares his reader for a narrative closure that will free them both from the seemingly inescapable cycle of freedom and bondage.

Bibb's bid for closure comes through the decisive declarative act of pronouncing Malinda "theoretically and practically dead to me as a wife." Only by successfully performing this act in his autobiography can he justify the new marriage to Mary Miles, which will deliver him from the cycle of tragic return to the South and reward his pathetic faithfulness to Malinda with a new wife worthy of him. By claiming that Malinda "had finally given me up" in becoming a slave concubine, Bibb shifts moral responsibility for the maintenance of their marriage onto *her* for the first time. Now *she* had failed *him*, which opens the way for him to declare her "dead to [him] as a wife." Only a declarative act outside and independent of the normal, instituted rules governing language transactions can empower and justify Bibb's freedom from Malinda. Their bond had never been "sanctioned by any loyal power" and could not be "cancelled by a legal process" (192). It could only be annulled by the same kind of speech act that had brought it into effect. Everything recounted in the narrative up to the climactic declarative act of annulment establishes the requisite appropriateness conditions that allow Bibb to do what he needs to do—conclude his life story as he had his fugitive career, in a new marriage free of the guilt of the past. The *Narrative* reconstructs a history of self-sacrifice designed to qualify its author as the best of husbands. In the face of such exemplary fidelity, Malinda's unexpected, unexplained "adultery" seems all the more a moral failure on her part, justifying Bibb's disqualification of her for the name of wife. Labeling Malinda's relationship with her master simply as adultery, without considering the special "wrongs, sufferings, and mortifications" that Harriet Jacobs's autobiography pleads on behalf of the sexually tyrannized slave woman,[74] let Bibb close his case with a much needed moral and legal conclusiveness, "according to the law of God and man." The more he insists on Malinda as an adulteress, the more disingenuous he sounds when he says, "Poor unfortunate woman, I bring no charge of guilt against her, for I know not all the circumstances connected with the case." To brand Malinda as an adulteress was certainly to use a highly charged term of moral opprobrium against a married woman, a term admitting of no mitigation through circumstance, and Bibb must have known it. On the other hand, he also knew that if death was the only parting that "the law of God" allowed a husband and wife, then the only way he could marry legitimately and to start a new life was to declare Malinda's "death." Thus to escape the guilt of bigamy, by declaring himself a widower to slavery, Bibb wrote his autobiography as an elaborate bill of divorce intended to clinch his case for freedom from the wife of his youth.

But what of the fate of his daughter? How could Bibb resolve the problem of his relationship to her? There was no declarative means of dissolving the ties that held her "bone of [his] bone, and flesh of [his] flesh." The only way that Bibb could approach the future unencumbered by moral responsibility to and for her was to let her die an undeclared death in his narrative. The last we know of her is that she was with her mother in 1845. After this, she disappears into silence, a kind of narrative repression. To continue futilely to speak the "obnoxious word" of her fate as a slave would leave this narrative unresolved and defeat its creator's self-liberating purpose. For this reason Mary Frances must be entombed in the record of the past so that her father's autobiography can close around her and her mother—instead of Henry Bibb.

The last important fugitive slave narrative of the 1840s was James W. C. Pennington's *The Fugitive Blacksmith*, a road narrative that confronted directly and dramatically a problem that had been debated with increasing regularity during the decade—to what lengths could one justifiably go in pursuit or defense of freedom? On the heels of the Nat Turner insurrection, Garrisonian abolitionists took a pacifistic stand against violence and argued that "moral purity," not "physical resistance," was the only right and lasting way to combat the "moral corruption" of slavery. "We reject and entreat the oppressed to reject the use of all carnal weapons for deliverance from bondage; relying solely upon those which are spiritual and mighty through God to the pulling down of strongholds."[75] By the 1840s, however, some abolitionists had stopped drawing lines between carnal and spiritual weapons. In 1844 Amos Phelps, a white Boston minister, confided in a letter to Charles Torrey, later an abolitionist martyr, "I agree with you fully in the doctrine that the slave laws & all other wicked laws, are to be habitually & everywhere *disobeyed*. In their *requirements & prohibitions they are in equity & before God, a nullity and to be treated as such.*"[76] The Reverend Henry Highland Garnet, one of the most militant of the black abolitionists of the period, counselled a more extreme policy than civil disobedience based on an appeal to the higher laws of God. In an address to a national Negro convention in 1843, Garnet exhorted his countrymen in chains to "let your motto be resistance! *resistance*! RESISTANCE!" While he was convinced that it was preferable to "*die freemen* [rather] *than live to be slaves*," the New York minister stopped short of calling for outright revolution against the master class. "What kind of resistance you had better make, you must decide by the circumstances that surround you, and according to the suggestion of expedience."[77] Let it be ethical or expedient, the idea of the justifiability of overt, perhaps even forcible, resistance to slavery was steadily gaining open adherence among abolitionists in the 1840s. It remained for the slave narrator to flesh out in specific, human terms the conflict between morality and expedience that the problem of resistance to slavery entailed. At stake was the conversion of white moral indignation into sympathetic identification with a fugitive slave resister.

Douglass's *Narrative* depicted forcible resistance to a tyrant like Edward Covey as a heroic gesture. When the choice was between manhood or utter degradation, Douglass extolled the rightness of resistance in self-defense. Here expedience and morality coincided, but in the autobiographies of Brown, Bibb, and Pennington, the choices became less clear-cut. Sandford's mode of self-defense might have been estimably expedient, but it was not justifiable, William W. Brown concluded, implying that there had to be some moral brake on expedience in a slave's resistance to injustice. Henry Bibb wrestled with but could not resolve independently the problem of the moral priority of self-interest versus family responsibility when the slave resister happened to be a husband and a father. Pennington, a Presbyterian minister in New York, pictured his flight to freedom in 1827 as "my *Exodus*" from slavery,[78] thereby appropriating scriptural precedent for his act of resistance to slavery. He went so far as to argue that "the exodus of the slaves from the South" by means similar to his own was "the divinely ordered method for the effectual destruction of American slavery." Fugitives had "the right of the question upon Christian principles," when "God, the spirit of peace, the love of order, and the spirit of liberty say to us, come out from among them."[79] But when "the spirit of peace" clashed with "the spirit of liberty" on the road, could expedience and self-interest take precedence over "Christian principles"? This was the problem that Pennington addressed himself to in *The Fugitive Blacksmith*. He designed his autobiography as "an humble harbinger to prepare and keep the way open" for whites to sympathize with fugitives like himself.[80] To open the way, Pennington had to open up key words in slave experience to new definitions freed from the contexts that had traditionally determined their meanings and moral connotations.

Pennington's narrative draws on the tradition of the black spiritual autobiography to recount the rise of an untutored slave artisan in Maryland to freedom, salvation, and a preaching vocation in the North. Like Henry Bibb, Pennington was haunted by guilt over the repercussions of his flight to Pennsylvania at the age of twenty. His parents and siblings were quickly sold after he fled in order to prevent him from trying to liberate them. Later the family was permanently divided. In 1846 Pennington tried to buy the freedom of his parents "to relieve myself from liability" and "to part this world in reconciliation" with them and with God (61–62). That failing, the minister employed the underground railroad to get his father and two of his brothers to Canada. His mother died in slavery.

Pennington had worried before he fled that his family would suffer in the wake of his deed, but nothing could curb his fear that to stay in slavery any longer would leave him "self-doomed" forever. In a desperate state of mind, he set out for the North, plunged into "a deep and melancholy dream." The road was as dark and unforgiving as his psychological condition: "It was cloudy; I could not see my star, and had serious misgivings about my course" (16). Twenty-four miles north of Baltimore the fugitive's erratic trek led to his capture by farmers who judged him a runaway since he carried no free papers. This turn of events thrust Pennington into a "great moral dilemma" that remained such a "case of conscience" to him twenty years afterward that he made it the crucial event in his narrative of the road. In response to his captors' demand for the truth, Pennington had three options. "I must now do one of three things —I must refuse to speak at all, or I must communicate the fact, or I must tell an untruth" (22). The fugitive's decision was that, "the facts in this case are my private property." Consequently, the white men who wanted to know his story had "no more right to them [the facts] than a highway robber has to my purse." In their possession the facts would be worth a $200 reward. "Is not my liberty worth more to me than two hundred dollars are to them?" The answer for Pennington, as he expected it would be for his reader, was to insist that he was a freeman.

Concocting a story to explain himself, Pennington proves himself a rival to Sandford in resourcefulness, invention, and self-preservation. To keep from being jailed, the fugitive stalls the Maryland farmers with a tale about being part of a coffle of slaves traveling through Virginia to Georgia when the trader in charge took sick with smallpox. After he died along with several members of the coffle, the local whites became alarmed about the possiblity of epidemic and would have nothing to do with the remaining blacks. At that point, Pennington claims to have left the gang and headed north to "get work."

The lie achieves its purpose. "It was evidently believed by those who were present." "Several who had clustered near me moved off to a respectful distance. One or two left the bar-room, and murmured, 'better let the smallpox nigger go'" (24–25). In answer to questions about the identity of the deceased slave trader, Pennington lies so convincingly that several in his audience attest to having met this fictional character. This further satisfies his captors that he need not be further detained. Only one man remains to hold him; he proposes to take the Negro to a tavern four miles away to work as an ostler "'till we see what will turn up.'" While agreeing, the fugitive resolves on another plan—to go only part way with the man and then fight him, to the death if necessary, for his freedom. Fortunately, he does not have to go to these lengths to get away; a well-timed bit of deception the next day gives him the chance to escape into the countryside at dusk and renew his journey to Pennsylvania.

Before recounting his "final deliverance," however, Pennington as narrator feels obliged to apologize for and defend his Sandford-like behavior on the road. He imagines himself interrogated by a righteously indignant fictive reader. "If you ask me whether I had expected before I left home to gain my liberty by shedding men's blood, or breaking their limbs? I answer, no! and as evidence of this, I had provided no weapon whatever. . . . I cannot say that I expected to have the ill fortune of meeting with any human being who would attempt to impede my flight." This exonerates the fugitive from the charge of premeditating violence if necessary to the accomplishment of his own personal ends. But what of the fugitive's plans to resist to the death the "tiger-like" white men who desperately hunted him across the northern Maryland countryside? Pennington calls this "self-defense." He was "trying to escape peaceably" from men who were determined that he should not do so. They forced him into the morally questionable position of having to "gain [his] liberty by shedding men's blood." Only the slave's skillful use of deception saved him from having to act on a survival ethic whose viability remained a "case of conscience" for a Christian.

At final issue, then, was the matter of the fugitive's lie about smallpox. "If you ask me if I expected when I left home to gain my liberty by fabrications and untruths? I answer, no! my parents, slaves as they were, had always taught me, when they could, that 'truth may be blamed but cannot be shamed.'" "I had no habits of untruth," the minister maintains. But when arrested, he knew "the fatal use these men would make of *my* truth," so he concluded "that they had no more right to it than a highwayman has to a traveller's purse" (30). Did this mean that the ex-slave minister "now really believe[d] that [he] had gained [his] liberty by those lies?" Pennington's resounding "no" to this question suggests his deference to conventional ideas about honesty being the best policy and faith in the power of the truth to make one free. But previous references to "*my* truth" and "the facts" being "my private property" raise doubts about Pennington's professed allegiance to traditional notions about truth and one's moral obligations to it on "autobiographical occasions" such as the fugitive found himself in before the Maryland farmers.[81]

By calling the facts of his past "my private property," Pennington implicitly defines truth in this case as his own possession, which he may disburse in accordance with subjective considerations alone. There is no higher, absolute claim of Truth on his disposition of "*my* truth." His italicizing of the pronoun that refers truth back to a possessing self is very provocative. We may first conclude from this that no one has a moral right to the self's "private property" unless the self wishes to yield that chattel up. As a black autobiographer among suspicious whites, Pennington was not morally obliged to deal truthfully with his audience if that meant putting himself in jeopardy. On such "autobiographical occasions," self-interest takes priority over truth by claiming it, appropriating it, to its own needs. In an ultimate, that is, in a survival, sense one could lie and still be true—to oneself. Under such conditions willed autobiographical concealments and/or deceptions might be the truest form of self-expression. They would denote, through silences or false declarations, strong and creative misreadings of autobiographical facts designed to restore those facts to the self in a condition in which they could be turned to the self's existential advantage, there being no immediate moral essence preceding it in authority.

Pennington was the first slave narrator to propose and defend an idea of priorities in black autobiography that demoted facts as an independent, objective standard of truth and promoted self as a point of reference to which all facts of the past would be relative. Pennington was politic enough not to claim that *The Fugitive Blacksmith* had been written according to the rationale that let him lie about the past with justification when surrounded by the Maryland farmers. Nevertheless, he does not repudiate the idea that he attributes to himself as a fugitive, namely, that a fugitive's autobiography is his only property in a society dominated by the principle of commodity exchange and that as his "private property" the facts of his life may be disposed of with complete freedom whenever necessary. To refuse the fugitive the right to make free with the facts of his life in this fashion would be to deny the right near-sacred to bourgeois America, the right to do as one wished with one's chattel. Thus through the declarative act of defining autobiographical truth as one's inalienable private possession, Pennington, with consummate irony, turned the chattel principle to his rhetorical advantage.

In concluding the episode of his "great moral dilemma," Pennington denounces slavery as "a system which can put a man not only in peril of liberty, limb, and life itself, but which may even send him in haste to the bar of God with a lie upon his lips." This possibility would seem to make the lie a guilty matter indeed, which ought to make Pennington's next directive unnecessary: "Whatever my readers may think, therefore, of the history of events of the day, do not admire in it the fabrications; but *see* in it the impediments that often fall into the pathway of the flying bond-man." Slavery "tempt[ed] him to shed blood and lie" and thrust "evil" upon him when "he would do good" (30). That being the case, why should the narrator need to warn his readers against admiring a man who played false to the truth? The answer lies in the mixed message that emerges from this confession-celebration of the fugitive as trickster.

Like William Wells Brown, Pennington allotted more narrative space to an episode centering on his transgression of the truth than to any other single event in his autobiography. He dramatized the incident and recon-structed dialogue for it so that it could be fully appreciated (and enjoyed) by his reader. The narrator knew, as a result, that he had made it more than possible for his reader to "admire" the demonstrated ingenuity of a black autobiographical fabricator. In his role as abolitionist clergyman, Penning-ton tried to get his reader to see in the event only the "impediments" that slavery thrust in the way of the "flying bondman." But as self-celebrating autobiographer, Pennington had already shown his audience how to read the event in a much less orthodox context, wherein the mode of over-coming those impediments becomes the thing one notices and delights in. The abolitionist clergyman asks us to see himself twenty years earlier as another pathetic hero, caught up like Henry Bibb in moral dilemmas that he resolved through decisions the morality of which continued to trouble him until he confessed. But the autobiographical champion of "*my* truth" invites us to "admire" his self-possession on the road and the audacity of his appropriation of the morality of private property to pro-tect himself from becoming property. By highlighting and rationalizing such acts of freedom, Pennington removes himself as fugitive from the status of pathetic hero to a more uncertain and fluid position vis-à-vis his audience, somewhere between a rogue and a romantic, depending on how one evaluates the justifiability of his devotion to what might be called (borrowing from Quentin Anderson) his "imperial self."

As we have seen, the narratives of William Wells Brown and Henry Bibb maneuver us into a similarly unsteady relationship to their pro-tagonists. In the main, Brown, Bibb, and Pennington subscribe to the tra-ditional rhetorical strategy of antebellum black autobiography. Each tries to effect consubstantiation with the white reader by portraying himself, in Bibb's words, "as a man and not a thing," or, in Pennington's words, as just as much desirous of "justice, truth, and honor as other men." Each confesses to morally compromising behavior in slavery or on the road to freedom, but each takes steps to preserve his bond with the reader by repudiating that behavior and requesting the reader's sympathy for the slave in his excruciatingly pathetic or tragic moral dilemmas. Yet each narrator celebrates his supposedly compromised behavior in a way that implies that in the midst of his apology he feels entitled to the reader's admiration as well as the reader's forgiveness and sympathy. In these moments the autobiographer seems to savor the sufficiency of his powers of invention, performance, and manipulation, which protect and advance his (guiltily acknowledged) egoistic needs. This celebration of self-sufficiency and the power to manipulate whites works at cross-purposes to the strategy of consubstantiation. The one tends to look down from a detached self-confidence toward the reader; the other tends to play up to that reader so as to qualify for his sympathetic identification. In the self-celebratory moment, the autobiographer declares his independence from the reader; he frees himself from the bondage of his white reader's moral approval. Apart from this bond, he observes himself at his best when doing the worst and begins to hint ever more strongly at the primacy of his own standard of self-judgment. Instead of soliciting his reader's confidence, he reminds the reader of how easily he can be conned by one who understands the power of names in "this gullible age" (Brown), who remembers to keep "the bold front" and "the best side out" (Bibb), and who performs the autobiographical act according to "*my* truth" (Pennington). All this indicates that by the end of the 1840s, the slave narrative had begun to make its first tentative steps away from its white readership, whose embrace meant suppression as well as success. The most self-conscious black autobiographers were beginning to wonder openly whose truth they were to speak, thus revealing the strains to which the genre's traditional social and moral proprieties subjected them. In the next decade their successors would move further outside the margins of propriety in search of greater narrative freedom and more usable truth.

5

The Uses of Marginality,
1850–65

On July 5, 1852, Frederick Douglass delivered a Fourth of July address to a gathering of between 500 and 600 people at the Corinthian Hall in Rochester, New York. At this point in the mid-nineteenth century, the temptation to indulge in the excesses of the American jeremiad had become particularly strong for American Independence Day orators. Social and political discord prompted orators from Maine to South Carolina to lament current trends and call the nation back to the sacred text of the Constitution and the ideal of controlled progress that it sanctioned as the only means of achieving America's predestined political millennium. As sectional strife grew, the Independence Day address as a form of jeremiad appealed for national consensus by reminding the American, "'the anointed civilizer'" of the world, of his special identity as "'Liberty's chosen apostle.'"[1] Douglass's speech began in this vein by comparing the thirteen colonies to Israel, England to Egypt, and Independence Day to the Passover, an event that typified, Douglass told his audience, "your great deliverance" from the British Pharaoh.[2] The black speaker paid his respects to the Founding Fathers of the Republic as "statesmen, patriots and heroes." "For the good they did, and the principles they contended for, I will unite with you," he continued, "to honor their memory." However, this was about all the unity that Douglass could see between himself and those he addressed as "fellow-citizens." "Pardon me," he inquired in tones of mock innocence, "allow me to ask, why am I called upon to speak here to-day? What have I, or those I represent, to do with your national independence? Are the great principles of political freedom and of natural justice, embodied in that Declaration of Independence, extended to us? and am I therefore, called upon to bring our humble offering to the national altar, and to confess the benefits and express gratitude for the blessings resulting from your independence to us?" (367). The movement from innocence to sarcasm in the tone of these rhetorical questions suggests that although Douglass knew what was expected of him, he would not play his appointed part in a Fourth of July ritual of national consensus. He would no longer pretend, as the end of his 1845 autobiographical "offering to the national altar" had implied, that he was one with the chosen and the free. It was no longer the affinity but "the disparity between us" that he hammered home to his 1852 American audience.

This day of celebration "is *yours* not *mine*," Douglass maintained. He punned ironically on not being "included within the pale of this glorious anniversary!" Everything about Independence Day "only reveals the immeasurable distance between us" (368). Thus he could not identify himself with the chosen people of the American jeremiad, but rather with the captive people of Psalm 137. America was not a new Jerusalem but a corrupt Babylon by whose rivers a captive people wept in their chains and alienation. "'How can we sing the Lord's song in a strange land?'" Douglass asked in the words of the psalmist. His answer was to call for a song with the power of "the storm, the whirlwind, and the earthquake." The estrangement of black people from the promise of America was not being ameliorated but exacerbated. "By an act of the American Congress, not yet two years old, slavery has been nationalized in its most horrible and revolting form." The opposition between North and South, on which Douglass's 1845 *Narrative* had rested much of its faith in American progress, had disappeared in the Compromise of 1850. "By that act, Mason & Dixon's line has been obliterated; New York has become as Virginia." "The power to hold, hunt, and sell men, women, and children as slaves" had become "co-extensive with the star-spangled banner and American Christianity" (375). Should a man in Douglass's position continue to abide by the proprieties of discourse, hoping somehow "to make a favorable impression on the public mind"? Should he "argue more, and denounce less," "persuade more, and rebuke less"?

At this late date in the antislavery crusade, Douglass had concluded that there was nothing left to be argued. "Must I undertake to prove that the slave is a man?" This had been the burden of black American orators and writers, especially in autobiography, for more than half a century, and Douglass was convinced that "that point is conceded," even by the slavocracy. If the slave were not "a moral, intellectual and responsible being," the slave states would not punish his or her disobedience to authority so severely, as seventy-two capital offenses in Virginia's slave code plainly bore witness. "Must I argue the wrongfulness of slavery?" Douglass asked further. "Is that a question for Republicans?" "The time for such argument is past," he pronounced; what was needed was "scorching irony, not convincing argument," "not light," but "fire, . . . not the gentle shower, but thunder" (371). Thus Douglass uttered his own version of that "NO! in thunder" for which Herman Melville had so extravagantly praised Nathaniel Hawthorne's "power of blackness" a year earlier. But if Hawthorne's imagination was fired by a "Calvinistic sense of Innate Depravity and Original Sin," Douglass's literary nay-saying in the 1850s emerged from a less cosmic and intellectual, and a more social and experiential, vision of what Melville called "the absolute condition of present things." Melville saw Hawthorne (and himself) seeking answers to "the Problem of the Universe" in "the blackness of darkness beyond" the boundaries of American intellectual orthodoxy and literary decorum. During a parallel renaissance in Afro-American letters of the 1850s, figures like Douglass sought answers to the Problem of America by undertaking similar critiques of mainstream thinking, written from the perspective of marginal observers. From 1850 to 1865, Afro-American autobiography played a crucial role in the revelation of a "blackness beyond" the margins of previous literary discourse, whether by white or Negro Americans.[3] To signify and interpret the shadowy borders of other-consciousness became increasingly the central concern of black autobiography in the crisis years leading up to the Civil War.

The year 1850 was a turning point in Afro-American history, a time when blacks felt obliged to engage in radical reassessments of their traditional sociopolitical and rhetorical strategies. The compromise passed by Congress in September of that year included the infamous Fugitive Slave Act designed "to insure a speedier return of runaway bondsmen to the South; any claimant who could establish affidavit proof of ownership before a special federal commissioner could take possession of a Negro." The former slave had no recourse to judicial hearing or jury trial. Proof of ownership might not amount to anything more than a sworn statement from a white person alleging a Negro's former status as a slave. Federal officers were empowered to demand the aid of any citizen in the enforcement of the law and could fine or imprison anyone who impeded disposition of the law.[4] The rescues of Shadrach (Frederick Wilkins) in Boston and Jerry McHenry in Syracuse soon after the Fugitive Slave Act went into effect illustrated the willingness with which the more militant black and white abolitionists would defy the government in the name of principle.[5] Nevertheless, the upshot of the passage of the "kidnapping law," as many blacks termed it, was the conclusion advanced from many segments of the northern black community that there was no place for the Negro in America.

The most vociferous proponents of this view were early black nationalists like H. Ford Douglass (no relation to Frederick) and Martin R. Delany, both of whom argued that blacks should emigrate to Central or South America or to Africa rather than remain in a country that did not want them. These men embraced exile as a badge of honor to be worn only by those who had finally learned to reject the lie that was America. H. Ford Douglass affirmed his right to hate his own government "because it treats me as an ALIEN and a STRANGER." An "outcast" from the Atlantic to the Pacific shores, he said he was willing to forget home and country and as an exile "seek on other shores the freedom which has been denied me in the land of my birth."[6] Delany's experience as a civil rights activist and antislavery journalist led him to predict that Central and South America would become the future homes of the Afro-American. In *The Condition, Elevation, Emigration and Destiny of the Colored People of the United States* (1852), he surveyed the racial status quo and found no real difference between the situation of southern slaves and northern freemen. The latter "occupy the very same position politically, religiously, civilly and socially, (with but few exceptions,) as the bondman occupies in the slave States." The "true condition" of black people in America was "as mere nonentities among the citizens, and excrescences on the body politic." Identityless and alienated, blacks could not expect their supposed friends in the antislavery movement to help them reverse the situation. Twenty years in the movement had left Delany with the disillusioning conclusion that freemen occupied "a mere secondary, underling position" in the eyes of white abolitionists. It was time, therefore, to "express our mind freely, and with candor" and to ignore "the custom of concealing information upon vital and important subjects, in which the interest of the people is involved." When William Lloyd Garrison accused Delany of advocating separatism, the proud black man showed just how far he was prepared to separate himself from the American Christian ethos: "I have no hopes in this country—no confidence in the American people—with a *few* exceptions—therefore, I have written as I have done. Heathenism and Liberty, before Christianity and Slavery."[7]

The Fugitive Slave Act made Canadian emigrants out of approximately 20,000 black Americans in the decade of the 1850s;[8] no one is sure how many fled to sanctuary in Central and South America at that time. The heightened emigrationist mood in black America gave rise to a new form of first-person writing in Afro-American letters—the narrative of travel and exploration. This new genre evolved out of the European travel correspondence, amounting to almost weekly reports, that prominent ex-slaves published in the American abolitionist press, similar to the letters that correspondents for larger dailies wrote for American readers who could not afford to tour the Old World themselves. Frederick Douglass and William Wells Brown were the first of these correspondents. Their letters from abroad—Douglass's in 1846–47 and Brown's in 1849–51—anticipated the perspective and tone of the increasingly alienated black autobiographer of the 1850s and 1860s.

The most salient of Douglass's letters was the one he wrote to the *Liberator* on New Year's Day, 1846, from Belfast during a triumphant speaking tour of the British Isles. The recently published *Narrative* had been hailed in England, and the welcome he received from practically everyone, in contrast to the threats and anxiety the fugitive had known in America, primed Douglass for a comparative estimate of the two countries. What is remarkable is the divergence of this letter from the *Narrative*'s image and assessment of America and Douglass's place in it. His "prejudices in favor of America," Douglass announced to Garrison, had all but disappeared because in the United States "all is cursed with the infernal spirit of slaveholding." Even in "the Northern states," the black man was "doomed by an inveterate prejudice against color to insult and outrage on every hand." As a result Douglass declared himself "an outcast from the society of my childhood, and an outlaw in the land of my birth." Once in England, Douglass proclaims, "Behold the change. . . . I breathe, and lo! the chattel becomes a man." Echoing the rhetoric of the turning point of the *Narrative*—"You have seen how a man was made a slave; you shall see how a slave was made a man"—Douglass updates the crucial transformation of his life to England, well beyond Covey's farm. Outside America "I seem to have undergone a transformation. I live a new life." "I gaze around in vain for one who will question my equal humanity."

Beyond the boundaries of America and his restricted situation in it, this newly "transformed" Douglass sets about immediately revising the version of his northern past that the closing pages of the *Narrative* had pictured so positively. He calls up a series of humiliating episodes in Massachusetts when he was refused admission to popular entertainments, public conveyances, a worship service, and an eating establishment, in each case because, in the words Douglass attributes to his refusers, "*We don't allow niggers in here'!*" The line becomes a bitter refrain for Douglass in the letter, driving home his sense of not belonging "in here"—in America, North or South. The letter ends with his entering Eaton Hall in Liverpool, "the residence of the Marquis of Westminster, one of the most splendid buildings in England," the traveler proudly notes, where neither servant nor aristocrat treats him as an alien. In England, Douglass asserts, "They measure and esteem men according to their moral and intellectual worth, and not according to the color of their skin."[9]

William Wells Brown's Anglophilic *Three Years in Europe* (1852), the first travel book to be published by a black American, exceeded Douglass's

travel letters in its identification with things English. Brown's loosely connected narrative, composed primarily of sight-seeing letters and sketches,
pictures the black exile very much at home in Europe, where caste and
color are not determinants of personal worth or success. Intent on self-
improvement, Brown visits the shrines of the guidebooks—the Crystal
Palace, Westminster Abbey, Versailles, and various cathedrals and castles
in France, Ireland, and Scotland—and hobnobs with aristocrats and prominent intellectuals like Harriet Martineau. From the freedom of its press to
the manners of its people and the beauty of its women, Europe becomes
a standard of civilization to which the land of slavery cannot measure up.
After three years of being treated as a man, not an inferior or an alien,
Brown thinks of America as a foreign land whose bigotry places it outside
the sphere of civilization as defined by the European norm. England displaces the United States as "indeed, the 'land of the free, and the home of
the brave.'" [10]

Despite the fact that Brown had come to feel himself "an Englishman
by habit, if not by birth," he returned to America in November 1854, after
a total of five years of "ease and comfort abroad." In *The American Fugitive in Europe: Sketches of Places and People Abroad* (1854), Brown explained why he had come back to the nation that had spurned him. It was
because of his allegiance to "more than three millions of my countrymen
. . . groaning in the prison-house of slavery." It is significant that Brown
should have referred to the slaves as "my countrymen," for from the point
of view of the U.S. government, the American slave was as much a "man
without a country" as a fugitive slave like Brown. By renaming slaves as
"countrymen," Brown invests them with an identity as a *people*, his
people, who *belong* somewhere, in a country to which the wandering
black fugitive gravitates at the end of his narrative. To reclaim his people
and regain that as yet undefined country, Brown says that he must relinquish the role of alienated "spectator" and become instead a "soldier" in
"moral warfare" against American "oppression." [11] We shall see that black
autobiographers of the 1850s often fought as much like guerrillas as conventional warriors of the pen, particularly because the liberation of their
psychosocial country from oppressive America necessitated first the creation of a cultural infrastructure on the margins of the dominant culture,
which would then make possible the assertion of Afro-America's raison
d'être and independence from the other America.

Subsequent antebellum black travel narratives do not yield very revealing glimpses into the structure of values and codes of signification that
the travel writings of Douglass and Brown imply. The cycle of departure
from and return to America is not portrayed as a time of self-discovery; it
is primarily the frame in which a pragmatic job of foreign promotion is

done. Little thought seems to have been given to the meaning of country and the problematic relationship of the American Negro to his roots, whether sought in North America, the Caribbean, or West Africa. Black explorers and travelers after Douglass and Brown set out on their journeys for a comparatively simple reason: they wanted to find a home for black emigrants. They devoted most of their literary efforts to extolling the opportunities of and scotching the myths about Liberia or the Caribbean Islands.[12] However, none of these writers had sufficient literary skill to make life outside America's borders seem attractive enough to warrant the abandonment of all that blacks had fought for in the United States. Many black leaders, among them Frederick Douglass, felt that to emigrate was to capitulate to white racist hopes of marginalizing the free Negro population right out of the country, the better to leave slavery undisturbed. Thus, even though Robert Campbell, a Delany protégé, tried to present his travels in central Africa as "a pilgrimage to my motherland," such a mission looked too much like a gesture of acquiescence to the alien status that racist America had been trying to impose on Afro-Americans for generations. The large majority of black writers of the 1850s and 1860s agreed with the National Negro Convention of 1853, which proclaimed: "We are Americans, and as Americans, we would speak to Americans," not as "aliens" or "exiles" but as "American citizens asserting their right on their own native soil."[13]

Four years later, however, the fragile hope that blacks could still assert their rights as Americans in their native land was crushed by the Dred Scott decision. The opinion of the U.S. Supreme Court, rendered by Chief Justice Roger B. Taney, was summarized in one infamous phrase that rang through the land: the Negro "had no rights which the white man was bound to respect." Taney asserted that Negro inferiority was a "fixed and universal" view in the Western world that determined that blacks were "altogether unfit to associate with the white race, either in social or political relations." The states of the Union might grant to their black denizens certain rights and protections, but as far as the U.S. Constitution was concerned, blacks had been barred from the beginning of the country onward from membership in the national "political family." Thus blacks were "not included . . . under the word 'citizens' in the Constitution," nor could they claim "the rights and privileges which that instrument provides for and secures to citizens of the United States." To Dred Scott, the Missouri slave who had sued for his freedom on the grounds that a slave transported into a free state or territory becomes a free man, the Taney decision meant a return to bondage. To abolitionists, the decision meant that the Missouri Compromise of 1820 had become a dead letter and slavery had been nationalized for all practical purposes. To Afro-

Americans, the Supreme Court had put the finishing touches on the national campaign of the decade—the complete political and social alienation of blacks from a common American identity with whites.

Robert Purvis called the decision a confirmation of the "well known fact" that under "the Constitution and the Government of the United States, the colored people are nothing, and can be nothing but an alien, disfranchised and degraded class." Another prominent black Garrisonian, Charles L. Remond, echoed Purvis's bitter denunciation of the U.S. government and stigmatized as "mean-spirited and craven" any Negro who persisted in claiming citizenship under a Constitution that treated people of color with such contempt. Having broken with the Garrisonians by this time over the question of whether the Constitution sanctioned slavery, Frederick Douglass argued that blacks should not spurn the Constitution solely because bad men had perverted it. It was "the wicked pride, love of power, and selfish perverseness of the American people" that had to be reformed, not the Constitution. News of slave revolts in the South assured Douglass that the Supreme Court's "open rebellion against God's government" could not stand. "The essential nature of things"—the right of every human being to liberty—could not be permanently reversed by Taney's words or James Buchanan's election. "The court of common sense and common humanity" would yet hear the Afro-American's plea for justice. No one could "close up against him the ear of a sympathizing world, nor shut up the Court of heaven." [14]

The dispiriting decade of the 1850s, therefore, demanded that many articulate and thoughtful blacks face the implications of the fundamentally alienated status of Afro-Americans in the United States. For years black writers, especially in autobiography, had hoped that once whites recognized the degree to which blacks identified with American religious, political, and moral ideals, the gap between the races could be closed and the Negro could be accepted as "a man and brother." But legislative and legal outrages like the Fugitive Slave Act and the Dred Scott decision seemed to preclude the consubstantiating rhetorical strategy of traditional black autobiography. As Frederick Douglass stated in 1852, there was no need to continue to argue over whether the southern slave was a man. By 1857 the issue had become whether the northern black freeman had not been de-Americanized into de facto slavery. Did the freeman have a national identity by virtue of his birth in the United States, or had he been rendered a nullity by virtue of his blackness? Should he re-identify himself, in accordance with the name of a black newspaper founded in Cleveland in 1853, as the *Aliened American*? [15] Through its history, black autobiography had celebrated lives of transition from outside in, from the marginality of sinfulness and slavery to a merging with the religious and socioeconomic mainstream of freedom and dignity. Could such a myth be maintained in the America of the 1850s? Much depended on the way black autobiographers interpreted the opposition of marginality and plenitude around which the genre's myth of assimilation had traditionally been structured.

Before mid-century the dominant myths of acculturation and assimilation in black autobiography posit the Afro-American, especially when marked as "structurally inferior" by slavery, as a descendant of Cain, the cursed and banished son, whose quest for self-realization and fulfillment requires that he gain admission into the charmed circle of an American identity. The system of slavery, in the view of most slave narrators, demands that the bondsman be thought of and think of himself as an "outsider, inhabiting a state permanently outside the social structure," yet regulated by it and dependent on it. The more thoughtful narratives of the 1830s and 1840s, however, argue that far from being the radical alien, the slave was actually a fundamental component of the social structure. Indeed, the slave was literally the basis on which the entire class and caste structure rested.

A great problem as well as a valuable opportunity for the slave was that his position in that social system had not been categorically defined, despite all the attempts to institutionalize it in southern law. The structure of caste and class was not fixed except in the abstractions of the statute books. In reality, the paternalistic model of the master-slave relationship that many slaveholders at least professed to follow lent a certain flexibility to institutionalized southern racism and the caste structure. The narratives of Douglass, Brown, and Josiah Henson, for instance, show that some slaves created for themselves a degree of social and economic mobility within the system. Such men realized that they were, in effect, interstitial figures in the social structure, identified primarily by an indefinite and often precarious position "betwixt and between all fixed points of classification." When a slave like Douglass wondered why, if he was qualified to labor as a man, he was not qualified to be rewarded as a man, that slave was confronting the tormenting contradictions of his own interstitiality. The slave realized that he was not other at the same time that he recognized that he had been rendered marginal, to both his advantage and disadvantage. When Douglass received Hugh Auld's permission to hire his time, he knew it was a "privilege," "a step toward freedom to be allowed to bear the responsibilities of a freeman." At the same time, such a privilege reminded Douglass cruelly of his own marginal condition: "I endured all the evils of a slave, and suffered all the care and anxiety of a freeman." In the larger analysis, however, the realization of his own forced marginality in bondage taught many a slave narrator a crucial truth early in life. His enslavement was not the result of his being essentially inferior to the human family or structurally alien to the forms and mores of human society. Enslavement had been the means of marginalizing the Afro-American into the condition of not knowing who he was essentially or what her rightful status ought to be, so as to shape him or her into the most adaptable instruments for white manipulation.[16]

In abolitionist literature by both blacks and whites, the enslaved black is often termed a "degraded" person, suggesting that he or she has been reduced in dignity from some prior standard that might have been maintained had normal conditions and opportunities applied. What is this standard from which the slave had been alienated at birth? Invariably, in the years before mid-century, when the slave narrative measures the slave's incompleteness as a total self, the standard of wholeness is that of the white implied reader, the truly democratic, Christ-imitating American. The monstrous marginality of the degraded slave is contrasted to and understood in terms of the presumed plenitude of the American democratic ideal, the free man who has the inalienable right to his own life, liberty, and pursuit of happiness. Consequently, the consubstantiating rhetoric of the great slave narratives of the 1840s says to the American implied reader: Compare my life, my values, my expression—all that signifies my self—to the ideals you hold dear as an American. Have I not realized those ideals in this life and in this discourse that you read? Slave narratives like Douglass's, Brown's, and Henson's portray the black other's divestiture of his own marginality through autobiographical acts designed to reidentify him as a fulfillment of the essence of Christian American selfhood. Though the nation may fail to recognize this and afford him its full respect and protection as a citizen, the black autobiographer before 1850 usually rests his case for personhood and justice on proof that he was no stranger to, but in all essential ways the personification of, the principles (though not the current application) of the New Testament and the Declaration of Independence.

Events like the Fugitive Slave Act and the Dred Scott decision made it increasingly problematic for black autobiographers of the 1850s to talk about escaping the marginality of southern slavery and fulfilling themselves within the structure of perverted northern democracy. It was clear enough that above the Mason-Dixon line the black freeman was being systematically remarginalized and divested of his American rights and identity. The depletion rather than the completion of self seemed to be the theme of his story as long as his standard of measuring civil and social selfhood remained in alignment with the predominant culture. Blacks during the 1850s and 1860s continued to protest these trends, but the most important development in black autobiography is the decision to explore the uses of marginality rather than simply to deplore the fate of the marginal black man or woman. Among the mid-century autobiographers we may identify three kinds of narrators who both identify with and make rhetorical use of Afro-American marginality.

The large majority of autobiographers narrate or, in some performative manner, act in and through their texts to establish an outside vantage point from which to analyze and criticize the circle of privileged assumptions and standards on which the perverse idea of America as plenitude was based. This effort to get outside the boundaries of the thought and discourse that governed American writing on race can be seen as an attempt to resolve the classic double consciousness of the Afro-American in some new plenitude, some higher sphere of value to which America's ideals have only a peripheral relationship. Some of these autobiographers, like the travel writers we have already glanced at, record literal journeys outside and beyond America and all it represents. Others undertake psychological and intellectual quests for standards of manhood or selfhood that do not defer to what were increasingly regarded as alien white ideals. We encounter in some of these narratives a search within as well as without for truly indigenous standards of valuation independent of white precedents or proprieties.

I shall term these autobiographers *outsiders manqué* because none attained a fully detached and liberated perspective on the American plenitude, despite their varied strategies of dissociation from it. The result of the aspiring outsider's narrative is to project himself into a marginal relationship with the American plenitude, not to identify himself with something distinct or more inclusive. What may seem at first a new plenitude is revealed as only a reformed supplement of a former plenitude; what seems to be discovery turns out to be recovery; heading outside seems to be just another way of heading inside. Because of the "law of supplementarity," narrators bent on escaping the imprisoning plenitude find themselves caught up in an endless, linked chain of clanging, contradictory variations on all too familiar themes.[17] Led by Samuel Ringgold Ward, these writers were at their best in exposing facets of the perverse American plenitude in a language and tone that few before them had dared to use. Yet the problem of telling a free story within the American "prison-house of language" was not something that these writers reckoned with. As a result, their metaphors and myths and in some cases their own unguarded honesty about themselves compromised the very writers who spoke out most strongly for non-compromise.

A second and much smaller group of writers, which I shall term the *interstitial* autobiographers, depict themselves as "betwixt and between" standard identifying classifications and norms, whether they are recalling their situations in the South or the North. In the cracks and crevices of the social hierarchy, the interstitial figure creates his own fluid status and unlikely freedom. On the boundaries of behavior, he reveals to us what Martin Heidegger meant when he said that "boundary is not that at which something stops but . . . that from which something *begins its essential unfolding*." Such figures mediate and often reverse the binary oppositions that define differences between the hierarchical states to which they are marginal. Contrary to the conventional wisdom, which believed that marginal figures like the octoroon were psychologically disjoined by their dual origins and identifications, the interstitial figure often defies expectations by conjoining and, we might say, confusing that which culture and society demand remain separate, distinct, and valorized according to rank. The most familiar manifestation of this figure in black autobiography is the trickster, who repeatedly confounds and makes a chaos of the enclosing norms of slavocratic culture. By mid-century, however, a slave narrator like Jacob D. Green pushed the tradition of the trickster beyond the limits that William Wells Brown would take it; Green would celebrate himself as the violator of black, as well as white, social taboos. We will need to consider seriously the function and possible purpose of such a trickster narrative, in particular its uses in the creation of what Victor Turner has called "communitas," that is, a "direct, immediate, and total confrontation of human identities" within a model of society that is unstructured and not "segmentalized into roles and statuses."[18]

One might also describe as marginal a third group of autobiographers who review their past from the standpoint of the *liminal* stage of personal or social development. The structure of black autobiography, like that of much first-person writing, often buttresses Arnold van Gennep's analysis of the "rites of passage" that inform the crises of life that individuals in many cultures must negotiate in order to cross thresholds from one status to another. In the first half of the nineteenth century, for instance, the slave narrative usually takes shape in conformity to the three rites of passage van Gennep made familiar: the "rite of separation" (the slave's resistance to his status and flight from it), the "rite of transition" (the period of lonely fugitiveship, defined as neither slave nor freeman), and the "rite of incorporation" (when the fugitive attains social validation in the North, perhaps via marriage, antislavery work, or purchasing his freedom).[19] Between 1850 and 1865 the slave narrative did not diverge radically from this plot structure, but the transitional or liminal phase of Afro-American passage tends to expand, if not crowd out, the climactic "rite of incorporation" in key texts like Douglass's *My Bondage and My Freedom* and Harriet Jacobs's *Incidents in the Life of a Slave Girl*.

Given the deepening sense of frustration and injustice expressed by Afro-Americans in the 1850s, it is not surprising to discover black autobiographers increasingly depicting their fugitive careers as a lingering limbo of dreams deferred, not as a linear quest leading to a new world. Ironic reversal becomes a basic motif of the liminal autobiographer. Nevertheless, an insistence on the advantages of liminality, as well as its discontents, becomes one of the strategies of reversal that such an autobiographer plays on his comfortably situated reader.

Autobiography may perform several functions for blacks caught in this kind of marginal condition. First, the pen of the writer may carve out a category of Afro-American experience in between the presumed plenitudes of property and person, bondage and freedom. Second, the narrative may realize and justify, through language acts, the state of liminality as a condition of psycholiterary freedom, irrespective of its indefinite sociopolitical status. Finally, the writing of such autobiography may enact its own [w]rite of transition, allowing the liminal narrator to pass over various thresholds into a new relationship with his or her reading audience. In the present chapter, in which we will concentrate on the narratives of outsiders manqué, we will not see autobiography put to such venturesome purposes as the interstitial and liminal writers, whom we discuss in Chapter 6, create for the genre. We begin in this chapter with a look at various manifestations of the outsider perspective and literary program at mid-century, leading up to Samuel Ringgold Ward's compelling account of his own frustrated escape from marginality. In the next chapter, the work of Jacob D. Green, Frederick Douglass, and Harriet Jacobs will reveal the usefulness of autobiography's own marginal character to three blacks at mid-century whose literary priorities—freedom of expression over facts of experience—pushed their narratives beyond generic borders into "fictions of factual representation."

In the early 1850s Harriet Beecher Stowe provided a powerful impetus to the revolution of literary priorities that would impel black autobiographers further and further away from white precedents. Liberal whites in America and England, longing for a standard by which to judge slavery and comprehend that exotic being, "the Negro," embraced *Uncle Tom's Cabin* as a kind of literary plenitude. From its appearance in 1851, the image of Uncle Tom took precedence in the popular mind over all previous black portraiture in American literature, including the tradition of self-portraiture built up in the slave narrative. Stowe's saintly hero outdid Josiah Henson, whom the novelist dubbed as one of Tom's prototypes, in self-renunciation. The Byronic George Harris of the novel exceeded his presumed models, Lewis Clarke and Frederick Douglass, in steely-eyed, intrepid self-determination. Critics who denounced the one-sided characterization of whites and blacks in the novel did not bother the millions in America and Europe who took Tom and Cassy and Topsy and George and Eliza Harris to heart. Reviewers in *Putnam's* and the London *Times* insisted that *Uncle Tom's Cabin* was singular in its delineation of character and its "scope of observation" of southern American life. The London *Times* reviewer found much to doubt and deplore in the novel, but this he was confident of: "We know of no book in which the negro character finds such successful interpretation, and appears so life-like and so fresh."

One indication of the immense conviction with which the novel was received is the amount of "anti-Tom" fiction that was published to disprove Stowe's version of "life among the lowly." The slight attention that almost all of these books received, when compared to the international readership of *Uncle Tom's Cabin*, is testimony to the completeness with which Stowe's image of black life and character in the South carried the day. The "romantic racialism" of Stowe's images of Uncle Tom, Aunt Chloe, the converted Sambo and Quimbo, and Topsy prepared her reader sentimentally for her particular program for the emancipation and education of the slave in the North, followed by his resettlement in Africa. Stowe's portrait of the Negro suggested that he or she would willingly emigrate to Africa after having received "the educating advantages of Christian republican society and schools." This "outcast race" did not demand a permanent home in America, only a temporary "refuge" where it could attain "moral and intellectual maturity" before working out its providential destiny as Christianizers of Africa. In other words, America provided the African his spiritual rite of passage to full moral and intellectual maturity—which was then to be exercised outside America. By implication, Uncle Tom's martyrdom signalled the passing of his spiritual test, his achievement of full moral maturity in the South, whereupon he could die and be "incorporated" (to use van Gennep's term) into heaven. George Harris's spiritual test would be completed only with his incorporation in Africa. This was clearly the most comforting and popular way for white America to think about black liminality in the crisis years of the mid-nineteenth century. Stowe's myth reconciled black progress with black alienation without threatening the white status quo.[20]

The black literary community was divided in its reaction to the Uncle Tom phenomenon. At the Rochester Colored National Convention of 1853, Frederick Douglass, speaking for the Committee on Declaration of Sentiments, spoke warmly of the novel as divinely inspired. William Wells Brown happily reported the salutary effect of *Uncle Tom's Cabin* on the British conscience in the *Liberator*.[21] What troubled some black abolitionists, however, was the inapplicability of the morality of Uncle Tom to their own sense of a freeman's sociopolitical mission in the North. Writing from the safety of England, where he had fled early in 1853 after having married a white woman in New York,[22] William G. Allen welcomed the celebrated novel as a "wonder of wonders." He especially favored the book's acknowledgment of color prejudice among supposed friends of the slave in the North. The former literature professor thought the simple Tom "a good old soul" but too "perfectly pious." Allen himself confessed to "more of 'total depravity.'" He told Douglass, "I believe, as you do, that it is not light the slaveholder wants, but fire, and he ought to have it," even if it meant "resistance" to the death.[23] Martin R. Delany insisted that however ably and "pathetically" Stowe had depicted "some of the sufferings of the slave," the best that could be said of her with regard to the northern freeman was she "*knows nothing about us.*" Delany concluded, in fact, that her colonization plan disclosed her callous attitude toward the "thrice-morally crucified, semi-free Negro in the North."[24] Allen's identification of Douglass as a native standard of heroism, whose perpetual resistance to slavery was quite distinct from that of Uncle Tom or the expatriate Harris, complements in at least one sense Delany's skepticism about the sensitivity of Stowe or the relevance of her book to the actual situation of free blacks. These responses to *Uncle Tom's Cabin*, as soon as its impact on white consciousness could be foreseen, point to a campaign of literary revisionism in black autobiography of the 1850s, an unacknowledged but evident effort to prevent Stowe's novel from becoming a literary plenitude, the final statement on black character and the black experience in America.

About a year after *Uncle Tom's Cabin* was published, the narrative of Solomon Northup, a free-born black New Yorker who had been kidnapped in Washington, D.C., and sold to a succession of Louisiana slaveowners, became the first of several slave autobiographies to promise to outdo Stowe in the full factual reportage of slavery. The kidnapping and sale of free blacks had been protested in the *Liberator* for two decades,[25] but *Twelve Years a Slave* was unique in its detailed, unchallenged account of not only the outrage but also the restoration of the abused black man to his family. Moreover, the book was dedicated to Mrs. Stowe and invited comparision to *Uncle Tom's Cabin*, as several reviewers were quick to note, if for no other reason than that the Red River plantation where Northup had been a captive was located in the same region in which Uncle Tom had suffered and died under the lash of Simon Legree.[26] Northup's ghostwriter, David Wilson, did not let the first page of the narrative go by without both capitalizing on the fame of Stowe's novel and using it as a precedent that his own book would try to surpass. The narrator of *Twelve*

Years a Slave remarks approvingly on "the increasing interest throughout the Northern States, in regard to the subject of Slavery. Works of fiction [such as *Uncle Tom's Cabin*], professing to portray its features in their more pleasing as well as more repugnant aspects, have been circulated to an extent unprecedented, and, as I understand, have created a fruitful topic of comment and discussion." Against the background of this discussion based on "works of fiction," the narrator's object, he claims, is simply "to repeat the story of my life, without exaggeration, leaving it for others to determine, whether even the pages of fiction present a picture of more cruel wrong or a severer bondage."

Hard at work on *The Key to Uncle Tom's Cabin* when *Twelve Years a Slave* came out, Stowe cited the new narrative, as she had most of the other famous slave autobiographies, as further proof of the reliability of her novel. She stressed that Northup's account of Red River plantation life formed "a striking parallel to that history" of slave suffering that she had recorded in the latter pages of *Uncle Tom's Cabin*. It is equally striking to notice that in comparing Northup's autobiography to her work of fiction, Stowe labeled the latter "that history." To the difficult task of verifying "that history," the slave narrative was crucial, for narratives like Northup's contained the facts that would support and vindicate Mrs. Stowe's fictions. Thus, in *The Key to Uncle Tom's Cabin* she encouraged the reading of black autobiography as a gloss on her own novel, the more to convince people that her novel could be treated "as a reality." [27] In the process she treated the slave narrative in the familiar, circumscribed manner of her era—as a source of facts best employed as signifiers of some prior reality (slavery) or some higher reality (myths about slavery valorized by white writing). The first page of *Twelve Years a Slave*, however, suggests that this story would not play merely a supportive role in the drama of Mrs. Stowe's literary defense. Wilson virtually guarantees his reader that the memory of Solomon Northup will outstrip the imagination of Harriet Beecher Stowe in the depiction of cruel wrongs done to a slave. *Twelve Years a Slave* would challenge Stowe's capacity to tell the whole truth about slavery.

In *The Key to Uncle Tom's Cabin* Stowe admits that "for the purposes of art" she had deliberately avoided telling the entire ugly truth about slavery in her novel. The artist who wishes to "succeed" must "draw a veil" over the most "dreadful" features of slavery; the book that failed to do so "could not be read." [28] However, Northup's narrative asked to be read as "a candid and truthful statement of facts," not a work of art, implying in the process that the black autobiographer would not be inhibited in the way that the white novelist was. That is, one could assume Northup's narrative to be more accurate than Stowe's because the former implicitly promised not to "draw a veil" or otherwise observe the proprieties that Mrs. Stowe felt obliged to abide by. This statement by Wilson on Northup's behalf anticipates a new discursive contract that evolves in the autobiographies of the 1850s and 1860s. For decades the slave narrator had asked to be believed on the basis, at least in part, of his ability to restrain himself, to keep to the proprieties of discourse that required the ugliest truths of slavery to be veiled. At mid-century, however, the black autobiographer would begin to claim credibility *because* he or she had violated those same proprieties of discourse. The further this new autobiographer placed himself or herself outside the conventions of the standard discourse on slavery, the more truthful this autobiographer claimed to be. I am to be trusted, this new black narrator seemed to be saying, because what I tell you is shocking and ought not to be said. That which "could not be read" would no longer be suppressed out of a fear of its being dismissed as a lie. An ever-heightening severity of subject or tone would now be invested with the illocutionary force of authentication itself.

The more obvious cases of this new severity in mid-century slave narratives had to do with more and more horrendous testimonials of man's inhumanity to man. *Slave Life in Georgia*, dictated by John Brown to Louis Alexis Chamerovzow, secretary of the British and Foreign Anti-slavery Society, achieved the unpleasant distinction of unveiling the most appalling atrocities yet seen in Afro-American autobiography. "Many people say that half of what Mrs. Stowe and others have written about the punishments inflicted on slaves is untrue," Chamerovzow wrote on behalf of Brown. "Unfortunately it is too true; and I believe half of what is done to them never comes to light." The prose of *Slave Life in Georgia* renders the unspeakable almost commonplace. In addition to the many floggings, paddlings, brandings, and burnings recounted in his story, Brown exposed in clinical detail a manifestation of nineteenth-century racism that is particularly chilling to the consciousness of post-Holocaust readers: sickening "experiments" done on Brown himself by a renowned Georgia doctor intent on ascertaining "how deep my black skin went." [29] Slave narrators at mid-century seemed almost to vie with each other to prove William Craft's accusation against the American South, namely, that in that region "there is a greater want of humanity and high principle amongst the whites than among any other civilized people in the world." Thus the opening pages of Craft's *Running a Thousand Miles for Freedom* argues that white southerners were so degenerate that they would traffic in the persons of free white girls, if necessary, to satisfy the lust of slavery for more bodies. The official justification of slavery as the condition appointed by God for the subhuman Negro was exploded by Craft's assertion, "I have known worthless white people to sell their own free children into slavery."[30] Some slave narrators strained for shocking effects that would demand the attention of even the most indifferent reader. This was the title that leaped off the cover of William Anderson's autobiography: *Life and Narrative of William J. Anderson, Twenty-four Years a Slave; Sold Eight Times! In Jail Sixty Times!! Whipped Three Hundred Times!!!* Sexual perversion as well as sadism was prominently featured in *Louisa Picquet, the Octoroon*, which recorded the Reverend Hiram Mattison's unprecedentedly explicit interviews with a near-white former slave concubine from the Deep South.[31]

In the face of these revelations, black autobiographers became less hesitant to recommend violence as a tool of resistance to tyranny. As far as Samuel Ringgold Ward was concerned, given the history of black treatment in America, "the white has no personal claim to anything else than the most cordial hatred of the black." And yet, "Some white persons wonder at and condemn the tone in which some of us blacks speak of our oppressors." Were these whites expecting blacks to conform to the standard of Uncle Tom's pacific lovingkindness? Ward's reply was, "Such persons talk as if they knew but little of human nature, and less of Negro character, else they would wonder rather that, what with slavery and Negro-hate, the mass of us are not either depressed into idiocy or excited into demons. What class of whites, except the Quakers, ever spoke of *their* oppressors or wrongdoers as mildly as we do?" That mildness of rhetoric ended in the 1850s in a militancy of tone that prophesied and, in its extremest manifestations, advocated what the slave revolutionary hero of Delany's novel *Blake* (1859–62) called "war upon the whites."[32]

James Roberts, who claimed to have served in the Revolutionary War and to have fought in the Battle of New Orleans, offered himself in 1858 as a model of the black hero as a warrior for freedom. According to his account, Roberts, along with a number of other Natchez slaves, was recruited in 1814 by Andrew Jackson himself for the defense of New Orleans. Should the Americans win the victory, Jackson promised these slaves their freedom. Their actual reward for their valiant efforts in protecting the city, however, was betrayal and a return to bondage. When Old Hickory revealed himself a liar, Roberts says he tried to shoot his perfidious commander, only to discover that his rifle lacked priming. "Had my gun been loaded, doubtless Jackson would have been a dead man in a moment. There was no fear in my soul, at that time, of anything, neither man, death, nor mortal. The war-blood was up. I had just two days before cut off the heads of six brave Englishmen, and Jackson's life, at that moment appeared no more to me than theirs." As narrator, Roberts does not apologize for any of this; he is determined to give black "war-blood" the credit for the victory of New Orleans. In the process he exposes and displaces a national symbol of white military and political honor, President Andrew Jackson.[33]

In *My Bondage and My Freedom* Douglass offered a justification for violent slave actions, such as Roberts's act of attempted murder, that accepted the premise of the slave's structural alienation from southern society and then turned it to his advantage. After defending the slave's right to steal from his master, Douglass stated categorically: "The morality of *free* society can have no application to *slave* society. Slaveholders have made it almost impossible for the slave to commit any crime, known either to the laws of God or to the laws of man. If he steals, he takes his own; if he kills his master, he imitates only the heroes of the revolution." In his fictionalized narrative of Madison Washington, leader of a successful slave mutiny aboard the *Creole* in 1841, Douglass had his hero articulate a justification of violence that was often repeated by blacks in the 1850s. When accused by the captain of the ship of being nothing more than a murderer, Washington replies, "I am not a murderer. God is my witness that LIBERTY, not *malice*, is the motive for this night's work. I have done no more to those dead [white] men yonder, than they would have done to me in like circumstances. We have struck for our freedom, and if a true man's heart be in you, you will honor us for the deed." Samuel Ringgold Ward honored Washington as comparable not only to the American Revolutionary patriots from whom he took his name but also to the heroes of European liberation movements in the 1840s.[34]

Douglass and Ward were leaders in a campaign undertaken by more militant blacks at mid-century to prove the traditional abolitionist claim that the Negro was "a man and a brother," this time by citing his courageous use of force to seize or preserve his freedom. This was undoubtedly unsettling to many white readers in a tense time, especially when "romantic racialists" were propagandizing the essential "Negro nature" as superior to the Anglo-Saxon only in the "feminine virtues" and religious sensibility. Nevertheless, on the eve of the Civil War, this new insistence on black manhood in terms of the traditional masculine attributes of aggressive, willful self-determination helped prepare white America for the role the black soldier was to play in the coming conflict. Four years before the war, Austin Steward concluded his autobiography by prophesying that blacks were "rising" after years of oppression—"coming up to an elevated standard, and are fast gathering strength and courage, for the great and coming conflict with their haughty oppressors."[35] The rhetorical problem for the militant black writer of the 1850s was to provide a moral rationale for the use of force as an elevated standard above and beyond the Christian fortitude of Uncle Tom.

The revolutionary ideals of the civic religion of the United States, embodied in the American jeremiad's celebration of controlled violence for progressive ends, offered itself to black writers as a ready alternative to Uncle Tom's pacific pieties. Distancing Madison Washington from all that Tom represented, Douglass allied his "heroic slave" from Virginia to the principle emblazoned on the state's conquering shield: "Sic Semper Tyrannis." This black man's violence deserved the same sanction as those who led the American Revolution because he was "a man who loved liberty as well as Patrick Henry,—who deserved it as much as Thomas Jefferson,—and who fought for it with a valor as high, an arm as strong, and against odds as great, as he who led all the armies of the American colonies through the great war for freedom and independence." Douglass's strategy was designed to domesticate a violence that easily could have been judged as alien and threatening to everything from Christian morality to the law of the high seas.

William Parker's "The Freedman's Story," a narrative defense of the celebrated Christiana, Pennsylvania, Fugitive Slave Law resisters, also urged admiration of a group of blacks who fought to the death in emulation of traditional American resistance to tyranny. In flight to Canada after having shed the blood of white men, Parker, under an assumed name, strikes up a conversation with a white man on board a train to Rochester. With the Christiana shootout on everyone's lips, the fugitive asks his companion what he thinks should be done with Parker, if the authorities are successful in apprehending him. According to Parker's account of the conversation, the white New Yorker replies with hearty approval of Parker's violent defense of himself and his family against the slaveowners at his door. It doesn't matter that federal law was on the side of the slain Edward Gorsuch, who claimed Parker as his absconded property. "'Had I been in his place, I would have done as he did,'" the New Yorker continues. "'Any good citizen will say the same. I believe Parker to be a brave man; and all you colored people should look at it as we white people look at our brave men, and do as we do. You see Parker was not fighting for a country, nor for praise. He was fighting for freedom: he only wanted liberty, as other men do.'" [36] By placing this advice to blacks in the mouth of a white man, Parker was able to send a message to blacks about Afro-American standards of heroism while also obtaining the endorsement of those standards by an American citizen. Parker's plea was that, after all, he had only done what any white man would do; in respecting him, blacks would be endorsing a precedent of citizen-heroism that had already been valorized in white American civic mythology. Thus, although his act of resistance might appear to have been that of an outlaw, the author claimed the American sanction of "fighting for freedom" upheld him firmly within the boundaries of justifiable violence.

What we see in Douglass and Parker—two men bent on justifying black violation of white norms—is an almost automatic intellectual as well as rhetorical dependence on white precedent for the sanctioning of acts of black violence. At the same time that these men glorify an act of violating, of breaking out of, an imprisoning norm, namely, that of obedience to white authority, they come perilously close to endorsing yet another white authority prior to the norm to be violated. They are prone to citing as precedent for an act of violation prior acts of whites that helped establish the norm that the black man must violate. For instance, while praising his heroic slave protagonist as comparable to the great American Revolutionary War leaders, Douglass fails to note also that the norm by which he measures his liberty-seeking hero is three slaveholders. If Madison Washington "loved liberty" only as much as Patrick Henry or Thomas Jefferson or George Washington, all of whom deprived hundreds of their right to enjoy liberty, then one might naturally question from the outset of his story whether Madison Washington is an exemplar at all. What can liberty mean anyway, if it is only defined according to the norm of Jefferson or George Washington, whose love of liberty inhibited them from allowing others to have it. As long as the norm to be violated was established by and for whites and the precedent for violating it was authorized by whites, black writers like Douglass and Parker ran a serious rhetorical risk. To violate a white norm as "any good [white] citizen" would do was, in effect, not to break out of the punishing contradictions of white American polity; it was to join in and tacitly accept the rationale for a culturally sanctioned act, a ritual, Sacvan Bercovitch might call it, of controlled revolution that inevitably reinforced the moral authority of the white majority—a majority that in the 1850s acquiesced in the steady violation of its own professed norms in the Declaration of Independence and the Constitution.

Douglass and Parker in these two texts thus exemplify one kind of outsider manqué in mid-century black narrative. Even as they violate the ideals of Uncle Tom's pacifism and declare blacks free from bloodguiltiness for killing their masters, they justify such actions by an appeal to the authorizing mythology of an oppressive culture. We may interpret this as a masterstroke of freemen's rhetoric or as a link in the "chain of supplementarity" binding black narrators to the white cultural tradition. Neither alternative excludes the other, which is why, like intersecting sets that create a marginal realm of shared values, the relationship of these kinds of autobiographies to the dominant culture always seems to turn our attention in two directions at once. When the writer's myths and metaphors of authority depend on the culture from which he desires to be liberated, is this ultimately a sign of the autobiographer's unknowing complicity in culture or his unacknowledged duplicity with culture? Does rhetoric, by its very nature as an appeal to another, chain the rhetorician to the words that the other can hear, or are those words themselves uttered merely as a script adopted for a performance, played out but not ingrained? On this interpretive threshold, withholding the key of intentionality, the outsiders manqué leave us to our own arbitrary and subjective devices.

In the autobiographies of a number of blacks at mid-century, we find the record of a search for a country, a community in which the black exile will find completion in a home separate and free from the corrupt and duplicitous world of the road. This quest invariably leads these autobiographers into more and more exalted realms of the white world where true acceptance and brotherhood seem to reside. From the South to the North was only the first step up the ladder. By the 1850s and 1860s blacks were recording their search for their rightful place in ever-higher (morally and socially) planes of the white world: among the American abolitionists, among the Canadians, and even among the English aristocracy itself. Nevertheless, for every narrator who seems to have found himself at home in one of these realms of the white world, there was another to deny such a hope by showing its failure in his own experience. Thus, mid-century black autobiography both confirms and refutes the Afro-American transcendental ideal that maintained that one could break out of a realm of racist perversity to discover, beyond the margin, a Canaan-land of freedom, fairness, and brotherhood with whites. The persistently hopeful liminal figures in this group of black autobiographers could never quite "get over," for every time they thought they had crossed Jordan into campground, they found themselves deceived by a mirage and sojourning still in the same old desert. The pattern of this irony and the search that it occasioned for another country within is important to our understanding of the outsiders manqué.

The antebellum slave narrative abounds in singular examples of humanitarian whites in the North like Wells Brown or David Ruggles (whom Douglass honored in the 1845 *Narrative*), who seem untainted by racism and provide an ideal by which the white reader might measure himself. As mid-century approached, however, black autobiographers joined William Wells Brown when he said of America's national complicity in slavery: "I am not willing to draw a line between the people of the North and the people of the South."[37] Uncompromising writers like Samuel Ringgold Ward declared after the Fugitive Slave Act that "nowhere in the world has the Negro so bitter, so relentless enemies, as are the Americans." "Parties having the least to do with the South, or with slavery," he asserted, "are among the fiercest opposers of the anti-slavery cause." The passage of the Kansas-Nebraska bill in May 1854 convinced Ward of "the impossibility—by any means now extant, and they are as wise as human ingenuity can invent—of reforming that country" [the United States]. "The only hopeful spot in the American horizon" that he could see was "the growing, advancing attitude of the black people. From the whites, as a whole, I see no hopes."[38] It was just such a despairing conclusion that led Ward to expatriate to Canada in 1851 after being indicted for his role in the rescue of Jerry McHenry.

Could the northern United States reform itself, if not the southern slavocracy, so as to become a truly Christian and democratic land hospitable to the black freeman? In the 1850s black autobiographers testified loudly and long against the infestation of racism endemic in the North, for which there seemed no ready cure. When Levin Tilmon denounced the conditions of the slave in the South and "the nominally free colored man in the North," he expressed the feelings of many former fugitives who had failed to find the promised land in the North.[39] Austin Steward's espousal of traditional middle-class values did not pacify "the bitter prejudice which every man seemed to feel against the negro" in Rochester, New York. "No matter how industrious he might be, no matter how honorable in his dealings, or respectful in his manners,—he was a 'nigger,' and as such he must be treated, with a few honorable exceptions." Steward devoted an entire chapter of his autobiography to a discussion of the "Persecution of the Colored People" in Ohio under the notorious Black Codes. "The fact is, that the African race there, as in all parts of this nominally free Republic, was looked down upon by the white population as being little above the brute creation." Although states like New York were not as officially hostile to free blacks as Ohio, Steward recommended that in general blacks in the North should disperse into the countryside to escape "the crushing weight of prejudice" in the cities. Anticipating Booker T. Washington's agrarian social philosophy, Steward promised that "if [free blacks] would but retire to the country and purchase a piece of land, cultivate and improve it, they would be far richer and happier than they can be in the crowded city," where bigotry impinges on all their initiatives. James Watkins echoed this judgment of the great urban centers of the North in an appendix to his autobiography, where he pictured New York City as a rigidly and systematically segregated society in its schools, public conveyances, housing, restaurants, and cemeteries. In *My Bondage and My Freedom* Douglass stripped Massachusetts of its liberal pretensions by reprinting in toto his January 1,

1846, letter to Garrison in which, as we have seen, he revisited with an anger unrepressed the closed doors and minds of Boston and New Bedford where *"They don't allow niggers in here!"*[40]

More damning than these criticisms of the North's alienation of the Negro, however, were the many indictments in mid-century black autobiography of the hypocrisy of white abolitionism. Over the previous decades, the cloak of brotherhood shared by blacks and whites in the antislavery movement had been stretched to the breakingpoint by divisiveness born of racial prejudices of many sorts. In the 1850s a few outspoken black autobiographers summed up their disillusionment with America by recalling their climactic realization that the cloak of abolitionism had been as much their burden as their blessing. The mantle of cooperation awarded them by whites seemed to have muffled and veiled the disquieting evidence of white paternalism and elitism that was all too detectable in the abolition movement, once the Afro-American was willing to acknowledge it. Acknowledge it they did, sometimes in the broadest of terms, as when Thomas Smallwood accused white abolitionists of harboring "national pride" in their discouraging fugitives from escaping to Canada, but more often in specific personal terms, as in Douglass's charges against Garrison in *My Bondage and My Freedom*.[41]

The usual purpose of these attacks was to unmask abolitionism as another god that had failed the black pilgrim in his search for the true gospel of brotherhood and a reliable model of that gospel somewhere in the Western world. As a result of this disillusionment, those autobiographers who felt betrayed by abolitionism either took refuge in philosophies of self-help within America or carried their quests for community beyond the borders of the now totally discredited republic. The Douglass-Garrison schism, whose significance to the formal structure of *My Bondage and My Freedom* is discussed in more detail in the next chapter, impelled Douglass to the position, similar to that of Ward, Delany, and Steward, that "OUR ELEVATION AS A RACE IS ALMOST WHOLLY DEPENDENT UPON OUR OWN EXERTIONS."[42] At the end of his second autobiography, Douglass emphasized that events in the last decade of his life had demanded that he attend more "to the condition and circumstances of the free colored people than when [he] was the agent of an abolition society." This had produced "a corresponding change" in his sense of mission. To achieve "the universal and unconditional emancipation of my entire race," he would labor especially "to promote the moral, social, religious, and intellectual elevation of the free colored people." Having become convinced by 1855 that "the self-appointed [white] generals of the Anti-Slavery host" were inimical to "the Idea of our Equality with the whites," Douglass concluded that the emancipation of the slaves in the South could only be effected by those who had liberated themselves from the role of "understrapper" and had developed their manhood to the point of leading a "self elevation movement" in the North. Men like Ward, Henry Highland Garnet, and Alexander Crummell, all expatriates, had the makings of such leadership if they would "come home and help us" redeem the race.[43]

Douglass knew from experience how difficult it would be to attract American blacks in England or other parts of the British Commonwealth back to the land of their birth. Recalling his own time abroad, Douglass admitted, "It is very *pleasant* to be where one can inhale a pure atmosphere, and lift up the voice against oppression, wafted as it were to the skies, upon the gratulations of the sympathising multitude." Douglass had been among the first Afro-American exiles in England to discover his ideals of equality and community realized in Queen Victoria's realm. He had gloried in his assertion to Garrison in 1846 that "the people here know nothing of the republican negro hate prevalent" in the so-called democracy of the United States. William Wells Brown, Josiah Henson, and William G. Allen enjoyed the same kind of welcome from the high-born and well-situated of English society, and they all responded in print with portraits of the English as a people untainted by bigotry. Allen's Anglophilia was representative: "That in Englishmen which most favorably impresses the colored man from America is the entire absence of prejudice against color. Here the colored man feels himself among friends, and not among enemies;—among a people who, when they treat him well, do it not in the patronising (and, of course, insulting) spirit, even of hundreds of the American abolitionists, but in a spirit rightly appreciative of the doctrine of human equality. Color claims no precedence over character, here; and, consequently, in parties given by the 'first people' in the kingdom may be seen persons of all colors moving together on terms of perfect social equality." Allen concluded, with Douglass in 1846, that English behavior proved "that prejudice against color is entirely a local feeling, generated by slavery." Thus if the black fugitive-pilgrim were willing to take the most drastic step of all—complete separation from the locale of slavery and racism—he or she could reach true fulfillment by "the light of British liberty."[44]

The romance of British royalty and American fugitives notwithstanding, more than a few black autobiographers discounted as myth the ideal of an England unblemished by racism. Samuel Ringgold Ward recalled that his "first experience of English dealing was in being charged treble fare by a Liverpool cabman, a race with which I have had much to do since." James Watkins arrived in England with joy "unbounded" and "perfect confidence" that at long last "NOW I AM FREE!" He soon learned Ward's lesson in Liverpool, however, when he discovered how much of a persona non grata he was in the eyes of the workers and merchants of the city. "English mothers and servants threaten a naughty child with being handed over to 'Black Sam,' or 'The Black Man,'" Watkins pointed out in his autobiography; Liverpool merchants refused to hire "'a nigger who would steal.'" The presumption of his disposition to thievery was based on the sympathy of British businessmen with their counterparts in the slave states of America. "By obtaining my freedom I had *robbed* my master," which was the reason why "my having escaped from slavery was looked upon as a heinous offence by these gentlemen." Jobless and friendless, Watkins had to take up antislavery lecturing and writing to support himself and his family. His success in these capacities (his autobiography went through nineteen printings between 1852 and 1860) testifies to the popularity of a number of black abolitionist writers and speakers in England, but the reason for his entering this line of work in the first place belies the idea of England as an interracial utopia.[45] Men like Watkins and Ward refused to conceal the existence of discrimination on every level of the English class structure. Even William Wells Brown's travel books contain the haunting image of a fugitive slave from Maryland who, after begging six pence of Brown for food, declares, "'You are the first friend I have met in London.'" Brown's reaction to this experience was to send a letter to *Frederick Douglass' Paper* in July 1851, urging that fugitive slaves not flee to England unless they wished to become beggars. Significantly, Brown did not include this letter among the others he wrote from the Old World in either *Three Years in Europe* or *American Fugitive in Europe.*[46]

Ward's was the most balanced treatment of England as a potential home for the Afro-American fugitive. Welcomed by British reformers of every stripe and feted by the nobility, Ward stressed that he had never felt so much "an equal brother man" in any country before his arrival in England. Prominent names drop persistently from page after page of his narrative of his social activities: dinners with Lord and Lady Ebrington, train rides with the duke of Argyll and the earl of Elgin, introductions to the Earl Waldegrave and Lord Shaftesbury and the earl of Carlisle, a stroll with Lord Blantyre through his picture gallery, tea with Lady Dover on the queen's birthday. "The kind interest taken in the coloured people by these distinguished personages, being to me an entirely new thing, kept me in a state of most excited delight." When the duchess of Sutherland informed Ward that "she had received abusive letters from American slaveholders," he quickly concluded "that English abolitionists, of whatever rank, suffer for the slave as well as feel for him a kind sympathy." One might necessarily ask, however, whether this "suffering" on the part of wealthy British liberals extended beyond having to peruse an occasional letter of criticism from an American slaveowner.

Ward insists in his autobiography that he knew a number of British abolitionists who, "in spite of opposition, and at large expense to their pocket," maintained their principles. Nevertheless, the fugitive could not ignore how often Britons compromised themselves and "pandered" to American racism in their dealings with "Yankees" (a generic term for all Americans in Ward's vocabulary). The humanitarianism of many Britons was "mere sentimentality"; Ward deduced this from the fact that when these good people went to the United States they kept their opinions of slavery to themselves. It was precisely this fellow-feeling between the English and the Americans that gave Ward his greatest doubts about what Britain might truly signify to the alienated Afro-American. Despite his admiration of British abolitionism, Ward was troubled by the receptiveness of the average Englishman to "Negro-hate" American-style once introduced to it. "Englishmen, Irishmen, and Scotchmen, generally become the bitterest of Negro-haters, within fifteen days of their naturalization [in the United States]—some not waiting so long," he averred. Class origins helped Ward explain this kind of racism, whether it appeared among "the lowest, the least educated, of all the white population" in Canada, England, and the United States. "The early settlers in many parts of America were the very lowest of the English population: the same class will abuse a Negro in England or Ireland now." By contrast, "the best friends the Negro has in America are persons generally of the superior classes, and of the best origin." Moreover, "so far as my experience goes (and that is considerable)," the fugitive confided, "*the British gentleman* is a gentleman everywhere, and under all circumstances." Thus, Ward argues on several occasions, the "petty jealousy" of racism is possible among any whites, European or American, who "have not the training of gentlemen, are not accustomed to genteel society, and, as a consequence, know but little, next to nothing, of what are liberal enlightened views and genteel behaviour." [47]

The readiness with which "lower"-class whites in Canada, England, and America resisted the aspirations of people of color caused Ward to cast his lot with "the middling and better classes of all Europe," since they "treat a black gentleman as a gentleman." But did they? Ward's own autobiography challenges his class generalizations in the recounting of the manner in which he was barred from eating with the white passengers aboard the English steamer *Europa* during his first journey to Great Britain in the spring of 1853. The rationale for this discrimination came from Edward Cunard, "a fine gentlemanly-appearing Englishman," who, in deference to the many Americans who traveled on his line, ruled that all blacks would be required to eat in their staterooms. This was Ward's first encounter with an Englishman, and it proved to him that such a man could be easily "perverted" like the Yankee to "make the dollar come before right, law, or anything." "Mr. Cunard's case, in its likeness to and connection with those of many other Englishmen," showed that accommodation to racism was very much in the economic interest of "the middling classes" of England. Cunard might genteelly deny Ward a seat at the captain's dining table while professing privately a liberal's aversion to discrimination. No matter—at bottom "Mr. Cunard is a man of business; so are the mass of Englishmen. What interferes with or threatens a diminution of the gains of business must be avoided." Only when blacks had attained sufficient economic power to "become of some value as customers," Ward instructed his black readers, would they be able to ensure that white gentlemen in Europe or America would behave according to their training and principles. Thus, while Ward might speak in glowing generalities of the fraternity of the white and black gentleman in Europe, he urged more practically that "the *chief*, almost the *only* business of the Negro, is to be a man of business." At the end of his story, Ward pictures himself in pursuit of this goal outside of England, in Jamaica, where he planned to become an independent farmer.[48]

The journey of Samuel Ringgold Ward from Maryland to New York, Toronto, the British Isles, and ultimately to fifty acres of uncertain opportunity in Jamaica epitomizes on an international scale the search of the antebellum Afro-American for what Ward called his "own appropriate place of duty." Educated black men like Ward were regularly upbraided for being "'out of their place'" in America; Ward wanted to believe that the place of such black men was beside those Europeans of "liberal enlightened views and genteel behaviour" who distinguished themselves as "*real* gentlemen and noblemen." People of this class stood above the meanness and prejudice of the "inferior" classes of Western Europe and America, and during his tour of Great Britain, Ward delighted in his own temporary exemption from the constant irritations and outrages of racism as he recorded them in the American sections of his autobiography. Still, the fugitive knew that the "demon" of racism flew with the American eagle on the green back of the dollar. He also knew that England was a land of businessmen, not of royalty, and their dependence on American trade militated against the egalitarianism and abolitionism of men like Ward. The expansive character of British capitalism, exemplified in Cunard's transatlantic shipping venture, had linked the interests of the gentleman entrepreneurs of Liverpool to those of Savannah planters and Boston doughfaces.[49]

Great Britain, therefore, was not at all free from the American slavocracy, and it could not be cited as an independent, uncorrupted standard of sociopolitical morality. England represented simply another compromised ideal from which fugitives like Ward fled when they realized, to use the metaphor of Ralph Ellison's twentieth-century fugitive Negro, that they "had boomeranged" once again. England was the place where Ward thought he had found an end to his quest, but he soon discovered himself there on yet another threshold, which led back to his origins in the Americas. Ward's quest for his "appropriate place" in the white world had taught him a variety of roles he might play but nothing fundamental on which he could base his fulfillment as a "true man" underneath the supplemental roles. He had "smattered away" at law, medicine, teaching, divinity, and public lecturing, but "I am neither lawyer, doctor, teacher, divine, nor lecturer." Thus, the writing of his autobiography on the eve of another phase of his life's journey forced Ward to take stock in a way that only the most thoughtful of the marginal men and women of black autobiography did at mid-century. When the prospective Jamaican farmer wrote, "I am glad to hasten back to what my father first taught me, and from what I never should have departed—the tilling of the soil," he was admitting that the final leg of the fugitive's journey was not to a place but to the past (33–34).

This kind of Afro-American "journey back" (to apply Houston Baker's broadly descriptive term to a specific instance) is routed through the past in narratives like Ward's toward a destination that seems to lie in original resources, primary principles, and essential truths. "What my father first taught me" is but one way of encoding this enduring plenitude of primary values grounded in black identity and experience to which the world-weary traveler looks back with nostalgia and faith. Ward might have just as readily cited his mother as the personification of a standard or ideal, departure from which had launched him on his career as a marginal man. What is important to us is the recognition that the failure of every level of ideals to which the marginal Negro aspired in the white world did not destroy his or her enduring faith in the existence of a fulfilling plenitude somewhere. They clung to the romantic idealism that had inspired their own brand of transcendentalism, their own faith in the power of the black spirit to overcome its confinements and move beyond its limitations to find self-completion. The disillusionment of Ward, the quintessential outsider manqué, did not cause him to recant his faith in idealism; he simply reversed his quest for the wellspring of that idealism. Instead of searching "out far" he would look "in deep" for the center of a plenitude from which he could draw the meaning and value of his career as a marginal man and, more profoundly, write himself into fulfillment.

The pundits of mid-century black journalism helped call attention to the black community's need for serious soul-searching over the question of the efficacy of its traditional deference to white ideals. Thomas Hamilton, editor of the *Anglo-African Magazine*, foresaw the "glorious destiny" of blacks in the United States as nothing less than "to purify the State, and purify Christianity from the foul blot which here rests upon them." Before Afro-Americans could assume this status as the moral leaders of the republic, however, some explanation had to be advanced as to why, as yet, blacks had failed "to manifest force of character equal to the whites." "The source of our degradation" Hamilton attributed to the failure of black imagination to commit itself to a truly original and independent ideal. The ideal of white America—"this Universal Yankee Nation" —was nothing less than "to excel all mankind—to do more than man ever did." In their drive to excellence and dominance, whites reject all models, precedents, and standards for their "character or conduct." Thus they had derived a "force of character" superior to all other peoples and races. By contrast, the black editor asked his readership, "What is the colored man's ideal?" It was merely to gain equality with the white man. "We have not heard of a higher [ideal], and there are very few that aim so high." In other words, "we have a lower IDEAL than the whites. We aim less high, and, therefore, require and use less force, in attaining our aim." Hamilton deplored as "imitative," "artificial," "limited," and "confined" this endowment of whites with normative priority. There was nothing "original," "expansive," or "ennobling" in the desire simply to equal whites, particularly when blacks devoted themselves to the tawdry objects of desire that whites set up as their ideals. "Must we bow down and worship the golden image along with them?" Hamilton asked rhetorically. Was this the way in which "we must excel our oppressors"? Hamilton hoped instead that his people would elevate themselves over the whites "in all that is noble, and prudent, and upright." By the end of his article, the editor was obliged to specify the noble and prudent actions he wanted his fellow blacks to undertake if they were to stand upright and even a little taller than whites. His recommendation was: "We know no better ideal for our choice, than to be true men, and useful citizens. We know no ambition worthier of us than to be the best citizens the State contains. The State has need of such, and will reward them—will advance them—will give them their place among the select few worthy of admiration." Therefore Afro-Americans should adopt "the ideal of good citizenship, of true, upright, thrifty manhood—clear, self-dependent, self-reliant manhood" and inculcate that ideal in their children.[50]

As his editorial shows, Hamilton was acutely aware of the self-limiting and feckless character of black aspiration and idealism defined in terms of equality with whites, since equality seemed just another word for imitation of whites. Somehow blacks had to "look up, above, and beyond the whites" for guiding principles. Ironically, however, the more Hamilton tried to enunciate this lofty aim, the more he lapsed into the flatulent language of bourgeois civic and moral idealism. He did not consider truth to the self and service to the republic contradictory, nor did he question whether being "useful" to the country was not putting oneself at the disposal of the whites who controlled it, thus placing one's advancement and elevation once again in the hands of those whom Hamilton knew were the "oppressors" of blacks. Hamilton groped for a way to define the "true man" for his black readers, but he had to appropriate the language of popularized Emersonian idealism—"self-reliant manhood"—to do it. He exemplifies the problem of establishing a distinct ideal of black selfhood that did not trace itself back to and thus endorse a prior white standard.

Black writers who took a more separatist position vis-à-vis whites had problems of their own in staking out standards for citizenship in the distinctly Afro-American nation that they sought to advance. An emigrationist might plump for Haiti as a place where blacks could preserve their identity against the forces of "subordination and absorption" in North America and thus create "a distinct people and a homogeneous nation." But a persuasive counterargument could be advanced to the effect that urging blacks to go to Haiti was not to point them to a higher ideal but a lower one. Didn't black Haiti evidence its continuing sense of inferiority to the whites by maintaining "a proverb, universal among the masses, 'Aprez bon Jo—blanc'"—"Next to God is the white man"? Austin Steward might ask the black reader of his autobiography why the Negro had been created "if not to fulfil his destiny *as a negro*, to the glory of God?" Yet after exhorting his countrymen "to cease looking to the white man for example and imitation," Steward could not or would not say what he meant, exactly, by his advice to "stand boldly up in your own national characteristics." Was there anything peculiarly "national" about the "perseverance and industry," "honor and purity" that he urged blacks to abide by, so as to prove "that you are men, colored men, but of no inferior quality"? When Steward entreated blacks "to band yourselves together in one indissoluble bond of brotherhood," he did not explain the basis on which he would have blacks see themselves as brothers. In light of the internecine conflicts within the black Canadian settlements whose history he chronicled unofficially in his autobiography, Steward's failure to discuss the meaning and character of racial solidarity makes for a glaring omission in his argument.[51]

Perhaps no black autobiographer at mid-century professed a more uncompromising belief in the abstract superiority of the Negro over the

197

Caucasian than Samuel Ringgold Ward. Under no circumstances, he informed the reader of his narrative, would he "degrade" his people to the point of asking pity for them from their "oppressors," the Americans. "Nor could I degrade myself by arguing the equality of the Negro with the white; my private opinion is, that to say the Negro is equal morally to the white man, is to say but very little." Ancient black thinkers and writers like Cyprian, Augustine, Tertullian, Euclid, and Terence exhibited "intellect beyond the ordinary range of modern literati, before the present Anglo-Saxon race had even an origin." This supported Ward's contention that in essence the Negro had always been a moral and intellectual plenitude in need of nothing extrinsic that the white man could bestow on him. "What the Negro needs is, what belongs to him—what has been ruthlessly torn from him—and what is, by consent of a despotic democracy and a Christless religion, withholden from him, guiltily, perseveringly." Thus to take their rightful place in the human family, blacks needed only to have "restored" to them what had been robbed of them. What is interesting here is not Ward's analysis of what had been "torn from" the Negro—he seems also deliberately to avoid defining it—but rather the scenarios he offers in which both free and enslaved blacks restore themselves to themselves through their own efforts. Journeying back through the stages of his own life, Ward isolated a pattern of black experience in America which he then endowed with virtually archetypal significance in an attempt to provide the Afro-American community a sustaining myth of its progress toward an ideal of its own.

We find this myth outlined and rationalized in the middle chapters of the *Autobiography of a Fugitive Negro* when Ward discusses the trials and achievements of black emigrants in Canada. Ward's aim in this section of his story is to show how in making their flight from slavery and the land of the Fugitive Slave Act, the black settlers of Canada West had attained "real true manhood," despite the prejudices that assigned to the escaped bondman only a life of wretched incompetency in freedom. Having raised himself above and beyond the hold of the perverse Yankee realm, the black man in Canada had not become merely a displaced alien outside the border of his homeland. He had come into his own, as Ward stressed of himself in becoming a Canadian citizen. At Dawn and Chatham, the former slave was creating community in a country that he could call "my own." This community, moreover, did not depend on whites for its leadership or its ideals; it had its indigenous standards of heroism that had evolved out of its own common experience and traditions. The foundation of that shared communal experience was, in Ward's analysis, a tripartite rite of passage from slave to fugitive to freeman that ensured not merely the escape of a slave from oppression but the "transformation" of that slave into a new and superior person, a "physical and moral hero"— the freeman. By defining the black exodus to Canada according to this archetypal pattern, Ward seized on a novel and compelling rhetorical strategy by which to argue the corporate progress of a people (not simply an exceptional individual like a Frederick Douglass) *out of* the degradation of slavery and *through* the marginality of their fugitiveship *into* an actual culmination of individual and corporate identity within a plenitude outside the borders of corrupt America.

Ward was at pains to endow the self-emancipated blacks in Canada with a new status liberated from identifying terms like ex-slave or fugitive slave. He knew that many whites resisted the idea that escaped slaves could ever qualify for any other status in the white world, and he scornfully quoted ministers who ruled that "'a man's running away from slavery is *prima facie* evidence of his being a bad man.'" Ward's counterargument was that running away from bondage was a "sublime" act that not only proved the fugitive an extraordinary man but also set in motion an initiation process that had molded many into "the most admirable of any race." Whites had to understand the differences between the slave and the fugitive and ultimately the freeman as stages in the development of the black self. Ward set up "this peculiar nomenclature for the sake of perspicuity and logical correctness. The fugitive is different on the plantation from what he is flying. When he reaches Canada, he is no longer either a slave or a fugitive, but a freeman," that is, a new creation, free not only from his literal chains but also from the grip of slavery on his essential self.[52]

Ward defines the slave who does not try to make a break for freedom as an "ordinary man" who submits to and tries to make the best of what he suffers. "Oppression cramps and dwarfs the mind" of such a man in slavery so that he becomes "mean enough" to accept his lot "without very vigorous efforts" to better himself. By contrast, "the slave intending, planning, determining to escape" distinguishes himself as an aspirant to something higher. He "grows" with his plan and becomes "more of a man for having conceived it." Acting on the plan proves him "to be superior to those generally surrounding him." During his fugitive experience he must exercise "patience, fortitude, and perseverance," which promote further growth of manhood within the former slave. The many "furnaces of trial" through which the fugitive must pass on his journey to freedom all serve to "purify and ennoble the man who has to pass through them." By the time he reaches Canada "he is, first, what the raw material of nature was; and, secondly, what the improving process of flight has made him." He has become, in sum, a "hero" as well as a freeman, worthy of comparison to the heroes of European liberation movements like Lajos Kossuth in Hungary and Giuseppe Mazzini in Italy.

Ward's delineation of this process follows the outline of the classic rite of passage in which one is detached from a defined status in a social structure to enter into an ambiguous liminal stage of transition before emerging into a new and "relatively stable state once more" with the rights and obligations that accrue to one in that new state. In the liminal stage all the inscriptions on the self that previously assigned its status are erased; one becomes a tabula rasa preparatory to being redesignated a new and fully mature person in a society of one's peers. The purification and ennoblement of the self of which Ward speaks corresponds to the "destruction of the previous status" of those who undergo liminality and the "tempering of their essence in order to prepare them to cope with their new responsibilities." [53] Ward's freeman represents the fulfillment, therefore, of a process of both the recuperation and maturation of the essential self ("the raw material of nature") no longer alloyed by the degradation of slavery but instead refined by the upgrading experience of fugitiveship. In Ward's freeman we find manifested once again the romantic ideal of antebellum Afro-American narrative: the slave freed not just from slavery but from his or her past as a slave and thereby empowered to discover and realize the potential of the original, pristine self before it was "dwarfed and cramped" in bondage.

And yet, no sooner had Ward penned his tribute to the self-restorative powers of the black rite of passage than he began to hedge his claims for the entire process. Many ex-slaves who had undergone the fugitive phase of initiation had not arrived in Canada as changed men, Ward admits, nor had they become new men in freedom. Many bore "with them the indelible marks of the accursed lot to which they have been doomed, in early life." It was "almost impossible" to grow up in slavery and "to any great extent ever become free from" its impact on the character. This was as true of slaveholders as it was of slaves. Most painful of all for Ward was the admission that it was also true of himself. "Though I recollect nothing of slavery, I am every day showing something of my slave origin." His parents had rescued him from slavery when he was barely more than an infant, yet in his "superstitions," his "narrow view," and his "awkwardness of manners" he felt "the infernal impress is upon me." "I fear I shall transmit it to my children, and they to theirs! How deeply seated, how far reaching, a curse it is!" (169–70).

In this moment of anguished reflection, Ward called into question black autobiography's romantic ideal of the recuperation of an essential self that would, through a process of liminality, enable a fugitive to transcend his dwarfed self in slavery and become someone different—the freeman. As propagandist for an abstract, idealized freeman, Ward could posit in every former slave an original plenitude of selfhood, temporarily "dwarfed and cramped" by slavery but not essentially or permanently marked by it. In his myth of the slave's psychological self-becoming, the conditioning of slavery could be labeled a perverse, but not necessarily perverting, supplement to the self. Because this supplement did not invest the self, it could be divested by it, and it was, Ward implied, during fugitive liminality. In freedom, "purified and ennobled," the self would assume or, more accurately, resume its rightful status among freemen.

When Ward applied this myth to specific cases, however, particularly his own, he could not sing such a paean to the recuperative powers of the self. What he wanted to believe about the self he could not testify to in his own autobiographical self-portrait. Even after nearly a lifetime of fugitive liminality, Ward had not undergone the transforming self-restoration he attributed to the freeman in the ideal. A look within revealed the lingering "infernal impress" of bondage on his psyche. Instead of identifying with the "purified" freeman, he associated himself with those who had been marked "indelibly" by their oppression. Likening the effects of racism to that of a "curse" affirmed the precedence of an unafflicted self in every black man and woman, but declaring his fear of an unconscious transmission of the curse through generations of his posterity suggested that the evil had become deeply rooted in the self and could not be readily extirpated. Nor did Ward suggest how he would become a man free from this profound, "deeply seated" stigma. Contrary to the myth he propounded, his own fugitive career had neither eradicated the marks of the past nor recuperated a "purified," essential self nor empowered his transformation into a fulfilled man.

The upshot of these revelations by Ward is an implicit model of the self different from the one he proposed in his myth of the making of the transcendent freeman. We might make the following inferences from what Ward says about this unidealized self. First, although everyone is born with an uncorrupted essence of selfhood, the "slave origin" of Afro-Americans like Ward was virtually coexistent with it from birth and thus profoundly inscribed it. As a hardy tree could grow around an iron stake driven into its taproot, so the selfhood of the slave could develop despite its "deeply seated" wound, but it would of necessity bear scars at the core of its being. What had been impressed unconsciously from the beginning of a life could not be escaped or completely supplanted through the kind of rite of passage that Ward embodied in the flight to Canada pattern. The impress of the slave origin was formative, not merely supplemental; that was the great outrage of slavery, the most compelling argument for its abolition. What slavery robbed of its victim, the freeman could not necessarily restore. As James W. C. Pennington stated in *The Fugitive Blacksmith*, when slavery "robbed" him of his primary education in his youth, it did him an "injury" that was "irreparable," for he felt his "deficiency more especially as I can never hope to make it up." This kind of intellectual foundation could not be established after the super-structure of the mind had been built.[54] In freedom, therefore, one's real or imagined intellectual and psychological deficiencies were not fully restored. Ironically, as men like Ward and Pennington became more and more self-conscious in freedom, they became supremely aware of the absences in their awareness and could not help but define themselves partly in terms of this absence, despite their need to identify with a recoverable ideal essence within.

Ward's devising of his myth of the black rite of passage is understandable in light of a natural desire to imagine and restore the absent essence within. At the same time, his contradiction and subversion of his own myth stand as an act of great candor in black autobiography, particularly since it is not in harmony with the tenor of his time in both black and white literature. From William Wordsworth to Emily Dickinson, white romantics affirmed a self anterior and superior to time, while, as we have seen in the case of a William Wells Brown, major black autobiographers often proclaimed a self that was proof against time. It was left to someone like Ward (supported by an equally candid Pennington) to insist that the self was perpetually, inescapably, a function and product of time. As such, it could not pass through the traumas of slavery or fugitiveship without being somehow permanently impressed by them. The self did not take passage through these states and stages to become a purified distillation of itself. It became, instead, a complex accretion of all it had passed through. Nor could the evolution of life be structured according to discrete stages of linear progression eventuating in the transformation of the old into the new. The progress of a life like Ward's seems to have been cumulative, not climactic, incremental, not transcendental.

Thus, for people like Ward the idea of a self-restorative rite of passage remained an ideal, while life continually reminded them of their persistent liminality. Having rebelled against and fled from slavery, these transitional figures could and would define themselves proudly as not-slave. But they could not redesignate themselves to their own satisfaction as free men or women until they could find ways, through the autobiographical act itself, to affirm their liminality as a "potentialising" phase in which indeterminacy signifies a host of possibilities, not simply a loss of center. Unlike a J. D. Green or a Frederick Douglass, Ward could not see, or at least could not take comfort in, this potential in liminality. The most eloquent of all the outsiders manqué whom we have examined in this chapter, he could not break out of the limits that his own nostalgia for an essential plenitude of self imposed on his capacity to imagine himself anew. In the same year that Walt Whitman celebrated the "simple separate" "One-Self," a "kosmos" of personal plenitude, Ward embraced that same ideal in his myth of the transformed fugitive and his fond hope of recovering his true self in Jamaica. Nevertheless, as we have seen, he was too honest about the absences that tormented him from within to claim for himself the resolution and fulfillment that he mythologized for many black fugitives. It is just this painful acknowledgment of his neither-slave-nor-freeman liminality that makes Ward important as a threshold figure in the history of Afro-American autobiography. He points toward key questions that would have to be raised about the romance of fulfilled selfhood, that secularized variation on the Christian conversion theme, which so few fugitive slave narrators could fully endorse except in some sort of mythic or fantasy form.

An audacious admission like Ward's, stating that one's life quest had not reached its goal and virtually disqualifying oneself for the blessedness of "One-Self," did not have to signify a confession of failed individual purpose in the face of oppressive environmental forces. Ward might have used his admission as a rhetorical gambit leading into a criticism of the myth of an attainable "one-selfhood" in the white world. An autobiographer who admits that he is not "One-Self" may imply that in his liminality he is no-self— but only as long as he accedes to the assumption that valorizes "One-Self" as an ideal. What is assumed in such an ideal is that the parameters of selfhood are one and none and that this bipolar opposition constitutes the totality of the field of selfhood. If an autobiographer defines himself in terms of absence, however, he may be saying more than that he is no-self. He may be declaring, indeed, turning to account, the great advantage of his liminality—his potential to become multiple recombinant selves. Only in the precarious phase of liminality can such potential be energized and experimented with. Only while one maintains an interstitial position on the margins of fixed and secure statuses in a social structure is it possible to try out different roles. Only the liminal autobiographer has the insight and the power to declare that self and role are but two sides of the same (authentically American) coin, payable always on the acceptance of face value. The slave learns this lesson first, as many slave narrators of the 1830s and 1840s attest. Recognizing this, the wisest of the marginal writers of the 1850s, people like Douglass and Harriet Jacobs, did not delude themselves into thinking that life outside slavery would ever deliver them wholly from role-playing or leave them free and complete in "One-Self." They understood better than

Ward that the black American's individual quest was unlikely to reach a definitive climax or denouement alone, outside of or apart from blacks in the United States. They realized that there would be no final break-through, no ultimate arrival, no essential transformation of self or transcendence of roles unless they found some form of "communitas," some form of interstitial community in America that they, as liminal figures, could claim as their special kind of home. For J. D. Green, Frederick Douglass, and Harriet Jacobs, autobiography was a way, the best and perhaps the only way, of creating that community and then affiliating themselves with it, so that the full potential of their literary as well as social marginality might be set free.

Culmination of a Century: The Autobiographies of J. D. Green, Frederick Douglass, and Harriet Jacobs

Perhaps it was the unique marginality manifested in his 1864 narrative that made Jacob D. Green a forgotten figure after the first century of Afro-American autobiography. Although at least 8,000 copies of the *Narrative of the Life of J. D. Green* were published in England,[1] the story of this trickster par excellence apparently received slight if any notice in America during the waning days of slavery. No historian or critic has mentioned it since then either. Yet Green's unabashed account of his roguish behavior vis-à-vis the black as well as the white community in the world of slavery exhibits a most pronounced case of interstitiality and celebrates that condition in a very remarkable way. One of the first tricks he recounts puts us in mind of the methods of Sandford, William Wells Brown's guileful alter ego in slavery. Like Sandford, young Jacob had offended his master so as to require punishment by flogging, and like Sandford, Jacob knew that the note he was given to take to Mr. Cobb, the overseer, conveyed instructions as to the beating that its bearer was to receive. The shifty Green agrees to do a fellow-slave a favor in return for his taking the note to Cobb. The unsuspecting victim receives thirty-nine lashes on his bare back while Green returns to his master in the carriage to drive him and his family home from Baltimore. Surprised to see his slave available for service, Mr. Earle inquires how the youth feels, to which Green replies with a hearty, "First-rate, sir." " 'Nigger, did Mr. Cobb flog you?' " asks the enraged master. " 'No sir,' " answers the slave innocently; " 'I have done nothing wrong.' " Master confronts the overseer with his failure to follow orders, but Cobb insists that he whipped the slave who brought him the note. Eventually the two white men realize that the wrong slave took the beating, and Mr. Earle summons Green to explain himself. The young slave coolly admits that because "I thought there was something in the note that boded no good to me, I did not intend to give it to" Cobb. The measure of the master's defeat in this battle of wits is the shrill threat he makes before throwing the trickster out of the house with only a tongue-lashing: "'You black vagabond, stay on this plantation three months longer, and you will be master and I the slave'" (9). As for Green's relationship with Dick, his black victim, "we had continual fightings for several months." The episode ends with no expression of contrition from Green the narrator for having exploited his fellow slave in such a cruel way.

What this episode illustrates is J. D. Green's liberation of the slave trickster from the role of the slave picaro. During the first century of black autobiography, the picaro becomes an increasingly familiar figure, for, as Raymond Hedin has argued, it is the justification of picaresque actions, or what we might call the survival ethic of fugitive slaves on the road, that preoccupies writers like William Wells Brown, Henry Bibb, and James W. C. Pennington.[2] However, the more the slave narrative of the 1840s "purified" (in Hedin's term) the black picaro of his "out-and-out roguishness," the less accurately we may denote this figure a true trickster. As Barbara Babcock-Abrahams characterizes the trickster, he or she is most notably not "justifiable" according to conventional moral or logical categories or social sanction. Henry Louis Gates, Jr., demonstrates in particular that the African trickster's interstitial relationship to *all* community makes him or her a perpetual anomaly and ambiguity with no steady alliances to either side of the basic binary oppositions—order/disorder, creation/destruction, good/evil, life/death—that structure culture. The trickster's interstitiality enables him or her to play both sides of these oppositions against the middle, which the trickster alone occupies, not in order to reconcile opposites but to embody their coexistence in a kind of irreducible dialogue. This dialogue can serve many functions, not the least of which is the stimulation of free thinking about the necessity of any traditional opposition or hierarchy valorized by culture.[3]

When fugitive slaves like William Wells Brown or Pennington defend their violations of Christian morality on the road by blaming slavery for their moral ignorance or their compromised integrity, they are very much concerned with explaining away their picaresque pasts so as to foist off their culpability onto slavery. They leave no ambiguity about their respect for social order and conventional moral standards; their purpose is to saddle the South with the responsibility for disorder and immorality. Thus, the confessions of former picaros like Brown or Pennington reinforce the basic binary oppositions that sustained the culture of their readers. These writers only want to reverse the relationship between these oppositions and the slave and slaveowner, to the obvious detriment of the latter. The lingering contradictions we find between William W. Brown, slave narrator, and Sandford, his alter ego, belie the efforts of William Wells Brown to reduce the dialogue within his autobiography to a less shifty single voice, that of the reformed picaro.

It is not the reformed picaro, however, but the unremorseful trickster that we hear in the narrative voice of Jacob D. Green. In the episode just recounted, the narrator displays no more sense of guilt over having sent an innocent fellow-slave to the whipping post than he shows in having deceived his master out of that whipping. To cheat, steal from, or otherwise trick a slaveowner was considered quite defensible, of course, as numerous slave narrators and students of slave culture have stressed. But to deceive or take advantage of a fellow bondman was judged the lowest thing a black person could do, since it weakened the code of solidarity that the slave quarters relied on in the survival struggle against the power of the plantation big house.[4] In the folklore of the slaves, the black trickster-hero, usually named John, is celebrated because he can make a fool of his master and gain some tangible, though temporary, reward in the bargain. Only rarely did slaves picture the trickster-hero trying out his wiles on his fellow blacks. In their animal tales, however, the slaves gave the trickster full latitude to make his "assault upon deeply ingrained and culturally sanctioned values." Tricksters like Brer Rabbit delight in their amoral manipulation and deprivation of strong and weak alike. Rabbit lives to gratify his own insatiable appetite for "wealth, success, prestige, honor, and sexual prowess," and he does not care how he achieves his ends. His vanity makes him the duped instead of the duper sometimes, but he is too nimble-witted to remain in anyone's power for long. When he turns the tables on his adversaries, his triumph is often vindictive and violent.[5] In several important respects, Green draws on the energy and ambiguity of the animal trickster tradition to create a bold and unprecedented identity for himself in his narrative.

The key episode in Green's career as a human version of Brer Rabbit occurs when, at the age of sixteen, he decides to attend "a negro shindy or dance" in grand style. He owns a good pair of trousers and a jacket; he steals from a black cook a checked apron from which he fashions a necktie and a pocket handkerchief; and to his collection of twenty-four pennies he adds fifty large brass buttons to carry in his pockets so that when he dances he will make all the yokels "stare to hear the money jingle." On the night of the clandestine dance he steals one of his master's horses and rides away "confident, of course, that I should have my pick among the best looking [women], for my good clothes, and my abundance of money, and my own good looks—in fact, I thought no mean things of my self"

(11). Unfortunately, upon his arrival at the meetinghouse, he accidentally catches his trousers on a nail in the hitching fence and splits his pants all the way up to the seat. He is able to borrow enough pins to hold the pants together and join the dancing, but during one flashy turn with one of "the pretty yellow and Sambo gals," his breeches give way and his shirt tail falls out. "What made my situation still more disgraceful was the mischievous conduct of my partner, the gal that I was dancing with, who instead of trying to conceal my shame caught my shirt tail behind and held it up." This brings on a loud roar of laughter from everyone, and none of the women will let the humiliated youth escape until she has had a chance to lead him a step or two around the room by the shirt tail. The same women whom he thought he would impress so much also turn out his pockets to discover the brass buttons, thus completing his inglorious unmasking and mockery.

Alone outside the meetinghouse, "the first thing I thought of now was revenge." Like Green, the slaves at the dance have come from all over the area on horseback, leaving approximately 100 animals appropriated from the stock of many unconsulted masters loosely tethered at the hitching fence. Green knows that all these horses must be returned to their proper places before dawn the next morning with no sign of their unauthorized use, and he knows that slaves who fail in this will receive severe punishment. For this reason, he cuts all the horses loose, runs them off, and then sets out for home on his own horse regretting only that he could not be on hand to see the dancers' faces when they discover the horses gone.

Ironically, when Green gets back to his master's stable he loses control of his own horse while removing the saddle and bridle and spends the rest of the night futilely chasing his mount in the fields nearby. At dawn he gives up and turns out all the rest of the horses in the stable to join the lone runaway. Then he returns to his quarters to await his master's discovery of the escaped horses. Since all the horses are entrusted to Green's care, Mr. Earle directs all his exasperation and anger at the teenaged slave, but, as Green recalls their encounter, "I put on an expression of such wonder and surprise—looking first into the meadow and then at the stable door, and to master's satisfaction, I seemed so completely confounded that my deception took upon him the desired effect." Green claims that some enemies of his among the slaves must have turned the horses out after he had stabled them properly the night before. Summoning all the blacks on the plantation, Earle demands a confession from the guilty ones, and when he hears none he sends all the slaves except Green into the fields to retrieve the horses and clean them up again. After a second fruitless demand for the identity of those who had perpetrated the time-consuming and costly trick, the master has all of his slaves except Green tied and given thirty-nine lashes. Green admits that "my poor guilty heart, already bleeding for the suffering I had caused my fellow slaves, was now almost driven to confession." But when Earle asks him whom he has the most reason to suspect, Green decides not "to satisfy my conscience at the expense of a very sore back." "I happened to be one of those boys who, among all even of my mother's children, loved myself best, . . . so I very soon thought of Dick, a negro who, like Ishmael, had his hand out against every man, and all our hands were out against him" (14–15). Because Dick is a despised informer for the master, "he was just the proper sacrifice for me to lay upon the altar of confession." Consequently Dick receives an additional thirty-nine lashes before confessing to the crime he never committed. And what of the stranded slaves at the clandestine dance the night before? "The forebodings of the awful consequences if they dared to go home induced many that night to seek salvation in the direction and guidance of the north star. Several who started on that memorable night I have since shook hands with in Canada. They told me there were sixteen of them went off together, four of them were shot or killed by the bloodhounds, and one was captured while asleep in a barn; the rest of those who were at the dance either went home and took their floggings, or strayed into the woods until starved out, and then surrendered" (15).

As Green unfolds this episode, he pictures himself initially as a cocky and ostentatious young swell whose vanity and craving for adult respect make him amusingly sympathetic. When he unveils his vengeful side, however, he complicates his reader's response considerably. The trick that the youth played on his fellow slaves at the dance was malicious and disproportionate to the humiliation he had received at their hands. As narrator Green makes no attempt to justify his revenge, either. Instead, he plunges directly into another ironic reversal for his protagonist, which forces him into a predicament similar to the one he had created for the dancers. Having watched the youth fall prey to the elemental, poetic justice of the biter bit, we are subtly drawn back into a sympathetic interest in him as we wonder whether he can conjure up another deception to escape his master's wrath. Our sympathy turns to outrage when we realize that the trickster's slick mode of dodging the whip brings cruel retribution to every other Negro on the plantation. How much can we trust Green's profession of a guilty conscience at the time when it is paired with his blatant acknowledgment of self-love as the prime motivating factor of all his behavior? The complexities introduced into our judgment of this young man are compounded by the almost admirable neatness with which he resolves his conflict between self and community interest. One must admit that by selecting Dick the informer as his final victim, Green was able to turn at least part of the needless suffering he had brought to the black community to some community advantage. Our moral judgment of Green as a betrayer of his people is complicated by the implicit narrative invitation we receive to compare Dick's mode of community betrayal with the young trickster's. Which figure is most alien to our respect—the "lickspittle" who serves white authority or the rogue who loves himself best over any authority? The sheer effrontery of the trickster's individualism and triumphant self-will, when contrasted to the craven nature of the informer's equally marginal role vis-à-vis the black community, places Green in a distinctly interstitial moral position somewhere between our outright condemnation and approval.

Then, too, our response to the protagonist of this narrative is further complicated by what we learn of the fates of the dancers whose horses he ran off. Unintentionally, Green's revenge had a salutary outcome for some of those slaves who chose flight to Canada over return to their masters' punishment. On the other hand, a number died in the attempt to reach Canada, and the large majority of the stranded dancers suffered painfully as a result of the trickster's vindictiveness. If we judge the trickster according to his intentions in this whole affair, we may very well condemn him, but at the same time we cannot ignore the fact that the crisis he precipitated that night compelled many slaves to break out of their appointed roles and in various ways to resist and even escape their bondage. Here again Green's behavior exemplifies one of the central contradictions of the trickster's power: while it threatens his community with the possibility of chaos, it also may endow a community with "vitality and other boons." Whatever beneficence he creates depends on the destruction of order, at least temporarily, and the violation of taboos.[6]

The trickster in Green's narrative brings the possibility of freedom, but only to those who are willing, as he is, to step outside of community, which is inevitably to weaken it for the sake of self. Thus the true trickster in the slave narrative represents both the creative *and* destructive potential of freedom in the context of both the black *and* white communities. Moreover, just as Green neither justifies nor repudiates his own unrestrained will to power, so his narrative prevents us from idealizing a slave's individual quest for freedom without simultaneously recognizing the possible community consequences of the growth of self-will in any slave, particularly one as cunning as Jacob Green. We may never know the extent to which slaves determined to be free had to liberate themselves from their obligations to the black community as well as violate the rules of the white social order in order to realize their private ambitions.[7]

If there is one leitmotif that pervades Green's story, it is the principle of reversal, of things and people transformed into their opposites, of events cycling from humor to horror and back again. What goes around usually comes around with a terrible, fateful logic in the world of J. D. Green, and triumph seems almost an inevitable prelude to tragedy. Everyone, white as well as black, must dance to an often-violent rhythm of metamorphosis. Green's narrative tone remains remarkably equable (another manifestation of marginality) as he recounts farcical and appalling incidents of slave life in unmediated succession, without the kinds of moral pronouncements we usually find framing the episodes of conventional slave narratives. Green rarely feels obliged to explain even the transformations that occurred in his own life. We can only wonder why, after the ample evidence he gives us of his disreputable youth, he insists that "from 18 to 27 I was considered one of the most devout Christians among the whole Black population," firmly convinced that "to run away from my master would be to sin against the Holy Ghost" (22). Unlike the usual conversion narrative, Green's tells us nothing about his reformation of character. We can be sure, however, that it will not last, for, when his wife and children are sold away without warning or explanation, Green begins stealing from his master to raise money for passage to freedom. Once on the road he puts his training in chicanery to the ultimate test against whites who are as deceitful and as desperate as the black trickster himself. The latter pages of his narrative read much more like a conventional picaresque narrative as the wily fugitive matches wits with would-be captors of all stripes before finally reaching safety in Toronto in 1848, after his third escape. At this point his narrative abruptly stops; in place of a conclusion, we are given an excerpt from a three-year-old article in the London *Times* concerning the secession of South Carolina from the Union.

What we might like to know most by the end of our reading of this narrative we will never learn. Who, finally, was Jacob D. Green? Can he be trusted any more as slave narrator than as slave? What could have been his purpose in identifying himself with the polymorphous and perverse identities of the trickster, betwixt and between the oppositions we employ to define identity? Green hints at an answer in the exclamation of his master upon learning how his slave had thwarted his plans to have hi.n flogged: "He said, 'you black vagabond, stay on this plantation three months longer, and you will be the master and I the slave.'" Most likely Earle did not fear a literal reversal of status between his slave and himself, but rather a more generalized threat to order, appointed status, and authority embodied in a trickster who refused to stay in his place. When the trickster's activities level hierarchies, dissolve distinctions, and reverse roles even temporarily, an alternative modality of social relationship is created, which, following Victor Turner, I have called "communitas." As noted in Chapter 5, when communitas supplants the normal structure of instituted relationships in a social unit, the bonds between people become "anti-structural in that they are undifferentiated, egalitarian," and liberated from "obligation, jurality, law and constraint." This, of course, constitutes a grave danger to the exploitative relationship of white and black in slavery, for in the state of communitas even the lowest ranks of society see themselves as "concrete, idiosyncratic individuals . . . equal in terms of shared humanity" with their supposed betters.[8] Under such liminal circumstances, when all social classifications and proprieties are suspended if not reversed, one has the chance to gain fresh insight into the provisional character of those sociocultural institutions that define identity. If there is anything essential in identity, anything knowable apart from sociocultural institutions, this fundamental self will be comprehensible only in communitas with another, when we place in abeyance the assumptions that we ordinarily use to judge identity according to the roles people play in the normal world of noncommunal values.

This, in turn, speaks to the relationship of white reader and black writer in Afro-American autobiography. When J. D. Green plays the trickster, he confounds the expectations and preferences of both those who tried to master him in the past and those who expect him to serve their interests and needs in the present. Earle's fear of a reversal of status and power may very well be analogous to the consternation that a reader of autobiography will feel if he or she suspects that the writer is no longer "your humble servant" to the truth. Such distrust and consequent resistance stem, at least in one important sense, from the reader's proprietary assumption that the grounds on which the autobiographical discourse takes place are his "plantation," where all the sowing and reaping are to be done according to his norms and needs. The reader may believe that all he or she is demanding is the truth, but having read James W. C. Pennington's *Fugitive Blacksmith*, we should remember that property rights to the truth can become a matter of intense dispute during autobiographical occasions involving blacks and whites. We have wanted to think of these as discursive occasions, but Green's narrative questions this easy assumption, too, by arguing implicitly that real discourse, a truly mediative dialogue, cannot take place on such a literary plantation. Hence, Green must break away from it and liberate his reader from it as well, even though this may be the only place we feel at home, before any genuine discourse can ensue. For a short time at least, Green's conduct toward his reader pushes us into a kind of liminal reading situation, in which the usual cues for a reader's response are suspended or even contradicted. In spite of, indeed, because of his refusal to join the pseudo-discourse of the conventional *en*slaved narrative, Green leaves open the possibility for a greater communitas of discourse between blacks and whites in autobiography.

Other slave narrators contemporary with Green celebrated the tricks and role reversals they played to achieve freedom, but none risked their discursive relationship with their readers in the manner of Green. One of the most famous mid-century picaresque slave narratives was William Craft's *Running a Thousand Miles for Freedom* (1860), which recounted the unique stratagem that the author and his very light-skinned wife Ellen devised to enable them to travel from southern Georgia to freedom in Philadelphia in December 1848. Ellen Craft disguised herself as a male slaveowner bound for medical attention in the North; her husband played the role of her faithful slave. As narrator, Craft sensed that white readers would be troubled by the example of a temporarily "unsexed" woman artful and devious enough to pass for male as well as white. Thus, in the tradition of the "justified picaro," he assured his reader: "My wife had no ambition whatever to assume this disguise, and would not have done so had it been possible to have obtained our liberty by more simple means."[9] Part of Craft's argument is that, contrary to its profession, the slavocracy willfully nullifies distinctions between black and white or wife and whore when an unprotected white girl can be passed off as an octoroon for sale. His narrative begins with an account of just such a blurring of opposites in a New Orleans case early in the century. He and his wife, therefore, simply exploited reversals already inherent in the perversities of the slave system—they did not themselves introduce some new and degrading role for woman to play. By referring to his wife as "my master" and "he" throughout his account of their escape, Craft actually savors the convincingness of her charade while also suspending, during his narration of the liminal phase of their lives, the equation of mastery and maleness on which societal power in the North and South had been traditionally predicated. The freedom that he and his wife extracted from the margin between male and female, white and black, and master and slave empowered Craft as autobiographer to make free with his reader in these literary ways. Once they reached Philadelphia, the Crafts returned to their conventional roles and the autobiographer to a traditional relationship to his characters and readers. Still, the Crafts' creation of identities that temporarily confuse the lines separating sexual, racial, and social classification in America mark them as interstitial figures in Afro-American autobiography, though their trickiness is not as shocking or as free as J. D. Green's. He is the supreme interstitial subversive of Afro-American autobiography in its first century.

Reversals in Frederick Douglass's life since his 1845 *Narrative* spurred the most famous black man of the era to undertake a fresh autobiographical stock-taking in the mid-1850s, the result of which was *My Bondage and My Freedom* in 1855. During the decade between his two books, Douglass underwent a rite of passage totally unanticipated by the pattern of events in the *Narrative* and wholly unprepared for by Douglass himself. Beginning in the summer of 1847, when he returned from his triumphal British speaking tour, Douglass found himself increasingly at odds with William Lloyd Garrison and the ideology of the Garrisonians. With money raised by his English supporters, the ex-slave had planned to start an antislavery weekly, but the *Liberator* counseled against it on the grounds that a new paper would only drain support away from existing abolitionist periodicals, in the unlikely event that such a paper, edited by a colored man, succeeded at all. Besides, a journalistic career would only divert Douglass from his true calling as a platform lecturer against slavery. Douglass temporarily acquiesced in this ruling by his Massachusetts associates, but by September he resolved to go ahead with the project as a way of disproving the "alleged inferiority" of black people in freedom and demonstrating "their capacity for a more exalted civilization than slavery and prejudice had assigned them." Garrison was not pleased. Nevertheless, in November Douglass moved to Rochester, New York, where he set up his newspaper, *North Star*, well outside the orbit of the Boston-centered American Anti-Slavery Society.

Although he maintained cordial relations with the Garrisonians for a few years, he could not hide his growing dissent with them over such questions as the interpretation of the Constitution (Garrison called it a proslavery document; Douglass decided that if strictly interpreted it was not so), the necessity of secession from the free states' "union with slaveholders" (Garrison demanded it; Douglass opposed dissolution of the Union), and the value of political action as a means of abolishing slavery (Garrison avowed "the non-voting principle" as an act of conscience; Douglass decided that the ballot should be used to overthrow slavery). Their open rupture took place in May 1851 at the eighteenth annual meeting of the American Anti-Slavery Society, when Douglass announced that in the future his paper would embrace the Constitution as an instrument of emancipation and would urge its readers to use political as well as moral means to abolish slavery. Outraged, Garrison exclaimed from the rostrum, "There is roguery somewhere," and successfully moved the

Frederick Douglass (circa 1855), from an ambrotype by an unknown artist. (National Portrait Gallery, Smithsonian Institution)

prohibition of further funding of the *North Star* by the society. A month later, the *Liberty Party Paper* merged with Douglass's to become *Frederick Douglass' Weekly*, a clear indication that the black editor was allying himself with political abolitionists like the Liberty party leader Gerrit Smith, whom the Garrisonians regarded as mischievous rivals. By the end of the next year, Douglass would be viewed by Wendell Phillips as "completely estranged from us [the Garrisonians]" and labeled by another Garrison intimate, Oliver Johnson, as "the most malignant" of "all the seceders and apostates from our ranks." [10]

From the vantage point of the outsider, reviled not only by proslavery interests but also by many of the most respected black and white antislavery spokesmen and women, Douglass in the early 1850s was forced to reconsider both his future and his past in the abolition movement. For the future, he felt himself obliged to impress upon the northern black community the necessity of economic "self-reliance" and sociopolitical "self-elevation" as basic means of group advancement. He had learned from individual experience that neither personal nor social progress was possible unless blacks would "commit the provoking sin of *impudence*" and exert themselves "to get out of our sphere." In an 1850 editorial Douglass exemplified this needful "sin" in his self-motivated passage "through all the grades of [southern] servitude" on the way to attaining the goal of freedom. By the fall of 1852, however, he would write privately of another "school through which I have passed, a school which has many good qualities, but a school *too* narrow in its philosophy and too bigoted in spirit to do justice to any who venture to differ from it." That school, of course, belonged to Garrison. The former slave's respect for the man who had been his inspiration for so long was such that he forbore censuring Garrison directly until the eve of the publication of *My Bondage and My Freedom*. In the spring of 1855, however, Douglass justified his editorial assertion that "OUR ELEVATION AS A RACE, IS ALMOST WHOLLY DEPENDENT UPON OUR OWN EXERTIONS" by noting that "we have called down upon our devoted head, the holy (?) horror of a certain class of Abolitionists, because we have dared to maintain our Individuality, and have opened our own eyes, and looked out of them, through another telescope." Accusing "American Garrisonianism" of being only theoretically, not practically, in favor of "the Idea of our Equality with the whites," Douglass called on all blacks to "help us perform the '*disagreeable duty*,' of telling the truth, and the whole truth, though its promulgation make enemies of 'our best friends' [i.e., the Garrisonians]." In open battle with his erstwhile sponsors, Douglass now pleaded for the support of men like Samuel Ringgold Ward to help him redeem "our whole race, from every species of oppression, irrespective of the form it may assume, or the source whence it may emanate." [11] Clearly, in Douglass's mind, the arena in which the black struggle for freedom in America was being contended had expanded considerably since 1845. It was in the spirit of this revelation that he wrote *My Bondage and My Freedom.*

Douglass's second autobiography is in many respects a greater testimony of freedom "from every species of oppression" than his first. The 1845 *Narrative,* for all its impressiveness as an autonomous autobiographical act, should not be read without acknowledging, as Robert Stepto has been the first to do, the subtle "tension" between Garrison's preface, which takes credit for inspiring Douglass in the antislavery cause, and Douglass's own text, which seeks to flesh out a portrait of its author as something much more than an abolitionist mouthpiece. In a very troubling sense, the alpha and omega of the 1845 *Narrative* is Garrison, whose words, we are told on the last page of the *Narrative* proper, became Douglass's "meat and drink" in the North and whose sentiments, concerning political action, for instance, are echoed in intervening chapters of the *Narrative.* What we are speaking of here is not so much an enclosing presence as a crucial parameter in the text that dictated in an inevitably restrictive way the range of Douglass's thinking about some key questions and the rhetorical form of his expression of that thinking. So long as Garrison and all he symbolized remained an unquestionable standard for the ex-slave, he would not be able to pen a truly free story, for he would not feel himself at liberty to declare himself independent of the claims of Garrisonianism on his loyalties. Once Douglass broke with his quondam "best friends," however, and "opened [his] own eyes" to his past and present, he gained a perspective that allowed him to see signs of "oppression" in the very "form" of the fugitive slave narrative that he had written in 1845. The first indication of this in *My Bondage and My Freedom* is the supplanting of Garrison by a vehemently anti-Garrisonian black abolitionist, James McCune Smith, as prefacer of Douglass's memoir.[12] From its introductory pages one can see that *My Bondage and My Freedom* was not meant to serve the *Narrative* as an updating second installment. In its tone, dominant metaphors, and structure, the new book represents a quiet but thorough revision of the significance of the life of Frederick Douglass.

A cursory comparison of the *Narrative* and *My Bondage and My Freedom* indicates that the latter book is larger, roomier, more detailed, and more leisurely written, befitting the more reflective mood of its author in 1855. Having lived an additional decade in the North, Douglass expands to seventy pages the few paragraphs allotted in the *Narrative* to his life in freedom and then appends a generous selection of speeches and other writings published since 1845. What is perhaps more remarkable, however, is the second autobiography's expansion in scope and depth of Douglass's memories of slavery. In 1855 Douglass did not have many new incidents from his slave experience to bring to light. What he wanted to do was cast the familiar incidents of the *Narrative*, and especially the ac- tors in those incidents, in a different light. Douglass was now an accom- plished man of letters, a sophisticated journalist as well as orator, and it was only natural that the ex-Garrisonian editor would want to revise the Garrisonian autobiographer. The editor had no intention of retracting anything substantial that he had said in judgment of slavery ten years ear- lier. In fact, after having disavowed his Massachusetts mentor and the pacifism that all Garrisonians were bound to maintain, Douglass went so far as to justify slaves' murdering their masters in *My Bondage and My Freedom*, displaying neither qualm nor qualification in making such a statement.[13] Still, there was much that Douglass did want to qualify from his 1845 depiction of slavery and much that he wanted to elaborate from it as well.

The young jeremiad-writer had painted his past in stark and striking outline; the older autobiographer wanted to shade in deeper dimensions to add proportion and perspective to the total portrait. The central char- acter would remain essentially the same as he had been portrayed in 1845, but his background, particularly the *human* environment in which he developed as a youth, would be given greater prominence. By 1855 Douglass had become convinced, as he wrote in *My Bondage and My Freedom*, that "a man's character greatly takes its hue and shape from the form and color of things about him" (80). The *Narrative* had pictured its protagonist in slavery as a heroic loner whose relationship to his environ- ment was largely adversarial. Slavery was "hell," a state of deprivation epitomized by the absence of mother, father, family, and, except during a short interlude at Mr. Freeland's, community with others. In the "heaven" of freedom, according to the *Narrative*, the black isolato was restored to community not only with blacks but with right-thinking whites. In 1855, however, the severe simplicity of this scheme underwent much modifica- tion with the result that the environment of "bondage" takes on much more of a presence in the second autobiography and the world of "free- dom" loses its plenary status. In sum, what was largely missing from the *Narrative*—a sense of the complex relationship of its protagonist to his environment, especially in the South, along with an understanding of the significance of that complex relationship to the evolution of his character and the meaning of his life—is infused into *My Bondage and My Free- dom*. What Douglass wanted to probe in 1855 was the dynamics of au- thority and power in each of the major relationships of his life. His un- spoken but implicit purpose was to revise the myth of his life so as to make his rebellion against Garrison a climactic moment, both under-standable and justifiable according to Douglass's new sense of his past and his mission in the North.

The first important relationship that Douglass discusses in *My Bondage and My Freedom* is one he says little about in the *Narrative*, his relation-ship to his grandmother Betsey Baily. Capable, energetic, and highly es-teemed for her self-sufficiency, this woman, along with her free husband Isaac, created a home for the young slave boy separated from his mother. Douglass nostalgically reminisces at some length about "MY HOME—the only home I ever had" (44). It was a place of "the veriest freedom" and "sweet content" within "the joyous circle under her care." Betsey Baily's authority was benign, allowing her charge to do "whatever his boyish nature suggests," but all the time the child knew that another had a claim on him, a "mysterious personage, called by grandmother, with every mark of reverence, 'Old Master.'" In the first of many religious metaphors that he would use to describe his relationships to the authorities in his life, Douglass likens his transfer from his grandmother's "joyous circle" to "Old Master's" realm to a ritual sacrifice. The old woman must play the role of "a priestess" bearing her grandson as "a meet offering to the fear-ful and inexorable *demi-god*" (45). To ease the separation, Betsey Baily does not tell seven-year-old Fred why he must go with her, one summer morning, on the twelve-mile journey from Tuckahoe to Colonel Lloyd's plantation on the Wye River. When the slave boy discovers that he has been deserted without explanation, he gets his "first introduction to the realities of slavery." "I had never been deceived before; and I felt not only grieved at parting . . . but indignant that a trick had been played upon me in a matter so serious" (49).[14]

This incident, "apparently so trivial" that it goes unmentioned in the *Narrative*, assumes its priority in *My Bondage and My Freedom* as a re-sult of Douglass's revisionistic decision to treat the ideal of "home" as well as "freedom" as the ambiguous, often mutually exclusive objects of his life's journey. "MY HOME," from which the slave boy had been so rudely thrust at such a crucial period in his life, remained for the adult Douglass a resonant symbol of what Houston Baker terms the imagined "prior unity" that has been so often "the object of black America's quest." This is not acknowledged in the *Narrative*, where "freedom" encompasses all that the protagonist seeks. But by 1855 Douglass realized that before freedom had beckoned him there had lain within him the hunger for a home, whetted by his bittersweet memory of his grandmother's "circle" with him at the center. Within this plenitude he had enjoyed the ideal of total freedom from restraint yet secure attachment to a nurturing, pro-tective authority. The betrayal of that authority illustrated the vanity of any such idea of home for a slave child subject to the whims of god-like whites. The author of *My Bondage and My Freedom*, however, was bound to reveal how powerfully that idea of home had motivated him throughout his youth and young manhood. It was also important to show that "every time the young tendrils of my affection became attached, they were rudely broken by some unnatural outside power" (186–87).

Douglass persevered through his youth and young manhood in quest of a paradox, a locus of psychological oppositions somehow reconciled in the nostalgic image of his grandmother's home, where he recalled the blessing of simultaneous freedom from and attachment to a nurturing authority in whom he could place complete trust and belief. In the *Narrative* we see how slavery's assaults on his emotional attachments tempered the steel within the young Frederick, thus empowering him to become the black rebel-individualist celebrated in that story. *My Bondage and My Freedom* gives us the other side of Douglass, the side that responded to his emotional losses by creating new attachments to others whom he identified unconsciously with the recovery of all that home signified. The structure of Douglass's life in the second autobiography is patterned after an evolving dialectic between these two sides of the man: the side that sought plenitude within, through some sort of ideal of the free self, and the side that sought plenitude outside, through an ideal of communal attachment. Douglass romanticized his defiance of authority throughout the *Narrative* as a way of building up his heroic image. In 1855, however, he would depict himself often as a seeker of authority, though persistently betrayed by it, even "something of a hero worshiper, by nature," to use his own phrase, who, like the protagonist of Ralph Ellison's *Invisible Man*, kept trying to find someone who could show him a way home.[15]

The slave boy found little to call home on Colonel Lloyd's plantation, though its grandeur impressed him a good deal. His mother had been hired out to a planter twelve miles away; with the other black children of the plantation, Fred was placed under the authority of Aunt Katy, the "sable virago" who presided over Old Master's kitchen. The black cook's "meanness, injustice, partiality, and oppressions" introduced the young Douglass to the rigors of power on the plantation well before he ever saw an overseer whip a slave. Her freedom to "beat, as well as starve" him, regardless of the fact that she was only a slave like himself, attests to a pecking order in the slave quarters whose character and function the narrator of *My Bondage and My Freedom* is at some pains to bring to light. Neither Aunt Katy nor her black counterpart in cruelty, Uncle Isaac Copper, makes an appearance in the *Narrative*. In 1845 Douglass preferred to emphasize the corrupting nature of power in the hands of white slaveowners alone. Ten years later he analyzed the entire plantation as a quasi-feudal hierarchy of authority and obligation that entangled many levels of its caste structure in abuses of power. In a social system in which "everybody," even the victimized slave, "wants the privilege of whipping somebody else" (72), nobody is exempt from the abuse of what little authority he or she may accrue. Copper's laudable aim of teaching the black children the Lord's Prayer is corrupted by his quick employment of hickory switches to force his pupils' close attention to their task. The old slave enjoys the prestige of having a surname and functioning independently as the quarters' "doctor of medicine, and doctor of divinity as well." Yet he is also a tool of the masters who gives his underlings their first lessons in respecting the absolute authority of the whip. Aunt Katy exploits her position in the kitchen by "cramming" her own offspring with food, though it means "starving" little Fred and the other black children who depend on her. Though in principle her master's slave with no right to deny other chattels in his property their sustenance, she behaves in fact more like his vassal, in a relationship parallel to that of Old Master and his lord, Colonel Lloyd. "What [her master] was to Col. Lloyd, he made Aunt Katy to him" (74). The cook "was often fiendish in her brutality" to the children of the quarters, but she exercised near-absolute power in her sphere because "she had a strong hold on old master," who "considered her a first rate cook" and therefore granted her special favors and power (74).

Douglass's description of the chains of privilege and obligation that linked slave to master and master to overlord on Colonel Edward Lloyd's "baronial domains" is designed to show us how the peculiar institution worked as a paternalistic system. Douglass might have provided a paradigm for Eugene D. Genovese's explanation of the way in which paternalism "afforded a fragile bridge across the intolerable contradictions inherent in a society based on racism, slavery, and class exploitation. . . . For the slaveholders paternalism represented an attempt to overcome the fundamental contradiction in slavery: the impossibility of the slaves' ever becoming the things they were supposed to be. Paternalism defined the involuntary labor of the slaves as a legitimate return to their masters for protection and direction. But the masters' need to see their slaves as acquiescent human beings constituted a moral victory for the slaves themselves. Paternalism's insistence upon mutual obligations—duties, responsibilities, and ultimately even rights—implicitly recognized the slaves' humanity."[16]

Douglass recalls a number of slaves in addition to Uncle Isaac and Aunt Katy who found ways to gain a modicum of recognition and advantage from their masters through the quid pro quo arrangements of paternalism.[17] He makes it clear that as just a boy he soon proved adept at making the system work to his benefit, too. If the "termagant" in the kitchen refused to feed him, he would sing under his mistress's window, whereupon Miss Lucretia Auld was likely to reward him with bread. By ingratiating himself to Master Daniel Lloyd, son of the great paterfamilias himself, he "got protection from the bigger boys" and occasionally a share of young master's cakes and biscuits. Even Old Master, Captain Aaron Anthony, whom the boy had learned to fear from an early age, "showed an affectionate disposition" toward him. "Could the reader have seen him gently leading me by the hand—as he sometimes did—patting me on the head, speaking to me in soft, caressing tones and calling me his 'little Indian boy,' he would have deemed him a kind old man, and, really, almost fatherly" (80). In 1845 Douglass indicted Anthony categorically as "a cruel man," in no wise humane to his slaves. But in 1855, a different figure appears from Douglass's pen, "a wretched man, at war with his own soul, and with all the world around him" (81). It seemed as though Old Master were "possessed by a demon," for while he "could be kind," his "temper," "subjected to perpetual trials," could explode and his "passions run wild." This Douglass learned firsthand when he witnessed Anthony's hideous flogging of Esther (Aunt Hester in the *Narrative*). By courting a slave named Ned Roberts after she had been forbidden to do so by Old Master, the beautiful slave woman directly defied the paternal authority and male "pride" of her owner, the result of which was an especially sadistic punishment fueled by the passions of "envy, jealousy, and the thirst for revenge."

The "demon" that set Anthony "at war with his own soul" had its origins in the grotesque contradictions on which his paternalistic relationship to his slaves was based. A slaveholder who could be kind and fatherly toward his blacks could, when provoked by an affront to his patriarchal honor and prerogative, turn on them with the ferocity of the devouring demigod of Douglass's metaphor. Paternalism fostered varying degrees of intimacy between masters and slaves, ranging from the quasi-familial, in young Fred's case, to the outright sexual, as Douglass broadly implies in his discussion of Anthony's demands of Esther in both his autobiographies. Under such circumstances, Genovese stresses that "every act of impudence and insubordination—every act of unsanctioned self-assertion"—could escalate into "an act of treason and disloyalty." When Esther repudiated the principle of submission that bound not only the slave to the master but also, more fundamentally, the female to the male, then she struck at the heart of Anthony's self-esteem as the first male claimant on her loyalties. She had placed her own limits on the "doctrine of reciprocity," which the white pater-masters demanded the authority to administer by their interpretation alone.[18]

In 1845 Douglass wrote that watching the whipping of Aunt Hester unveiled to him "the blood-stained gate, the entrance to the hell of slavery, through which I was about to pass." In 1855 the narrator of *My Bondage and My Freedom* did not invest the scene with the significance of an initiation. Perhaps this was because to speak of being dragged through such a lurid, Dantesque portal into bondage seemed no longer an accurate way of imaging the manner in which he had been socialized as a slave. At any rate, in 1855 Douglass narrated a more gradual and insidious intellectual and emotional binding of the black boy to white oppressors whose methods elicited both his submission and resistance, respect and disdain, gratitude and resentment, praise and reproach. From this point through the rest of the story of his bondage and his freedom, Douglass would trace the crooked path of losses and gains down which the paternalistic powers of his life had led him to his ultimate liberating revelations of the 1850s.

As the young slave boy witnessed more and more of the sufferings of his fellows in bondage, he began to ask questions about the source of ultimate responsibility for his condition next to that of his white masters. The answers he received from some slaves reflected their belief in a sort of Great Chain of Paternal Authority that reached all the way up to God, the Big Master in heaven. This God made whites to be masters and blacks to be slaves; because He "was good," and "knew what was best for me, and best for everybody" (90), to question His ordinances was folly. The slave boy doubted this means of justifying the ways of God to man, however, because he knew of blacks who were not slaves and whites who were not slaveholders. Besides, how could God be good if He permitted blacks to suffer as Aunt Esther had? The seven-year-old decided that "not *God*, but *man*" was the root cause of slavery, a conclusion that "filled [him] with a burning hatred of slavery" and also "increased [his] suffering" as his awareness of the injustice of his condition dawned on him. From a very early age then, Frederick Douglass found himself confronted with a two-tiered problem of authority arising from the idea of a paternalistic cosmos overarching a paternalistic earthly sphere. He was determined "to accept God as a father," and "to regard slavery as a crime" (134), but how could one render one's duties to the good Heavenly Father while refusing to do the same to the evil earthly fathers? Religious instruction for the slave in the South always predicated salvation by the Heavenly Father on faithful service to His earthly surrogate, the white master.[19]

Douglass's surprise removal to Baltimore in the spring of 1826 soothed such worries as these with the balm of an affection he had never known before. Sophia Auld's motherly tenderness and encouragement of Fred's talents drew him into what seemed a "new home" of the brightest prospects. On Fell's Point, at least for a while, he lived under the mildest of paternalistic—or, we should say, maternalistic—regimes. Mrs. Auld could not think of young Fred as a chattel; in many ways she tended to treat him more as the "half-brother" to her son than as his slave. However, as had been the case in Fred's relationship to his grandmother, this idyllic home proves transient. The demands of paternalism for a dutiful slave override its sense of familial obligation to the young Negro in its charge. Discovering that his wife has been teaching young Fred to read, Hugh Auld asserts his paternal authority over both his woman and his slave and forbids further lessons on the grounds that "'learning . . . would forever unfit him [young Fred] for the duties of a slave'" and make him "'disconsolate and unhappy'" in the bargain (146). Auld, of course, is prescient: the slave boy's subsequent covert reading not only "unfits" him for slavery but also arouses in him the spirit of "rebellion." Through "a new and special revelation," young Fred realizes that knowledge and the expanded awareness that accompanies it constitute "the direct pathway from slavery to freedom."

It also becomes clear to the boy that this pathway to knowledge leads diametrically away from home. To attain the knowledge that he craved for himself, he would have "to resort to indirections [deceits and concealments] by no means congenial to my nature" (151). It was not in the boy's nature to spurn his petted status under Sophia Auld and, by defying the paternal edict, to be cast out of yet another maternal Eden, as it were, in exchange for the forbidden fruit of knowledge. The more light that reading cast on his consciousness, the more distressed and tormented the black boy became. "Too thoughtful to be happy," Douglass says that he "almost envied [his] fellow slaves their stupid contentment" (160). They remained inside the circle of unconscious contentment that paternalism reserved for any slave who was willing to accept that as his home. Young Frederick had taken his first willed step outside.

Emotional alienation from the paternalistic authority of the Aulds sends young Frederick in search of compensation for the loss of his blighted home. The speeches anthologized in the *Columbian Orator* thrill him with their "brilliant vindication of the rights of man," but however much they enhance his sense of self-worth and unmask the false pretenses of his "good, *kind* master," they also leave a void, or rather, leave the awakened black youth with a growing consciousness of what we might call today his existential bereavement of community as a consequence of (1) his being a slave, and (2) his refusal of the paternalistic social relationships offered him as a perverse substitute for community. These are terrible revelations for the young black who learns to read slavery aright. Let him discover the *aporia*, or logical impasses, that belie the privileging of paternalistic and racist powers over him, and he will, in effect, deconstruct the authoritarian ideology that imprisons him. But do not expect that the light shed on his condition as a result of this demolition will be a great comfort to him. Such a revelation of his existential aloneness will almost of necessity send him in search of a compensating essence around which he might reconstruct an alternative sphere of meaning and community. In a very limited sense young Douglass would try to do this with the abolitionists, of whom he learned indirectly by hearsay and by reading reports in the *Baltimore American*. He derived "a deep satisfaction" from this knowledge that "I was not alone" in a deep revulsion against slavery (165). But prior to this, and more fundamental than this, was the slave boy's decision, by the age of thirteen, that he was in "need of God, as a father and protector." If the earthly fathers and mothers had failed him, he could still reach out to the paternal "authority of God" above them in the ultimate hope of securing an indestructible heavenly home.

A white Methodist minister was the catalyst to Douglass's conversion, but it was a black drayman, Charles Lawson, who became Douglass's "spiritual father" and "chief instructor, in matters of religion" (168). "Father Lawson" was the first to inspire the teenaged black youth with a sense of destiny and calling; "he had been shown that I must preach the gospel." When Douglass wondered how such a thing could ever be, the old man replied simply, "'*Trust in the Lord.*'" When the young slave argued that his future was already determined, Lawson told him, "'If you want liberty, . . . ask the Lord for it, *in faith*, AND HE WILL GIVE IT TO YOU.'" As a result of this counsel, Frederick took new hope, "believing that my life was under the guidance of a wisdom higher than my own." He felt sure that "in His own good time," his heavenly Father would "deliver [him] from [his] bondage" (169). Meanwhile, he found more and more of his "attachments . . . now outside of our family," for example, among a handful of young Baltimore blacks whom he taught to read. Unfortunately, when Hugh and Thomas Auld quarreled early in 1833 over the disposition of Douglass's crippled cousin Henny, all the black youth's newly formed attachments were obliterated in one command from Thomas Auld—that his brother immediately return to St. Michael's the slave on loan named Frederick.

Before Douglass went back to the Eastern Shore, he had already lost his faith in his earthly southern masters and their paternalistic pretensions; at

St. Michael's, his faith in a heavenly Father who would "deliver [him] from [his] bondage" also collapsed. Ironically, but appropriately, his religious disillusionment came at the hands of two very demonstrably Christian masters, Thomas Auld and Edward Covey, who used their public piety to underscore their image as firm but fatherly slaveholders. Auld's stingy meanness in his food allotments to his few slaves caused Douglass to start stealing with a clear conscience, despite the commandments he heard from the pulpit of the St. Michael's Methodist chapel, which both he and his master regularly attended. As a further index to his growing self-reliance, Douglass notes that he pondered the genuineness of Auld's conversion by "appealing to my own religious experience, and judging my master by what was true in my own case" (194–95). Douglass adopted a worldly, pragmatic test of his master's piety, very much in line with the religious morality of the slave community,[20] and Auld failed it miserably. After his profession of salvation, Captain Auld made his house "the 'preachers' home,'" but while he "stuffed" the white ministers at his board, he "starved" the black slaves in his kitchen. Douglass's contempt for such hypocrisy was shown by his bold and refractory manner toward his owner, which forced Auld to the decision to have the young blood broken by Edward Covey.

Reviewing the disjunctive series of events that had carried him to his new home at Covey's on the first of January 1834, Douglass recalls having been troubled by serious doubts about his heavenly Father's solicitude for his welfare. "'I am,' thought I, 'but the sport of a power which makes no account, either of my welfare or of my happiness'" (206). More alone than he had ever been in his life, the strong-willed teenager finds in the implacable slave-breaker the sternest test yet to his dignity and hope. After six months of beatings and humiliation, culminating in Covey's savage attack on his heat-stricken slave in the "treading yard" under the August sun, Douglass limps back to St. Michael's to beg Auld's "interposition of his power and authority, to protect me from further abuse." Master's refusal to interfere extinguishes Douglass's "last hope" in paternal succor from the big house; the next day, in the forest on his way back to Covey's, the slave finds that he cannot "pray for help for deliverance" either. "The sham religion which everywhere prevailed, cast in my mind a doubt upon all religion" (235). Cut adrift now from his appointed earthly and heavenly fathers, Douglass turns to a third paternal alternative, a black conjure man named Sandy Jenkins, whose belief in voodoo power the Christian Douglass would have once regarded as "dealings with the devil." The desperate slave puts his last remaining faith in paternal authority into Sandy, an "old advisor" similar to Father Lawson except that the one affiliates himself with the power of the Christian God and the other with the potency of the African supernatural. In accepting the protective roots given him by the "genuine African" plantation shaman, Douglass was trying to summon to himself the last source of other or outside power to which he had any access, the power of roots, symbolically signifying his African origins, which no longer seemed devilish once all his white attachments, earthly and cosmic, had betrayed him.

We know from reading the *Narrative* that in the end nothing was to avail Douglass against Covey except the black man's innate will to resist tyranny and thus revive within himself his own manhood. In 1845 Douglass stated that he did not know "from whence came the spirit" that caused him to fight back. In 1855, even as he wonders about the origins of that "daring spirit," he gives his readers good reason to identify it with "the devil." Douglass informs us that the morning he fought back against Covey was his first opportunity "to make my fallen state known" to those in power over him. This lapse from grace was the slave's liberation; "my hands were no longer tied by my religion" (241). Douglass was sufficiently outside the boundaries of the paternalistic moral order that he could reenact Lucifer's primordial *non serviam* and become the Rebel, the essential character of the Christian devil. Moreover, once he had defeated Covey, he "purposely aim[ed] to provoke [his master] . . . by refusing to keep with the other hands in the field." This "somewhat reckless" behavior gave him the reputation of having "*got the devil in me*," which distinguished him from his "servile brethren." While most slaves were "trained from the cradle up, to think and feel that their masters are superior, and invested with a sort of sacredness," Douglass prided himself on having "got free from it." Barren of Christian lovingkindness, "I hated slavery, slaveholders, and all pertaining to them; and I did not fail to inspire others with the same feeling, wherever and whenever opportunity was presented" (250–51).

As a preacher of hatred, not love, toward white authority, Douglass fulfilled another satanic office, that of the estranger, the alienator of superior and subordinate, the opposer of order, the lord of antistructure. As soon as the chance presented itself on Mr. Freeland's plantation, he set about "mischief," addressing his companions as to "the advantages of intelligence over ignorance" and, in general, doing his best to "disturb the quiet of the slaves and slave-masters of the neighborhood of St. Michael's." Just as the devil is a "slanderer" or "accuser" who labors to seduce others into his own orbit, so Douglass turns a handful of slaves against Mr. Freeland, "a man of many excellent qualities . . . quite preferable to any master [Douglass] ever had." None of the five slaves in his band of rebels "would have dreamed of escape as a possible thing" except at Douglass's instigation. He is their Prince of Light who inspires in them "incendiary" thoughts, but in the end he leads them to "perdition" in the Easton jail, where they are tormented by "fiends" and "imps" who mock their failed rebellion against the instituted authority of slavery. There Douglass is denounced by his master's mother, Mrs. Betsey Freeland, as a "*long legged yellow devil*" for having lured two of her favorite slaves, Henry and John, away from their home ("they having been reared from childhood in her house") and into reprobate status with himself.[21]

Douglass gladly embraces this characterization of himself as a devil at the climax of his slave career because it gives him a basis on which to do some devilish turning of metaphors and meanings without which he cannot have a complete turning point for his autobiography. Aside from recounting Mrs. Freeland's epithet, Douglass did little in the *Narrative* to associate himself with the devil. The first autobiography's emphasis is on Douglass as a savior, resurrected from "the tomb of slavery" by "bold defiance," it is true, but without the satanic attributes of defiance that *My Bondage and My Freedom* claims for its hero. Nothing is said in 1845 of Douglass's "fallen state," his purposeful provocations of Covey, his preaching of hatred and appeals to the "pride" of his disciples (289), his "mischief"-making and determination, upon arrival at Freeland's, to be "up to my old tricks" (264). In 1845 Douglass led his readers to believe that the Sabbath school he opened at Freeland's was the result of pressure from fellow slaves who longed to learn to read. *My Bondage and My Freedom* brings out Douglass's selfish motives; he "wanted a Sabbath school, in which to exercise my gifts" as well as to teach his brother slaves their letters. *My Bondage and My Freedom* also does not neglect to mention Douglass's preference for self-interest over the welfare of those he would have to leave behind in the slave quarters, people he knew were likely to suffer to some extent whether he succeeded or failed in his escape.[22] In sum, the second autobiography deliberately brings to the fore the contradictions in Douglass's role at the turning point of his life that are at most only hinted at in the first autobiography.

Douglass is determined to confront his reader with an image of himself as both savior and devil whose gospel threatens order throughout the plantation, whose leadership is shot through with the motives of hatred and the methods of violence, and whose unshakeable pride refuses to accept any status or seek any outside justification that conflicts with the desire of self. In light of these admissions, it is not surprising that the narrator of *My Bondage and My Freedom* was "not sure that some kind reader will not condemn me for being over ambitious, and greatly wanting in proper humility," in refusing to adapt himself to his improved lot at Freeland's and, in effect, spurning every blessing except that which would gratify his personal desire for total freedom (274). In this remark

Douglass designedly gives his northern readers grounds for seeing him as his southern masters did—as a man guilty of satanic sins and unrepentent of them, indeed, blithely turning them into virtues, in yet another imitation of the father of lies.

The obvious question we must address is, why did Douglass portray himself this way? Clearly, he is taking a risk in revealing this shadow self in his past, with all its satanic, destructive potential. Unlike a William Wells Brown or a Josiah Henson, he neither apologizes for this shadow as wayward self-will, nor does he try to explain it away as a temporary aberration brought on by the extreme pressures of slavery on his consciousness. Douglass is most devilish at Freeland's, where the rule of the master is comparatively mild. What makes Douglass original is his proud espousal of this subversive shadow and, more importantly, his repeated association of it with creative energy for the building of a black community. By contrast, Douglass's predecessors in the slave narrative interpret the shadow as antisocial, destructive of the Negro's saving relationship with his God (in the case of Henson and Pennington) or his communal relationship with his fellows in bondage (in the case of William Wells Brown).

The rebellious shadow comes to the fore in Douglass only when all his gods and fathers fail and he must become his own self-authorizing presence in a world bereft of legitimate structure or sanction. Douglass's behavior under these circumstances parallels that of the fictional Henrico Blacus, the rebel-hero of Martin R. Delany's revolutionary novel *Blake; or the Huts of America* (1859–62):[23] once outside the social structure and ideational superstructure of the white gods, the black alien becomes a kind of Promethean figure, a man-maker and light-bringer among his people by virtue (and I use the word advisedly) of transgressing the will of the supreme father of the gods. Thus, when we consider Douglass's devilish behavior, we should remember that these are but the satanic aspects of the larger Promethean mythic identity that he accrues to himself at the turning point of *My Bondage and My Freedom*.

Douglass's emphasis on the satanic in Prometheus is in keeping with the views of many of his Romantic literary contemporaries, like the black Delany or the white Percy Bysshe Shelley, both of whom admire and accentuate the proud antiauthoritarian *daimon* of their Promethean heroes and show aversion to only one element of the purely satanic rebel, namely, what Shelley calls his exclusive "desire for personal aggrandisement." From the time of Aeschylus's *Prometheus Bound*, the Western literary tradition has felt both pity and fear for the tragic rebel who pronounces defiantly: "I am the enemy of all the gods that gave me ill for good."[24] White as well as black nineteenth-century readers could be drawn to a bold transgressor of the established moral order if his fall, like that of self-sacrificial Prometheus, ensured the elevation of others. After all, as Harold Bloom has noted, the same Prometheus who was often regarded by nineteenth-century Romantics as a type of Lucifer had also been read traditionally "as an analogue of the crucified Christ," a savior of benighted humanity.[25] In keeping with both sides of this view of Prometheus, Douglass strongly suggests through his narration of his fall and his rebellion against the paternal gods above him that this satanic prelude was necessary not only to his personal resurrection from slavery but also to the creation of a community of slave disciples to whose redemption he would be equally dedicated.

We can see in *My Bondage and My Freedom* that as Douglass became progressively disillusioned by the false godliness of his Eastern Shore masters, he was impelled by his unsatisfied desire for nurturing relationships to seek a home in alternative religious communities for blacks alone. This is the context in which we may interpret his leadership of two Sabbath schools, one near the town of St. Michael's before Douglass went to Covey's and a second near Freeland's farm after the triumph over the slave-breaker. In both schools Douglass was the teacher of reading and the leader of thinking, first on religious topics but eventually (in the case of the latter school) on much more secular concerns. It is clear, however, from his description of the Freeland's experiment that what started out as a gesture of largesse from the educated teenager to his ignorant fellows ended up becoming the most mutually beneficial and egalitarian community that Douglass had heretofore experienced. "I never loved, esteemed, or confided in men, more than I did in these. . . . [N]o band of brothers could have been more loving. There were no mean advantages taken of each other, as is sometimes the case where slaves are situated as we were; . . . and no elevating one at the expense of the other. We never undertook to do anything, of any importance, which was likely to affect each other, without mutual consultation. We were generally a unit, and moved together" (269).

Here was a new model of home in a fraternal instead of paternal social arrangement, one in which power was distributed laterally, not vertically. While paternalism tended to fragment relationships with one's peers in favor of the cultivation of one's immediate superiors and inferiors, the fraternalism of Douglass's Freeland band cemented a bond of unity among the oppressed that weakened the chains that held them to their oppressors. For these disciples of freedom Douglass risked his own future by including them in his escape plot. He was the serpent who tempted them to rebel when none was "self-moved" to do so; he also made himself their potential savior—by showing them the way to freedom—and their potential partner in tragedy should their attempt fail. From the Christ-like side of Douglass's Promethean persona, the pathetic escape leader who moans in the Easton jail—"Where now is the God of justice and mercy?"—echoes Jesus in his passion on the cross—"My God, My God, why hast thou forsaken me?" From this perspective, Douglass figuratively went to hell in a futile but self-ennobling attempt to redeem his black brothers from their damnation in slavery.[26]

By appropriating the Prometheus metaphor and deliberately exploiting its tensions, Douglass gave evidence of his intellectual and artistic maturation beyond the boundaries of binary thinking that govern his 1845 *Narrative.* Before him, ever since the eighteenth century in fact, the Christian tradition and the politics of race had forced Afro-American autobiographers to make self-defeating (in two senses of the word) choices between Cain and Christ as metaphors of self: since there was inevitably something satanic about aspiring individualism in the Negro, the image of the altruistic Suffering Servant became the autobiographer's safest refuge from censure. The narratives of Douglass, Brown, and Bibb in the 1840s all indicate a gathering resistance to this invidious paradigm and the dilemma it posed for the depiction of a complex self. Meanwhile, the religion of the slaves themselves took the lead in creating an alternative. Black Christianity in the South assimilated the self-sacrificial Jesus with the idea of Moses as a communal deliverer in order to reconcile "spiritual freedom" and "earthly deliverance" while instilling in black folk "a spirit of pride and love in each other" that could sustain community until Canaan was reached.[27] In 1855 Frederick Douglass became the first black autobiographer to work out a similar kind of reconciliation of oppositions in his self-portrait by adopting the Prometheus metaphor, which he could freely turn in contrary directions at his literary will. When he turns the savior inside-out to reveal the devil to us, he becomes another manifestation of the trickster,[28] refusing to identify himself wholly or finally with either the insider or outsider but only with the freedom to move back and forth across the margin. There is no way to undo this Douglass-doubling short of making an arbitrary choice ourselves between the savior/satan alternatives that define the poles of interpretation of the Prometheus figure. In offering us this choice, Douglass turns the tables on his readers and gives them the same untenable choices between binary oppositions that the black autobiographer traditionally had to make. Thus the turning point of *My Bondage and My Freedom* becomes as much a matter of what choice the reader turns to, once faced with the savior/satan duality in Douglass, as it is a matter of the choices Douglass himself made at Covey's and Freeland's in 1833–34. Not to accept Prometheus as the metaphor of Douglass's marginality during his transition from slave to freeman is to restrict the potential "emergent meanings" (in Monroe Beardsley's terms) of this very maneuverable figure when applied to Douglass's subsequent Garrisonian career.

During the last phase of Douglass's experience in bondage, he received perhaps the most preferential treatment that slavery as a paternalistic system could offer. He was not punished for plotting escape; if anything, he was rewarded by being sent back to the Baltimore Aulds to learn a trade. For the first time in his 1855 autobiography Douglass reveals that Thomas Auld verbally assured him that if he behaved himself he would be manumitted in eight years, at the age of twenty-five. Even these heightened prospects, however, were but ashes in the mouth of one whose thirst for freedom could not be slaked by anything less than complete independence. The only inhibition on Douglass's plans for flight was "the painful sensation of being about to separate from a circle of honest and warm hearted friends" in the all-black East Baltimore Mental Improvement Society. This was another circle in which Douglass would have happily created a home for himself had not his enslaved status and obligations to Hugh Auld prevented him from free communal participation. Douglass's only alternative was to step outside once more, to seek in the North that elusive plenitude in which freedom and community dwelt harmoniously together.

In recounting his first impressions of freedom in New York City, Douglass makes it clear that despite his "joyous excitement" on arriving there, he was soon "oppressed" by "a sense of loneliness and insecurity." "In the midst of thousands of my fellow-men, and yet a perfect stranger" who felt he could "trust no man," Douglass once again had discovered himself "homeless" (340). The freedom he had achieved had come with an anxious awareness of his existential alienation, covering him "with something bordering on despair." The irony of getting "free from slavery" was that "I was free from home, as well." This sort of radical alienation was almost as intolerable as slavery itself, for while the one isolated him from "friends," "work," and "succor," the other estranged him from the ideal self he hoped to become in freedom.

Douglass began the process of rectifying this situation by marrying, taking a new name, and settling in New Bedford, Massachusetts, as a self-supporting day laborer. He also sought a church home with the Methodists on New Bedford's Elm Street, among whom he hoped to reverse his "backslidden state" in slavery and rejuvenate his dormant "religious faith." Although he was initially refused a seat in the sanctuary because of his color, Douglass thought that after his official conversion and uniting with the church, the whites would treat him "as a man and a brother." Observing the Methodists' segregated communion service, however, disabused the hopeful freeman of this illusion while unveiling to him the old racist paternalism in a new quasi-religious guise. As Douglass recalls the incident, the white Methodists were served the Lord's Supper while the black members of the church were kept "penned" in a back corner "like sheep without a shepherd," awaiting their invitation. When "pious Brother Bonney" condescended to call them, they came forward—the "poor, slavish souls"—but as for Douglass, "I went *out*, and have never been in that church since" (353). Following a now-familiar pattern to readers of his second autobiography, Douglass sought more satisfying communion in a black African Methodist Episcopal Zion church of New Bedford, where he soon became a class leader and local preacher. When he found, however, that even this church "consented to the same spirit which held my brethren in chains," he concluded that he could not unite permanently with this black community either and thus broke away from his attachments there.[29]

This renewed alienation from religious community, black as well as white, in the North provides the background in *My Bondage and My Freedom* for Douglass's introduction to Garrison. This context, followed by the extensive religious terminology that Douglass employs to characterize his first impressions of Garrison and the *Liberator*, is designed to call our attention to a strongly personal motive, emotional, not ideological, that propelled Douglass into the Garrisonian orbit. This motive is nowhere alluded to in the final pages of the 1845 *Narrative*, nor is the Douglass-Garrison relationship couched in any sort of religious metaphor in that book. But in *My Bondage and My Freedom*, Douglass discusses the origins and development of his Garrisonian career in a manner that insistently harks back to his previous patterns of attachment to and withdrawal from patrons who had exploited his propensity for "hero worship" and his craving for the special communion of home.

Douglass first learned of Garrison four or five months after reaching New Bedford, when he was shown a copy of the *Liberator* by a subscription agent. The paper "preached human brotherhood" and "denounced oppression," in particular chattel slavery, with a "holy fire." It soon ranked in the fugitive's mind "next to the bible"; through the paper, Douglass "learn[ed] to love" Garrison before ever having met him. Upon hearing the white abolitionist speak, the twenty-one-year-old former slave was powerfully moved by Garrison's "heavenly countenance" and his "exalted piety," as well as by his uncompromising perfectionism and immediatism with regard to the extirpation of slavery from the land. "Here was one, on first sight, to excite my love and reverence," Douglass continues, hinting that this extreme emotional response was precipitate and not based on sufficient knowledge or reflection. The narrator goes on to admit here that he was "something of a hero worshiper, by nature" (354) and that this propensity was very much at work in inspiring his "reverence" for the "exalted" Mr. Garrison. No wonder, then, that in the admiring eyes of the young freeman, Garrison loomed large as "the Moses, raised up by God, to deliver his modern Israel from bondage" (355). After all, Father Lawson had primed the young slave in his early teens to look to God for protection and for ultimate deliverance from slavery. It is not surprising to see Douglass, ten years later and in search of a fit object for his long-suppressed and often betrayed religious idealism, invest it in Garrison and his movement. Douglass's "spontaneous" elevation of Garrison to the status of Old Testament patriarch and secular saint is consistent with his conditioning as a slave taught to endow white authority with sacredness and to receive a master's words as commandments from God. That so many fatherly pretenders had failed the fatherless slave did not leave Douglass any less susceptible to a paternalistic attachment to Garrison, particularly at this transitional stage of the fugitive's life and especially since the great abolitionist seemed so eminently deserving of a black man's love and fidelity. At any rate, as Douglass confided privately to Charles Sumner in 1852, the relationship between himself and Garrison soon became "something like that of a child to a parent." [30]

Of course Douglass did not join the antislavery movement as a full-time lecturer just because of a near-worshipful feeling about Garrison. The "holy cause" of abolitionism encompassed, at least initially in Douglass's view, three great psychological desiderata of home. Authority, community, and freedom are the triple coordinates of home in *My Bondage and My Freedom*, whether we think of home as historically locatable, as in the case of Betsey Baily's "joyous circle," or as a *genius loci*, discoverable on the "symbolic geography" of this black quester's journey toward renewal and fulfillment.[31] Joining the abolitionists meant Douglass's immersing himself into an evolving movement instead of simply changing his status and position on the American social landscape, as his journey from Maryland to Massachusetts had done. Becoming a Garrisonian meant entering a new phase of liminality for the self-emancipated freeman, who would now be called upon to recreate himself and his life as a slave for curious white audiences all across the North. This very public "new life" was both experimental and dangerous for a fugitive slave, but it attracted Douglass because it seemed to embody the psychosocial plenitude that he had long sought: a union of (1) divinely sanctioned benevolent authority, (2) a community of interracial brotherhood, and (3) a message of freedom and hope. With God and His vicar Garrison leading a cause in which "for a time" Douglass "was made to forget that [his] skin was dark and [his] hair crisped," the ideal of freedom within a fellowship of truly color-blind comrades seemed very near to the self-described "ardent" young "enthusiast" (359–60). However, as the fugitive slave began to realize the limited role that his abolitionist associates expected him to play in the cause, the familiar process of disillusionment, alienation, and resumption of the search for home was triggered once again.

As usual, reading and thinking on his own, beyond the boundaries that his speech-making for the Garrisonians required, placed the initial strains on Douglass's relationships with those in authority over him. According to *My Bondage and My Freedom*, while his white co-workers on the platform tried to "pin [his speeches] down" to simple, factual narrations of his personal experience, Douglass "was growing, and needed room" to address a wider variety of topics with all the "moral indignation" at his command (361–62). As soon as he got outside the United States and arrived at Liverpool to begin his speaking tour of the British Isles, Douglass felt himself freer than ever before to go where he wished, associate with whom he wished, and speak out as he wished. English abolitionists raised the money for the purchase of his freedom from the Auld brothers, despite the objections of some of the more "uncompromising" antislavery people in America.[32] English reformers also put $2,500 in Douglass's hands for the establishment of the newspaper "devoted to the interests of my enslaved and oppressed people" for which he would never gain more than Garrison's grudging support. The sense of having been admitted and embraced by a truly nonracist people, the exhilaration of which Douglass reported in the letter to Garrison that we have examined earlier in the previous chapter, survived the black man's entire stay in Great Britain. In his farewell address to the British people in London, March 30, 1847, after contrasting the "deference" and "kindness" of England to the discrimination and hostility he expected to encounter when he returned to America, Douglass promised his cheering audience that he would proclaim in his native land, "wherever else I may be a stranger, that in England I am at home."[33] Why, then, was he leaving the one place that had offered him "the right hand of fellowship" in tangible acknowledgment of his "humanity and equality"?

The reason stemmed from Douglass's realization, undoubtedly heightened after nearly two years in England, that he could never feel completely at home apart from a black community that he could both serve and lead. The only fulfilling interludes during his life's quest that had not been spoiled by disillusionment had been those among blacks. From his grandmother to Father Lawson, from the Sabbath school at St. Michael's to the first experience of real brotherhood within his Freeland's band, Douglass had consistently found black people his most reliable authorities, his most sustaining and admirable fellows, and his most sympathetic supporters in the cause of their mutual freedom. Thus, when Douglass told his London audience, "I choose rather to go home; to return to America," he described home exclusively in terms of Afro-America. "I will go back, for the sake of my brethren. I go to suffer with them; to toil with them; to endure insult with them; to undergo outrage with them; to lift up my voice in their behalf; to speak and write in their vindication; and struggle in their ranks for that emancipation which shall yet be achieved." It was prophetic that Douglass spoke of struggling "in their ranks" and not within the ranks of the Garrisonians. Within six months of his return from England, he would found the *North Star* and thus initiate the final liminal stage of the life reconstructed in *My Bondage and My Freedom*.

Douglass's autobiography invites his readers to compare the behavior of his Boston friends and his Maryland masters in their responses to a black man seeking freedom of expression and independence of view. First of all, the reaction of Hugh Auld to young Fred's learning to read anticipates the Garrisonians' opposition to the mature Douglass's starting to write: the former fears that reading will "unfit" his servant for his "duties"; the latter also argue that editing a newspaper will only detract from Douglass's "usefulness as a lecturer" since he was "better fitted to speak than to write" (393). Both Douglass's southern and northern authorities, as *My Bondage and My Freedom* presents them, have a definite and imposing idea of what is "fitting" for a Negro under their supervision. It is just this notion of "fitness" that proves very binding to Douglass in the North as well as the South and thus impels him to break out, first by reading, then by writing. The slave with a mind of his own "has the devil in him"; the freeman who aspires to an independent pen is deemed "ambitious and presumptuous" by those who expect his compliant loyalty (394). Douglass pictures his "apostasy" from Garrison as proceeding on a psychological course parallel to that which brought about his "backsliding" from obedience to the white "demi-gods" of the South. The more he read, thought, and later wrote, the less "bound" he was by anyone's "superior knowledge." Douglass uses the same kind of antithetical construction to summarize the "radical change" that took place between him and the two major paternalistic authorities of his life, Hugh Auld and William Lloyd Garrison. Of Auld: "*He* wanted me to be *a slave*; I had already voted against that. . . . That which he most loved I most hated; and the very determination which he expressed to keep me in ignorance, only rendered me the more resolute in seeking intelligence" (147). Of Garrison: "To those with whom I had been in agreement and in sympathy, I was now in opposition. What they held to be a great and important truth, I now looked upon as a dangerous error" (396). The outcome of this opposition to his white patrons also followed parallel courses. The momentum of his flight from Auld led to a freedom in which Douglass would identify himself, on both written and spoken occasions, with his three million enslaved "brethren" in the South.[34] The freeman's estrangement from Garrison became a crucial impetus behind the decision that forms the conclusion of *My Bondage and My Freedom*: to "change . . . the disposition of my time and labors" so as to concentrate more on "the condition and circumstances of the free colored people than when I was the agent of an abolition society" (405).

This signals a key transition in Douglass's sense of himself, of black community, and of his mission in the mid-1850s. As Garrison's agent, Douglass had proudly accepted his designated role of representative of and advocate for the enslaved black people of the South. He worked hard to prove that he had "been one with them" in all their suffering and therefore knew their needs. So long as he played this role in the abolition society, however, Douglass was encouraged to identify more with the black people of his past than of his present as his closest brethren in spirit. Seeing American racism through the Garrisonian perspective, he was led to think that fulfillment for displaced freemen like himself lay in working under the direction of paternalistic white reformers for the welfare of black slaves far away. Black solidarity in the pursuit of the rights of northern blacks violated the virtue of self-forgetfulness demanded of northern blacks by white reformers in the name of total dedication to the cause of their southern brethren.[35] Once outside of Garrison's society, however, Douglass could see that blacks in the North were as much his spiritual and political brethren as the slaves of the South. He, like many of his fellow blacks in the quasi-free states, was as much in need of community, and in some senses, had less community, less solidarity, less sense of home, than the more obviously exploited and deprived Negroes of the South. On the basis of his own experience among the Garrisonians, Douglass recognized that northern blacks could not escape the subtler forms of white paternalism in the free states without a refuge of their own, without a communal alternative to a compromised, humiliating society with whites like Garrison.

The first step toward such a refuge, for Douglass the literary man, lay in the reclamation of the spirit of the lost homes of the past. The writing of *My Bondage and My Freedom* would allow him to expose and spurn the paternal, while idealizing the fraternal, models of community that he had tested through his experience as a slave and freeman. Simultaneously he could explore the powerful need within himself to attain not only freedom but also a home, indeed, to be so fascinated by the prospect of recovering some semblance of the latter that he could jeopardize the former. At the end of this most demanding of all his autobiographical self-examinations, Douglass had concluded that he was now a man as much in need of a community as he had once been in need of freedom. Just as important to the end of *My Bondage and My Freedom* is his implicit additional conclusion that after the many disillusionments of the last decade, the sense of alienation, isolation, and displacement that haunted "free" Afro-America in the 1850s constituted the profoundest threat yet to his people's sense of identity *as* a people, without which they could no more survive than could an individual like himself, whether enslaved or free. Thus *My Bondage and My Freedom* ends with Douglass in the role of revivalist exhorting the black community to remember its peculiar destiny.

"Progress is yet possible," Douglass promises his black reader in the last lines of *My Bondage and My Freedom*, but it is not the sort of progress imaged at the end of the *Narrative*. The progress of Douglass's first autobiography is that of the "classic ascent narrative" in Afro-American literature, in which the questing figure forsakes "familial or communal postures" in the world of slavery in the hope of becoming "an articulate survivor" in the less oppressive world of the North. As Robert Stepto emphasizes, the fate of the protagonists of such narratives of ascent is "at best, one of solitude; at worst, one of alienation." [36] This, by the early 1850s, is what Douglass realized had happened to him. Having "forsaken" his communal ties to the South, he had hoped that the Garrisonians would welcome him into a more fulfilling community. When he realized that insistence on his individuality would of necessity alienate him from the "abolition society," he accepted this eventuality. He did not, however, accept "solitude" or "alienation" for long. He set out to reestablish his ties to the kind of nurturing black community that he had known and trusted before. If, as James McCune Smith stated in his introduction to *My Bondage and My Freedom*, a "wide gulf" had grown between Douglass and the black community as a consequence of his adherence to Garrison (xxiv), then the publication of an independent newspaper like the *North Star* would do much to restore its editor to fellowship with his people. But the revision of Douglass's life in *My Bondage and My Freedom* into the story of a black man's circuitous route toward black community was a much more direct argument on his part for the kind of social redemption and communal identity that Douglass needed by 1855.

Out of the "solitude" or "alienation" with which the "ascent narrative" concludes emerges "an immersion narrative" in black American literary history, Stepto maintains. In this type of story, a protagonist undertakes "a ritualized journey into a symbolic South" where he hopes to find "new-found balms of group identity" that can "ameliorate, if not obliterate, the conditions imposed by solitude." In a figurative sense, *My Bondage and My Freedom* is such a narrative of immersion. Although Douglass would not record a literal return to the South until his 1881 *Life and Times*, his second autobiography represents his imaginative journey into a South resonant with the symbols of the "group identity" that Douglass, in 1855, required with a special, poignant need. To create *My Bondage and My Freedom* was to retrace the arc of Frederick Douglass's ascent so that its coordinates became unmistakably communal, not merely individual, so that his apotheosis read immersion in the group identity of Afro-America.

My Bondage and My Freedom does not conclude with Douglass's having actually arrived at that state of immersion he aims for; he could not record in this book that which he hoped to achieve through the autobiographical act of writing it. *My Bondage and My Freedom* is the work of a man who is working his way toward the center of a new group identity from the margins of his Garrisonian past. The book concludes with assurances that this new identity subsumes the previous one: "one of the best means of emancipating the slaves of the south is to improve and elevate the character of the free colored people of the north" (405). To this new work (and this new role in the group) Douglass dedicates himself in the future. In doing so, he also pointed himself, for a final time in *My Bondage and My Freedom*, on the way home. At the same time, he appointed himself builder of and spokesman for the community in which he professed his faith. By 1855 Douglass had learned not only the lesson that he, the quintessential ascendant black man of his time, needed a communal anchor. He also recognized that the community he sought he would have to create, as he had first done so twenty years before on William Freeland's plantation. To create community for himself required that he recreate himself into a communal entity, one who was realized and empowered only in and through community. This is the burden of *My Bondage and My Freedom*. As a consequence, this autobiography represents the most communally as well as self-conscious stage of Douglass's progressive autobiographical recreation of himself, for by 1855 he was not trying just to prove who he had been in the past (as the *Narrative* was designed to do) but who he wished to become in the future—a man with a community-affirming mission for the truly free black men and women among whom he could feel fully and finally at home.

The quest for home, whether understood in terms of the homeland that sent black emigrationist writers exploring or the ideal black community on the free margin of American society that Douglass hoped to find, dominates the major black woman's autobiography of the mid-nineteenth century, Harriet Jacobs's *Incidents in the Life of a Slave Girl* (1861).[37]

Like Douglass, Jacobs nostalgically recalled the "snug little home" of a free grandmother in the South whose love and protection the slave girl rarely encountered again in the bleak houses of the whites with whom she had to live in later years. From her early childhood, Jacobs "longed for a home like" her grandmother's, not just because there she found hope, sympathy, and "sweet balsam for [her] troubles" (28), but because within that sphere of maternal protection she could feel safe and inviolable. Grandmother Martha's home lay on the margins of the power wielded by the white patriarchy of the South; on that margin she maintained an independence that would become in the mature mind of Harriet Jacobs the sine qua non of home, the quality that gave this psychosocial space its special significance and value. From her home Grandmother Martha "once chased a white gentleman with a loaded pistol, because he insulted one of her daughters" (47). Jacobs sought a home in which she could be similarly secure and free from the prerogative of men to insult her. For a black woman, a slave, and an unmarried mother of two in the first half of the nineteenth century, such a quest constituted as heroic a struggle against overwhelming odds as any male fugitive slave would ever record.

Because of the special nature of her struggle and the manner in which she had to fight what she called "the war of my life," Harriet Jacobs was confronted with probably the most difficult rhetorical problems of any slave narrator in the antebellum era. She wanted to indict the southern patriarchy for its sexual tyranny over black women like herself, yet she could not do so without confessing with "sorrow and shame" to her willing participation in a miscegenetic liaison that produced two illegitimate children. Displaying the divided loyalties that Alice Walker finds in many early black women writers,[38] she seemed very much of two minds regarding her own moral status vis-à-vis that of her fictive white female reader. She wanted to speak out frankly and fully, but she dreaded breaking her silence about the obscenities of slavery for fear that giving tongue to these "foul secrets" would impute to her the guilt that should have been reserved only for those who hid behind such secrets. Thus Jacobs wrote on a precarious margin as she composed her autobiography, hoping "to kindle a flame of compassion" in her female reader's heart without searing her sensibilities with a frank account of such inflammatory subjects as seduction, rape, and miscegenation. On page after page of her story, she wavers between the antipodes of "concealment" and "confidence" in her narrative posture before her reader. She had practiced concealment for so long as a slave and a fugitive that she was not at all sure how "confidence took the place of distrust." For decades slave narrators had worried publicly over their readers' distrust of them, but Jacobs was the first to acknowledge her distrust of the white reader as a brake on her candor. In the end, she resorted to the tactic of many a confider of unwelcome truths in women's literature: she concealed herself behind a pseudonym, "Linda Brent," and then promised her reader "to tell you the truth, and I will do it honestly, let it cost me what it may" (83).

Many of the ugly truths of the black woman's condition in slavery had been widely publicized before Jacobs's book, but her work made an important difference: never before had an American slave woman pleaded her own case.[39] Male slave narrators had given voice to her suffering, and abolitionists had echoed their protest, but neither group had defended the slave woman without leaning heavily on what Frances Foster has termed the stereotype of the female slave as sexual victim. Foster argues that most male slave narrators referred to slave women en masse rather than individually and said little to counter the idea that white abolitionists constantly hammered at in their propaganda, namely, that black women were "defenseless creatures" for whom "rape or seduction is virtually inevitable."[40] If we reread the stories of Cynthia in William Wells Brown's narrative or Patsey, "the enslaved victim of lust and hate," in Solomon Northup's or Antoinette in William Craft's or Hester and Caroline in Frederick Douglass's, we can find a representative sample of the way in which male slave narrators dealt with the theme of white sexual exploitation of black women. Their emphasis is on the woman's repugnance at the master's or overseer's advances, the futility of her continual resistance unless she chooses suicide as her ultimate recourse, and her eventual humiliation and betrayal after she finally yields or is worn down by force. It is worth noting, at least, that there were exceptions to this tragic portraiture of black womanhood, as attested by such a well-known autobiography as *My Bondage and My Freedom* and by lesser works like the narratives of Milton Clarke and John Thompson. The "bright mulatto" fieldhand Nelly is strongly distinguished from Douglass's pitiable aunt Hester in her noble resistance to a whipping and in her "invincible spirit" while under the lash, which, Douglass suggests, probably lessened the likelihood that she was whipped again. Thompson's sister repelled the sexual attack of her master, withstood the whippings he administered in revenge, and ultimately made a successful escape to Philadelphia, leaving behind her slave husband and one child rather than submitting further to her white tyrant.[41] Nevertheless, the price for such strong-mindedness was great, for Nelly could not expect her husband to risk defending her against a brutal overseer, and Thompson's sister Delia had to sacrifice her family ties in exchange for her own freedom.

Women abolitionists tried to fire the moral indignation of their northern sisters by showing how the chattel principle had denied the slave woman her rightful status in antebellum America's "cult of True Woman-hood." If, as Barbara Welter has argued, a "true woman" in America pos-sessed four cardinal virtues—"piety, purity, submissiveness and domes-ticity"—that valorized her socially as well as morally, then by dint of slavery, black women had been ruthlessly denied an opportunity to fulfill themselves as true women. Abolitionists like Harriet Beecher Stowe and L. Maria Child did not speak pejoratively of the black woman, but they did emphasize strongly that since the female slave had no protector in bondage, her chances of maintaining her purity and ensconcing herself in domesticity were virtually nil.[42] In her *Key to Uncle Tom's Cabin*, Stowe insisted, "It is true that the slave-woman has no protection from the foulest dishonour and the utmost insult that can be offered to woman-hood—none whatever in law or gospel; but so long as she has enough to eat and wear, our Christian fathers and mothers tell us it is not so bad!" Child pictured the slave woman's moral prospects as hopeless: "The negro woman is unprotected either by law or public opinion. She is the property of her master, and her daughters are his property. They are al-lowed to have no conscientious scruples, no sense of shame, no regard for the feelings of husband, or parent; they must be entirely subservient to the will of their owner, on pain of being whipped as near unto death as will comport with his interest, or quite to death, if it suit his pleasure."[43] Although it is unlikely that these early feminists believed wholeheartedly in the notion of woman's needing a male protector, they couched their rhetoric in terms of the "cult of True Womanhood" probably to win the support of northern female devotees of the cult. The price that Stowe and Child paid for this was their reinforcement of those tenets of the cult that bound American women, white and black, to the beliefs that chastity was the essential index to a woman's moral and social status and that, apart from a protector, woman's natural passivity would likely fail her in any prolonged attempt to maintain her virtue independently.

Abolitionists attacked slavery so often on domestic grounds, stressing its despoliation of the family and its degradation of woman, primarily be-cause so much of the proslavery battle had been advanced on the home front. Each side of the slavery issue claimed the institution of the family as its guiding ideal and the protection of the domestic well-being of black slaves as one of its chief reasons for existence. For every James A. Thome who complained that "no ties of sacred home" were allowed to exist in the slave quarters, there was a C. G. Memminger to reply that under slav-ery "domestic relations become those which are most prized," since "each planter in fact is a Patriarch" who views the welfare of his "children and servants" as part of his sacred familial duty. As Willie Lee Rose has shown, southern apologists labored to domesticate the so-called domestic institution of slavery by likening it to the idealized Victorian family, wherein one found "cheerful obedience and gratitude on the part of children (read slaves), and paternalistic wisdom, protection, and discipline on the part of the father (read master)." Masters compared themselves favorably to what Memminger would call "the Hebrew form" of patriarchal authority and claimed that they presided necessarily and benevolently over three interlocking domesticities: the blood family, the slave families, and the larger family of the entire plantation community. Some abolitionists responded by disputing the idea of Abraham, the first Hebrew patriarch, as a slaveholder; others by condemning the "patriarchal family" of slavery as "one of the lowest forms of civilization, just emerging from savageism." Most abolitionists were willing to grant the slaveowner his patriarchal pretentions, however, since only a little extension of inference was needed to turn his paternal preeminence into "unlimited sovereignty," the breeding grounds for his terrible "lust for power." Using such rhetoric, Garrison and the Grimké sisters stigmatized the "patriarchal institution" as a haven, indeed, a harem, of interracial libidinousness, in which the "absolute power" of the unholy patriarch combined with the male's supposedly innate "lust of dominion" to produce the lurid image of the "Erotic South."[44]

Given abolitionism's ready linkage of the South with Sodom, rhetorically accomplished slave narrators must have felt some temptation to exploit the prurient appeal of their knowledge of patriarchalism's perversities. However, despite Robin Winks's characterization of the slave narratives as "the pious pornography of their day," the overwhelming majority of male slave narrators drew a veil between their readers and the details of interracial sexual relations on the plantations. They would describe the physical torture of slaves in the most sensationalistic detail, but the manner in which the sexual abuse of black women was effected, through rape and other forms of coercion, was deemed too "disgusting" or "shocking" to expose to view.[45] On the eve of the Civil War, however, even this form of propriety fell before the shock tactics of militant abolitionism and the heightened candor of mid-century black autobiographers. As a result, not one but two autobiographical exposés of concubinage in slavery appeared in 1861—Jacobs's *Incidents* and the Reverend Hiram Mattison's *Louisa Picquet, the Octoroon; or, Inside Views of Southern Domestic Life.* To appreciate fully Jacobs's skill in deploying a subject whose potential prurience was a real liability for the woman who wrote about it all, let us first examine the way a white man handled the case of Louisa Picquet.

In May 1860 Hiram Mattison, a Methodist minister and antislavery activist, met Louisa Picquet, a former slave from New Orleans, for an interview in Buffalo, New York. Since her manumission through her master's will some eight years earlier, Picquet had been living in Cincinnati with her husband and four children while trying to buy her mother and brother out of bondage in Texas. After hearing Picquet's story, Mattison became so interested in her cause that he made personal appeals on her behalf to several Methodist bishops meeting in Buffalo in General Conference, but he failed to get this matter on the agenda of the conference. As an alternative means of publicizing her fund-raising effort, the minister turned his interview with Piquet into a sixty-page narrative in which he recorded the arduous process by which the dauntless daughter regained her mother. The reprinting of four letters from Elizabeth Ramsey to her daughter Louisa Picquet gives Mattison's narrative a special poignance as well as historical significance. The happy reunion of the two women in the conclusion of *Louisa Picquet* pays genuine tribute to their strength and perseverance against the power of male slaveowners to keep them apart. These heroic qualities, however, are not what Mattison brings out initially to attract his reader's attention to Picquet, nor is his "Conclusion and Moral of the Whole Story" designed to impress us with these attributes of black women. As far as the white preacher was concerned, the "most prominent feature of the whole narrative is *the deep moral corruption* which it reveals in the families concerned" because of their entanglement in slavery.[46]

Mattison backed up this claim by listing ten instances of miscegenation mentioned in his interview with Picquet and noting (for quick reference) the page numbers in the text on which these illicit relationships are discussed. Such evidence proved to Mattison that "there is not a family mentioned" in Picquet's memory, white or black, "that does not reek with fornication and adultery." The real significance of Louisa Picquet and all the other "tell-tale mulatto, and quadroon, and octoroon faces" in her story was as "testimony to the deep moral pollution of the Slave States" (51). As editor of Picquet's narrative, this scandalized white man made sure that whatever else we might discover therein, the first thing we associate with the slave woman is "fornication and adultery."

Mattison introduces Picquet as an attractive and "artless" woman, about thirty-three years of age, who, to every appearance, looks and behaves like "an accomplished white lady" (5). No one "can talk with her without becoming fully convinced that she is a truthful, conscientious, and Christian woman"; nevertheless, because she is "an octoroon, or eighth blood" of African descent, she is "consequently, one of the four millions in this land . . . who 'have *no rights that white men are bound to respect.*'" By pointing out in the next paragraph that Picquet was herself the fruit of a miscegenetic union, Mattison focuses on his main preoccupation: the sexual abuse of slave women's rights to chastity and voluntary pregnancy. When Picquet mentions that her mother had had children in Georgia and Alabama previous to her and her brother, Mattison queries, "Had she any one she called her husband while she was in Georgia?" To Picquet's negative reply, he responds, "Had she in Mobile?" Picquet's second "no" prompts Mattison to ask who her brother's father was (probably her mother's master, answers Picquet) and to conclude by inquiring, "Was your mother white?" which implies that Picquet's mother was probably the product of just such a union as her daughter was.

These facts, unaccompanied by any explanatory detail, foreground Picquet's narrative in such a way as to predispose the reader to think of slave families like Elizabeth Ramsey's solely in terms of absence, their lack of chastity, their deviance from Christian norms. However, had Ramsey's family been nothing more than a testimonial to southern "moral pollution," Louisa Picquet would not have resisted so firmly the advances and threats of her master Mr. Cook during their stay in a Mobile, Alabama, boardinghouse. Unfortunately, the minister's questions about this episode betray his curiosity about less edifying matters. With the help of the white woman who ran the boardinghouse, the fourteen-year-old Louisa was able to frustrate Mr. Cook's plans for getting her into his bedroom, but not without incurring a whipping. Mattison is not content to record the simple fact that young Louisa was whipped, in her words, "so that I won't forget another time" (12). "Well, how did he whip you?" "With the cowhide." "Around your shoulders, or how?" "That day he did." "How were you dressed—with thin clothes, or how?" "Oh, very thin; with low-neck'd dress. In the summertime we never wore but two pieces—only the one under, and the blue homespun over. . . ." "Did he whip you hard, so as to raise marks?" "Oh yes. He never whip me in his life but what he leave the mark on, I was dressed so thin" (12).

A reading of *Louisa Picquet* reveals its editor to have been a very inquisitive man when it came to ferreting out the salacious details of slavery. Whenever Picquet mentions a new black woman during their interview, he usually wants to know how white she was, how many children she had, and how she came to get so many. Picquet's replies help build the minister's image of the South as a seraglio of beautiful octoroons bountifully breeding a mixed race for the debauched pleasure of white slaveowners. To reinforce this idea of pervasive southern concupiscence, Mattison asks how many children Mrs. Cook, the slaveowner's lawful wife, had borne, and, through Picquet's reply, "I could not tell; they had a lot of them. I know I been nursin' all my life up to that time," he leaves the implication that southern whites were as carnally unrestrained among their own kind as they were among those of "African descent." Ironically, the northern preacher seems to have required some restraint himself as he pried ever more deeply into Picquet's most sensitive memories. Toward the end of her recitation of Cook's cruelties, the former concubine remarks that he once "whip me with the cowhide, naked, so I 'spect I'll take some of the marks with me to the grave. One of them I know I will" (14–15). Mattison must have felt himself on the threshold of yet another titillating moment in the interview, but Picquet disappointed him. His editorial brackets interrupt the flow of the story so that he may inform his reader: "[Here Mrs. P. declines explaining further how he whipped her, though she had told our hostess where this was written; but it is too horrible and indelicate to be read in a civilized country.]" Picquet's reticence on these private matters is apparent earlier in the interview, though in an effort to satisfy her interrogator she seems to have tried to be forthcoming. Eventually, however, she had to frustrate this white man's verbal penetration of her privacy just as she had had to repel Cook's physical assault on her person years before. Significantly, while she declined to satisfy Mattison's appetite for the sexually perverse, she confided in an unnamed hostess where the interview was conducted, which Mattison records with perhaps more than a trace of jealousy.

Whatever we make of Mattison's attitude toward Louisa Picquet, had his narrative of this reformed slave concubine been the only one of its kind published before Emancipation, one can easily imagine its doing as much harm as good. No doubt Mattison wanted to help Picquet and was righteously appalled by the violations to her body and soul that she and other mixed-blood women like her had suffered in slavery. On the other hand, one wonders how moved he would have been by her case if she had not been so white. Moreover, as the minister's questions insinuate themselves into prurient subjects, he does little as editor to counter an impression of Picquet supportive of the prevailing stereotype of black women, especially the "dark-eyed," "easy and graceful" (5) quadroon or octoroon in slavery, namely, that they were tools and objects of sexual gratification, altogether too "easy and graceful" for anyone's good.[47] Mattison dutifully records Picquet's conversion to true Christian womanhood after leaving the South with the last two of the four children she bore her New Orleans master. But while the preacher does not portray the freed Louisa Picquet as morally tainted by her past, he does not ask her the kinds of questions that would let her reveal just who she was in the past, how she felt and what she thought about herself and her relationship to the world, aside from the role she played as her master's mistress. What Mattison wants to know about Picquet's relationship with Mr. Williams is how many children she had by him and "Were your children mulattoes?" But when Picquet characterizes her life with Williams as a time when "I had no peace at all" (19), her interviewer shows no interest in probing the meaning of "peace" to a doubly enslaved woman—except to invite its comparison to the peace of redemption or of death. A woman who had gone through the battles that Picquet had endured would need the kind of amanuensis and editor who could interpret her longing for peace as something more than a death wish or a sign of her need for Christ. Women like Picquet and Jacobs needed a sense of an empathetic female audience, not an interrogating male one, before they could speak or write freely about the woman behind the veils of silence and shame.

Harriet Jacobs found such an audience for her self-revelations in L. Maria Child and Amy Post, two "whole-souled" antislavery women in whom she confided her hopes and fears for her unpublished autobiography from 1852 to 1860. Post provided the initial suggestion and the steady encouragement for the writing of a book that would take almost five years to complete. Child lent her considerable prestige to the project by acting as the manuscript's editor and by contributing a preface, which Jacobs believed the work would need in order to be taken seriously by a publisher.[48] Professor Jean Yellin's research has effectively laid to rest the skepticism that has attended Child's claim in her preface that she only "revised" Jacobs's manuscript "for purposes of condensation and orderly arrangement" (7).[49] Now that we can dismiss the idea that Child was Jacobs's ghostwriter, we can appreciate more intelligently the role that she and Post did play in the evolution of *Incidents in the Life of a Slave Girl*.

It is very likely that Post and Child embodied demonstrably the kind of implied reader who Jacobs needed to believe was out there in the white world ready to listen empathetically to her story. It is equally likely that for two feminist-abolitionists like Post and Child, the publication of Jacobs's autobiography constituted a double opportunity, for as woman and slave, Jacobs dramatized the feminist analysis of the parallel slavery of race and sex. Thus her career furnished strong support for the antebellum feminist argument that chattel slavery was only the most egregious manifestation of the tyranny of patriarchal power in America, the subjection of women being a more genteel and less plainly institutionalized form of the same oppressive impulse in the North as well as the South. For two decades Angelina Grimké had been referring to politically silent women in the free states as "the white slaves of the North"; by 1857 Elizabeth Cady Stanton had denounced the unequal status of the wife in marriage as "nothing more nor less than legalized prostitution."[50] White women who had been thus prepared to think of themselves as their husbands' slaves, with no legal right to their own bodies, might be able to see in Harriet Jacobs not an outsider pretending to sisterhood but a metaphor of woman's plight South and North, black and white, married and single. From the feminist point of view, which labeled true womanhood white slavery and submissive wifehood prostitution, Jacobs's multiply marginal identity qualified her amply as one of the most truly representative women of her time.

Women on the cutting edge of American social reform had plenty of reason to embrace Harriet Jacobs, therefore, and as a result of her battles with patriarchal power she had good reason to find in them friendly advisors and sponsors. Nevertheless, the black woman was not overly sanguine about the responsiveness of the average female reader of the North, especially because she knew that the usual censure that slave autobiographers incurred—charges of "presumptuousness" and an egotistical desire "to attract attention to [one]self" (6)—would be leveled with extra vehemence on a female slave narrator. Moreover, the protagonist of *Incidents* could not, and the narrator of the book would not, proudly loft the banner of true womanhood. Harriet Jacobs was, in conventional perspective, a "fallen woman"; unlike Louisa Picquet, she had not legitimized herself or her children by marrying in freedom and establishing herself in a traditional domestic role. Expressions of bitterness and vengefulness in the book raise doubts about the depth of Jacobs's womanly piety, while her advice to colored domestic servants like herself to stand up for their rights in the North sets her at odds with feminine submissiveness. Besides, the idea of a mere domestic servant, and a mulatto to boot, placing herself and her opinions and judgments at the center of a book—why, this completely flew in the face of accepted and proper literary practice in American women's writing. Servants were social auxiliaries; they could not be heroines or pretend to lecture middle-class women on their moral duties. Certainly not *this* servant who, in addition to her own distasteful past, willfully and repeatedly transgressed every standard of literary decorum in the Victorian era by bringing to light a whole cellar-full of odious subjects, many of them suggestive of unnatural sex.[51]

Given both the encouragement of a feminist minority and the likely indifference, if not abhorrence, of the female majority to her book, the apprehensiveness of Jacobs as she approaches her reader is understandable. She does not feel at liberty to speak out; "on the contrary, it would have been more pleasant to me to have been silent about my own history." At several intervals in the narrative, particularly as she confesses the motives that led her, at the age of fifteen, to take a white lover, she asks for her reader's pardon and sympathy, though she also insists that slave women "have wrongs, and sufferings, and mortifications peculiarly their own" (119). Naturally, Jacobs would like to break the silence that surrounds these "wrongs," "sufferings, and mortifications," and her story shows her search in the South as well as the North for someone in whom she could confide. *Incidents* attests, however, to a more excruciating irony that besets the slave woman in Jacobs's situation: the more enormous the crimes committed against her, the less receptive people are to hearing about them, especially from the victim herself. This fact is dramatized in several confession scenes that Jacobs incorporates into her narrative for both structural and rhetorical purposes. There are two major scenes of this type, one occurring while Jacobs is in the South and can still confide in her grandmother and another that takes place after she escapes to Philadelphia, where she must risk her safety by taking a black minister into her confidence.

As a nurturing and benevolent guardian of home, Jacobs's grandmother plays something of the same role in *Incidents* as Douglass's does in *My Bondage and My Freedom*. But while Betsey Baily consistently signifies protective maternal authority in Douglass's autobiography, "Aunt" Martha plays a more complex part in Jacobs's memory as both protector and censurer, defender and judge. When young Harriet's master, Dr. Flint, first began "to whisper foul words in [her] ear" in order "to corrupt the pure principles" that "grandmother had instilled" in her, the slave girl "would have given the world to have laid my head on my grandmother's faithful bosom, and told her all my troubles" (46). But Flint had threatened her should she ever divulge his proposals to her. Then too, "although my grandmother was all in all to me, I feared her as well as loved her." To broach "such impure things" to a woman who was "very strict on such subjects" made the granddaughter feel "shamefaced about telling her." Consequently, she kept silent and remained so even as Flint applied more and more pressure. Feeling that she had no one else to turn to, fifteen-year-old Harriet accepted as her lover "an unmarried white gentleman" whom she calls Mr. Sands, partly because she believed he would help her get free of her "old tyrant." By contrast, her grandmother urged Harriet "to pray for contentment" in slavery (28) and "was strongly opposed" to any escape plans that members of her family might confide in her (66). Only the knowledge that she is pregnant by Sands overrides Harriet's "dread" of confessing to Aunt Martha.

At first the old lady banishes her granddaughter from her home when she hears Harriet accused of being Dr. Flint's mistress. After several days of alienation, however, Aunt Martha relents and listens "in silence" to Harriet's entire story and her supplication for forgiveness and pity. The outcome of the episode is the slave girl's reinstatement in her grandmother's home, where she receives love and "pity," though no outright statement of forgiveness. Still, exoneration is not as important to the "fallen" woman as is her restoration to a loving female community, symbolized by her grandmother's home. The first confession scene in *Incidents* suggests that the great danger to that community is the "respect bordering upon awe" with which the younger woman "looks up to" the older one, for it is this trembling awe and shame that causes the younger woman to conceal the truth about herself rather than risk rejection as one "no longer worthy of her love" (86). For Jacobs's female reader there was a lesson here, which, if applied to their discursive relationship in this written autobiographical confession (of sorts), could lay the foundation for the development of real understanding between them.[52] All that stood between them, in effect, was the white female reader's moral pedestal.

The second key confession scene in the text bears a similar message for Jacobs's implied male reader. The Reverend Jeremiah Durham, minister of the Bethel A.M.E. Church in Philadelphia, serves as a model for the male reader of *Incidents*, just as Aunt Martha figures as an object lesson for female readers. Durham meets Jacobs by accident soon after her escape from the South. Though she is a complete stranger, he invites her home where his wife receives her warmly "without asking any questions." The minister proves more inquisitive later on while helping the rather mysterious southern woman look up some friends in the city. After his guest refers inadvertently to her daughter, Durham seems poised to ask about Jacobs's husband, which causes her to debate inwardly, "if I answered him truly what would he think of me?" She resolves not to deceive him, for "if he was desirous of being my friend, I thought he ought to know how far I was worthy of it" (244). After listening to her story, Durham explains that his questions were motivated by a desire to be of service, not to indulge "idle curiosity." "'Your straightforward answers do you credit,'" he continues, "'but don't answer every body so openly. It might give some heartless people a pretext for treating you with contempt.'" Burned "like coals of fire" by "that word *contempt*," Jacobs professes her belief that God will forgive her for her past and that in the future she will "'be a good mother'" and "'live in such a manner that people cannot treat me with contempt.'" Durham declares his respect for these "sentiments" and offers some advice: "'Place your trust in God, and be governed by good principles, and you will not fail to find friends'" (245).

This confession scene poses an implicit question for the male reader of *Incidents*: will he be a respectful "friend," or merely peruse Jacobs's past with "idle curiosity," if not "contempt"? Are faith in God and highly principled behavior in freedom enough to assure a female fugitive slave of a friendly hearing from men? Does a woman with Jacobs's past gain "credit" (another variation on credibility) by giving "straightforward answers" to her reader's implicit questions, such as those that center on her sense of culpability for her relationship with Sands? Or would the wiser course in autobiography be not to answer all such implied questions "so openly," especially if declaring one's belief in God's forgiveness of one's sexual transgressions could be read as an act of facile self-exculpation? Jacobs's maxim as narrator is, "It is always better to trust than to doubt" (166), but in light of the rarity of trustworthy men in her life, Jacobs may very well have doubted the wisdom of answering openly the kinds of questions that many men might have wanted to pose. On the other hand, believing that she could gain credit with her female reader by responding straightforwardly to the kinds of questions that a woman would more likely put forward, Jacobs constructed her autobiography in such a way as to draw in a certain kind of woman-identified reader while turning away those motivated by only a demeaning form of "curiosity."

Although *Incidents* alludes to more varieties of perverse sexuality than any other antebellum slave narrative, it offers the merely curious reader little in the way of voyeuristic titillation. There are no teasing references to thin, low-necked dresses, hidden marks of the whip on women's bodies, or parades of half-naked octoroons on New Orleans auction blocks, such as one finds in Mattison's little book. Jacobs "was twenty-one years in that cage of obscene birds" (81), but in recalling those years, she concentrated on the psychological source, not the physical manifestation, of the obscenity of slavery. That is, she grew eloquent in denouncing the lust for and corruption of power in the "patriarchal institution," as she scornfully referred to slavery (114, 222). On the other hand, she adopted a deliberately conventional and moralistically stilted manner whenever she described the sexual expression of that power. For instance, she refuses to be specific about the "low" and "revolting" suggestions that Dr. Flint whispered to her or the "vile language" that another slaveholder, Mr. Hobbs, poured into the ears of her nine-year-old daughter Ellen. It is not the text but the subtext of Flint's propositions that Jacobs articulates. The doctor is not simply the "Byronic seducer" he has been labeled.[53] Jacobs shows how he first struck a paternalistic pose before fourteen-year-old Harriet, promising his "poor child" that he " 'would make a lady of [her]' " and place her under his direct protection in exchange for her sexual submission. When Harriet refuses, Flint unmasks the obverse side of his fatherly prerogative —a recriminatory jealousy and capacity for violence reminiscent of Aaron Anthony, which qualifies the doctor for the bestial imagery that Jacobs, like many other slave narrators, used to characterize white men whose unbridled power as slaveholders brutalized their feelings and gave free rein to their appetites. Jacobs is not interested in developing Flint's depraved character, which is one reason why his speeches are nearly all of a piece. The function of the man is as a signifier of patriarchal power at its most dehumanized extreme, immitigable and irredeemable. In Flint's monomaniacal harping on a single string, namely, "that I was made for his use" (29), Jacobs points her reader toward the origins of all obscenity—the objectification and instrumentalization of another for one's personal gratification.

Jacobs also drains her affair with Sands of all its pornographic potential by disclosing only the psychological motives that carried her into the relationship, not the manner in which the affair was conducted. The "educated and eloquent" white man is not cast in the role of seducer, for however much he may have concealed from young Harriet the ulterior motives behind his "sympathy" and "kindness," his is not the triumph of the seduction novel's proud, scheming gallant over the ingenuous and passive virgin. Fifteen-year-old Harriet knew where Sands's attentions were taking her, and in her acknowledgment of the motives of "revenge" and "calculations of interest" behind her accepting Sands as her lover, Jacobs deromanticized the potentially sensational liaison. This beautiful octoroon was no helpless shrinking violet, no sister of Cooper's simple-minded Hetty Hutter or George Lippard's Mary Byrnewood, the seduced innocent of that classic of the overheated American imagination, *The Monks of Monk Hall* (1844).[54] Those male readers who sought a little stimulation for their power fantasies probably would not be titillated to find Harriet Jacobs using her sexual favors as a weapon of vengeance on her "tyrant." To accept Sands was "to triumph over" Flint (85); it was also to take a very calculated step toward freedom, since Harriet assumed that in his jealous rage, the doctor would sell her, Sands would buy her, and then "my freedom could be easily obtained from him." All this suggests that the affair with Sands was as much an act of subversion as of surrender. Even Harriet's subsequent pregnancies can be seen as gestures of defiance and aids to liberation from the "patriarchal institution." Indeed, the most sensationalistic instance of miscegenation in Jacobs's story, and probably in all the slave narrative tradition, underlines her suggestion in the Sands affair that when the sex act becomes politicized, as patriarchal power inevitably makes it, it can be best interpreted as a weapon, either of oppression or rebellion.

Jacobs cites the example of a slaveholder "whose head was bowed down in shame" after his neighbors learned that his daughter had selected "the most brutalized" slave on his plantation "to be the father of his first grandchild" (80). In addition, when the outraged master tried to exact revenge on the offending black man, the daughter gave her lover free papers and dispatched him well beyond her father's power. On the face of it, this incident illustrates Jacobs's contention that not only the slaveholder's sons but also his daughters can be corrupted "by the unclean influences every where around them." The most sordid of all these influences is the idea of "father's authority" over his female slaves, which the daughter then appropriates to justify her own perverse instrumentalization of a male slave. Only slightly below the surface of Jacobs's commentary is the strong implication that while corrupted by the example of patriarchal authority on the plantation, the daughter may have also been waging some form of rebellion against her father's authority over her. What better way to bow the patriarch's proud head than to prefer the love of "the most brutalized" servant to the respect of the seignior himself and to flout the patriarch's obsession with lineage by presenting him a mixed-blood illegitimate as his first descendant?

These are some of the ways in which Jacobs forestalls the wrong kind of reading of her book; we need now to examine what kind of implied reader her text does inscribe and what sort of relationship she tries to develop with that reader. I have stated that *Incidents* is written in a manner to appeal (in both senses of the word) to a woman-identified reader. By this I mean a reader who is capable of identifying, first, with the woman who narrates and plays the central role in this autobiography, and, second, with the community of women to whom the book is addressed as both a criticism and an appeal. The status of this particular female community in *Incidents* is very similar to that of the northern black community in *My Bondage and My Freedom*. In both books, a homeless black fugitive creates an autobiography that pictures as a partially realized goal of fulfillment a community on the margins of the perverse American social sphere. For both autobiographers, that community offers a truly familial kind of fellowship untainted by the traditional authoritarianism that puts blacks and women to the service of cognate masters pretending to paternal or patriarchal office. Both autobiographers want very much to qualify themselves for admission into that idealized marginal community. But neither writer seems confident of the existence of such a community unless its rituals and values are articulated and reinforced through the narrative act of autobiography itself. It appears as though Jacobs and Douglass appeal for acceptance into communities, of women and blacks respectively, whose viability depends greatly on declarative autobiographical acts that create historical models for the desired community, and directive autobiographical acts that attempt to recreate the implied readership into a contemporary model of that community.[55] Moreover, the two dimensions of autobiographical action in which this remodeling takes place, namely, the historical and the discursive, gravitate toward an uneasy union in the plot structure of both Jacobs's and Douglass's narratives. For both writers, the pattern of the past involves (1) an initiatory separation from the community of home; (2) successive periods of isolation and alienation within oppressive hierarchies, interrupted by brief glimpses of redeeming community; and (3) a final recognition, from the liberating perspective of liminality, of the conditions on which lasting community had to be predicated. *Incidents in the Life of a Slave Girl* was written as much to assert the power and potential of women's community in the South and the North as to denounce the state of commonage under which all resided under the patriarchy of slavery.

Harriet Jacobs's quest for freedom, from chattelism in the South and from the tongue-tying sense of moral unworthiness that was slavery's legacy to her in the North, could not have been successful without the support of women's community. The fugitive slave's revelations about this community in the South and the North furnish an important commentary on what Carroll Smith-Rosenberg has called "the female world of love and ritual" in nineteenth-century America. Rosenberg found access to this world by examining "women's private letters and diaries" wherein she discovered "a very private world of emotional realities" central to women's lives, though often screened off from men's perceptions. This intimate world was "built around a generic and unself-conscious pattern of single-sex or homosocial networks. These supportive networks were institutionalized in social conventions or rituals which accompanied virtually every important event in a woman's life, from birth to death." [56] Rosenberg's sources introduce us to the female support networks that conducted the socializing rituals that white middle-class women underwent in the nineteenth century. *Incidents* unveils for us not just a private but a clandestine set of women's support networks, often interracial in their composition, which presided over perilous black female rites of passage in which the stakes were, quite literally, life and death. The homosocial networks of Smith-Rosenberg's research enjoyed a "complementary" relationship to the male-dominated heterosexual world. The parallel homosocial networks of Jacobs's autobiography are maintained clandestinely outside of male awareness because they are subversive of the patriarchy in varying degrees. This covert women's community did not document itself through private written sources; it was knit together by oral means, Jacobs informs us, through the most private and personal of all communications—secrets. Jacobs approaches her woman-identified reader with a personal history of secrets whose revelation, she hopes, will initiate that reader into the community of confidence and support that nineteenth-century women needed in order to speak out above a whisper against their oppression.

Although Elaine Showalter has noted that in Western myth and folklore "the essence of women's language is its secrecy," there has been more discussion in women's literary history of binary oppositions like silence versus speech or repression versus expression than there has been of modes of utterance betwixt and between them, such as the secret. Yet, as Nina Auerbach has argued, while male communities in literature posit their codes of living in a "most explicit, formulated, and inspirational sense," female communities treat their codes like "a whispered and a fleeting thing, more like a buried language than a rallying cry, whose invocations . . . have more than a touch of the impalpable and the devious." In other words, some of the most important codes of the female community are articulated ("whispered") as secrets, "buried" in language for many purposes, some "devious," yet resuscitable for "inspirational" use as well. The secrets that women harbor and share among themselves and shield from men in *Incidents* help to distinguish their situation as a "muted group" in the male-dominated social structure of both the slavocracy and the so-called free states. This "mutedness" is "not some condition of linguistic silence," but a mode of expression on "a reduced level of perceptibility" to the dominant group and only marginally connected to "the dominant communicative system of the society." In the sub rosa zone of knowledge and communication that women occupy in *Incidents*, all sorts of muted truths traffic about, some to the benefit, others to the detriment of women's community. What Adrienne Rich has posited as paradoxical axioms of women's muted expression, namely—"Women have always lied to each other. Women have always whispered the truth to each other"; and "Women have always been divided against each other. Women have always been in secret collusion."—Harriet Jacobs dramatizes in such a way as to explain how the "lies, secrets, and silences" of women can deliver them into community or alienate them from it.[57]

Patriarchalism spawns secrecy. Male social as well as sexual intercourse with women under patriarchal constraint teems with guilty secrets that women are expected to bear. In *Incidents* there are the vile proposals that Dr. Flint makes secretively to young Harriet; the clandestine letters that white masters send to female slaves that the latter are required to read and then destroy; the secret mulatto children that a Congressman asks his slave mistress to hide from his visiting Washington friends; the hidden identity of Jacobs's white lover who deceitfully neglects his fatherly responsibility to their children; the secret that Jacobs keeps for years from her own daughter concerning her paternity lest the mother suffer a diminution of her child's love and respect. The entire slave population is big with secrets begat by the patriarchal institution and crying for acknowledgment, but northern travelers, like northern readers, do not make the right kinds of inquiries, and southern women, black as well as white, sometimes perpetuate the conspiracy of silence by viewing each other more as the cause than the conduit of these obscenities.

Women prostitute themselves for men in this way, Jacobs suggests, because of their misplaced allegiance to the supposedly feminine virtue of discreetness. The bearing of male secrets may render a woman honorably discreet in male-dominated society, but it will leave her pathetically discrete from women's community, as *Incidents* proves. All secrets, Jacobs seems to have realized, stem both etymologically and psychologically from the act of separating, of putting apart or out of the way. Secretiveness, discreetness, discretion—all tend toward the creation of a discrete, or separate and potentially secret, thing.[58] The question for Jacobs and many other women in her life was, would a woman allow herself to become a discrete, isolated entity, dependent on men, for the sake of bearing male secrets with discretion? Or would she use her hard-won discernment and discretion to separate herself from patriarchal control so as to cherish and foster the confidences that maintained the sub rosa women's community? Would she dare finally to bare the misbegotten secrets of the patriarchy to the world?

In the first one-third of *Incidents*, Jacobs portrays the process by which the secrets that she bore so discreetly for Flint gradually separated her from communion with her grandmother, leaving her alone and desperate for a confidante and protector. It is significant that young Harriet next turned to a white woman, Mrs. Flint, for sympathy and aid. The slave girl could see that it was in their mutual interest to confide in each other against their common harasser, but after Harriet disclosed to her mistress the secrets of her husband's infidelity, Mrs. Flint responded with false promises of protection and "constant suspicion and malevolence." Her knowledge of her husband's character might have been used "to counsel and to screen the young and the innocent among her [female] slaves" (49), but instead, Mrs. Flint suppressed it to protect her individual pride. While Harriet felt genuine pity for her, Mrs. Flint only "pitied herself as a martyr" (53), thus hoarding for herself alone the emotional support that she might have shared and received among the black women whom her husband oppressed in common with her. Though outraged by her husband's behavior, Mrs. Flint preferred to identify herself in terms of her relationship to him (as the "martyr" to his infidelity), not to the slave girl subordinate to her, whom she regarded simply as "an object of her jealousy." It is only when both black and white sources of potential female support fail her that young Harriet turns to the patriarchy for "sympathy" and "protection" by becoming Mr. Sands's lover.

The second part of Jacobs's narrative begins with Chapter XI, after the birth of her son Benjamin. Although Sands "promised to care for [their] child, and to buy [Jacobs], be the conditions what they might," the slave mother soon learns that she will not be able to rely on the weight of her lover's purse, for Dr. Flint "loved power more" than the money he might receive from Sands for Jacobs and her child. Her grandmother naively believes that Flint will be moved to negotiate once reminded of the faithfulness with which she had served him for so long, but such an effort assumes that ties of obligation bind the white patriarch to his female slave, when in fact no such familial feeling exists in the symbolically named Flint. Jacobs becomes convinced that "I must fight my battle alone," using her "woman's pride" and her "mother's love for [her] children" to brace her for the struggle to escape Flint's grasp (130). Her plan is to conceal herself for a few weeks at the house of a friend until the doctor gives up trying to find her, at which point he would be forced to sell her, rather than lose her value entirely, and the children as well, for fear of their following their mother in a second escape. Through an intermediary, Sands would then buy them all. It is a daring plot, and it must be concealed from her grandmother Martha because she neither trusts Sands nor believes that a mother should "forsake her children," even if doing so seems the only way to reunite them all in freedom. Martha's well-meaning pressure on her granddaughter to submit to social prescriptions for true motherhood indicates another way that patriarchal power could pit maternal affection against itself and isolate one mother from another. After Jacobs makes her escape, her relatives also advise her to return to Flint; the doctor does not give up the search after a week, and the house of the friend (whose gender is not given in the text) where she is concealed seems unlikely to protect her for long from her master's inquiries.

At this point, when her prospects seem the dimmest since her flight from Flint, Jacobs is rescued by the first manifestation of a liberating female community in the slavery-ridden South. Grandmother Martha, whose friendly connections with white women are brought out early in *Incidents*, takes into her confidence a slaveowning woman long acquainted with the trials of the old black woman's family. Out of pity for both Martha and her granddaughter, the white woman promises to conceal the runaway in a small room over her own bedroom that she uses "'to store away things that are out of use'" (153). Betty, the southern lady's black cook whose allegiance to her is absolute, is also enlisted in the scheme; she takes great pleasure in outwitting the white constables who try to discover Jacobs on the premises. Thus an interracial women's community of interlinking confidences is formed among four women of differing status: a free white, a free black, an enslaved black, and a fugitive black. After having been the bearer of so many male secrets, Jacobs is transformed into a women's secret, protected by women who unite around her in complicity against the caste and class distinctions that ordinarily hold them separate in the patriarchy. The wife of a slaveholder identifies more with a runaway slave mother than she does with patriarchal interests. She is not free, however, to speak of this, which is why she adjures Jacobs "'never [to] tell my secret; for it would ruin me and my family.'" True to her charge, the narrator of *Incidents* leaves her "kind benefactress" anonymous in the text and blesses her as an exemplar of "Christian womanhood" (Jacobs's term for true womanhood).

During Jacobs's stay with her white female protector, she learns of Flint's sale of her children and their purchase by Sands. She rejoices to think that her children are "saved," but she lives in great apprehension lest a meddlesome black housemaid named Jenny should discover her hiding place. Now her family, male and female, come to her rescue, spiriting her away at night to an airless, mice-infested garret, nine feet long, seven feet wide, and three feet high, attached to the roof of her grandmother's house. Here she exists for the next seven years, visited only by her brother, an uncle, an aunt, and her grandmother, suffering acutely from extremes of summer and winter weather, taking only as much exercise as the crawling space in her "den" will allow, and having no firsthand contact with the world except through a one-inch gimlet hole in the wall of her living tomb. In the fictions of Ann Radcliffe, the Brontës, Charlotte Perkins Gilman, or the female Gothicists whom Ellen Moers has analyzed, there is no more stifling and oppressive "imagery of entrapment," "enclosure," and "powerlessness" than that which appears in the middle chapters of Jacobs's autobiography. Sandra M. Gilbert and Susan Gubar have demonstrated that nineteenth-century white women writers' "anxieties about space" caused them to project into their work a "mad double" through whose violence "the female author enacts her own raging desire to escape male houses and male texts."[59] In her situation Harriet Jacobs had little choice but to accept the "dismal hole" above her grandmother's house as "my home," though there seemed to be "no justice or mercy in the divine government" that permitted her to suffer such persecution. During this period of virtual burial alive, the fugitive woman begins to question God as a "compassionate Father" (186), another step away from passive reliance on the Great Chain of Patriarchal Power. By the time she would write her autobiography, the fantasy of a "Queen Justice," to whose righteous edicts the president of the United States would be subject, displaces prayer to God the Father for racial justice at the end of Chapter VIII.

Instead of going mad, Jacobs finds ways to turn her marginalized situation to advantage. She monitors Sands's decisions regarding the disposition of Benjamin and Ellen and, from a hiding-place in her grandmother's storeroom, accosts her former lover with a plea for their immediate emancipation. Through her tiny window to the outside world she becomes privy to the suppressed conversations of slave-hunters plotting how to catch a fugitive slave. She overhears the solitary muttering of a slave woman, "'It's his own, and he can kill it if he will'" (184), which reminds her of the continuing misery of black women betrayed by white men. Hers is not, therefore, a totally sequestered and impotent condition; she accrues to herself through her marginality a narrow zone of scrutiny and influence wherein she holds the power to penetrate secrets. No mere voyeur on the world, Jacobs turns her "loophole of retreat" (the title of Chapter XI) into a keyhole through which she unlocks further mysteries of the power relationships in her world. She also finds that her disembodied presence in patriarchal society lets her become for the first time Dr. Flint's manipulator instead of his tool. In a chapter entitled "Competition in Cunning," we see Jacobs writing devious letters to her master about her life in the North, having them mailed from a post office in New York, and then watching, with secret amusement, Flint's maneuvers to obtain further information about the slave who he is now convinced lives in Boston. Using her pen in this manner helps to divert the doctor's attentions away from her refuge and her family, which, in turn, helps keep alive her hope of escape. Thus Jacobs's first experiments in writing let her play the role of slave trickster lodged in the interstices of a social structure that she pries apart with her spying eyes and ventriloquistic voice. She takes the power that comes from the point of a pen to project an alter ego in freedom up North, not a lunatic self raging in rebellion in a psychic attic. In her garret, where she reads and sews, she wields a literary needle that injects her master's mind (instead of her own) with poisonous "delusions."

Though Jacobs makes a great deal out of her limited resources, she does not discover a way, during her seven-year imprisonment, to free her children or extract from Sands a guarantee that he will manumit them. The best she can do is agree to have Ellen sent to Brooklyn, New York, where a cousin of Sands promises to care for her and send her to school. Not long thereafter, Jacobs hazards everything on a night journey by boat to Philadelphia and freedom. Spurred by her likely discovery by the mischievous black housemaid, Jenny, she leaves her son behind and, trusting the judgment of a black male friend, puts herself in the hands of a southern sea captain. For once, she experiences "some justice in man" (216) and is brought safely to freedom with another black female runaway who also had to leave her loved ones to be free. "Alone in the world," she goes in search of friends in Philadelphia, meeting the Durhams and receiving a warm introduction to the North.

In the last ten chapters of *Incidents*, Jacobs depicts life in the North punctuated by trial and triumph; like many fugitive slave narrators she records removal to the "free states" as a blessing, albeit a mixed one. Dr. Flint and his agents dog her movements, and humiliations on account of northern prejudice make her feel as though she is still being "trampled under foot" by white "oppressors." Her great sources of support are women and her family.[60] On her arrival in New York she finds Ellen in the company of the daughter of a woman who formerly lived with Grandmother Martha. They join with another female friend of Jacobs in New York to welcome her. "They laughed, they cried, and they shouted. . . . How different from the silent days" she had passed in solitary confinement in the South (251). This provides a foretaste of the receptiveness of other women to Jacobs, especially the two white women who employ her as a nurse and protect her as resourceful guardians against Flint's machinations. With the first woman, Mrs. Bruce, she finds "a home," and after setting aside her suspicions of white people and confiding in this "excellent friend," she receives the additional offer of "a home for Ellen." Although Ellen's position as a waiting-maid with Sands's cousin, Mrs. Hobbs, distresses Jacobs because of its vulnerability, she refuses Mrs. Bruce's generosity until she can "make a home" for her children herself. Freedom defines itself to Jacobs as the power "to act a mother's part towards my children," i.e., to support them and protect them herself without relying on any outsider (256). Friendship and community with women, white and black, she treasures, but what she longs for is a home modeled on her grandmother's, where a woman of color retains both her freedom and her privacy and is beholden to no one for her economic welfare or that of her children.

At the end of *Incidents*, Jacobs has not yet reached this goal. Benjamin arrives safe and legally free from the South, is entered into a trade school, and eventually goes with his uncle William to California. William also offers to pay for Ellen's education in a boarding school, which is too good a chance for her mother to let pass, especially considering the paltry learning that Ellen's years in service to the Hobbses gave her. As a seamstress Jacobs can earn enough to support one child but not to underwrite the education of both. She must put by part of her earnings to meet Dr. Flint's purchase price for her; otherwise she can never feel that her freedom is a certainty. When Mrs. Bruce dies, the fugitive is deprived of another of her most cherished emotional supports, though in Mr. Bruce's second wife she discovers a "generous, sympathizing lady" who equals her predecessor in defending the fugitive slave woman against the depredations of Flint. Ultimately, with the deceased doctor's successor hard on the trail of both the fugitive and her daughter, Mrs. Bruce decides to pay Jacobs's purchase price herself, though the former slave vigorously opposes the idea: "being sold from one owner to another seemed too much like slavery; [moreover] such a great obligation could not easily be cancelled" (299–300). Rather than consent to be traded again like "an article of property," Jacobs tells Mrs. Bruce that she would rather go to her brother in California.

Nevertheless, without the fugitive's knowledge or agreement, the white woman goes ahead with the transaction that nets Jacobs her freedom. In the closing paragraphs of her narrative, Jacobs pay tribute to her "sacred" friend for bestowing on her the "precious, long-desired boon" of liberty. And yet, she cannot recall the episode without great ambivalence and a sense of anticlimax. "So I was *sold* at last!" she writes, evoking in her tone and narrative context the nineteenth-century colloquial sense of being "sold"—to be cheated or duped. Was it not an ironic trick of fate that, after all she had been through, a female friend, with the best intentions, had broken confidence with her and secretly negotiated with the patriarchal institution on its own terms? In a letter to Amy Post, excerpts of which appear in the appendix to *Incidents*, Jacobs alluded bitterly to the irony of her release from slavery. "The freedom [she had] had before the money was paid was dearer" to her than the liberation that came of being sold. She had "served for [her] liberty as faithfully as Jacob served for Rachel," but whereas the Hebrew patriarch had ended his fourteen-year indenture to Laban with a wife and "large possessions," the American black woman had finished her struggle only to be "robbed of my victory." "I was obliged to resign my crown, to rid myself of a tyrant" (305). It was this act of obligatory resignation, this renouncing, which Emily Dickinson would grimly label a "piercing virtue," a "Choosing/Against itself," that the black woman felt had denied her a clear "victory" against the patriarchy. Instead of the proud independence of a victor, Jacobs felt the "great obligation" of a debtor who owed her freedom to another. Freed from Flint and his ilk, she was now obliged to Mrs. Bruce in just the way she had feared "could not easily be cancelled." To use, once more, the language of Ralph Ellison's *Invisible Man*, she "had boomeranged again," from one marginal status, that of the unfree freedom of the fugitive slave, to another kind of marginality, the obligated freedom of a charitably purchased slave.

Of course, Mrs. Bruce told Jacobs that she had not bought her for her services and that she was free to sail for California anytime she wished. But Jacobs could not do so, at least, not immediately.[61] She stayed with Mrs. Bruce, putting the best possible face on her situation by proclaiming that her story ended "with freedom; not in the usual way" of women's fiction, "with marriage." This was Jacobs's way of iterating the freedom she did have—no man had a claim on her now. However, in terms of the profounder quest of her life, the quest for an independent home, Jacobs's story ends with a dream deferred. "I do not sit with my children in a home of my own. I still long for a hearthstone of my own, however humble. I wish it for my children's sake far more than for my own." Three times repeated, "my own" expresses Jacobs's still-frustrated, consuming desire for the possession and control of self and circumstance that evil men in the South and, the supreme irony, a "sacred" woman in the North had as yet prevented her from achieving. The black woman tries to strike a note of narrative resignation. "God so orders circumstances as to keep me with my friend Mrs. Bruce. Love, duty, gratitude, also bind me to her side. It is a privilege to serve her who pities my oppressed people, and who has bestowed the inestimable boon of freedom on me and my children" (303).

This is a brave rhetorical effort on Jacobs's part, this attempt to secrete behind a mask of true womanhood her resentments against God the Father for his having ordained that Mrs. Bruce "keep me." Nevertheless all her protestations about "love, duty, and gratitude" do not conceal her lingering sense of constraint, of being bound in obligation to a white woman. It may be a spiritual "privilege to serve her," but in a social sense such service to a boon-grantor, however morally enforced, did not sort well with previous relationships of female community that had been so liberating. The idea of the "privilege" of service harks back uncomfortably to the paternalistic models analyzed earlier in *Incidents* and in *My Bondage and My Freedom*. Thus, like Douglass, Jacobs becomes an analyst of some of the many modes of paternalism in American race relations on both sides of the gender line. After a long struggle for independence from patriarchal power she found herself in the most unexpected sort of love-bind, on an emotional and moral margin between serving out of gratitude for freedom bestowed and rejecting that obligation in the name of freedom inherently deserved. To write herself off this margin Jacobs could either re-sign herself at the conclusion of *Incidents* as the thankful, dutiful true woman, thus cancelling out the character of the feminist that evolves through the text, or she could design for herself a new role, liberated from the obligations of true womanhood to its binding protectors, female or male, and ready to accept the consequences of such an act of radical feminist self-creation. Instead of making either of these moves, however, the narrator of *Incidents* decided to portray poignantly and subtly her dilemma itself. This gives her story that open-ended quality that forces *Incidents*, like the best nineteenth-century problem fiction, back into the hands of its reader for resolution.

This decision also constitutes an important advance in the sophistication of narrative and rhetorical technique in Afro-American autobiography. The usual kinds of choices that black autobiographers asked their readers to make by the end of their stories, either implicitly or through direct exhortation, were ones involving morally unambiguous opposites: between the reader's salvation or damnation if the story were a spiritual autobiography; between black emancipation or white spiritual degradation in the case of the slave narrative. In these terms most early black autobiography concludes on a unitive rhetorical note with a clear moral option available to the reader. Certainly we have seen gaps and seams in a number of texts, attesting to the structural strain that an unresolved perception of a past incident incurs when it is refashioned and tensely fitted into a morally unambiguous binary opposition. William Wells Brown's manner of explaining away Sandford's trickiness exemplifies such a textual seam. Still, Brown and virtually everyone else who faced such a predicament were determined to resolve these problems *in* their texts, to bury them, in effect, deep within the text, so that they could not haunt the conclusion of the story. The ending was where everything of a personal nature was to appear settled, so that nothing detracted from that singular image of freedom finally achieved that proved so uplifting to many readers, black and white, in the antislavery movement. However, when Harriet Jacobs left her reader with only hard questions about the subtler forms of bondage encountered by free blacks in the North, she joined Douglass's literary resistance to the conventional slave narrative's "sense of an ending." At the end of *Incidents*, she seems to straddle the opposition between true womanhood and that fallen-freed female other that beckons to her from the far side of her imagination. While paying lip service to the true woman self, the words she mouths at the end of the text connote a secret longing to seize the power to become that other. On the final page of *Incidents*, in this tense, covert discourse between such crucial words of woman's definition as "love," "duty," "privilege," and "serve," we see this other emerging from its liminality and seizing the linguistic terrain on which to declare itself empowered to be born.

Edmonia Lewis's *Forever Free*, marble, 1867. (Gallery of Art, Howard University)

"Free at Last": From Discourse to Dialogue in the Novelized Autobiography

The claim advanced in the previous chapter that J. D. Green's *Narrative*, Frederick Douglass's *My Bondage and My Freedom*, and Harriet Jacobs's *Incidents in the Life of a Slave Girl* represent the culmination of black autobiography in the first major period of Afro-American literary history does not sort well with the current state of criticism regarding this genre and the crucial era in which it developed. Green's narrative has either been forgotten or ignored since its original publication; in the 1960s and 1970s, when a host of slave narratives were given new currency in reprint editions, Green's little book remained off the lists. This is no doubt a principal reason why he has fallen outside the boundaries of scholarly discussion, apparently an unknown to the many critics participating in the reconstruction of black American literary history. One wonders if perhaps he has been discovered, but because he seems so unrepresentative—a subverter of black as well as white community and authority—his work has not been revived. As critic after critic has informed us, the slave trickster is to be interpreted as a kind of culture hero for a black community that asserted itself through "puttin' on old Massa."[1] The self-aggrandizing motives of Green, which led him to put on anyone and everyone who stood in his way, do not fit that heroic mold; yet, as we have seen, he cannot be dismissed as a villainous betrayer of his people either. Falling between these two stools, Green's interstitiality makes him a problem in classification, especially because so much criticism of the slave narrative has been devoted to the celebration of heroic fugitives whose status vis-à-vis the oppressor and the oppressed is fixed, not shifty. Precisely because Green's behavior as trickster and his treatment of that behavior as narrator resist enclosure within the convenient classifying norms that underlie the evolving canon of early black autobiography, his *Narrative* must be regarded as a ground-breaking, precedent-defying work. An act of literary freedom in its own right, this brief, quirky book should also help to liberate us today from a too narrow range of reference as we study the way black people became tellers of free stories in the nineteenth century.

While Green remains invisible, Douglass now enjoys the privileged status of a canonical writer. The *Narrative* has been analyzed and lionized in more than a dozen articles and chapters of scholarly books; it seems to be regarded currently as the epitome of the slave narrative genre. There is no reason to quarrel with this belated recognition of Douglass as an outstanding literary figure, except to wonder why the first of his autobiographies has received such meticulous attention while the second is treated with virtual benign neglect. The exigencies of contemporary publishing and the politics of academic scholarship have something to do with this state of affairs. As Douglass's star rises and more people wish to read and teach him, paperback reprints of the *Narrative* proliferate, since this is the shortest and most approachable of his books as well as the one most easily assimilated into crowded student reading lists. The more the *Narrative* is read and taught, the more it is written about by students and their instructors. The more it is discussed in critical journals and scholarly forums, the more it will be read and taught in the classroom. This is the way a literary classic is made these days, and in the case of Douglass's *Narrative* one might well feel that, for once, the inertia of academe is moving in the right direction. Unfortunately, in the process Douglass is too often viewed as a one-book author.

Only one critic has thus far taken the time to evaluate the *Narrative* in light of *My Bondage and My Freedom* and the *Life and Times of Frederick Douglass* (1881, expanded in 1892), and his conclusion is that after the "excellence" of the *Narrative*, we find only "declining literary merit" in the efforts of 1855 and thereafter. *My Bondage and My Freedom* offers us "a sad index of the wearying struggles and frustrations" of its author's later years. James Matlack is aware of J. Saunders Redding's remark in 1939 that neither of Douglass's later autobiographies had been adequately appreciated, particularly as reflectors of the black man's maturity as a stylist. Nevertheless, Matlack argues that *My Bondage and My Freedom* "is diffused and attenuated by an enormously loosened sense of structure and stylistic control." He dismisses the book with the epithets of a cursory, impressionistic reading. *My Bondage and My Freedom* isn't "taut and crisp"; "its pace lags"; its narration is "rambling"; its rhetoric is "puffy"; "there is no punch to it." Such a commentary would scarcely be worth noting here but for what it suggests about the privileged status that the *Narrative* may be assuming as the paradigm by which everything else Douglass wrote is now being measured. When Matlack complains that "the terseness so appropriate to describing life under the hardships of bondage" has been squandered in the "complex and sloppy" sentence structure of *My Bondage and My Freedom*, he assigns moral and political as well as literary correctness to only one of the many stylistic devices Douglass exploits in the *Narrative*. To Matlack, the 1845 autobiography was the first and final Word, whose purity Douglass could never restore as he wearily ground out his later memoirs. Matlack is appalled to discover the desecration of the textual temple of 1845 throughout the revisions of 1855, whether in the section on slavery, "padded" as it is with "anecdotes and verbiage" that only "clog the narrative flow," or in the section on freedom, which is "choppy and fragmented" as a result of all those "letters, speeches, and extracts from the press" that Douglass crammed into his story. Next to the *Narrative*'s pristine leanness of phrase and tone of "righteous anger," *My Bondage and My Freedom* can only be rated a tired and "flabby" sequel that supplements the original text with "verbiage" that only "stretches out" and "dilutes" that good "old material from the *Narrative*." [2]

It would not be necessary to put Matlack's essay in this kind of critical spotlight were it not for the fact that it presides over the present state of literary judgment of *My Bondage and My Freedom* by default, since little else has been written about this book. Stephen Butterfield, Frances Smith Foster, and Kenny J. Williams have a kind word for the book, but for them, as for almost all the other Douglass critics who note the book at all, it is treated as a successor to the *Narrative*, which, as the earlier text, is automatically accorded priority as well. [3] It is time to rethink this assumption and to ask, if the second autobiography can be seen as the successor of the first, why can't the *Narrative* be examined as the precursor of *My Bondage and My Freedom*?

Unlike *My Bondage and My Freedom*, *Incidents in the Life of a Slave Girl* had no predecessor to overshadow it; unlike Green's *Narrative*, it has often been cited among the significant documents of slave literature. Yet these two male-authored works, ignored or neglected as they have been, have never been mentioned and then dismissed with the suspicion and condescension that Jacobs's book has repeatedly received. In 1931 Vernon Loggins's pioneering literary history, *The Negro Author*, plucked Jacobs out of invisibility by including *Incidents* among the few slave narratives that were "readable." This was "probably because of the 'editing' of Lydia Maria Child," Loggins hastened to add. The observation is doubly invidious, implying first that without Child's aid Jacobs could not have written an intelligible book on her own, and second, that the white woman's editing amounted to a euphemism (which is why Loggins put the word in quotation marks) for ghostwriting. Quoting Child's introduction to *Incidents*, in which she delimits specifically the extent of her editorial role, Charles H. Nichols defended Jacobs's story against the latter of Loggins's charges. However, the black scholar prefaced this defense with a condescending caution to Jacobs's prospective reader: "any reasonably well informed reader can separate the facts from the sentimental moralizing of an editor whose meddling tended to mitigate the stark realities narrated rather than to exaggerate them."[4]

L. Maria Child's traditional identification with literary sentimentalism—which critics (especially male) have persistently and reductively equated with mere sentimentality—has been a liability for *Incidents* until very recently. Even now, in the only sustained literary evaluation of *Incidents*, Jacobs is viewed as having failed to "write openly about her own experience" in her autobiography because she gave into the demands of "the domestic novel," which forced her to "trivialize" her achievement of freedom by apologizing for it at the end of her story. The implication of these remarks by Annette Niemtzow is that Jacobs the autobiographer wrote like a novelist in the Richardsonian tradition (domestic and seduction fiction being one in the same in Niemtzow's view) in order to escape the inadequate narrative formulas of male slave narrative. Unfortunately, Jacobs was not resourceful enough to see through the blandishments and keep clear of the pitfalls of the "domestic novel" (where was Child when Jacobs needed her?). Instead, the black woman "ran straight to the arms of" this seductive genre, accepting nearly indiscriminately the voice, structure, and language of "domestic fiction" and losing her individuality in it. H. Bruce Franklin has given Jacobs more credit for independent thinking regarding her literary models. He believes she retailed "all those accumulated conventions of the literary romance" of her time in order to expose them ironically, especially at the end of her story. However, all this evidence of fictionalizing in *Incidents* caused John W. Blassingame to reject the book as altogether "too melodramatic" to be taken seriously. Had it not been for Jean Fagan Yellin's research corroborating Child's and Jacobs's claims for the book's authenticity, even the meager critical response that *Incidents* has drawn to itself might not have come forward in the face of Blassingame's interdiction. As it is, the woman Nichols labeled "a latter-day Pamela, prey to a master's lust" goes unmentioned in three of the most important contemporary collections of literary and historical essays on Afro-American women: Bert James Loewenberg and Ruth Bogin's *Black Women in Nineteenth-Century American Life* (1976), Sharon Harley and Rosalyn Terborg-Penn's *The Afro-American Woman*

(1978), and, except for one brief remark, in the highly regarded *Sturdy Black Bridges: Visions of Black Women in Literature* (1979).[5]

There is a common thread that runs through the critical response to these three autobiographies by Green, Douglass, and Jacobs: in different ways and for different reasons, each has been treated as a supplement to an original tradition or text that holds the privilege of priority. As a supplement, each of these autobiographies is viewed (when commented on at all) as an "adjunct" to something else, a "surplus" that may, at most, enrich our sense of what was already there inherent in some previously present plenitude.[6] In her critical history of the slave narrative, Marion Wilson Starling treats all female slave autobiographies as supplementary to male ones. She saves her discussion of the "bizarre addenda" of women's narratives until after she has apprized her reader of "the grotesque essentials of the slave experience by way of the male slave." Similarly, in its largely cumulative relationship to the 1845 *Narrative, My Bondage and My Freedom* is praised mostly for giving "more details about the incidents and facts" in the *Narrative* and "additional and more elaborate accounts" of Douglass's life in freedom. Though less full and complete than Douglass's second memoir, the *Narrative* still "stands on its own," a "complement" to *My Bondage and My Freedom*. Even when the latter book improves on the former, it loses "punch" or "impact," a testimony to the vitiating effect of supplementation. When Matlack condemns *My Bondage and My Freedom* as a "puffy" and "flabby" work of "stylistic inflation," he is describing what the supplement can do to endanger, by substitution and amplification, the essential text it follows. When Matlack complains that the pure and "simple prose narration" of 1845 has gone to fat in "Douglass' swelling style of the 1850s," he suggests that the supplement can be a sign of decline. Its earmarks are formal disintegration, stylistic elaboration, and "manipulative appeals" to the inessential, like "sentiment," instead of outrage, in Matlack's opinion.[7]

In the history of the criticism of Afro-American autobiography, many books that seemed too good to be true, on the basis of stylistic sophistication, self-characterization of the narrator, or structure and outcome of the plot, have been regarded as fictional supplements to the real thing, i.e., the authentic slave narrative itself. Nowadays, as we learn how canny slave narrators and their editors were in the employment of authenticating strategies for texts, we realize that we can no longer judge credibility by measuring a narrative against some general and arbitrarily defined standard of literary sophistication presumably appropriate to the scope of an ex-slave. In the past, critics have culled from the ranks of autobiography certain works like Mattie Griffiths's *Autobiography of a Female*

Slave (1856) and Emily Catherine Pierson's *Jamie Parker, the Fugitive* (1851) because they "read like novels, replete with reconstructed dialog and false sentiment."[8] This has been a valuable service, enabling one to discriminate between two kinds of antislavery narrative: those that represent specific historical personages and instances and those inspired by less immediate historical precedents. The problem, however, is that a few narratives of this first group, notably *Incidents in the Life of a Slave Girl*, have been routinely discounted as inauthentic, hence unreliable, because they employ the narrative techniques most identified with the second group.

This is what lies behind Blassingame's rejection of *Incidents* for being "too orderly" and "too melodramatic," with a conclusion in which "all live happily ever after." Blassingame's eminent scholarship has judged many another slave autobiography credible despite the presence of considerable melodramatic incidents, careful ordering of plot, and a happy ending for the central black characters concerned. For instance, the narrative of Solomon Northup is undoubtedly more melodramatic, more firmly controlled in its plot, and more improbable in its happy ending than Jacobs's story. However, David Wilson was a more experienced writer than Jacobs, with two books already published, a somewhat different sense of audience, and a much less difficult set of rhetorical problems to solve than had Jacobs. With readers like Blassingame, Wilson has the extra advantage that comes of the corroboration of Northup's story in mid-nineteenth-century legal history. But even without that, *Twelve Years a Slave* is likely to sound more convincing than *Incidents* because the fictionalizing of the former does not call attention to itself so much, nor does it make appeals to the kind of sentiment that often discomfits and annoys twentieth-century critics.

The most obvious kind of fictionalizing in early black autobiography is dialogue, reconstructed years after the fact and usually dramatized to heighten the emotional impact of a scene and underline the themes illustrated by it. Some very popular slave narratives, like Charles Ball's and Douglass's 1845 autobiography, eschew dialogue almost entirely. Others, like Northup's, Jacobs's, and Douglass's 1855 memoir, feature a significant number of dramatized conversations, often between masters and slaves, which one can hardly believe the ex-slave could have recalled after so many years. The supplement of reconstructed dialogue has not been uniformly condemned as a telltale sign of a narrative's fictitiousness; otherwise, *Twelve Years a Slave* would be a prime candidate for suspicion. However, when reconstructed dialogue is accompanied by, or seems to exist to elicit, some sort of sentimental appeal, then animadversions on the fictionalizing of black autobiography and its resultant loss of credibility usually arise. In this variation on the centuries-old objection to fiction as a subverter of the truth, some critics sound like latter-day Puritans while others mask their ambivalences with an urbane but still condescending stance.

Historians have provided most of the spokesmen for this first camp of critics, beginning with Ulrich B. Phillips, who thought virtually all slave narratives were fictionalized, editorialized propaganda, and leading up to John W. Blassingame, who has suggested criteria by which to distill the truth from the "literary flourishes," "stirring appeals," and other violations of "verisimilitude" that appear in slave narratives.[9] In the second critical camp are such literary scholars as Charles Nichols, Frances Smith Foster, and James Matlack. By stating that books like *Archy Moore* (1836) or *Jamie Parker* can be spotted as unreliable because they are packed with "reconstructed dialog and false sentiment" that makes them "read like novels," Nichols suggests both a convenient and a very ambiguous way of segregating fictitious and true slave narratives. What, exactly, *is* "false sentiment"? Foster also links dialogue and sentimentality in her discussion of *Incidents in the Life of a Slave Girl*, one of "many slave narratives," she claims, that are "full of long passages of dialogue and of discussions of the moral and spiritual dangers which assailed every slave of sensibility." By supplementing their narratives with such "literary embellishments" from "the sentimental novel," autobiographers like Jacobs gave us "black Joseph Andrews [*sic*] and Pamelas faced with the continuous assaults upon their virtue and sensibilities." Echoing Nichols in his linkage of Jacobs and Richardson's heroine, Foster betrays her conflicting sympathy and condescension toward the protagonist of *Incidents* by stating that "no heroine of any sentimental novel of that day could have displayed more virtue or more sensibility than Brent." The annotation to *Incidents* in Erlene Stetson's useful "Bibliography of Female Slave Narratives" also hints at a certain uneasiness about how to take that autobiography's literary mode. "Interesting for its romantic-realistic elements," Stetson observes somewhat ambiguously, before adding "considered by many to be a 'bogus' narrative."[10]

The developments we are discussing here—the supplementation of one narrative by a sequel, or one style by another; the intrusion of suspect voices into black autobiography, especially those that appeal to diversionary sentiments of any sort; the deliberate fictionalizing of texts in the 1850s and 1860s, notably through the use of reconstructed dialogue; the problem of interpreting the dialectic of "romantic-realistic elements" that all these kinds of supplements introduce into autobiography—are actually different manifestations of a single phenomenon. They are all features of what M. M. Bakhtin has called the "novelization" of narrative genres, which the Russian critic has traced throughout the history of Western narrative literature. Here is his summary of what happens when genres undergo novelization: "They become more free and flexible, their language renews itself by incorporating extraliterary heteroglossia and the 'novelistic' layers of literary language, they become dialogized, permeated with laughter, irony, humor, elements of self-parody and finally— this is the most important thing—the novel inserts into these other genres an indeterminacy, a certain semantic openendedness, a living contact with unfinished, still-evolving contemporary reality (the openended present)." In many respects (though not all), this constitutes an instructive description of what we see taking place in the culminating texts of black autobiography in the mid-nineteenth century. The work of Green, Douglass, and Jacobs shows us a genre in transition, becoming something novel, indeed, something that reads and appeals to us like a novel and invites comparison to the earliest Afro-American novels, such as William Wells Brown's *Clotel* (1853) and Harriet E. Wilson's *Our Nig* (1859). The gradual novelizing of black autobiography helped to liberate the genre from the inevitable processes of conventionalizing and stylizing that tend to ossify genres in any era. The price of this renewal, however, was just such indeterminacy and openendedness as Bakhtin alludes to, particularly in the relationship of literary form to the "still-evolving contemporary reality" of the social world and the self in autobiography.[11]

The autobiographies of Green, Douglass, and Jacobs incorporate into their narrative texture forms of discourse that extend well beyond the basic rhetorical relationship between narrator and reader that we have examined in so many early black autobiographies. In addition to the implicit discourse they create between prefatory and appended matter and their narratives per se, these three writers "dialogize" their renditions of the past in ways that admit the "social diversity of speech types," i.e., what Bakhtin calls heteroglossia, into their stories. Within this diversity of social speech types, we can find "authorial speech" (in the form of various kinds of speech acts), "the speeches of narrators" (such as the interpolation of passages from the 1845 *Narrative* into *My Bondage and My Freedom*), "inserted genres" (Dr. Flint's reward notice regarding the fugitive Harriet Jacobs reprinted in *Incidents*), and "the speech of characters" (reconstructed in dialogues in all three autobiographies).[12] The interaction among all these voices and types of speech acts multiplies the channels through which a narrative communicates whatever message it holds for its readers. It becomes increasingly difficult to tell who speaks for whom the more a narrative becomes dialogized. On the other hand, without incorporating the fullest possible diversity of social speech into autobiography, one could not dramatize the fundamental sociolinguistic reality within and against which all black speech action had to contend for authority. Reality, therefore, is not merely supplemented (or vitiated) by the many kinds of fictionalized dialogism we find in novelized black narratives. On the contrary, dialogue evokes reality by dramatizing for us the sociolinguistic context in which all discourse takes on form and meaning.

The crucial fact attending all concrete discourse in Bakhtin's view is this: "language, for the individual consciousness, lies on the borderline between oneself and the other. The word in language is half someone else's." Before someone appropriates a word for his or her own purposes "it exists in other people's mouths, in other people's contexts, serving other people's intentions: it is from there that one must take the word, and make it one's own." Thus, whenever a word is directed toward some object, it enters "a dialogically agitated and tension-filled environment of alien words, value judgments and accents" with which it "intersects" and "recoils" alternately in ways that "crucially shape discourse" and "influence its entire stylistic profile." To speak or to write is "to become an active participant in social dialogue." It is also to engage in a power struggle, for "language is not a neutral medium that passes freely and easily into the private property of the speaker's intentions." It belongs to the other, and "expropriating it, forcing it to submit to one's own intentions and accents, is a difficult and complicated process."[13]

Consider, for example, the dialogue between William Wells Brown and his St. Louis master, Dr. John Young, after the latter informed his slave that he intended to sell him. Appealing to the doctor's sense of fair play and familial responsibility, Brown's expostulation with his master concludes with "'will you sell me to be carried to New Orleans or some other place?'"

> "No," said he, "I do not intend to sell you to a negro trader. If I had wished to have done that, I might have sold you to Mr. Walker [a slave-trader to whom Brown had been hired out the previous year] for a large sum, but I would not sell you to a negro trader. You may go to the city, and find you a good master."
> "But," said I, "I cannot find a good master in the whole city of St. Louis."
> "Why?" said he.
> "Because there are no good masters in the state."
> "Do you not call me a good master?"
> "If you were you would not sell me."
> "Now I will give you one week to find a master in, and surely you can do it in that time."

Having extracted this concession from his master, Brown went to St. Louis, spent a couple of days visiting his mother and his incarcerated sister, and then ran away to Illinois. After his apprehension and return to slavery, Brown's master summoned him and "asked me where I had been? I told him I had acted according to his orders. He had told me to look for a master, and I had been to look for one. He answered that he did not tell me to go to Canada to look for a master." [14]

This is a prototypical instance of the dialogizing of black autobiography. What we witness here is something more than a conventional verbal transaction of power between a master and slave. Young is not simply dictating to Brown; there is a genuine exchange between two interlocutors that immediately belies the idea of the unquestioned authority of the one over the other. In fact, this is a verbal sparring match in which the white and black men are contending for mastery of the word "master." Young unwittingly introduces this loaded word into the discourse, assuming that he has control over the word, assuming implicitly that this word is exempt from Bakhtin's "dialogic imperative," which keeps all signification in flux and subject to "competing definitions for the same things." As soon as Young lets the word out of his mouth, Brown snatches it and starts to "signify" on it. That is, he dialogizes it in a manner peculiar to the oral culture of black America. Signifying on the term "good master," Brown reiterates Young's language in order to reverse and confuse the relationship between himself and *his* master. Like all signifying, Brown's constrains Young (and the implied reader of the *Narrative*) "to attend to all potential meaning carrying symbolic systems in speech events—the total universe of discourse," or, what Bakhtin would call the heteroglossia surrounding the word master. [15] Expropriating the white man's language, tricking it out in his own sly idiom, and then returning it dialogically, the signifying slave lays claim to the right to redefine terms like master and slave. This is the prelude to redefining himself as a freeman.

To facilitate the enslavement of people, the ideology of slavery must first master the potential meanings of key words in the language of the oppressing culture. Slavery must constrict the free play of meaning that normally informs words like master, home, lady, or freedom so as to reduce the multivalent to the univocal. In dialogic instances such as the one we have just noted, we see, momentarily at least, a crack in the wall surrounding words and a subsequent dispersion of what Paul Ricoeur might call "potentialised" meanings. What takes place is a grave challenge to authority, but because the slave selects a verbal, rather than physical, ground on which to assert himself, his insubordination does not seem so threatening. Moreover, his weapon is wit, the signifying riposte, not the outright insult. The slave seems only to be making fun by butting heads with master over the figurative or literal interpretation of his commands.

However, to make fun is to make free, at least temporarily. Beneath the play of dialogue the slave is flexing his mental muscles in a power struggle the significance of which is crucial to our understanding of slavery as major black autobiographers like Brown, Douglass, or Jacobs wanted it understood.

For ex-slaves like these, it was essential to show that the master-slave relationship was not monologic, but rather dialogic. Though standard abolitionist propaganda stressed the absolute power of master over slave, novelized slave narratives insisted, through repeated instances of dialogue between whites and blacks, that the terms of the master-slave relationship were not dictated from the one to the other in an "I talk—you listen" fashion. In fact, those terms were often the subject of negotiation in and through dialogic verbal jousts, some taking the form of jokes, others escalating into speech acts of defiance.[16] During such dialogic negotiation, the appropriateness conditions of master-slave discourse were suspended along with the rules that limited the language of that discourse to the master's meanings. Dialogue, therefore, often became a liminal phase in the master-slave relationship, when neither master nor slave was in full control of the situation, when they implicitly agreed to an indeterminacy of outcome to their verbal combat. Under these circumstances the slave seizes the opportunity to use all his performing skills, including irony, humor, and elements of parody, anything to wrest a comic advantage from the tragedy of his status outside the liminal sphere. Ex-slaves that dialogize their narratives do so to create a similar comic advantage out of *their* status as black autobiographers expected to keep to the monolithic facts in a monologic voice.

To analyze thoroughly the many ways in which black autobiographers dialogized their texts would require another book-length study of this genre. Short of this, one can only point to salient examples of this phenomenon in the hope that this initiates further discussion. Through Green's autobiography, for instance, we can trace what amounts to a kind of by-play that punctuates the deadpan, objectified narrative voice with roguish asides that seem to wink ironically at the reader. This implicit dialogue is never resolved into a united, monologic narrative voice. Green introduces more buffoonery into his portrait of himself as a youth than any other early black autobiographer; indeed, he seems to revel in it. Even his desperate escapes from slavecatchers sometimes have an element of the madcap in their narration.

> On starting up the hill I met my master's nephew, who at once seized hold of me, and a sharp struggle ensued. He called for help but I threw him and caught a stone and struck him on the head, which caused him to let go, when I ran away as fast [as] my legs could carry me, pursued by a numerous

crowd, crying "stop thief." I mounted a fence in the street, and ran through an alley into an Irishman's yard, and through his house, knocking over the Irishman's wife and child, and the chair on which she sat, the husband at the time sat eating at the table, jumped into a cellar on the opposite side of the street without being seen by any one, I made my way into the back cellar and went up the chimney, where I sat till dark, and at night came down and slept in the cellar.[17]

Green's zesty comic view of himself at some of the most serious times of his life (as in the ridiculous perspective in which he pictures his near-suicidal courtship of a slave woman) does much to disqualify him for a place in Benjamin Quarles's "heroic fugitive school of American literature."[18] Many slave narrators modestly declined to claim heroic status for themselves regardless of their fugitive exploits, but Green was the first to make so much of his nonheroic, even antiheroic past. Was this done just for the amusement of his reader? Or was Green signifying on someone and something previously exempt from the laughter in slave narratives that punctures unfounded fear, respect, and piety? Was the idea of self-hood—essential, indivisible, and authoritative in autobiography—now under the siege of comic demolition?

Regardless of how we answer this, we must pay attention to the fact that novelized black autobiographies take an increasingly revisionist attitude toward authority of all kinds, moral, social, intellectual, and aesthetic. Dialogizing autobiographies in novel ways may very well have arisen out of doubts about the capacity of the slave narrative in its traditional form to render certain aspects of reality in an authoritative way. Early in the history of black autobiography, questions about the capacity of this genre to represent the reality of slavery arose in response to the challenge that the ugly facts and monstrous truths of slavery posed to mimesis. After autobiography was judged capable of admitting and authenticating such material, it was faced with a new challenge. Could its capacities be stretched again to accommodate bitter expressive and self-authorizing declarative speech acts that reflected not the objective past but the autobiographer's subjective sense of the present and need to realize himself or herself in it? Again, the genre proved itself capable of accommodating these seeming violations of its generic borders. By the middle of the nineteenth century, novelizing narrators made a further demand of the genre. Could it become not just an authenticator of certain truths and an authorizer of certain speech acts but also, simultaneously, a mode of deauthorizing, of dissenting even from its own authority at times, in order to hint at the insufficiency, if not the collapse, of recognized authority in the world experienced by people like Green, Douglass, and Jacobs? Let us examine a scene or two of dramatized dialogue in *My*

Bondage and My Freedom and *Incidents in the Life of a Slave Girl* as a way of answering this question.

There is more dialogue in *Incidents* than in any other black autobiography of the antebellum era. Many of these interchanges occur between Jacobs and Dr. Flint on occasions when the white man hopes to cajole or coerce his slave into submitting to his various demands. It should be noted that most of these dialogues pivot on an argument over the slave woman's right to speak certain words in certain contexts, to define herself through language that Dr. Flint denies is applicable to her. It should also be noted that in none of these debates is the verbal struggle resolved absolutely in favor of the master. Between Jacobs and Flint the word "love" is constantly at issue. "'Do you love this nigger?'" the doctor impatiently inquires when young Harriet asks permission to marry a free Negro carpenter. When she replies, "'Yes, sir,'" Flint thunders, "'How dare you tell me so!'" [19] By putting these words in Flint's mouth, Jacobs underlines the fact that it is the *telling* as much or more than the *feeling* of love that angers the master. He can tolerate the idea of her pairing up with a black man (so long as it is one of his slaves), but he cannot abide hearing her talk about love, for this is a word that signifies a feeling to which he would deny her access. To name the feeling is to know the difference between what Flint and the young carpenter desire of the slave woman. Flint tries immediately to reclaim the empowering word: "'I supposed you thought more of yourself; that you felt above the insults of such puppies.'" Jacobs neatly parries the attempt to redefine love as "insult": "The man you call a puppy never insulted me, sir; and he would not love me if he did not believe me to be a virtuous woman.'" The doctor's response is to give his slave "a stunning blow," an obvious sign that, having lost the verbal combat, his only recourse is physical violence. The slave woman makes a verbal rejoinder, "'How I despise you!'" which caps the argument over whom she loves by identifying unmistakably whom she hates. Shrieking "'Silence!'" and demanding never to hear Harriet speak of the freeman again, Flint tries once more to repress the dialogic imperative that underlies the competition between the master and slave for the right to define and apply the word love. However, he cannot simply take the word out of commission; it is the only route through which he can learn anything about the slave woman's secret affections. Thus, after the birth of Jacobs's first child, with the doctor desperate to know who his rival is, he tries first to shame, then threaten, then wheedle the information out of her, but with no success. Finally, after extracting her admission that the child's father is white, he returns to the crucial word. "He sprang upon me like a wolf, and grabbed my arm as if he would have broken it. 'Do you love him?' said he, in a hissing tone." Jacobs's reply is the perfect squelch, "'I am thankful that I do not despise him'" (92). This evades the question of how she feels about the unnamed white man while echoing the conclusion of her previous interview with Flint. It is an act of verbal obfuscation that leaves Flint tormentingly ambivalent about the manner and degree of his response to Jacobs. Nothing that Jacobs can say in these interviews can free her of her master, but her repeated dialogic struggles with Flint testify to the power she could and did exercise against his attempts to manipulate and dominate her.

By dialogizing her narrative exposé of "the patriarchal institution," Jacobs illustrated graphically the discursive nature of male-female power relationships such as that which linked her to Dr. Flint. The white man does not simply issue commands that the black woman silently obeys. The vagaries of patriarchalism may require that in some cases he talk her into submission to him. If the slave woman seizes the right opportunities with presence of mind, she may talk her way out of the most abject forms of humiliation. The relationship of master and concubine, for instance, is interstitial, somewhere between that of master and slave and husband and wife. The source of the power of the master over his concubine is not sanctioned in law or instituted in recognized praxis; it is relative only to the individual instance and the informal ties that bind the two parties together. Under such circumstances, power is much more likely to be negotiable than to be absolutely fixed in either party. And power, as Jacobs shows us, is negotiated through speech acts, through dialogue in which the woman constantly matches wits with the man to define a margin of option for herself. Jacobs does not imply that the average slave woman could have done what she was able to do in her verbal bouts with Flint. Few slave women could risk talking back to their masters as she did; one who forgot "that it was a crime for a slave to tell who was the father of her child" is sold away from Dr. Flint's plantation early in *Incidents*. This victim of Flint upbraids him with his promise "'to treat me well,'" but the white man is immovable. "'You have let your tongue run too far; damn you!'" he replies (24). Jacobs, by contrast, knows just how far her tongue can get her, and when to use it to purpose.

Instances of dialogue provide moments of comic release from the oppressive pattern of white-to-black dictation that threatens to enclose many slave narratives in tragedy. Though Jacobs's discourse with Flint is almost never humorous, it plays a comic role in her story nonetheless by reinforcing her inner resources and preparing her for her eventual triumph over patriarchal slavery at the end of her book. Moreover, through dialogue we sometimes receive a distinctly comic perspective on patriarchal authority that reduces it through ridicule to a level that makes it easy for the black protagonist to talk down to it condescendingly. This

occurs in Jacobs's account of her repartee with a gang of white ma-
rauders who use Nat Turner's insurrection as an excuse to rob, horse-
whip, and kidnap unprotected blacks in the area. When these "low
whites" arrive, spoiling for a chance to "exercise a little brief authority"
over Jacobs and her grandmother, both women indulge themselves in
sassy rejoinders to the "soldiers," knowing that they are "in the midst of
white families who would protect us" (99).

> My grandmother had a large trunk of bedding and table cloths. When that
> was opened, there was a great shout of surprise; and one exclaimed,
> "Where'd the damned niggers git all dis sheet an' table clarf?"
>
> My grandmother, emboldened by the presence of our white [male] pro-
> tector, said, "You may be sure we didn't pilfer 'em from *your* houses."

Upon discovering the young slave woman can read and write, the captain
of the patrol demands all her letters.

> I told him I had none. "Don't be afraid," he continued, in an insinuating way.
> "Bring them all to me. Nobody shall do you any harm." Seeing I did not
> move to obey him, his pleasant tone changed to oaths and threats. "Who
> writes to you? half free niggers?" inquired he. I replied, "O, no; most of my
> letters are from white people. Some request me to burn them after they are
> read, and some I destroy without reading." (101)

This unwelcome, unexpected knowledge "put a stop to our conversation." The white men complete their search by sampling Grandmother
Martha's preserves and then depart, pronouncing "a malediction on the
house."

In this comic scene the black women skillfully play off one class of
male power against another, and for a time they enjoy the freedom of
their interstitial position between the "better" and the "low" class whites
in their region. As narrator, Jacobs reconstructs the scene with a freedom
approaching that of a caricaturist. First she recounts in general terms the
ruthlessness of these troops of feral white trash "terrifying and tormenting the helpless." Then, through their dialogue with the black women,
she transforms these rampaging "demons" into bumbling dimwits who
are easily made the butts of ridicule. For once, southern whites, not
slaves, speak in a dialect removed from dignified English; the narrator
must intervene editorially to help us make sense of cracker vernacular
like: "'Don't wonder de niggers want to kill all de white folks, when dey
live on 'sarves' [meaning preserves]'" (101). For a moment, the power of
the word backed by women's wit seems more than a match for the crude
strength of these gabbling male ignoramuses. But how seriously can we
take this as history? Was it actually so deliciously easy to vanquish such
men verbally? Or is the chief significance of this scene structural, provid-

ing, as it does, comic relief from the steadily downward turn of Jacobs's fortunes in the first half of *Incidents*? Does the narrator's appeal to comic sentiments here undermine her veracity more or less than the appeals she makes to other kinds of sentiments through her dialogic struggles with Dr. Flint?

However we choose to answer these questions, we should recognize this scene as an instance of Jacobs's releasing her voice into dialogue, exchanging her fixed narrating role for role-playing, authorizing herself to become other, and then making free with that terrible white male other through comic caricature. Whether we call this narrative tricksterism something positive, like novelizing, or something negative, like outright fictionalizing, will be a function of our own sense of how much an autobiography owes to the past or to the self when fidelity to each makes a conflicting demand on the writer. By the mid-nineteenth century black autobiographers had learned that they could not serve two masters—the past and the self—equally. Self-expressiveness presides over retrospective mimesis in the autobiographies of Jacobs and Douglass because of these writers' commitment to the ideal of freedom, not just as the theme of their life quests or as the moral aim of their narratives, but as the distinguishing characteristic of their style of storytelling.

The dialogic relationship of *My Bondage and My Freedom* to the *Narrative* of Frederick Douglass is pervasive and profound. In the previous chapter we have noted some aspects of this, but none so obvious as the incorporation of key passages from the *Narrative* into the 1855 memoir. The voice of 1845 engages in a dialogue with the voice of 1855 most notably in three interposed passages: (1) the pathetic image of Douglass's grandmother languishing alone in a "little hut, before a few dim embers" (*MBMF*, 179–81); (2) Douglass's "apostrophe" to the sailing vessels on the Chesapeake Bay across from Covey's farm (*MBMF*, 219–21); and (3) the cacophonous scene at Gardiner's shipyard in Baltimore, where a dozen white voices demand Douglass's attention at once (*MBMF*, 308–9). In reprinting these passages from the *Narrative*, Douglass was preserving some of the most novelized material in the *Narrative* to enhance the novelization of *My Bondage and My Freedom*. The first passage invites the reader, through carefully wrought sentimental appeals, to contemplate the death of Betsey Baily as a result of Thomas Auld's indifference. As early as 1849 Douglass had acknowledged in an open letter in the *North Star* that contrary to his prediction in the *Narrative*, his grandmother had not met her end alone and unattended but had been taken into the Auld home where her master was caring for her "in a manner becoming a gentleman and a Christian." Two months after publication of this letter, Betsey Baily died in the home of Thomas Auld. In spite of what he knew about his grandmother's last days, the author of *My Bondage and My Freedom* refused to alter the image of betrayal and despair that he had first introduced to public consciousness in 1845. He would not portray, as he had in the *Narrative*, his grandmother's death by the cold and lonely hearth of a desolate slave hut. But he allowed nothing he had learned since 1845 to mitigate the potent melodrama of blighted domesticity that had served him so well in the *Narrative*.[20]

The second novelized passage from the *Narrative*, equally a tribute to Douglass's imaginative dramatization of the past, also makes a strong sentimental appeal through the slave's soliloquy to the "moving multitude" of "freedom's swift-winged angels" of the sea. When the bondman exclaims, "O, that I were free! O, that I were on one of your gallant decks, and under your protecting wing! Alas! betwixt me and you the turbid waters roll," we know that we are not reading the spontaneous outburst of a wretched slave. We are being consciously reminded of the sophistication of the freeman who deploys such "literary flourishes" to transform a supposedly broken slave into a Romantic hero. Through the third novelized passage from the *Narrative*, Douglass introduces into his second memoir the voices of working-class white men that easily put us in mind of the bullies who ransack the house of Jacobs's grandmother. Like Jacobs, Douglass flavors his narrative with white vernacular here for comic purposes, creating a running dialogue between his own free voice and that of the enslaved on Colonel Lloyd's plantation (see the interpolated passage in *MBMF*, 99) and the exploited whites on the Baltimore docks.

In all three of these interpolated passages, we see Douglass retrieving material from the *Narrative* that displays his imaginative and dramatic powers most overtly in melodramatic as well as comic literary instances. In creating *My Bondage and My Freedom* Douglass treats the *Narrative* as though it were a first rehearsal for his performing self, which by 1855 had evolved into an even more freely novelizing narrator. *My Bondage and My Freedom* was a text in which he wanted to feature his novelizing performance closer to center narrative stage than in any previous book. A look at the revisions of the climax of the *Narrative*—the battle with Covey—for *My Bondage and My Freedom* highlights Douglass's achievement as a black literary freeman.

The *Narrative* recounts the entire struggle with Covey in the following single paragraph.

> Mr. Covey entered the stable with a long rope; and just as I was half out of the loft, he caught hold of my legs, and was about tying me. As soon as I found what he was up to, I gave a sudden spring, and as I did so, he holding to my legs, I was brought sprawling on the stable floor. Mr. Covey seemed now to think he had me, and could do what he pleased; but at this mo-

ment—from whence came the spirit I don't know—I resolved to fight; and, suiting my action to the resolution, I seized Covey hard by the throat; and as I did so, I rose. He held on to me, and I to him. My resistance was so entirely unexpected, that Covey seemed taken all aback. He trembled like a leaf. This gave me assurance, and I held him uneasy, causing the blood to run where I touched him with the ends of my fingers. Mr. Covey soon called out to [William] Hughes for help. Hughes came, and, while Covey held me, attempted to tie my right hand. While he was in the act of doing so, I watched my chance, and gave him a heavy kick close under the ribs. This kick fairly sickened Hughes, so that he left me in the hands of Mr. Covey. The kick had the effect of not only weakening Hughes but Covey also. When he saw Hughes bending over with pain, his courage quailed. He asked me if I meant to persist in my resistance. I told him I did, come what might; that he had used me like a brute for six months, and that I was determined to be used so no longer. With that, he strove to drag me to a stick that was lying just out of the stable door. He meant to knock me down. But just as he was leaning over to get the stick, I seized him with both hands by his collar, and brought him by a sudden snatch to the ground. By this time, Bill came. Covey called upon him for assistance. Bill wanted to know what he could do. Covey said, "Take hold of him, take hold of him!" Bill said his master hired him out to work, and not to help to whip me; so he left Covey and myself to fight our own battle out. We were at it for nearly two hours. Covey at length let me go, puffing and blowing at a great rate, saying that if I had not resisted, he would not have whipped me half so much.[21]

These twenty-four clipped sentences of terse narrative exhibit Douglass's style at its most factual and economical. Other than one conventional simile (Covey's trembling like a leaf), he employs no embellishing imagery. Only once ("Covey seemed all taken aback") does Douglass interrupt his blow-by-blow description of events to characterize any of the agents of all this action. We do not know who Hughes and Smith are other than that they were present earlier along with "a slave named Eli," in Covey's treading yard when Douglass first collapsed in the heat and precipitated the whole episode (107). All the discourse in the scene, with the exception of Covey's "Take hold of him. Take hold of him!" is indirect, unaccompanied by modifiers that could suggest how the words were spoken or received. This is about as close as one comes in the 1845 *Narrative* to an undeviatingly assertive speech act.[22]

The first thing we notice in the 1855 version of the fight with Covey is the carefully modulated narrative pace that intersperses commentary of various kinds into the original blow-by-blow recitation of events. After recounting, in the manner of the *Narrative*, Covey's initial seizure of Douglass in the stable loft, *My Bondage and My Freedom* postpones the telling of what happened next in favor of providing an interpretive context for the rest of the action. "I now forgot my *roots* [given him for protection by Sandy Jenkins], and remembered my pledge to *stand up in my own defense.*"[23] Standing up turns out to be difficult, however, when a man is "endeavoring skillfully to get a slip-knot" around one's legs. Covey "seemed to think he had me very securely in his power. He little thought he was—as the rowdies say—'in' for a 'rough and tumble' fight; but such was the fact." These statements hold up the narrative to characterize Covey in the first sentence, but it is the second one, in which the narrator characterizes himself implicitly, that is the more noteworthy. Here we see Douglass adopting the vernacular tongue to foreground a serious moment in his autobiography. Though he quarantines the argot of the rowdies in quotation marks, as most proper antebellum writers did,[24] he had to know that this only pointed up the presence of the vernacular and its comic incongruity in the serious context in which he was using it. Douglass's use of the vernacular is both diverting and diversionary; it is only the first of a number of comic distractions that he will introduce into the 1855 version of the fight with Covey, distractions that compete with the serious narration of the fight to keep the reader very much off balance.

Douglass's description of his initial resistance to Covey is told in 1855 with much attention to its "strictly *defensive*" character [Douglass's italics]. While Douglass "felt as supple as a cat, and was ready for the snakish creature at every turn," he was wise enough to do no more than parry the slave-breaker's blows and deal "no blows in turn." This emphasizes the limited nature of Douglass's rebellion in a way the *Narrative* does not make clear. The slave youth knew that if he tried to choke Covey into submission, his eventual punishment was sure and lethal. Thus he resorted to a kind of psychological as well as physical jujitsu to gain a more powerful advantage over the white man's mind and heart than he could risk taking over his body. We can see this at work in the verbal exchange that Douglass next writes into *My Bondage and My Freedom*.

"Trembl[ing] in every limb"—not like a leaf—Covey asks, "'*Are you going to resist*, you scoundrel?'" "To which, I returned a polite '*yes sir.*'" Once again, Douglass diverts his reader with the comic incongruity of such well-mannered speech in such ill-mannered (at least from Covey's point of view) behavior. One starts to sense a certain playfulness in the intent of a narrator who would write this into what had been a decade before a climactic moment of high seriousness in his autobiography. More evidence follows in *My Bondage and My Freedom* to enhance this spirit of verbal play. Covey cries out "lustily" (a nice word choice in this context, reflecting comically on Covey) for help from "his cousin Hughes." The *Narrative* does not inform us that Hughes was a white man, much less the kin of Douglass's antagonist, but *My Bondage and My Free-*

dom characterizes him as "youthful" and, after catching a kick from the defiant slave, a "poor fellow." Are we then to feel a bit sorry for this assailant of Douglass? Or can the narrator of *My Bondage and My Freedom* indulge himself in the luxury of this kindly epithet because he now recalls the whole episode with a detachment that defuses old resentments and diverts them into comic sympathy and ridicule? Some of this humorous perspective colors the narrator's characterization of himself as he struck out against Hughes. "Since I was, in any case, to suffer for resistance, I felt (as the musty proverb goes) that 'I might as well be hanged for an old sheep as a lamb.'" Reading this proverb into the slave's resistance to his two white adversaries puts his action once again into a vernacular context. Comic incongruity arises again as we try to apply something homely to something potentially heroic and as we confront the improbable association of Douglass the rebel with a sheep or a lamb.

My Bondage and My Freedom places the second verbal exchange between Douglass and Covey into more direct discourse than appears in the *Narrative*. However, the wording in both texts is almost the same, as is the narration of Covey's maneuvering to reach a stick that could help him gain the upper hand over the fractious slave. Douglass informs his 1845 reader that he responded to Covey's maneuver by seizing him by the collar and bringing him "by a sudden snatch to the ground." *My Bondage and My Freedom* elaborates this direct statement of fact into a comic anticlimax: "with a vigorous and sudden snatch, I brought my assailant harmlessly, his full length, on the *not over* clean ground—for we were now in the cow yard." This dip in the dung reduces Covey, at least for a moment, from the threatening proportions of the *Narrative* to the status of a slapstick villain. The narrator of *My Bondage and My Freedom* plays up his coarse joke by pronouncing, with mock seriousness, "He [Covey] had selected the place for the fight, and it was but right that he should have all the advantages of his own selection."

At this point enter Bill, the hired man. The second autobiography makes a strategic pause to recapitulate the time elapsed in the entire struggle. Further adding to the suspense, the 1855 narrator gives us an insight into the minds of both Douglass and Covey as they consider the probable outcome of the struggle. After this, we return to the action: "Holding me, Covey called upon Bill for assistance." Then comes another foregrounding comment, which makes explicit what Douglass has been doing implicitly throughout his revised version of the battle with Covey. "The scene here, had something comic about it." First of all, Smith "knew *precisely* what Covey wished him to do" but "affected ignorance, and pretended he did not know what to do." By playing the dumb darky role for all it's worth, the hired slave tries to escape the all too obvious fate of

William Hughes, while also giving tacit support to his black comrade's rebellion. The *Narrative* makes nothing funny out of Smith's ploy; it does not even present it as a ploy but rather as an offer: "Bill wanted to know what he could do." *My Bondage and My Freedom*, on the other hand, develops between Smith and Covey a comic dialogue that accentuates the reversals initiated by young Frederick's rebellion.

> "What shall I do, Mr. Covey," said Bill [with feigned ignorance].
>
> "Take hold of him—take hold of him!" said Covey [with mounting exasperation].
>
> With a toss of his head, peculiar to Bill, he said, "indeed Mr. Covey, I want to go to work."
>
> "*This is* your work," said [a desperate] Covey; "take hold of him."
>
> Bill replied, with spirit, "My master hired me here, to work, and *not* to help you whip Frederick."
>
> "Bill," said I [warningly], "don't put your hands on me."
>
> "MY GOD! Frederick, I ain't goin' to tech ye," [Smith replied] leaving Covey and myself to settle our matters as best we might.

This reconstructed dialogue further dramatizes the comic demotion of Covey that *My Bondage and My Freedom* insists on as it pursues the story of Douglass's fateful fight with the slave-breaker. The once redoubtable white man is pictured as fairly pleading with, not ordering, a slave under his supervision. In their discourse, Bill Smith proves as much a verbal resister as Douglass is a physical one. That Covey and Smith have a discourse at all is Douglass's way of indicating what Jacobs also illustrated in the dialogues of Dr. Flint and herself in *Incidents*, namely, that this is another crucial instance of power negotiation through language between blacks and whites.

As a slave hired from another to do a specific job, not to be "broken," Smith knew that Covey was not free to beat him except for the most grievous offenses. Thus the black man felt free to engage the slave-breaker in a verbal quibble, a bit of solemn-faced play, over the meaning of the word *work*. Covey's word is no longer law; rebellious young Frederick's is. The unexpected final vernacular exclamation that Douglass puts into Smith's mouth adds one more bit of comic word-play to the scene, as Covey's formerly imperious expression "take hold of him" (which can signify the whipping of a slave) suffers a double affront, not just a refusal, but one couched in black idiom that affirms the solidarity of the hired man with his unruly fellow slave.

At this point, *My Bondage and My Freedom* brings into the scene a character who makes no appearance in the climax of the *Narrative*. Caroline, Covey's only female slave, is mentioned in the *Narrative* only as an illustration of black female humiliation in slavery. "A large, able-bodied woman, about twenty years of age," she was purchased by Covey to serve as a "breeder," an office she fulfilled to her master's satisfaction within a year of her forced cohabitation with Bill Smith. In 1845 Douglass spoke of Caroline simply as a "wretched woman" (105); in 1855, as he pictured her "coming to the cow yard to milk," she became "a powerful woman" who "could have mastered me very easily, exhausted as I now was." Douglass is most impressed by her moral power, however, which is put to the test when her master demands that she help him bind the insubordinate black teenager. The black woman answers Covey as Bill Smith had, which is a great favor to Frederick, especially because Caroline belongs to Covey and will not be able to escape his wrath later, as Bill Smith knew he could. In an irony that only belittles Covey even more, "he gave her several sharp blows" for her disobedience, while giving the main cause of all the trouble only a few more sharp words. "We were all in open rebellion, that morning," Douglass comments in 1855, an important modification of the 1845 image of Douglass as heroic loner in his battle with Covey. *My Bondage and My Freedom* does not make young Frederick's actions so singular or so distinctively prominent that they throw into the shadows of history the contributions of his fellow mutineers, Bill Smith and Caroline. True to its pervasive emphasis on the interdependence of freedom and black community, the second autobiography demonstrates that the rebel had to have black support to win his fight. Indeed, in admitting for the first time that Caroline "could have mastered me very easily" but chose not to, though the consequences for her were dire, Douglass built her up as a heroic figure at the expense of his own 1845 image of indomitable self-sufficiency.

My Bondage and My Freedom concludes the Douglass-Covey fight very much as the *Narrative* does, except that the later book puts Covey's parting words into direct discourse, which has the advantage of dramatizing his bluster more effectively than the earlier book does. *My Bondage and My Freedom* also follows the *Narrative* in analogizing the fight to a "resurrection" from the "tomb of slavery" to the "heaven of freedom" (although the second autobiography inserts the qualifier "comparative" before "freedom"). There is a salient difference, however, between the statements that each narrator makes to launch his concluding remarks about the inspirational significance of his rebellion. The *Narrative*'s conclusion begins: "This battle with Mr. Covey was the turning-point in my career as a slave" (113). *My Bondage and My Freedom* prefaces its conclusion with: "Well, my dear reader, this battle with Mr. Covey,—undignified as it was, and as I fear my narration of it is—was the turning point in my '*life as a slave.*'"

To characterize as undignified both the climax of his life as a slave and his narration of that climax was not just a gesture of self-depreciation or literary modesty on Douglass's part. *My Bondage and My Freedom*'s revisionary approach to the battle with Covey does tend to diminish the dignity of the *Narrative*'s version of that battle. The 1855 perspective on this episode neither debunks nor denies what Douglass had said earlier about the turning point of his slave life, but it does novelize it. That is, the narrator of *My Bondage and My Freedom* treats the episode with a certain "comic familiarity" which is, according to Bakhtin, both a cause and an effect of the continuous novelization of all literary genres that ensures "their liberation from all that serves as a brake on their unique development."[25] *My Bondage and My Freedom* deliberately "undignifies" through comic familiarity its protagonist and its narrator, Douglass in past action and Douglass in present autobiographical speech action. In doing this, Douglass's second autobiography, along with other dialogized narratives like William Wells Brown's, Green's, and Jacobs's, helped to launch a mode of literary realism essential to the development of Afro-American narrative into novel, fictional forms.

The turning point of *My Bondage and My Freedom* does not undignify its protagonist to demean him or his actions. Its aim is to divest him of singularity as a hero in order to endow him with more familiarity as a representative human being. The more details that the 1855 revision adds to the 1845 image of the slave in his rebellion, the less distance remains between the hero and the reader. As we hear his cheeky retorts to Covey, learn the musty proverb that spurred his resolution to resist Hughes, follow him into the cow yard for the finish of his wrestling match with an increasingly ridiculous antagonist, and discover Caroline a rival to him in strength and bravery, we begin to view Douglass on a level that seems nearer our own. We gain a glimpse of our common, undignified humanity with this hero, the climax of whose life moves us to comic empathy as well as respect, not just awe of or fear for him. We laugh to discover Douglass much more a man among men than the *Narrative*'s high seriousness allows him to be. The hero of *My Bondage and My Freedom* seems one of us in key moments such as this, when comic empathy helps us identify him with the heroes of Northrop Frye's "low mimetic mode" of narration, epitomized in "social comedy" and "realistic fiction."[26] Unlike the protagonists of many low mimetic narratives, Douglass never disqualifies himself as a figure of our admiration in his second autobiography, but by qualifying his heroic dignity in the ways we have noted, he inhibits our idealizing him to the extent that, too often, readers and critics of the *Narrative* have gone. By 1855 Douglass understood that the black autobiographer who bound his reader to him through comic sympathetic identification as well as admiration had found the most balanced means of affirming himself a man and a brother with whites. Whether, by 1855, this sort of affirmation was of much concern any longer to Douglass is debatable. However, given the focus of his second autobiography on building bridges to the black community, this same strategy of comic undignification (reinforced by other confessions of human weaknesses, such as his hero-worship of Garrison) could hardly have retarded his acceptance among northern blacks, either.

The simple gravity of Douglass's 1845 plainstyle is also undignified in 1855, mainly as a result of the implicit dialogue it holds with many competing voices that emerge from the cracks in the linked narrative chain of events forged for the climax of the *Narrative*. As we have seen, *My Bondage and My Freedom* allows the argot of the rowdies, homespun proverbial wit, ironic word-play, barnyard humor, near-blasphemous oaths, and southern black dialect to dialogize the narration of Douglass's battle with Covey. Consequently, the monologic voice of the *Narrative* disintegrates into a "social diversity of speech types" which is, for Bakhtin, the stylistic desideratum of the novel. The admission of all these voices into his text tends to deauthorize any single narrative voice as solely and exclusively Douglass's. Douglass can play the rowdy, the proverb-monger, the earthy humorist, the vernacular raconteur, without confining his consciousness to any of these narrative roles. When he wishes to, he can so dialogize his text that, like a novelist, he himself (assuming for a moment at least that there is some unitary self behind the dialogized utterance) "does not speak in a given language" so much as "he speaks, as it were, *through* language." The freedom that comes of using language this way leaves fewer and fewer "rock bottom truths"—in the form of linguistic "brute facts"—undialogized and unrelativized.[27] On the other hand, out of the multiple incongruities of voice that emerge from Douglass's, Green's, and Jacobs's dialogized autobiographies come the unpredictable pleasures of these unmanageable texts.

The most basic novelizing elements in *My Bondage and My Freedom*, as in the work of Green and Jacobs, are dialogue and dialect. As we have noted, each of these elements has a crucial comic role in mid-century Afro-American autobiography, a role that extends beyond the eliciting of humor to the prefiguring of triumph for those who can harness the power of wit and words in dialogic competitions. The dialects that break into the three culminating texts of early black autobiography belong to white as well as black social groups and range from the patronizing discourse adopted by white preachers when they speak to slaves (dissected satirically in Green's *Narrative*) to the "Guinea" patois of Colonel Lloyd's slaves that Douglass translates for the reader of his second autobiography. Most antebellum prose writers introduced dialect into their writing for the purpose of "condescending amusement,"[28] but Jacobs and Douglass, as representatives of an alienated people, would not treat the vernacular that they had heard as merely an alien tongue incapable of profound utterance. For them, as for a growing number of American writers after the Civil War, vernacular utterance, especially when dramatized in dialogue, became an epitome of that which was distinctive and genuine in a particular person or social group. This does not deny that Harriet Jacobs entered the dialect of "low" white men into her story primarily to ridicule the social class from which they came and to affirm her superiority to it. Nevertheless, the vernacular of the lowest of all classes in America, that of the slave, she treats with respect. Recalling an old slave woman who, after slapping her dead mistress while she lay in her coffin, then seethed, "'The devil is got you *now!*'" Jacobs invests in black dialect a power of expressiveness to which her more conventional narrative prose rarely compares. Similarly, when Douglass wanted to render the trauma of his separation from his grandmother at the age of seven, he made a black child's dialect—"'Fed, Fed! grandmammy gone! grandmammy gone!'"— the medium through which tragic awareness entered his life. Even the italics that nineteenth-century dialecticians so often used to intensify a vernacular word in the punch line of a joke become, in the hands of Douglass and Jacobs, a means of stressing the heightened poignancy of black vernacular utterance. This is evident in *My Bondage and My Freedom* when "the wild screams" of slave children in defense of their mother—"'*Let my mammy go*'"—are placed in pathetic dialogue with an overseer's obscene promise to "'teach the d——d b——h how to give a white man impudence.'"

Both Douglass and Jacobs recognized the vitality that dialect takes on when it is put in a dialogic relationship with standardized usage that has become morally bankrupt or emotionally bogus. It was just such tensions between the standard and the vernacular view of the world that made Mark Twain the great stylistic innovator of his age. *Huckleberry Finn* epitomizes the native strain in American realism that arose between 1825 and 1925 when, according to Richard Bridgman, a "colloquial" style displaced the traditionally formal and genteel "literary" style. This process was initiated primarily through dialect writing and the rise of conversational, colloquial dialogue to a position of dominance over authorial exposition in American narrative.[29] For years antebellum white southerners like George W. Harris, Johnson Jones Hooper, and the contributors to William T. Porter's *Spirit of the Times* have been celebrated for their pioneering of these early forms of dialect and dialogue writing. Now it is time to recognize that the experiments with dialogue and dialect that Jacobs, Douglass, and, to a lesser extent, Green and William

Wells Brown engaged in give these antebellum black southern writers a place of importance among the harbingers of American literary realism.[30]

The realism achieved by Afro-American autobiography by the end of the slavery era is rooted in the linguistic freedom that black narrators accrued to themselves as they took increasing control over a medium of expression that had been at first only nominally theirs. By the middle of the nineteenth century, black autobiographers had come to realize that the more freely a life story was told, the more insistently that telling affirmed black people's right to the tree of life—the saving and sustaining word—that only bloomed in freedom-land. One could not address the reality of black experience and speak of it truly unless one could speak of it freely.

The journey of black autobiography toward free telling first had to pass through the intervening consciousness of amanuenses and editors, then had to challenge generic conventions and discursive proprieties of writing itself, before finally undertaking the greatest task of all, the appropriation of language for purposes of signification outside that which was privileged by the dominant culture. By 1865 the leading writers in the tradition had sounded the resources of language to evoke both an external and an internal dimension of reality authorized uniquely by black perception. External or social reality in the work of these writers was not confined to the oppressive, often sordid brute facts of slavery and racism, though this was an area of black experience about which Jacobs and Douglass spoke with unabashed candor. Social reality in their eyes was not simply grim and fixed, an antagonistic force above and beyond black influence. Social forces and arrangements even in slavery could be, under certain conditions, manipulated and exploited through speech action. The social scene had its provisional dimensions that were not fully realized until linguistic transactions established and defined them. Likewise, the inner dimension of reality, the world of all that was signified in the word self, was also dependent on language for its reification. Self-realization for black autobiographers involved the finding of one's voice, the reclaiming of language from the mouth of the white other, and the initiation of the arduous process of fitting language to voice instead of the other way around.

No one can claim that after only a century of existence, black autobiography in America reached a fully liberated, and thus a fully realized, vision of the social and private dimensions of black experience in this country. What the genre did was to demonstrate to its readers how much was at stake in the creation of a realist literature for blacks in the United States as well as how the real might be appropriated and signified in and through the discursive and linguistic resources of first-person narrative.

Early black autobiography also provided literary precedents and models for the freedom with which black writers have continually adapted first-person narrative to their needs and purposes, beginning with James Weldon Johnson's *The Autobiography of an Ex-Coloured Man* (1912) and continuing through Richard Wright's *Black Boy* (1945), Ralph Ellison's *Invisible Man* (1952), Ernest Gaines's *The Autobiography of Miss Jane Pittman* (1971), and Alice Walker's *The Color Purple* (1982). The vitality of this tradition today represents a triumph not just for these twentieth-century writers but also for their forbears, who first came to the autobiographical form convinced, as John Marrant wrote in his *Journal* almost two centuries ago, that they "were at a loss for words," since "experience goes beyond expression." Now that we are recovering more and more the words of these pioneers and recognizing their expressive import, we can approach their work with a more complete appreciation of what it meant when Frederick Douglass finally wrote, "I must speak just the word that seemed to *me* the word to be spoken," and when Harriet Jacobs answered, "What a comfort it is, to be free to *say* so!" [31]

Notes

Chapter 1, The First Century of Afro-American Autobiography

1. Georges Gusdorf, "Conditions and Limits of Autobiography," in James Olney, ed., *Autobiography: Essays Theoretical and Critical* (Princeton: Princeton University Press, 1980), p. 36.

2. I use the term *oratorical* in the generic sense as it has been applied by William L. Howarth to a type of autobiography to be discussed in greater detail later in this chapter. See Howarth's "Some Principles of Autobiography," *New Literary History* 5 (Winter 1974), 367–81.

3. Henry David Thoreau, *Walden and Civil Disobedience*, ed. Owen Thomas (New York: Norton, 1966), p. 1.

4. Emerson could excuse Thoreau's "severity" and "dangerous frankness" as concomitants of his unbending idealism, his "noble soul," and his unsurpassed Americanism. However, when Frederick Douglass exhibited the same sort of severity and frankness in his writing, he was attacked for being supercilious, conceited, and "altogether too self-sufficient." See Emerson's "Thoreau," *Atlantic* 10 (Aug. 1862), 246, and John W. Blassingame, ed., *The Frederick Douglass Papers, Series I* (New Haven: Yale University Press, 1979), 1, pp. xxxvii–xxxix.

5. George M. Fredrickson, *The Black Image in the White Mind* (New York: Harper & Row, 1971), pp. 1–36.

6. Gerrit Smith, "Letter to Editor of the Union Herald," *Emancipator*, Jan. 3, 1839, p. 146, col. 2.

7. Samuel G. Howe, *The Refugees from Slavery in Canada West* (Boston: Wright and Potter, 1864), p. 3.

8. Houston A. Baker, Jr., *The Journey Back: Issues in Black Literature and Criticism* (Chicago: University of Chicago Press, 1980), pp. xv–xvii.

9. The most convenient resource for documents relating to the Kingsley-Newman dispute is Charles Frederick Harrold's edition of the *Apologia Pro Vita Sua* (New York: Longmans, Green, 1947). I quote from p. 358 of this edition, which reprints Kingsley's original charge against Newman, which appeared in Kingsley's review of James A. Froude's *History of England* for *Macmillan's Magazine*, Jan. 1864.

10. See Newman's "True Mode of Meeting Mr. Kingsley," in Harrold, ed., *Apologia*, pp. 385–92. All further quotations attributed to Newman are taken from this pamphlet.

11. The *Chronotype* quotation appears in a pamphlet, *Fugitive Slaves*, in the Leeds Anti-Slavery Series, no. 34 (London, 1849), p. 12.

12. As Theodore Weld, compiler of *American Slavery as It Is* (New York: American Anti-Slavery Society, 1839), an abolitionist handbook, wrote: "The North is so blinded it will not *believe* what we say about slavery, its horrors. . . . All the arguments drawn from the nature and history of mind, knowledge of human nature, etc., with such a flood of logic and mental philosophy" would not have as much effect as the "testimony" of eyewitnesses to slavery. Weld to Sarah and Angelina Grimké, May 22, 1837, in Gilbert H. Barnes and Dwight L. Dumond, eds., *Letters of Theodore Dwight Weld, Angelina Grimké Weld and Sarah Grimké, 1822–1844* (New York: Appleton-Century, 1934), 1:390. Angelina Grimké agreed that slave narratives "are greatly needed," for "many a tale of romantic horror can the slaves tell." *Ibid.*, 2:525.

13. Ralph Waldo Emerson, "Thoughts on Modern Literature," *Dial* 1 (Oct. 1840), 147.

14. The shadow as a vehicle of expression for the unconscious in black autobiography is discussed at several points in this book. This concept is outlined in Carl Jung, *Aion: Researches into the Phenomenology of the Self*, vol. 9 of *Collected Works of C. G. Jung* (Princeton: Princeton University Press, 1959), pars. 13–42.

15. See Ernst Robert Curtius's discussion of "affected modesty" and "inexpressibility" as *topoi* of Latin and medieval oratory in his *European Literature and the Latin Middle Ages*, trans. Willard R. Trask (New York: Pantheon, 1953), pp. 83–85, 159–62.

16. For the concept of "reportability," see William Labov, *Language in the Inner City* (Philadelphia: University of Pennsylvania Press, 1972), p. 370. "Evaluators" and "embedding" are discussed in Labov and Joshua Waletsky, "Narrative Analysis: Oral Versions of Personal Experience," in June Helm, ed., *Essays on the Verbal and Visual Arts* (Seattle: University of Washington Press, 1967), pp. 37–39.

17. Tillie Olsen, *Silences* (New York: Delacorte, 1978), p. 7.

18. See Paul Ricoeur, *Hermeneutics and the Human Sciences*, trans. and ed. John B. Thompson (Cambridge: Cambridge University Press, 1981), pp. 165–76; Monroe C. Beardsley, *Aesthetics* (New York: Harcourt, Brace & World, 1958), pp. 134–44; and Beardsley, "The Metaphorical Twist," *Philosophy and Phenomenological Research* 22 (Mar. 1962), 293–307.

19. James Olney, *Metaphors of Self* (Princeton: Princeton University Press, 1972).

20. Charles Feidelson, Jr., *Symbolism and American Literature* (Chicago: University of Chicago Press, 1953), pp. 58–61.

21. Karl J. Weintraub, *The Value of the Individual: Self and Circumstance in Autobiography* (Chicago: University of Chicago Press, 1978), pp. xv–xvi.

22. Olney, *Metaphors of Self*, p. 39.

23. Harold Bloom, *A Map of Misreading* (New York: Oxford University Press, 1975), pp. 3–4, 32, 54.

24. Wilson J. Moses, *Black Messiahs and Uncle Toms* (University Park: Pennsylvania State University Press, 1982), pp. 30–31; Leonard Black, *The Life and Sufferings of Leonard Black* (New Bedford, Mass.: Benjamin Lindsey, 1847), pp. 54–55; William Craft, *Running a Thousand Miles for Freedom* (London: William Tweedie, 1860), p. 9.

25. Curtius, *European Literature*, pp. 94–98.

26. Hayden White, "The Problem of Change in Literary History," *New Literary History* 7 (Autumn 1975), 97–112.

27. Jean Starobinski, "The Style of Autobiography," in Olney, ed., *Autobiography*, pp. 76–77.

28. Ulrich B. Phillips, *Life and Labor in the Old South* (Boston: Little, Brown, 1929), p. 219: "Ex-slave narratives in general . . . were issued with so much abolitionist editing that as a class their authenticity is doubtful." Although some scholars of the 1930s and 1940s used slave narratives as historical sources, it was not until the publication of Blassingame's *The Slave Community* (New York: Oxford University Press, 1972) and Genovese's *Roll, Jordan, Roll: The World the Slaves Made* (New York: Random House, 1974) that the predisposition against the slave narrative as documentary evidence was completely set aside.

29. John W. Blassingame, ed., *Slave Testimony* (Baton Rouge: Louisiana State University Press, 1977), p. xxxix.

30. Hayden White, *Tropics of Discourse* (Baltimore: Johns Hopkins University Press, 1978), pp. 121–25.

31. Lloyd F. Bitzer, "Functional Communication: A Situational Perspective," in Eugene E. White, ed., *Rhetoric in Transition* (University Park: Pennsylvania State University Press, 1980), p. 24.

32. These are the chief characteristics of "oratorical" autobiography as Howarth defines them in "Some Principles of Autobiography," pp. 92–95.

33. White, *Tropics of Discourse*, pp. 3–4. M. M. Bakhtin, *The Dialogic Imagination*, trans. Caryl Emerson and Michael Holquist and ed. Michael Holquist (Austin: University of Texas Press, 1981), pp. 281–84.

34. Francis R. Hart, "Notes for an Anatomy of Modern Autobiography," *New Literary History* 1 (Spring 1970), 490.

35. Hammon's fourteen-page *Narrative* was published in Boston by Green and Russell in 1760. The identification of Hammon as "Servant to General Winslow of Marshfield, in New-England" makes it unclear whether this is also the first slave narrative published in North America. See also Luther P. Jackson, "Religious De-

velopment of the Negro in Virginia from 1760 to 1860," *Journal of Negro History* 16 (Apr. 1931), 168–239.

36. Frances Smith Foster, *Witnessing Slavery: The Development of Antebellum Slave Narratives* (Westport, Conn.: Greenwood, 1979), p. 32. For a full discussion of "Adam Negro's Tryall," see Sidney Kaplan, ed., *The Selling of Joseph: A Memorial* (Amherst: University of Massachusetts Press, 1969), pp. 42–45. In Charles Evans, *American Bibliography* (1904; rpt. New York: Peter Smith, 1941), 2:283, a *Declaration and Confession of Jeffrey, A Negro* (Boston: T. Fleet, 1745) is listed, but I have been unable to locate a copy.

37. The following narratives are considered fictitious today, though in the antebellum era some exerted much influence on public opinion because of their ostensible validity: Richard Hildreth, *The Slave, or Memoirs of Archy Moore*, 2 vols. (Boston: J. H. Eastburn, 1836), revised and enlarged as *The White Slave: or, Memoirs of a Fugitive* in 1852; Jabez Delano Hammond's anonymously published *Life and Opinions of Julius Melbourn* (Syracuse: Hall and Dickson, 1847); Peter Neilson, *Life and Adventures of Zamba, an African Negro King* (London: Smith, Elder, 1847); Emily Catharine Pierson, *Jamie Parker, the Fugitive* (Hartford: Brockett, Fuller, 1851); Martha Griffiths Browne, *Autobiography of a Female Slave* (New York: Redfield, 1856); and Rev. S. H. Platt, *The Martyrs, and the Fugitive* (New York: Daniel Fanshaw, 1859).

38. I restrict the term *American* to the continental United States and therefore do not discuss black autobiographies from the Caribbean, such as *The History of Mary Prince, a West Indian Slave* (London: F. Westley and A. H. Davis, 1831); Simon Strickland, ed., *Negro Slavery Described by a Negro: Being the Narrative of Ashton Warner, a Native of St. Vincent's* (London: S. Maunder, 1831); Thomas Price, ed., *Narrative of the Cruel Treatment of James Williams, a Negro Apprentice in Jamaica* (London: John Haddon, 1837); and the *Narrative of Joanna; an Emancipated Slave, of Surinam* (Boston: Isaac Knapp, 1838), which derives from J. G. Stedman's *Joanna, or the Female Slave* (London: Lupton Relfe, 1824), a "West Indian tale" written by the Englishman Stedman about Joanna, a slave whom he married in Dutch Guiana in 1774.

39. Examples of antislavery annuals are: *The Liberty Bell* (irregularly published from 1839 to 1858), *Freedom's Gift* (1840), *North Star* (1840), *Liberty Chimes* (1845), and *Autographs for Freedom* (1853 and 1854). Representative anthologies of interviews with ex-slaves include, in addition to Howe's *Refugees from Slavery in Canada West*, Benjamin Drew's, *The Refugee: or the Narratives of Fugitive Slaves in Canada* (Boston: John P. Jewett, 1856), and James Redpath's, *The Roving Editor: or Talks with Slaves in the Southern States* (New York: A. B. Burdic, 1859).

40. Blassingame, *Slave Community*, 2d ed. (New York: Oxford University Press, 1979), p. 378.

41. Some of the more well-known antebellum diaries and unpublished memoirs by black Americans are: Edwin A. Davis and William R. Hogan, eds., *William Johnson's Natchez: The Ante-Bellum Diary of a Free Negro* (Baton Rouge: Louisiana State University Press, 1951); Ray Allen Billington, ed., *The Journal of Charlotte L. Forten* (New York: Dryden, 1953); Sheldon H. Harris, *Paul Cuffe:*

Black American and the African Return (New York: Simon & Schuster, 1972), which reprints Cuffe's journals of 1811 and 1812; and Jean McMahon Humez, ed., *Gifts of Power: The Writings of Rebecca Jackson, Black Visionary, Shaker El-dress* (Amherst: University of Massachusetts Press, 1981).

42. A representative selection of such edited narratives includes: Charles Ball, *Slavery in the United States* (New York: John S. Taylor, 1837), ghostwritten by Isaac Fisher; *Narrative and Writings of Andrew Jackson, of Kentucky* (Syracuse, N.Y.: Daily & Weekly Star Office, 1847), anonymously ghostwritten; *Narrative of Henry Box Brown* (Boston: Brown & Stearns, 1849), ghostwritten by Charles Stearns; *Slave Life in Georgia: A Narrative of the Life, Sufferings and Escape of John Brown* (London: W. M. Watts, 1855), ghostwritten by L. A. Chamerovzov; *The Life and Adventures of James P. Beckwourth* (New York: Harper, 1856), ghostwritten by T. D. Bonner; and James W. C. Pennington's *A Narrative of Events of the Life of J. H. Banks, an Escaped Slave* (Liverpool: M. Rourke, 1861). The line between ghostwritten black autobiography and biography proper is very thin. For a listing of Afro-American biographies published during the antebellum period, see the "Annotated Bibliography of Afro-American Biography, 1760–1865" that appends this book.

43. Blassingame, ed., *Slave Testimony*, p. xviii.

44. John Searle, *Speech Acts* (Cambridge: Cambridge University Press, 1969), pp. 50–51.

45. *Narrative of the Life of Moses Grandy*, ed. George Thompson (Boston: Oliver Johnson, 1844), p. iv; *The Life of Josiah Henson*, ed. Samuel A. Eliot (Boston: Arthur D. Phelps, 1849), pp. iii–iv; Solomon Northup, *Twelve Years a Slave*, ed. David Wilson (Auburn, N.Y.: Derby and Miller, 1853), p. xii.

46. Labov, *Language in the Inner City*, p. 355. Other factors affecting the "self-report" of an interviewee have been discussed by Arthur Combs and Daniel Soper, "The Self, Its Derivate Terms, and Research," *Journal of Individual Psychology* 13 (Nov. 1957), 135–45. These researchers stress the determinative effect of "social expectancy," "cooperation of the subject" (which is often masked, they note), and the subject's senses of "freedom from threat" and "personal adequacy" on the quality of a "self-report." These are some of the more indeterminate factors affecting the dictation of ex-slave self-reports.

47. For a detailed survey of the criticism of the methodology of the WPA interviews, see Blassingame, ed., *Slave Testimony*, pp. xlii–xlix, and Paul D. Escott, *Slavery Remembered* (Chapel Hill: University of North Carolina Press, 1979), pp. 7–9. Further discussion of the relationship of editor and narrator in slave narratives appears in James Olney's "'I Was Born': Slave Narratives, Their Status as Autobiography and as Literature," in Charles T. Davis and Henry Louis Gates, Jr., eds., *The Slave's Narrative: Texts and Contexts* (New York: Oxford University Press, 1985), pp. 158–66.

48. See Michel Foucault, "What Is an Author?" in Josué V. Harari, ed., *Textual Strategies* (Ithaca: Cornell University Press, 1979), pp. 148–53.

49. The silences I refer to in this context indicate not so much a thwarting of expression as a deliberate omission of evidence needed to reach conclusions about the ontogeny of the text.

50. Kenneth Burke, *A Rhetoric of Motives* (New York: Prentice-Hall, 1950), pp. 20–21, 43, 55–56, 146.

51. William C. Spengemann, *The Forms of Autobiography* (New Haven: Yale University Press, 1980), p. 167.

52. J. L. Austin, *How to Do Things with Words* (London: Oxford University Press, 1962), pp. 98–102.

53. Mary Louise Pratt, *Toward a Speech Act Theory of Literary Discourse* (Bloomington: Indiana University Press, 1977), p. 86.

54. Wolfgang Iser, *The Act of Reading* (Baltimore: Johns Hopkins University Press, 1978), pp. 53–58.

55. Searle, *Speech Acts*, pp. 54–64.

56. Elizabeth Bruss, *Autobiographical Acts* (Baltimore: Johns Hopkins University Press, 1976), pp. 20–29.

57. Iser, *Act of Reading*, pp. 61–72.

58. For an insightful look at authentication in four major antebellum slave narratives, see the first chapter of Robert B. Stepto's *From behind the Veil: A Study of Afro-American Narrative* (Urbana: University of Illinois Press, 1979).

59. Wayne Booth, *The Rhetoric of Fiction* (Chicago: University of Chicago Press, 1961), p. 138.

60. My definitions of "characterized fictive reader" and "implied reader" are from W. Daniel Wilson's clarifying article "Readers in Texts," *PMLA* 96 (Oct. 1981), 848–63.

61. Marion Wilson Starling, "The Slave Narrative: Its Place in American History" (Ph.D. diss., New York University, 1946), which was published in 1981 under the same title by G. K. Hall of Boston); Margaret Young Jackson, "An Investigation of Biographies and Autobiographies of American Slaves Published between 1840 and 1860" (Ph.d. diss., Cornell University, 1954); Charles H. Nichols, *Many Thousand Gone* (Leiden: E. J. Brill, 1963); Sidonie Smith, *Where I'm Bound* (Westport, Conn.: Greenwood, 1978); Stephen Butterfield, *Black Autobiography in America* (Amherst: University of Massachusetts Press, 1974); Foster, *Witnessing Slavery*. A recent collection of historical and critical essays is Charles T. Davis and Henry Louis Gates, Jr., eds., *The Slave's Narrative*.

62. I borrow the phrase from James M. Cox's article "Jefferson's Autobiography: Recovering Literature's Lost Ground," *Southern Review* 14, no. 4 (1978), 633–52.

Chapter 2, Voices of the First Fifty Years, 1760–1810

1. The most extensive study of the slave narrative, Marion Wilson Starling's *The Slave Narrative: Its Place in American History* (Boston: G. K. Hall, 1981), argues that Hammon had "a scribe" who wrote the opening and closing of his narrative. Frances Smith Foster's *Witnessing Slavery: The Development of Ante-bellum Slave Narratives* (Westport, Conn.: Greenwood, 1979) considers Hammon the author of his story.

2. See the preface to *A Narrative of the Most Remarkable Particulars in the Life of James Albert Ukawsaw Gronniosaw, An African Prince* (1770; rpt. Newport, R.I.: S. Southwick, 1774); the title page of the *Narrative of the Lord's Wonderful Dealings With John Marrant, A Black*, ed. William Aldridge (London: Gilbert and Plummer, 1785); the preface to *A Narrative of the Life and Adventures of Venture a Native of Africa* (New London, Conn.: C. Holt, 1798); and the remarks appended to *Dying Confession of Pomp, A Negro Man* (Newburyport, Mass.: Jonathan Plummer, 1795).

3. David Daggett, ed., *Sketches of the Life of Joseph Mountain, A Negro* (New Haven: T. and S. Green, 1790).

4. See Richard Slotkin, "Narratives of Negro Crime in New England, 1675–1800," *American Quarterly* 25 (Mar. 1973), 3–31.

5. Mary Louise Pratt, *Toward a Speech Act Theory of Literary Discourse* (Bloomington: Indiana University Press, 1977), 135–40. A narrator may relate a group of autobiographical facts without making them "tellable," i.e., without "displaying" them as unusual or problematic in such a way that the reader will want to contemplate, evaluate, or involve himself imaginatively in them.

6. Vernon Loggins, *The Negro Author in America: His Development in America to 1900* (New York: Columbia University Press, 1931), p. 31.

7. John Searle's concept of "appropriateness conditions" is explained in chapter 1 of this book. I use the terms "seam" or "cut" in a text in a way suggested by Roland Barthes in *The Pleasure of the Text*, trans. Richard Miller (New York: Hill and Wang, 1975), pp. 6–10.

8. Houston A. Baker, Jr., *The Journey Back: Issues in Black Literature and Criticism* (Chicago: University of Chicago Press, 1980), pp. 19–21.

9. W. E. B. Du Bois, *The Souls of Black Folk* (Chicago: A. C. McClurg, 1903), p. 3.

10. For discussions of the pervasive spiritual adventure theme in white autobiography of the eighteenth century, see James Levernier and Hennig Cohen, eds., *The Indians and Their Captives* (Westport, Conn.: Greenwood, 1977), pp. xv–xvix; Richard Slotkin, *Regeneration through Violence* (Middletown, Conn.: Wesleyan University Press, 1973), pp. 94–115, 241–59; Daniel B. Shea, *Spiritual Autobiography in Early America* (Princeton: Princeton University Press, 1968); Robert F. Sayre, "Autobiography and the Making of America," *Iowa Review* 9 (Spring 1978), 1–19; G. Thomas Couser, *American Autobiography: The Prophetic Mode* (Amherst: University of Massachusetts Press, 1979); Albert E. Stone, "The Sea and the Self: Travel as Experience and Metaphor in Early American Autobiography," *Genre* 7 (Sept. 1974), 279–306.

11. *The Life, and Dying Speech of Arthur, A Negro Man* (Boston, 1768), broadside.

12. John Winthrop, *The History of New England from 1630 to 1649*, ed. James Savage (New York: Arno, 1975), p. 229. See Alfred Adler, *Superiority and Social Interests*, ed. Heinz L. Ansbacher and Rowena R. Ansbacher (Evanston, Ill.: Northwestern University Press, 1964), pp. 23–40.

13. *Last Words and Dying Speech of Edmund Fortis, A Negro Man* (Exeter, Me., 1796); *The Life, Last Words and Dying Speech of Stephen Smith* (Boston, 1797), broadside.

14. See the preface to Venture Smith's *Narrative*.

15. For an exhaustive discussion of pre–nineteenth-century colonial views of blacks, see Winthrop D. Jordan, *White over Black: American Attitudes toward the Negro, 1550–1812* (Chapel Hill: University of North Carolina Press, 1968). Briefer treatments of the subject are David Brion Davis, *The Problem of Slavery in Western Culture* (Ithaca: Cornell University Press, 1966), pp. 446–82; and Milton Cantor, "The Image of the Negro in Colonial Literature," in Seymour L. Gross and John Edward Hardy, eds., *Images of the Negro in American Literature* (Chicago: University of Chicago Press, 1966), pp. 29–53.

16. See *The Narrative and Confession of Thomas Powers, A Negro* (Norwich: John Trumbull, 1796), p. 4.

17. *Confession of John Joyce, Alias Davis. . . . with an Address to the Public and People of Colour* (Philadelphia: Bethel Church, 1808), p. 18; *The Life and Confession of Johnson Green* (Worcester: Isaiah Thomas, 1786), broadside.

18. Allen described his youth in slavery and his ministerial career in *The Life, Experience and Gospel Labors of the Rt. Rev. Richard Allen* (Philadelphia: Martin and Boden, 1833), a work he is believed to have dictated to his son sometime in the 1820s. Allen's most famous literary defense of black people against racist slander appears in *A Narrative of the Proceedings of the Black People, During the Late Awful Calamity in Philadelphia, in the Year, 1793* (Philadelphia: William W. Woodward, 1794). Because the Pennsylvania district clerk named Allen as the depositor and "proprietor" of Joyce's *Confession* and because Allen's church, the Bethel A.M.E. Church of Philadelphia, published the *Confession,* I have judged it Allen's composition, as well as the "Address to the Public and People of Colour," which prefaces the confession of Joyce. In this address, Allen prophesies that many black "slaves of Sin" will imitate Joyce if they do not recognize the tendencies of "midnight dances and frolics" and "drunkenness and stealing." For another Afro-American denunication of slavery to Satan instead of to whites, see Jupiter Hammon, *An Address to the Negroes in the State of New-York* (New York: Carroll and Patterson, 1787).

19. See Romans 5:17–18, 22.

20. Marrant, *Narrative*, p. 25. Marrant's *Journal* (London: Author, 1790) is even less revelatory of the black identity of its author than the dictated *Narrative*.

21. Gronniosaw, *Narrative*, p. 46.

22. This assumption about Afro-American "pregeneric myths" is proposed by Robert B. Stepto in *From behind the Veil: A Study of Afro-American Narrative* (Urbana: University of Illinois Press, 1979), p. ix.

23. Sacvan Bercovitch, *The Puritan Origins of the American Self* (New Haven: Yale University Press, 1975), p. 13.

24. George White, *A Brief Account of the Life, Experiences, Travels, and Gospel Labours of George White* (New York: John C. Totten, 1810), p. 57. Further references to White's autobiography will be from this edition.

25. *The Life . . . of John Jea* was published by Jea in Portsea, England, probably in 1811, if internal evidence in the text is reliable. The title page of the ninety-six-page book has no date of publication. It is also misleading in stating that the narrative was "Compiled and Written by Himself," i.e., by John Jea. In the penulti-

mate paragraph of the book, the narrator states, "I cannot write, therefore it [the narrative] is not quite so correct as if I had been able to have written it myself." Thus I have judged this to be a dictated narrative. For a useful scholarly edition of Jea's *Life*, see Henry Louis Gates, Jr., ed., *The Collected Writings of John Jea, African Preacher* (New York: Oxford University Press, forthcoming).

26. The broadside on which *Dying Confession of Pomp* was printed is slightly mutilated as a result of having been folded. Some words are indecipherable and must be surmised.

27. See Jacques Derrida, *Of Grammatology*, trans. Gayatri Spivak (Baltimore: Johns Hopkins University Press, 1976), pp. xiv–xvii, 19–24.

28. Venture Smith, *Narrative*, pp. 26, 30.

29. To trace the development of the black bourgeois autobiographer in the pre-Emancipation period, one should proceed from Venture Smith's story to the *Narrative of Lunsford Lane* (1842), the *Narrative of the Life of Moses Grandy* (1844), Austin Steward's *Twenty-Two Years a Slave, and Forty Years a Freeman* (1857), and Israel Campbell's *Bond and Free* (1861). These writers were by no means unique among black autobiographers in putting their faith in the traditional Protestant work ethic and middle-class values as the key to individual advancement in America. More than most black memoirists, however, these men concentrate on their economic successes as a primary basis on which their readers might empathize with and respect them.

30. See Daniel A. Payne, *Recollections of Seventy Years*, ed. C. S. Smith (Nashville: A.M.E. Sunday School Union, 1888), and Booker T. Washington, *Up from Slavery* (New York: Doubleday, Page, 1901).

31. I have drawn my conclusions about the role of the exhorter in white Methodism from an examination of *A Form of Discipline, for the Ministers, Preachers and Members (Now Comprehending the Principles and Doctrines) of the Methodist Episcopal Church in America*, 6th ed. (Philadelphia: R. Aitken & Son, 1790), which I judge to be a statement of church policy contemporaneous with White's evolving career in the ministry.

32. For a detailed discussion of scenes of and allusions to talking and silent books in early Afro-American and Anglo-African texts, see chap. 4, "The Trope of the Talking Book," in Henry Louis Gates, Jr., *The Signifying Monkey* (New York: Oxford University Press, 1985). I shall discuss the *Interesting Narrative of Olaudah Equiano, or Gustavus Vassa, The African* (1789) later in this chapter.

33. See William L. Howarth's "Some Principles of Autobiography," *New Literary History* 5 (Winter 1974), 363–81, as discussed in chapter 1 of this book.

34. See William J. Walls, *The African Methodist Episcopal Zion Church* (Charlotte, N.C.: A.M.E. Zion Publishing House, 1974), p. 74.

35. Paul Edwards, ed., *The Life of Olaudah Equiano* (1789; rpt. London: Dawsons of Pall Mall, 1969), 2: 37. Further quotations are from this facsimile reprint of the first English edition.

36. See Ottabah Cugoano, *Thoughts and Sentiments on the Evil and Wicked Traffic of Slavery and Commerce of the Human Species* (London: the Author, 1787); Ignatius Sancho, *Letters of the Late Ignatius Sancho, An African* (London: J. Nichols, 1782); and James Walvin and Paul Edwards, eds., *Black Personalities*

in the Era of the Slave Trade (Baton Rouge: Louisiana State University Press, 1983).

37. Victor Turner, "Betwixt and Between: The Liminal Period in *Rites de Passage*," in his *The Forest of Symbols* (Ithaca: Cornell University Press, 1967), pp. 93–95.

38. *Samaide* was a term for a nomadic Asiatic tribe in northern Siberia, thought in Equiano's day to be cannibalistic.

Chapter 3, Experiments in Two Modes, 1810–40

1. For discussions of the secular ramifications of the spiritual, see John Lovell, Jr., *Black Song: The Forge and the Flame* (New York: Macmillan, 1972), pp. 220–40, and Lawrence W. Levine, *Black Culture and Black Consciousness* (New York: Oxford University Press, 1977), pp. 50–55. See also Albert J. Raboteau, *Slave Religion* (New York: Oxford University Press, 1978), pp. 246–51. For another way of reading tropological dimensions in early black autobiography, see Henry Louis Gates, Jr., *The Signifying Monkey* (New York: Oxford University Press, 1985), especially ch. 3 "The Figures of Signification."

2. Theodore Dwight Weld to Sarah and Angelina Grimké, May 22, 1837, and Weld to Gerrit Smith, Nov. 28, 1838, in Gilbert H. Barnes and Dwight L. Dumond, eds., *Letters of Theodore Dwight Weld, Angelina Grimké Weld and Sarah Grimké, 1822–1844* (New York: Appleton-Century, 1934), 1:390; 2:717.

3. Theodore Dwight Weld's *American Slavery as It Is* (New York: American Anti-slavery Society, 1839) sold more than 100,000 copies in its first year of publication.

4. John Greenleaf Whittier, ed., *Narrative of James Williams* (New York: American Anti-slavery Society, 1838), p. xvii. Further references to Williams's narrative will be taken from this edition.

5. See the preface to *Slavery in the United States* (New York: John S. Taylor, 1837). In the Dover reprint edition of this book (New York, 1970), Philip S. Foner points out in his introduction to the text that "Mr. Fisher," the editor of Ball's narrative, was Isaac Fisher, an attorney in Lewistown and Huntingdon, Pa. For further information on Fisher (d. 1858), see Albert M. Rung, *Rung's Chronicles of Penna. History* (Huntingdon, Pa.: Huntingdon County Historical Society, 1977), pp. 8–9. Further references to *Slavery in the United States* will be taken from the Dover reprint of the 1837 edition.

6. In M. H. Abrams's *The Mirror and the Lamp* (1953; rpt. New York: Norton, 1958), pp. 13–14, 31–34, the tradition of associating mimesis with the pictorial, as well as poetic, arts is discussed.

7. Paul Ricoeur, *Hermeneutics and the Human Sciences*, trans. and ed. John B. Thompson (Cambridge: Cambridge University Press, 1981), p. 185.

8. David Brion Davis, *The Problem of Slavery in Western Culture* (Ithaca: Cornell University Press, 1966), p. 90.

9. Ricoeur, *Hermeneutics*, pp. 142–44, 192–93. For Heidegger's concept of *Dasein*, or "being-in-the-world," see the translation of *Being and Time* by John Macquarrie and Edward Robinson (Oxford: Basil Blackwell, 1978).

10. Ricoeur, *Hermeneutics*, pp. 131–32.

11. For a brief summary statement of Gadamer's view of "belongingness" as a "transcendental relationship between being and truth," see *Truth and Method*, trans. and ed. Garrett Barden and John Cumming (New York: Seabury, 1975), pp. 416–18.

12. Paul Ricoeur, *Interpretation Theory: Discourse and the Surplus of Meaning* (Fort Worth: Texas Christian University Press, 1976), pp. 72–73. The concepts of explanation and understanding are also basic to Ricoeur's answer to the question, "What is a text?" in *Hermeneutics*, pp. 145–52.

13. Solomon Bayley's *Narrative* (London: Harvey and Darton, 1825) was "written by himself," as the title page points out, and edited by Hurnard, who notes in the preface to the book that he limited himself to "orthographical" corrections. Further references to Bayley's narrative are from the above-mentioned edition. For additional letters of Bayley and a sketch of his life after he became a missionary to Africa, see Abigail Mott, *Biographical Sketches and Interesting Anecdotes of Persons of Color* (New York: Trustees of Lindley Murray Estate, 1839), pp. 57–74.

14. *The Life, Experience and Gospel Labors of the Rt. Rev. Richard Allen to Which is Annexed the Rise and Progress of the African Methodist Episcopal Church in the United States of America* (Philadelphia: Martin & Boden, 1833). All quotations from the *Life, Experience* are from the 1960 edition of this autobiography, published by the Abingdon Press. The authorship of the *Life, Experience* is a matter of some dispute. The title page claims that the book was "Written by [Allen] Himself," but in *Segregated Sabbaths: Richard Allen and the Emergence of Independent Black Churches, 1760–1840* (New York: Oxford University Press, 1973), p. 24, Carol V. R. George claims that the text was the product of Allen's dictation to his son Richard Allen, Jr.

15. Jarena Lee, *The Life and Religious Experience of Jarena Lee* (Philadelphia: the Author, 1836), p. 24. Further quotations from Lee's *Life* are from this edition. For an annotated edition and additional analysis of the *Life*, see William L. Andrews, ed., *Sisters of the Spirit: Three Black Women's Autobiographies of the Nineteenth Century* (Bloomington: Indiana University Press, 1986).

16. Turner's only rival is Christopher McPherson, whose *A Short History of the Life of Christopher McPherson, Alias Pherson, Son of Christ* was first published in 1811 in Richmond, Va., and reprinted in Lynchburg, Va., in 1855. See Edmund Berkeley, Jr., "Prophet without Honor: Christopher McPherson, Free Person of Color," *Virginia Magazine of History and Biography* 77 (Apr. 1969), 180–89.

17. I am using the Derridean terms *différance* and *trace* to signify the basic notion, out of Ferdinand de Saussure, that "the signified concept is never present in itself, in an adequate presence that would refer only to itself. Every concept is necessarily and essentially inscribed in a chain or system, within which it refers to another and to other concepts, by the systematic play of differences. Such a play, then—*différance*—is no longer simply a concept, but the possibility of con-

ceptuality, of the conceptual system and process in general." See Derrida's essay, "Différance," in *Speech and Phenomena*, trans. David B. Allison (Evanston, Ill.: Northwestern University Press, 1973), p. 140.

18. *The Confessions of Nat Turner* (Baltimore: Thomas R. Gray, 1831) is most conveniently reprinted in Henry Irving Tragle, *The Southampton Slave Revolt of 1831* (Amherst: University of Massachusetts Press, 1971), pp. 301–21. Further references to the *Confessions* are from this edition. Gray's pamphlet was reprinted at least twice. By 1861 Thomas Wentworth Higginson, in an article entitled "Nat Turner's Insurrection" (*Atlantic* 8, pp. 173–87) estimated that 50,000 copies were in circulation. See Tragle, *Southampton Slave Revolt*, p. 346.

19. *Paradise Lost*, Book IV, lines 522–23, in Merritt Y. Hughes, ed., *John Milton: Complete Poems and Major Prose* (New York: Odyssey, 1957), p. 290.

20. The quotations are rough approximations of Luke 12:31, 47.

21. A useful overview of the approach to the Old Testament maintained by American typologists is offered in Ursula Brumm's *American Thought and Religious Typology*, trans. John Hoaglund (New Brunswick, N.J.: Rutgers University Press, 1970). The idea of fulfillment and displacement of the Old Testament by the New is discussed in Erich Auerbach's "Figura," in his *Scenes from the Drama of European Literature* (New York: Meridian, 1959), pp. 51–56.

22. For a concise discussion of the immediate social and political aftermath of the Turner rebellion, see Eric Foner, ed., *Nat Turner* (Englewood Cliffs, N.J.: Prentice-Hall, 1971), pp. 6–10.

23. For a review of the controversy over Styron's novelistic reworking of the Nat Turner affair, see remarks in James M. McPherson et al., *Blacks in America: Bibliographical Essays* (Garden City, N.Y.: Doubleday, 1971), p. 64, and a more recent bibliography of articles on Nat Turner's *Confessions* in Gregory S. Sojka's "Black Slave Narratives—A Selected Checklist of Criticism," in John Sekora and Darwin T. Turner, eds., *The Art of Slave Narrative* (Macomb: Western Illinois University Press, 1982), 145.

24. See "To The Public" in Grimes's *Life* (New York: the Author, 1825). Further quotations from Grimes's *Life* will be from this edition. The only scholarship that has been done on Grimes is by Charles Nichols, "The Case of William Grimes, the Runaway Slave," *William and Mary Quarterly* 8 (Oct. 1951), 552–60.

25. Fitzhugh's views on this topic are best represented in chapters III–VI in his book, *Cannibals All! or, Slaves Without Masters* (Richmond, Va.: A. Morris, 1857).

26. The 1855 edition of Grimes's narrative is conveniently reprinted in Arna Bontemps, ed., *Five Black Lives* (Middletown, Conn.: Wesleyan University Press, 1971), pp. 59–128.

27. Wolfgang Iser, *The Act of Reading* (Baltimore: Johns Hopkins University Press, 1978), pp. 71–72.

28. This is a central thesis in Roy Pascal's *Design and Truth in Autobiography* (London: Routledge and Kegan Paul, 1960).

29. Although Roger Rosenblatt's notion of "Black Autobiography: Life as the Death Weapon" (*Yale Review* 65 [1976], 515–27) is suggestive, I have borrowed his terminology, not his thesis, for my discussion of William Grimes.

30. Ralph Waldo Emerson, "Montaigne; or, The Skeptic," *Representative Men*, vol. 4 of *The Complete Works of Ralph Waldo Emerson* (Boston: Houghton Mifflin, 1903), p. 168.

31. Ball's *Narrative* went through five editions before 1860. See Marion Wilson Starling, *The Slave Narrative: Its Place in American History* (Boston: G. K. Hall, 1981), pp. 226–32. When the Reverend Charles E. Lester invited Peter Wheeler to recount his slavery experiences for publication in 1839, the ex-slave replied, "'You've got an idee of makin' out some sich a book as Charles Ball, and that has done a sight of good.'" Peter Wheeler, *Chains and Freedom: or, The Life and Adventures of Peter Wheeler*, ed. Charles E. Lester (New York: E. S. Arnold, 1839), p. 18.

32. John Searle's ideas about "assertives" and "directives" are summarized in his *Expression and Meaning: Studies in the Theory of Speech Acts* (Cambridge: Cambridge University Press, 1979), pp. 1–4, 12–14.

33. John S. Taylor's introduction to the 1837 edition of *Slavery in the United States*, p. ii.

34. Rung in his *Chronicles of Penna. History* points out that after Fisher was admitted to the Delaware bar, "while very young he began a tour of the settled parts of America, spending much time in the South" where he made "a careful study of conditions" in the slave states.

35. Searle, *Expression and Meaning*, pp. 15–16. For a broader application of the expressive to discourse, see James L. Kinneavy, *A Theory of Discourse* (Englewood Cliffs, N.J.: Prentice-Hall, 1971), 393–449.

36. The quotation from Grimes is on p. 14 of his *Life*. For Curry's story, see "Narrative of James Curry, a Fugitive Slave," *Liberator*, Jan. 10, 1840, pp. 5–6. In "The Slave Robert" (*Liberator*, May 10, 1839, p. 74), a fugitive is asked if slaves immediately after emancipation would cut their masters' throats in vengeance. Piously, Robert replies, "I would rather kneel down and pray for my master than to injure him." If slaves were emancipated immediately, would they migrate to the North? "O no," Robert assures his interrogator, "I would rather work there for six dollars a month than for twelve here" because the weather in the North is so harsh.

37. See Vernon Loggins, *The Negro Author in America* (New York: Columbia University Press, 1931), pp. 102–3.

38. Rittenhouse attacked Williams's narrative in letters of Mar. 29 and Apr. 5, 1838, in the Greensborough, Ala., *Beacon*. He was answered most fully in the *Emancipator* of Aug. 30, 1838, pp. 71–73, which published a lengthy defense of the narrative drawn up by the executive committee of the American Anti-Slavery Society. The quotation describing Williams himself appears on p. 71, col. 5, of that resolution.

39. This decision of an investigating subcommittee composed of James G. Birney and Lewis Tappan, prominent officers in the Anti-slavery Society, convinced the society's executive committee to withdraw the narrative from further promotion and printings. See Birney and Tappan, "'Narrative of James Williams.' Statement Authorized by the Executive Committee," *Emancipator*, Oct. 25, 1838, p. 104, cols. 5–6.

40. Ruth Miller and Peter J. Katopes, "Slave Narratives," in M. Thomas Inge et al., eds., *Black American Writers: Bibliographical Essays* (New York: St. Martin's, 1978), p. 46. In *Slave Testimony* (Baton Rouge: Louisiana State University Press, 1977), John Blassingame says that Williams's narrative was "proved" by southerners to be "an outright fraud." See his introduction, p. xxiii.

41. The first edition of Roper's *Narrative* was published in London by Harvey and Darton in 1837. The second edition, from which all subsequent quotations will be taken, appeared in 1838 with footnotes to the original edition inserted by Roper. By 1856 this narrative had gone through ten editions and had been translated into Celtic. Charles H. Nichols, *Many Thousand Gone* (Leiden: E. J. Brill, 1963), p. xiv.

42. Charles T. Davis, *Black Is the Color of the Cosmos: Essays on Afro-American Literature and Culture*, ed. Henry Louis Gates, Jr. (New York: Garland, 1982), pp. 88–89.

43. Roper calls himself "the author" of his narrative in the "Advertisement to the Second Edition," p. iv. The preface to his narrative, by Thomas Price, an English clergyman and the editor of an abolitionist periodical entitled *Slavery in America*, states that Roper had "drawn up" his narrative and that "it is his own production."

44. Roper deletes the conclusion of verse 7: "and spake roughly unto them; and he said unto them, 'Whence come ye?' And they said, 'From the land of Canaan to buy food.'"

45. The idea of the reader's self-understanding "in front of the text" and the concept of the "enlarged self" resulting from the reader's appropriation from the text are Ricoeur's. See *Hermeneutics*, pp. 142–44.

Chapter 4, The Performance of Slave Narrative in the 1840s

1. Ephraim Peabody, "Narratives of Fugitive Slaves," *Christian Examiner* 47 (July 1849), 64.

2. For more sales statistics on slave narratives in the 1840s see: Charles H. Nichols, "Who Read the Slave Narratives?" *Phylon* 20 (Summer 1959), 149–62; Arna Bontemps, "The Slave Narrative: An American Genre," in his *Great Slave Narratives* (Boston: Beacon, 1969), pp. xvii–xix; and Marion Wilson Starling, *The Slave Narrative: Its Place in American History* (Boston: G. K. Hall, 1981), pp. 32–39 et passim. In his edition of Douglass's *Narrative*, Houston Baker states that by 1850 30,000 copies of Douglass's book had been sold (see the Viking Penguin edition of the *Narrative*, 1982, p. 21). Starling notes that the first three editions of William Wells Brown's *Narrative* sold 11,000 copies in England alone by 1849 (*Slave Narrative*, p. 138).

3. Peabody, "Narratives," pp. 62–63. Theodore Parker, "The American Scholar," in George Willis Cooke, ed., *The American Scholar*, vol. 8 of *Centenary Edition of Theodore Parker's Writings* (Boston: American Unitarian Association, 1907), p.

37. "The American Scholar" was first delivered as a commencement speech at Colby College, Aug. 8, 1849. See Margaret Fuller's review of Douglass's *Narrative* for the New York *Tribune* of June 10, 1845, as reprinted in Bell Gale Chevigny, *The Woman and the Myth: Margaret Fuller's Life and Writings* (Old Westbury, N.Y.: Feminist Press, 1976), pp. 340–42.

4. Frederick Douglass, *My Bondage and My Freedom* (New York: Miller, Orton and Mulligan, 1855), p. 361.

5. George Fredrickson, *The Black Image in the White Mind* (New York: Harper & Row, 1971), p. 30. The pioneering study of the perfectionist and immediatist religious orientation of abolitionism is Gilbert H. Barnes's in *The Antislavery Impulse, 1830–1844* (New York: D. Appleton-Century, 1933). See also Louis Filler, *The Crusade against Slavery* (New York: Harper & Row, 1960).

6. The *Narrative of Henry Box Brown, Who Escaped from Slavery Enclosed in a Box 3 Feet Long and 2 Wide* (Boston: Brown and Stearns, 1849), pp. v–vi. This book was ghostwritten by Charles Stearns from a statement of facts that he received from Henry Brown. Hathaway's remarks appear in William Wells Brown's *Narrative* (Boston: American Anti-slavery Society, 1847), p. ix. Further quotations from Brown's *Narrative*, unless explicitly noted otherwise, will be taken from the 1847 edition.

7. For discussions of the rise of the fugitive slave to prominence on the antislavery platform, see Jane H. and William H. Pease, *They Who Would Be Free: Blacks' Search for Freedom, 1830–1861* (New York: Atheneum, 1974), pp. 33–46; Benjamin Quarles, *Black Abolitionists* (New York: Oxford University Press, 1969), pp. 56–67; and Larry Gara, "The Professional Fugitive in the Abolition Movement," *Wisconsin Magazine of History* 48 (Summer 1965), 196–204. In *Building an Antislavery Wall: Black Americans in the Atlantic Abolitionist Movement, 1830–1860* (Baton Rouge: Louisiana State University Press, 1983), R. J. M. Blackett examines the efforts of black Americans in England to advance the cause of freedom.

8. See Donald M. Scott, "Abolition as a Sacred Vocation," in Lewis Perry and Michael Fellman, eds., *Antislavery Reconsidered* (Baton Rouge: Louisiana State University Press, 1979), pp. 51–74.

9. John W. Blassingame, ed., *The Frederick Douglass Papers, Series I* (New Haven: Yale University Press, 1979), 1:xxxviii–xxxix.

10. William Lloyd Garrison, "The Cause of Emancipation," *Liberty Bell* (Boston: Metcalf, Torry, and Ballou, 1839), p. 97. See also Garrison's continuing argument for "a new and stronger dialect" of antislavery agitation in his essay "Hard Language," *Liberty Bell* (Boston: National Antislavery Bazaar, 1848), pp. 281–88.

11. Lawrence Buell, *Literary Transcendentalism* (Ithaca: Cornell University Press, 1973), p. 7; John L. Thomas, "Romantic Reform in America, 1815–1865," *American Quarterly* 17 (Winter 1965), 656–81.

12. See "The American Scholar," in Robert E. Spiller and Alfred R. Ferguson, eds., *Nature, Addresses, and Lectures*, vol. 1 of *The Collected Works of Ralph Waldo Emerson* (Cambridge, Mass.: Harvard University Press, 1971), p. 67; and "The Editors to the Reader," *Dial* 1 (July 1840), 4.

13. See the chapter on "Eloquence" in F. O. Matthiessen's *American Renaissance* (New York: Oxford University Press, 1941), pp. 14–24; and Buell, *Literary Transcendentalism*, p. 267.

14. Douglass's *Narrative*, ed. Baker, pp. 37–38. Further references to Douglass's narrative are from this edition.

15. Ideas about the "play" of a text, either in terms of implicit dialogues being played out (as maintained by Hans-Georg Gadamer and Paul Ricoeur) or in terms of a free dissemination of meaning in a hermeneutical "game" that cannot be won (as suggested by Roland Barthes and Jacques Derrida), are helpfully summarized in David Couzens Hoy, *The Critical Circle: Literature, History, and Philosophical Hermeneutics* (Berkeley: University of California Press, 1978), pp. 73–95; the essays on Barthes and Derrida by John Sturrock and Jonathan Culler, respectively, in Sturrock's *Structuralism and Since* (New York: Oxford University Press, 1979); and Culler's "Meaning and Iterability" in his *On Deconstruction* (Ithaca: Cornell University Press, 1982), 110–34, esp. pp. 122–34.

16. John Searle's discussion of declarative speech acts is in *Expression and Meaning: Studies in the Theory of Speech Acts* (Cambridge: Cambridge University Press, 1979), pp. 16–20.

17. "The Poet," in Edward Waldo Emerson, ed., *Essays, Second Series*, vol. 3 of *The Complete Works of Ralph Waldo Emerson* (Boston: Houghton Mifflin, 1904), pp. 8, 21. I borrow the Adamic metaphor, of course, from R. W. B. Lewis's *The American Adam* (Chicago: University of Chicago Press, 1955), in which the discussion of Walt Whitman as Adamic namer parallels in some ways my own treatment of some black autobiographers. A further important treatment of this subject is Kimberly W. Benston's "'I Yam What I Am': Naming and Unnaming in Afro-American Literature," *Black America Literature Forum* 16 (Spring 1982), 3–11.

18. Among the many useful treatments of the relationship of blacks and whites in the abolition movement are: August Meier and Elliott Rudwick, "The Role of Blacks in the Abolitionist Movement," in John H. Bracey, Jr., et al., eds., *Blacks in the Abolitionist Movement* (Belmont, Calif.: Wadsworth, 1971), pp. 108–22; Leon F. Litwack, "The Emancipation of the Negro Abolitionist," in Martin Duberman, ed., *The Antislavery Vanguard* (Princeton: Princeton University Press, 1965), pp. 137–55; William H. and Jane H. Pease, "Antislavery Ambivalence: Immediatism, Expediency, Race," *American Quarterly* 17 (Winter 1965), 682–95; and Quarles, *Black Abolitionists*, pp. 42–56.

19. Henry Bibb to James G. Birney, Feb. 25, 1845, in Dwight L. Dumond, ed., *Letters of James Gillespie Birney* (New York: Appleton-Century, 1938), 2:928.

20. Douglass, *My Bondage and My Freedom*, pp. 361–62. For further evidence of the restraints under which Douglass found himself among the Garrisonians, see Peter Walker, *Moral Choices: Memory, Desire, and Imagination in Nineteenth-Century American Abolition* (Baton Rouge: Louisiana State University Press, 1978), pp. 245–46, 257–59.

21. Quincy's remarks about Brown appeared in a letter to Caroline Weston, July 2, 1847, as quoted in William Edward Farrison, *William Wells Brown: Author and Reformer* (Chicago: University of Chicago Press, 1969), pp. 112–13.

Hathaway's comment appears in his preface to Brown's *Narrative*. May's remark appeared in a letter to John Bishop Estlin, May 21, 1849, and is quoted in Larry Gara's reprint of the 1848 edition of Brown's *Narrative* (Reading, Mass.: Addison-Wesley, 1969), pp. xii–xiii.

22. *Narrative of Lunsford Lane* (Boston: Lunsford Lane, 1842), p. iv. Henry Watson to Garrison, Feb. 28, 1848, as quoted in the *Liberator* (Mar. 17, 1848), 43. Grandy's amanuensis, George Thompson, stated the former slave's aim for his narrative in the introduction to *Narrative of the Life of Moses Grandy*, which was first published in England in 1842. I shall use the first American edition published in Boston by Oliver Johnson in 1844. Further references to the narratives of Lane and Grandy are from these editions.

23. The standard study of institutionalized racism in the antebellum North is Leon F. Litwack's *North of Slavery: The Negro in the Free States, 1790–1860* (Chicago: University of Chicago Press, 1961).

24. Peabody, "Narratives," pp. 74–76, 78–79, 92–93.

25. Richard Poirier, *The Performing Self* (New York: Oxford University Press, 1971), pp. xiii–xiv, 86–88.

26. Grandy dictated his narrative to George Thompson, a prominent English abolitionist; Henson dictated his to Samuel A. Eliot, a moderate antislavery man and a one-time mayor of Boston. Lane prefaced his narrative by stating that although he could read and write, he had been "obliged to employ the services of a friend, in bringing this Narrative into shape for the public eye." John W. Blassingame has suggested that Lane's editor was William G. Hawkins, who in 1863 published a biography, *Lunsford Lane; or Another Helper from North Carolina*. This, however, is quite unlikely because in July 1842, when Lane's *Narrative* was published in Boston, the eighteen-year-old Hawkins had only been a resident of the state for two months. See William's biography of his father, *John H. W. Hawkins* (Boston: E. P. Dutton, 1863), pp. 44, 222. In the preface to his 1863 biography of Lane, Hawkins says that his acquaintance with Lane was "quite recent." While Grandy's life remains unresearched by scholars, Henson's has received considerable attention. For a listing and critical evaluation, see "A Note on Henson's Biographers," in Robin W. Winks, ed., *An Autobiography of the Rev. Josiah Henson* (1881; rpt. Reading, Mass.: Addison-Wesley, 1969), pp. xxxiii–xxxiv.

27. Alexis de Tocqueville found the "love of wealth" to be "at the bottom of all that the Americans do," and the number of Americans "who seek to emerge from their original condition" an incalculable majority. See *Democracy in America*, trans. Henry Reeve and ed. Phillips Bradley (New York: Alfred A. Knopf, 1966), pp. 229, 243. The character of the self-made man in antebellum America is sketched in Irvin G. Wyllie, *The Self-Made Man in America* (New Brunswick: Rutgers University Press, 1954), pp. 8–54. In *Ancient Law: Its Connection with the Early History of Society, and Its Relation to Modern Ideas* (New York: Charles Scribner, 1870), Henry Sumner Maine, an eminent British jurist and legal historian, stated: "There are few general propositions concerning the age to which we belong which seem at first sight likely to be received with readier concurrence than the assertion that the society of our day is mainly distinguished from that of preceding generations by the largeness of the sphere which is oc-

cupied in it by Contract." He added, "The point . . . debated in the vigorous controversy still carried on upon the subject of negro servitude, is whether the status of the slave does not belong to by-gone institutions, and whether the only relation between employer and labourer which commends itself to modern morality be not a relation determined exclusively by contract" (295–96).

28. *The Life of Josiah Henson* (Boston: Arthur D. Phelps, 1849), p. 14. Further quotations from Henson's autobiography in this chapter will be from this edition.

29. The *Narrative of the Sufferings of Lewis Clarke* was originally published in Boston in 1845 and sold 3,000 copies in its first year. In 1846 it was reprinted with the narrative of Clarke's brother Milton and published by Bela Marsh of Boston as *Narratives of the Sufferings of Lewis and Milton Clarke*. I quote from pp. 62–63 of this edition.

30. Frederick Cooper, "Elevating the Race: The Social Thought of Black Leaders, 1827–1850," *American Quarterly* 24 (Dec. 1972), 604–25. The majority of black leaders possessed "a whole-hearted acceptance of the moral values of white middle-class America" (616).

31. See Fredrickson, *The Black Image in the White Mind*, pp. 97–109, for the ways in which "romantic racialism" manifested itself in the antislavery movement in the 1840s.

32. Horace Mann as quoted in Merle Curti, *Human Nature in American Thought* (Madison: University of Wisconsin Press, 1980), p. 147.

33. Hayden White, "The Forms of Wildness: Archaeology of an Idea," in Edward Dudley and Maximillian E. Novak, eds., *The Wild Man Within* (Pittsburgh: University of Pittsburgh Press, 1972), pp. 15, 21–22. For the idea of the shadow, see Carl Jung, *Aion: Researches into the Phenomenology of the Self*, vol. 9 of *Collected Works of C. G. Jung* (Princeton: Princeton University Press, 1959), pars. 14–15.

34. Harriet Beecher Stowe, *The Key to Uncle Tom's Cabin* (Boston: J. P. Jewett, 1853), pp. 42–43.

35. As the link between Henson and Uncle Tom fastened itself more firmly on the public consciousness, more installments of the Henson story found an ever-widening audience. In 1858 Eliot revised and expanded the *Life* into *Truth Stranger than Fiction: Father Henson's Story of His Own Life* (Boston: J. P. Jewett, 1858). This book was published in an English edition in 1859. A third installment of Henson's autobiography, ghostwritten by John Lobb, an English religious journalist, appeared in London in 1877 under the title *"Uncle Tom's Story of His Life": An Autobiography of the Rev. Josiah Henson (Mrs. Harriet Beecher Stowe's "Uncle Tom")*. Lobb saw into print several reprintings and children's versions of the Henson story before bringing out a final "revised and enlarged" edition of *An Autobiography of the Rev. Josiah Henson ("Uncle Tom")*, which was first published in London, Ontario, by Schuyler and Smith in 1881. The most informative discussion of the evolution of Henson's autobiographies is in Winks's edition of the 1881 *Autobiography*, pp. xiii, xx–xxv, xxxi–xxxiii, which has been my own source.

36. "The negro race is confessedly more simple, docile, childlike, and affectionate, than other races; and hence the divine graces of love and faith, when in-

breathed by the Holy Spirit, find in their natural temperament a more congenial atmosphere." Stowe, *Key to Uncle Tom's Cabin*, p. 41.

37. For the concept of "other-perception" see R. D. Laing, H. Phillipson, and A. R. Lee, *Interpersonal Perception* (London: Tavistock, 1966), pp. 4–6.

38. Wilson J. Moses, *Black Messiahs and Uncle Toms* (University Park: Pennsylvania State University Press, 1982), pp. 30–48, and Sacvan Bercovitch, *The American Jeremiad* (Madison: University of Wisconsin Press, 1978), p. 180. My discussion of the American jeremiad as a genre is dependent on Bercovitch's excellent study and draws liberally from it.

39. See Douglass's address, "Southern Slavery and Northern Religion" (Feb. 11, 1844), in Blassingame, ed., *Douglass Papers*, 1:25.

40. G. Thomas Couser discusses the "analogy between the process of conversion and that of liberation" in the *Narrative* in his *American Autobiography: The Prophetic Mode* (Amherst: University of Massachusetts Press, 1979), p. 53. See also Houston Baker's observation in *Long Black Song* (Charlottesville: University Press of Virginia, 1972), p. 78: "Douglass's work is a spiritual autobiography akin to the writings of such noted white American authors as Cotton Mather, Benjamin Franklin, and Henry Adams."

41. Robert G. O'Meally, "Frederick Douglass' 1845 *Narrative*: The Text Was Meant to Be Preached," in Dexter Fisher and Robert B. Stepto, eds., *Afro-American Literature: The Reconstruction of Instruction* (New York: Modern Language Association, 1978), pp. 192–211. O'Meally concentrates on the relationship of the *Narrative* to black sermonic traditions. For a discussion of Douglass's actual experience as a preacher, see William L. Andrews, "Frederick Douglass, Preacher," *American Literature* 54 (Dec. 1982), 592–97.

42. Bercovitch, *American Jeremiad*, p. 160.

43. John Seelye, "The Clay Foot of the Climber: Richard M. Nixon in Perspective," in William L. Andrews, ed., *Literary Romanticism in America* (Baton Rouge: Louisiana State University Press, 1981), p. 125.

44. *Life and Times of Frederick Douglass* (Hartford, Conn.: Park, 1881), p. 260.

45. For an example of Douglass's attacks on the racist Methodists of New Bedford, see his speech, "The Church Is the Bulwark of Slavery" (May 25, 1842), in Blassingame, ed., *Douglass Papers*, 1: 19.

46. Bercovitch, *American Jeremiad*, pp. 177–78.

47. Henry Louis Gates, Jr., "Binary Oppositions in Chapter One of *The Narrative of the Life of Frederick Douglass, an American Slave, Written by Himself*," in Fisher and Stepto, eds., *Afro-American Literature*, pp. 226–27.

48. Douglass's "Appendix" does question distinctions between Christianity in the South and the North through statements like "I can see no reason, but the most deceitful one, for calling the religion of this land Christianity." In this respect, Douglass was following the Garrisonian line of attacking all northern churches that maintained any sort of denominational "union with slaveholders." However, this hypocrisy of the northern church when linked with the corruption of the southern gave Douglass all the more reason to write as a Jeremiah lamenting the decline of present-day religion when contrasted to its opposite, "Christianity proper."

49. For an earlier discussion of Douglass's use of "language as a weapon," see Stephen Butterfield, *Black Autobiography in America* (Amherst: University of Massachusetts Press, 1974), pp. 65–89.

50. I use the terms *official* and *vernacular* in the way Henry Nash Smith does in *Mark Twain: The Development of a Writer* (Cambridge, Mass.: Harvard University Press, 1962).

51. Douglass's treatment of Thomas Auld occasioned controversy and denials from him and his family about certain allegations in the *Narrative*. Some of those allegations were softened in *My Bondage and My Freedom* and *Life and Times of Frederick Douglass*. See Dickson J. Preston, *Young Frederick Douglass: The Maryland Years* (Baltimore: Johns Hopkins University Press, 1980), pp. 110–11, 165–67, 172–73.

52. Philip Wheelwright, *The Burning Fountain: A Study in the Language of Symbolism*, 2d ed. (Bloomington: Indiana University Press, 1968), pp. 34–45.

53. Benjamin Quarles, *Frederick Douglass* (Washington, D.C.: Associated Publishers, 1948), pp. 55–56.

54. Richard Bridgman, *The Colloquial Style in America* (New York: Oxford University Press, 1966).

55. *Narrative of the Sufferings of Lewis Clarke . . . Dictated By Himself* (Boston: D. H. Ela, 1845), pp. 9–10, 40.

56. See Mark Twain's definition of the pose of the humorous storyteller in "How To Tell A Story," in Charles Neider, ed., *The Complete Essays of Mark Twain* (Garden City, N.Y.: Doubleday, 1963), pp. 155–60; Walter Blair's comment on the mid-nineteenth-century humorist as "simple Hans" in *Native American Humor* (1937; rpt. San Francisco: Chandler, 1960), p. 116; and Lawrence W. Levine, *Black Culture and Black Consciousness* (New York: Oxford University Press, 1977), pp. 121–33.

57. Lydia Maria Child, ed., "Lewis Clarke. Leaves from a Slave's Journal of Life," *National Anti-slavery Standard*, Oct. 20, 1842, p. 77, c. 5.

58. *Narrative of William Hayden* (Cincinnati: the Author, 1846); *The Life and Sufferings of Leonard Black* (New Bedford, Mass.: B. Lindsey, 1847); *Narrative of Henry Watson* (Boston: Bela Marsh, 1848).

59. See *Memoirs of the Life, Religious Experience, Ministerial Travels and Labours of Mrs. Zilpha Elaw* (London: the Author, 1846); *Incidents in the Life of the Rev. J. Asher, Pastor of the Shiloh (Colored) Baptist Church, Philadelphia* (London: Charles Gilpin, 1850); and *A Narrative of the Life and Travels of Mrs. Nancy Prince* (Boston: the Author, 1850). All quotations from Elaw's *Memoirs* are taken from the 1846 edition. For an annotated edition and further analysis of Elaw's work, see William L. Andrews, ed., *Sisters of the Spirit: Three Black Women's Autobiographies of the Nineteenth Century* (Bloomington: Indiana University Press, 1986).

60. *A Journal of the Rev. John Marrant from August the 18th, 1785 to the 16th of March, 1790* (London: the Author, 1790) begins where his dictated *Narrative* of 1785 leaves off, with his ordination in London and immediate removal to Nova Scotia on a preaching mission. Marrant's is the first published ministerial journal in Afro-American autobiography. The *Journal of Daniel Coker, a Descendant of*

Africa (Baltimore: Edward J. Coale, 1820) recounts, with edifying commentary, a trip to Sierra Leone in 1820 for the purposes of African colonization. For a sketch of the life and writings of this important early A.M.E. minister, see Matei Markwei, "The Rev. Daniel Coker of Sierra Leone," in David W. Wills and Richard Newman, eds., *Black Apostles at Home and Abroad* (Boston: G. K. Hall, 1982), pp. 203–10. The *Religious Experience and Journal of Mrs. Jarena Lee* (Philadelphia: the Author, 1849) adds to the 1836 autobiography a journal of preaching activities from approximately 1821 to the early 1840s.

61. Benjamin Quarles, ed., *Narrative of the Life of Frederick Douglass* (Cambridge, Mass.: Belknap Press of Harvard University, 1967), p. xvi.

62. Charles T. Davis stresses the ways in which the narratives of Douglass, Brown, and Bibb are "quite different" from each other in terms of the kind of threat that slavery posed to each man and the possibilities for resistance to it. Douglass stresses the threat of slavery to the evolution of human self-consciousness and the fulfillment of an individual in a community. Brown's view of slavery in the central part of America is uglier than Douglass's; there is no opportunity for self-education, successful defiance, or community, as Douglass pictured them in the Maryland slavocracy. Bibb has even less to say than Brown about "self-realization" for the individual; he stresses the subversion of "domestic virtues" by slavery and the impossibility of protecting the home against it. Davis's useful observations of these differences of subject matter and theme appear in his essay "The Slave Narrative," which appears in his *Black Is the Color of the Cosmos*, ed. Henry Louis Gates, Jr., (New York: Garland, 1982), pp. 89–102.

63. See Douglass's *Narrative* (Baker, ed.), pp. 106–7.

64. See *Narratives of the Sufferings of Lewis and Milton Clarke* (Boston: Bela Marsh, 1846), pp. 119–20; and *Narrative and Writings of Andrew Jackson, of Kentucky* (Syracuse, N.Y.: Daily & Weekly Star Office, 1847), pp. 28–29.

65. See Larry Gara's edition of the 1848 edition of Brown's *Narrative*, pp. 24–25.

66. The pretense of depicting rascally behavior to moralize over it is a convention of the literature of roguery from Elizabethan times forward. See George Sherburn, *The Restoration and the Eighteenth Century*, book 4 of Albert C. Baugh, ed., *A Literary History of England* (New York: Appleton-Century-Crofts, 1948), p. 796.

67. Gara, "Professional Fugitive in the Abolition Movement," p. 49.

68. Levine discusses the animal and the slave as trickster in *Black Culture and Black Consciousness*, pp. 102–33. For a useful collection of animal stories and "Old Marster and John" stories, see Richard M. Dorson, ed., *American Negro Folktales* (Greenwich, Conn.: Fawcett, 1967), pp. 66–171. Simon Suggs's motto appears in Johnson Jones Hooper's *Some Adventures of Captain Simon Suggs* (Philadelphia: Carey & Hart, 1845), p. 8.

69. *Narrative of the Life and Adventures of Henry Bibb* (New York: the Author, 1849), p. 159. Further references to Bibb's *Narrative* will be taken from this edition.

70. Raymond Hedin describes road narratives, in which the act of flight is central, as useful to the ex-slave who wishes to reveal his essential nature "away from

society," where he could "act as unrestrained agent" to his moral vindication or detriment. See "Strategies of Form in the American Slave Narrative," in John Sekora and Darwin T. Turner, eds., *The Art of Slave Narrative* (Macomb: Western Illinois University Press, 1982), pp. 26–27.

71. For more on the extension of the Indian captivity mythology to slave narratives, see Richard Slotkin, *Regeneration through Violence* (Middletown, Conn.: Wesleyan University Press, 1973), pp. 440–44.

72. It is worth noting, however, that according to Douglass's daughter, Rosetta Douglass Sprague, her father had help from his wife-to-be, Anna Murray, before he fled Baltimore for freedom in 1838. As a consequence of a romance that had blossomed between the slave and the free black woman who supported herself as a housekeeper in Baltimore, Anna Murray knit for Frederick the sailor suit that helped him masquerade successfully as a freeman on his way to port in New York. Money from her savings helped pay his fares and subsistence until she reached him in New York City soon after his arrival there. See Sylvia Lyons Render, "Afro-American Women: The Outstanding and the Obscure," *Quarterly Journal of the Library of Congress* 32 (Oct., 1975), 308. I am indebted to Professor Mary Helen Washington for pointing out this article to me.

73. Northrop Frye, *Anatomy of Criticism* (Princeton: Princeton University Press, 1957), pp. 38–39. Douglass would correspond to Frye's characterization of a hero in the "high mimetic mode."

74. Harriet Jacobs, *Incidents in the Life of a Slave Girl* (Boston: the Author, 1861), p. 119.

75. See "Declaration of Sentiments of the American Anti-slavery Society," *Liberator*, Dec. 14, 1833, p. 198, c. 1.

76. Phelps to Torrey, Dec. 10, 1844, as quoted in William H. and Jane H. Pease, eds., *The Antislavery Argument* (New York: Bobbs-Merrill, 1965), pp. lxxv–lxxvi.

77. Garnet published a revised version of his "Address to the Slaves of the United States of America" five years after he first delivered it in Buffalo, N.Y., in a volume with David Walker's *Appeal* and a biographical sketch of Walker that he drew up. J. H. Tobitt of New York printed the volume in 1848. I have used William Loren Katz's reprint of the 1848 edition, *Walker's Appeal in Four Articles and An Address to the Slaves of the United States of America* (New York: Arno, 1969), p. 96.

78. James W. C. Pennington, *The Fugitive Blacksmith*, 2d ed. (London: Charles Gilpin, 1849), p. 74. Further quotations, unless otherwise noted, will be taken from this edition.

79. Pennington's preface to the third edition of *The Fugitive Blacksmith* (London: Charles Gilpin, 1850), p. xviii.

80. Pennington's "object in writing" what he called his "tract" was "to show the reader the hand of God with a slave; and to elicit your sympathy in behalf of the fugitive slave" (56).

81. Albert E. Stone outlines a number of characteristic "occasions" or situations that impinge on twentieth-century American autobiographers in his *Autobio-*

graphical Occasions and Original Acts (Philadelphia: University of Pennsylvania Press, 1982), pp. 19–27.

Chapter 5, The Uses of Marginality, 1850–65

1. Sacvan Bercovitch, *The American Jeremiad* (Madison: University of Wisconsin Press, 1978), pp. 141–51. In this discussion of the Fourth of July address as jeremiad, Bercovitch quotes extensively from William Evans Arthur's Independence Day speech in Covington, Ky., in 1850 as a prime example of the genre. My references to the American as "anointed civilizer" and "Liberty's chosen apostle" are drawn from Bercovitch's quotations from Arthur's *Oration*.

2. Frederick Douglass, "What to the Slave is the Fourth of July?" in John W. Blassingame, ed., *The Frederick Douglass Papers. Series I:* (New Haven: Yale University Press, 1982), 2:360. Further quotations from this speech are taken from this edition.

3. See Herman Melville's "Hawthorne and His Mosses" (first published in *Literary World*, Aug. 17 and 24, 1850) and his letter to Hawthorne, Apr. 16, 1851, as transcribed by Julian Hawthorne. These two pieces are conveniently reprinted in *Moby-Dick*, ed. Harrison Hayford and Hershel Parker (New York: Norton, 1967), pp. 535–56. My discussion of the period from 1850–65 as a renaissance in Afro-American letters draws from my earlier essay, "The 1850s: The First Afro-American Literary Renaissance," in William L. Andrews, ed., *Literary Romanticism in America* (Baton Rouge: Louisiana State University Press, 1981), pp. 38–60.

4. This outline of the major provisions of the Fugitive Slave Act is taken from Leon Litwack's *North of Slavery: The Negro in the Free States, 1790–1860* (Chicago: University of Chicago Press, 1961), pp. 248–49. For further information see Stanley W. Campbell, *The Slave Catchers: Enforcement of the Fugitive Slave Law, 1850–1860* (Chapel Hill: University of North Carolina Press, 1970).

5. The two cases are discussed in greater detail in Jane H. and William H. Pease, *They Who Would Be Free: Blacks' Search for Freedom, 1830–1861* (New York: Atheneum, 1974), pp. 219–25.

6. *Speech of H. Ford Douglass, in reply to Mr. J. M. Langston before the Emigration Convention, at Cleveland, Ohio* (Chicago: W. H. Worrell, 1854), p. 16.

7. Martin R. Delany, *The Condition . . . of the Colored People of the United States* (Philadelphia: the Author, 1852), pp. 14, 27, 192. Garrison's criticism of Delany appeared in "New Publications," *Liberator*, May 7, 1852, p. 74. Delany's reply to Garrison is quoted in Victor Ullman, *Martin R. Delany* (Boston: Beacon, 1971), p. 147.

8. Fred Landon, "The Negro Migration to Canada after the Passing of the Fugitive Slave Act," *Journal of Negro History* 5 (Jan. 1920), 22.

9. Frederick Douglass to William Lloyd Garrison, Jan. 1, 1846, as reprinted in Michael Meyer, ed., *Frederick Douglass: The Narrative and Selected Writings* (New York: Random House, 1984), pp. 231–37.

10. William Wells Brown, *Three Years in Europe* (London: Charles Gilpin, 1852), p. 9.

11. William Wells Brown, *The American Fugitive in Europe. Sketches of Places and People Abroad* (Boston: John P. Jewett, 1854), pp. 303, 314–15.

12. See Samuel Williams, *Four Years in Liberia. A Sketch of the Life of the Rev. Samuel Williams* (Philadelphia: King and Baird, 1857), a defense of Liberia; J. Dennis Harris, *A Summer on the Borders of the Caribbean Sea* (New York: A. B. Burdick, 1860), a positive assessment of the Dominican Republic, Haiti, and British Honduras as black emigration sites; and Robert Campbell, *A Pilgrimage to My Motherland* (New York: Thomas Hamilton, 1861), a narrative of the author's journeys in Central Africa. The anonymously authored *A Colored Man Round the World* (N.p.: the Author, 1858), attributed to David F. Dorr, does not express the anti-American sentiments of emigrationist travel writers and betrays no apparent ideological purpose. Joseph Deane's *Sketch of the Life and Travels of Joseph Deane* (Lancaster, Pa.: Pearsol & Geist, 1857) attempts to capitalize in familiar ways on the author's adventures in Africa and the Far East.

13. Black nationalists and emigrationists were often attacked for furthering the aims of the American Colonization Society, whose desire to repatriate free blacks to Africa or the Caribbean without meddling with slavery seemed a double outrage to the antebellum free black community. For the responses of northern blacks to colonization and emigration schemes, see Litwack, *North of Slavery,* pp. 20–27, 252–62, and 272–78. See also *Proceedings of the Colored National Convention* (Rochester: Frederick Douglass, 1853), p. 8, in Howard Holman Bell, ed., *Minutes of the Proceedings of the National Negro Conventions, 1830–1864* (New York: Arno, 1969).

14. Dred Scott v. Sandford, 19 Howard 393, in Henry Steele Commager, ed., *Documents of American History* (New York: Appleton-Century-Crofts, 1973), pp. 340–42. See Litwack's discussion of the impact of the Dred Scott decision in *North of Slavery,* pp. 59–63. The remarks of Purvis and Remond are quoted in "Spirited Meeting of the Colored Citizens of Philadelphia," *Liberator,* Apr. 10, 1857, p. 59, col. 2–3. Douglass's comments are in his speech, "The Dred Scott Decision," May 11, 1857, in Philip S. Foner, ed., *The Life and Writings of Frederick Douglass* (New York: International Publishers, 1950), 2: 411–12, 415–16.

15. Representative documents from the *Aliened American* can be found in Martin E. Dann, ed., *The Black Press, 1827–1890* (New York: Capricorn, 1971), pp. 50–55.

16. I use the concepts of the *outsider* and the *interstitial* figure as Barbara Babcock-Abrahams outlines them in "'A Tolerated Margin of Mess': The Trickster and His Tales Reconsidered," *Journal of the Folklore Institute* 11, no. 1 (1974), 151. She acknowledges a debt to Victor Turner in the defining of these types of marginality. For a brief survey of outsiders in American autobiography, see William C. Spengemann and L. R. Lundquist, "Autobiography and the American Myth," *American Quarterly* 17 (Fall 1965), 504, 512–14. Quotations of Douglass's appear in Chapter XI of the 1845 *Narrative.* Brief, general comments on the marginality of the slave appear in Nathan Irvin Huggins, *Black Odyssey* (New York: Pantheon, 1977), pp. 114–18.

17. For this law of supplementarity, see Jacques Derrida's discussion in *Of Grammatology*, trans. Gayatri Spivak (Baltimore: Johns Hopkins University Press, 1976), pp. 152–57, where Derrida discusses "The Chain of Supplements."

18. Martin Heidegger, "Building Dwelling Thinking," in *Basic Writings*, ed. David Farrell Krell (New York: Harper & Row, 1977), p. 332. Victor Turner's discussion of "communitas," on which I will draw for my discussion of J. D. Green's narrative in Chapter 6, appears in *The Ritual Process* (Ithaca: Cornell University Press, 1969), pp. 94–130.

19. Arnold van Gennep, *The Rites of Passage*, trans. Monika B. Vizedom and Gabrielle L. Caffee (1909; rpt., Chicago: University of Chicago Press, 1960), pp. 11, 21. See also Victor Turner's "Betwixt and Between: The Liminal Period in *Rites de passage*," in his *The Forest of Symbols* (Ithaca: Cornell University Press, 1967), pp. 93–102.

20. Stowe linked Uncle Tom to Josiah Henson and George Harris to Lewis Clarke and Frederick Douglass in *The Key to Uncle Tom's Cabin* (Boston: J. P. Jewett, 1853). "Uncle Tomitudes," *Putnam's* 1 (Jan. 1853), 97–102, and the London *Times* review of *Uncle Tom's Cabin* (Sept. 3, 1852), 5, are both conveniently reprinted in Elizabeth Ammons, ed., *Critical Essays on Harriet Beecher Stowe* (Boston: G. K. Hall, 1980), pp. 25–42. A brief review of the "anti-Tom" literature of the 1850s appears in Francis Pendleton Gaines, *The Southern Plantation* (New York: Columbia University Press, 1924), pp. 45–49. The ideology of romantic racialism is discussed at length in George M. Fredrickson, *The Black Image in the White Mind* (New York: Harper & Row, 1971), pp. 101–70. Stowe's emigrationist program as part of her implicit notion of black liminality in America is put forward in "Concluding Remarks," the final chapter of *Uncle Tom's Cabin*.

21. Benjamin Quarles, *Frederick Douglass* (Washington, D.C.: Associated Publishers, 1948), p. 123. William Wells Brown to William Lloyd Garrison, June 3, 1853, as quoted in Carter G. Woodson, ed., *The Mind of the Negro as Reflected in Letters Written during the Crisis 1800–1860* (Washington, D.C.: Association for the Study of Negro Life and History, 1926), p. 360. Douglass also published a Virginia slave preacher's narrative, "Uncle Tom Anderson's Conversion and Experience, as Given by Himself," in *Frederick Douglass' Paper*, Feb. 9, 1855, in which a number of the virtues of Stowe's hero are exemplified in an apparently real life figure. The original version of this narrative appeared in 1854 in Virginia from an unacknowledged publisher under the title *Interesting Account of Thomas Anderson, a Slave, "Taken from his Own Lips,"* by a white man, J. P. Clark.

22. See Allen's autobiographical *The American Prejudice Against Color* (London: W. and F. G. Cash, 1853), a variant of the antebellum black "escape narrative," for an account of this sensational affair.

23. Allen's letter of Douglass appeared in *Frederick Douglass' Paper*, May 10, 1852. According to William C. Nell, the same kind of critique of Uncle Tom's "submission to tyranny" was uttered by a black Rhode Island minister during public meetings of the Free Soil party in Boston in December 1852. See Woodson, ed., *Mind of the Negro*, pp. 337–38.

24. See Delany's letters of Apr. 1, Apr. 29, and May 6, 1853, in *Frederick Douglass' Paper*. It is worth noting that while Delany attacked Stowe on a number of

grounds, he left himself open for Douglass's chiding by admitting that he had not actually read *Uncle Tom's Cabin!*

25. See Marion Wilson Starling, *The Slave Narrative: Its Place in American History* (Boston: G. K. Hall, 1981), pp. 171–72.

26. Reviews of *Twelve Years a Slave* are discussed in Sue Eakin and Joseph Logsdon's carefully edited reprint of *Twelve Years a Slave* (Baton Rouge: Louisiana State University Press, 1968), pp. xii, xiv. Further quotations from *Twelve Years a Slave* are taken from this edition.

27. Stowe, *Key to Uncle Tom's Cabin*, pp. 342, 1.

28. Ibid., p. 1.

29. L. A. Chamerovzow, ed., *Slave Life in Georgia* (London: the Editor, 1855), pp. 88, 48. For a useful modern annotated edition of this book, see F. N. Boney, ed., *Slave Life in Georgia* (Savannah: Beehive Press, 1972).

30. William Craft, *Running a Thousand Miles for Freedom* (London: William Tweedie, 1860), pp. 2–4.

31. *Life and Narrative of William J. Anderson* (Chicago: Daily Tribune, 1857); *Louisa Picquet, the Octoroon*, ed. Hiram Mattison (New York: H. Mattison, 1861).

32. See the chapter on "The Uses of Violence—The Rhetoric of the 1850s" in Pease and Pease, *They Who Would Be Free*, pp. 233–50. Samuel Ringgold Ward, *Autobiography of a Fugitive Negro* (London: John Snow, 1855), pp. 28–29. Martin R. Delany, *Blake, or The Huts of America*, ed. Floyd J. Miller (Boston: Beacon, 1970), p. 290.

33. *The Narrative of James Roberts* was dictated to an unknown black amanuensis in Chicago, where it was printed for Roberts's benefit in 1858. I quote from a 1945 reprint of the narrative, published by the Book Farm of Hattiesburg, Miss. Several of Roberts's claims in his narrative are of questionable historical authenticity. While Jackson did help to recruit two battalions of free black soldiers, who fought bravely in the decisive battle for New Orleans on Jan. 8, 1815, there is no official evidence that slaves were armed for such duty. Nevertheless, James Thomas echoes Roberts's accusation against Jackson in Loren Schweninger, ed., *From Tennessee Slave to St. Louis Entrepreneur: The Autobiography of James Thomas* (Columbia: University of Missouri Press, 1984), p. 69. The free black volunteers received, as Jackson promised, the same pay as white soldiers who fought in the Battle of New Orleans, but federal pensions and other bounties promised the black veterans of New Orleans were "endlessly delayed." See Jack D. Foner, *Blacks and the Military in American History* (New York: Praeger, 1974), pp. 24–25. For a military history of the nineteenth-century Afro-American from a black point of view, see Joseph T. Wilson's *The Black Phalanx* (Hartford, Conn.: American Publishing, 1890). Wilson notes that in New York slaves were allowed to enlist in the U.S. Army during the War of 1812 and were promised their freedom upon expiration of their service.

34. Frederick Douglass, *My Bondage and My Freedom* (New York and Auburn: Miller, Orton & Mulligan, 1855), p. 191. Douglass's *The Heroic Slave* first appeared in *Frederick Douglass' Paper*, Mar. 4–25, 1853. I quote from Ronald Takaki, ed., *Violence in the Black Imagination* (New York: Capricorn, 1972), p. 75.

A useful discussion of Douglass's novella is Robert B. Stepto's "Storytelling in Early Afro-American Fiction: Frederick Douglass' 'The Heroic Slave,'" *Georgia Review* 36 (Summer 1982), 355–68.

35. See James McPherson's discussion of works like Theodore Tilton's speech, "The Negro" (1863), in "A Brief for Equality: The Abolitionist Reply to the Racist Myth, 1860–1865," in Martin Duberman, ed., *The Antislavery Vanguard* (Princeton: Princeton University Press, 1965), pp. 162–66. Austin Steward, *Twenty-two Years a Slave and Forty Years a Freeman*, ed. Jane H. and William H. Pease (1857; rpt. Reading, Mass.: Addison-Wesley, 1969). p. 198.

36. William Parker, "The Freedman's Story," *Atlantic Monthly* 17 (Mar. 1866), 290. "The Freedman's Story" was serialized in two issues of the *Atlantic* beginning in February 1866. In his book *Resistance at Christiana* (New York: Thomas Y. Cromwell, 1974), Jonathan Katz argues that Parker's narrative "was composed with the aid of four black men" in the office of the Chatham, Canada, *Provincial Freeman* beginning in March 1858 (p. 285). Katz offers a detailed account of what some have regarded as a harbinger of the Civil War second only in importance to the John Brown raid on Harpers Ferry.

37. William Wells Brown, *A Lecture Delivered Before the Female Anti-Slavery Society of Salem* (Boston: Massachusetts Anti-slavery Society, 1847), p. 5.

38. Ward, *Autobiography of a Fugitive Negro*, pp. 39, 63, 128–29.

39. Levin Tilmon, *A Brief Miscellaneous Narrative of the More Early Part of the Life of L. Tilmon* (Jersey City: W. W. & L. A. Pratt, 1853), p. 2. See also the preface to Anderson's *Life and Narrative*.

40. Steward, *Twenty-two Years a Slave*, pp. 77, 106–12, 102–3; James Watkins, *Struggles for Freedom* (Manchester, England: the Author, 1860); Douglass, *My Bondage and My Freedom*, pp. 368–73.

41. *Narrative of Thomas Smallwood (Coloured Man)* (Toronto: James Stephens, 1851), p. 45; Douglass, *My Bondage and My Freedom*, pp. 395–98.

42. "Self-Elevation—Rev. S. R. Ward," *Frederick Douglass' Paper*, Apr. 13, 1855, as reprinted in Foner, ed., *Life and Writings*, 2: 360. Ward's endorsement of the self-help philosophy appeared in this same issue of *Frederick Douglass' Paper*. See also Delany's *Condition of the Colored People*, pp. 45–46, and Steward's *Twenty-two Years a Slave*, p. 199.

43. Douglass, *My Bondage and My Freedom*, pp. 405–6, and "Self-Elevation—Rev. S. R. Ward," p. 361. At the time of the writing of his "Self-Elevation" article, Douglass knew that Ward, who considered himself a Canadian citizen by virtue of his residence in Toronto, had been lecturing and fund-raising in England, Scotland, and Wales for the past two years. Garnet had been a Presbyterian minister in Jamaica since 1853, and Crummell, who had been preaching and studying in England from 1848 to 1853, had become an Episcopal missionary to Liberia.

44. See Douglass's letter to Garrison in *My Bondage and My Freedom*, p. 372; Brown's *American Fugitive in Europe*, p. 40; [Samuel A. Eliot, ed.], *Truth Stranger than Fiction: Father Henson's Story of His Own Life* (Boston: John P. Jewett, 1858), chaps. XX–XXIII; and William G. Allen to William Lloyd Garrison, June 20, 1853, as reprinted in *Liberator* (July 22, 1853), 116.

45. Ward, *Autobiography of a Fugitive Negro*, pp. 236–37; Watkins, *Narrative*,

pp. 42–44. The original edition of Watkins's autobiography was *Narrative of the Life of James Watkins* (Bolton, England: Kenyon and Abbatt, 1852), dictated to an English abolitionist. In this first installment of Watkins's story, the "leprosy" of English racism is only briefly mentioned and is attributed to Liverpool's frequent contact with American sailors. Eight years later, when Watkins authored his own autobiography, he was much more plainspoken about these matters.

46. See Ward's chapter on "Pro-Slavery Men in England" in his *Autobiography of a Fugitive Negro*, pp. 256–88. Further references to Ward's autobiography are taken from the 1855 London edition. The episode in which Brown meets the fugitive slave in London appears in letter IX of *Three Years in Europe* and chap. IX of *American Fugitive in Europe*. Brown's letter, "Don't Come to England," appeared first in *Frederick Douglass' Paper* and was reprinted in the *Liberator*, July 25, 1851, p. 118. See also Brown's letter "Fugitive Slaves in England," *Frederick Douglass' Paper*, July 24, 1851, in which he estimates that there were roughly 30,000 fugitive slaves in England, the majority of whom were unemployed and without decent prospects.

47. Ward, *Autobiography of a Fugitive Negro*, pp. 39–40, 143, 150. Ward's view of aristocracy is further explored in R. J. M. Blackett, *Building an Antislavery Wall: Black Americans in the Atlantic Abolitionist Movement, 1830–1860* (Baton Rouge: Louisiana State University Press, 1983), p. 152.

48. Ward, *Autobiography of a Fugitive Negro*, pp. 40, 231–33. For further information on Ward's life and work, see Ronald K. Burke, "Samuel Ringgold Ward: Christian Abolitionist" (Ph.D. diss., Syracuse University, 1975).

49. The strongest link in the economic chain that bound English capitalists to American slaveholding interests was, of course, cotton. No doubt informed blacks in England like Ward were aware that in the early 1850s virtually all of the usable raw cotton that textile manufacturers imported into Britain came from the American South. See Allan Nevins, *Ordeal of the Union* (New York: Charles Scribner's, 1947), 1:466.

50. See "Apology," *Anglo-African Magazine* 1 (Jan. 1859), 4, and "A Word to Our People," ibid., 1 (Sept. 1859), 296–98.

51. The exchange on Haiti appeared in the *Weekly Anglo-African*, Jan. 12, May 11, 1861 as quoted in Dann, ed., *Black Press*, pp. 263–68. See also Steward, *Twenty-two Years a Slave*, p. 199.

52. Ward's discussion of this process of development from slave to fugitive to freeman appears on pp. 157–66 of his autobiography.

53. Turner, *Ritual Process*, p. 103.

54. James W. C. Pennington, *The Fugitive Blacksmith* (London: Charles Gilpin, 1849), pp. 56–57. For a portrait of another freeman whose "superior faculties" were "prostituted by the sensuality imposed by Slavery," see the image of Israel Lewis set forth in Steward, *Twenty-two Years a Slave*, pp. 172–74.

Chapter 6, Culmination of a Century

1. *Narrative of the Life of J. D. Green, a Runaway Slave, from Kentucky* (Huddersfield, England: Henry Fielding, 1864). The title page of this edition is printed

"Eighth Thousand." Further quotations from Green's narrative will be taken from this edition.

2. Raymond Hedin, "The American Slave Narrative: The Justification of the Picaro," *American Literature* 53 (Jan. 1982), 630–45.

3. Barbara Babcock-Abrahams, "'A Tolerated Margin of Mess': The Trickster and His Tales Reconsidered," *Journal of the Folklore Institute* 11, no. 1 (1974), 159–60, provides a detailed characterization of the trickster proper. On p. 161 of her essay she acknowledges her debt to Mikhail Bakhtin and Julia Kristeva for her application of the idea of dialogic phenomena to tricksters and their stories. In his extensive discussion of Èsù-Elégbára, the divine trickster of Yoruba mythology, Henry Louis Gates, Jr., explains the many ways in which this ancestor of the protean trickster figure of Afro-American cultures serves as a mediator, though never a resolver, of oppositions. See the opening chapter of *The Signifying Monkey* (New York: Oxford University Press, 1988).

4. See Daryl Dance, "Wit and Humor in the Slave Narrative," *Journal of Afro-American Issues* 5 (Spring 1977), 125–34; Albert J. Raboteau, *Slave Religion* (New York: Oxford University Press, 1978), pp. 294–99; John W. Blassingame, *The Slave Community* (New York: Oxford University Press, 1972), pp. 207–11; and Keith Byerman, "We Wear the Mask: Deceit as Theme and Style in Slave Narratives," in John Sekora and Darwin T. Turner, eds., *The Art of Slave Narrative* (Macomb: Western Illinois University Press, 1982), pp. 70–82.

5. See Lawrence W. Levine's discussion of the human and animal trickster traditions in black folklore in *Black Culture and Black Consciousness* (New York: Oxford University Press, 1977), pp. 102–33.

6. Babcock-Abrahams, "'A Tolerated Margin of Mess,'" p. 148.

7. In *My Bondage and My Freedom* (New York and Auburn: Miller, Orton & Mulligan, 1855), Douglass asks his reader to "bear in mind, that, in a slave state, an unsuccessful runaway is not only subjected to cruel torture, and sold away to the far south, but he is frequently execrated by the other slaves," who charge him with "subjecting them to greater vigilance, and imposing greater limitations on their privileges." When a slave is known to have escaped, all his fellows are regarded with suspicion, and "they are sometimes even tortured, to make them disclose what they are suspected of knowing of such escape" (p. 288).

8. Victor Turner, *Dramas, Fields, and Metaphors: Symbolic Action in Human Society* (Ithaca: Cornell University Press, 1974), pp. 46–47, 49; and Turner, *The Ritual Process* (Ithaca: Cornell University Press, 1969), p. 177.

9. William Craft, *Running a Thousand Miles for Freedom* (London: William Tweedie, 1860), p. 35.

10. Douglass's convictions about the value of a black-run newspaper are quoted from *My Bondage and My Freedom*, p. 389. Further quotations from *My Bondage and My Freedom* in this discussion are taken from the 1855 edition published by Miller, Orton & Mulligan. This brief account of the split between Douglass and Garrison is taken from Benjamin Quarles's "The Breach between Douglass and Garrison," *Journal of Negro History* 23 (Apr. 1938), 144–54; Waldo E. Martin's *The Mind of Frederick Douglass* (Chapel Hill: University of North Carolina Press, 1984), pp. 25–48; and Philip S. Foner, ed., *The Life and*

Writings of Frederick Douglass (New York: International Publishers, 1950), 2:48–66. Douglass's alliance to Gerritt Smith is proclaimed in the effusive dedication of *My Bondage and My Freedom* to the Liberty party leader.

11. For Douglass's views on economic self-dependence, see his editorials, "Learn Trades or Starve" and "A Few Words More about Learning Trades," in Foner, ed., *Life and Writings of Frederick Douglass*, 2:223–25, 236–38. See also *Life and Times of Frederick Douglass* (Boston: DeWolfe, Fiske, 1892), pp. 353–59. My quotations from Douglass's advice to blacks and criticism of the Garrisonians are taken from "Prejudice Against Color" (*North Star*, June 13, 1850), Douglass to Charles Sumner (Sept. 2, 1852), and "Self-Elevation—Rev. S. R. Ward (*Frederick Douglass' Paper*, Apr. 13, 1855), as reprinted in Foner, ed., *Life and Writings of Frederick Douglass*, 2:129, 210, and 359–62.

12. See Robert B. Stepto, *From behind the Veil: A Study of Afro-American Narrative* (Urbana: University of Illinois Press, 1979), p. 18. In chap. II of the *Narrative* Douglass compares plantation slaves competing for the opportunity to run errands on the Great House Farm to "the slaves of the political parties" who compete for election to Congress. In 1855, no longer a Garrisonian scornful of political effort, Douglass dropped the analogy. For a discussion of the relationship of James McCune Smith to the Garrisonians, see Jane H. and William H. Pease, *They Who Would Be Free: Blacks' Search for Freedom, 1830–1861* (New York: Atheneum, 1974), pp. 90–93.

13. *My Bondage and My Freedom*, p. 191.

14. For further information on Betsey and Isaac Baily, see Dickson J. Preston, *Young Frederick Douglass: The Maryland Years* (Baltimore: Johns Hopkins University Press, 1980), pp. 3–21.

15. Houston A. Baker, Jr., *The Journey Back: Issues in Black Literature and Criticism* (Chicago: University of Chicago Press, 1980), pp. 1, 19–21. In the only extensive reading of *My Bondage and My Freedom* to date, Peter Walker stresses "a divided, conflict-torn Frederick Douglass" emerging from his second autobiography, but his interpretation of the psychological source of this conflict—namely, Douglass's "hopeless secret desire to be white"—reduces the man to just another version of the nineteenth-century "tragic mulatto," a reading that seems to me quite inadequate. We are in general agreement, however, that in the author's successive autobiographies "the past became the mirror of Douglass' ongoing life, reflecting his contact with the world which necessitated his re-definitions of self and the unfolding of self-consciousness," and which produced a "more revealing autobiography." See Peter Walker, *Moral Choices: Memory, Desire, and Imagination in Nineteenth-Century American Abolition* (Baton Rouge: Louisiana State University Press, 1978), pp. 228, 247.

16. Eugene D. Genovese, *Roll, Jordan, Roll: The World the Slaves Made* (New York: Random House, 1974), p. 5.

17. See Douglass's comments on the "black aristocracy on Col. Lloyd's plantation" in general and on the fate of William Wilks in particular in *My Bondage and My Freedom*, pp. 109–10 and 115–16. Even an ordinary field hand with sufficient boldness to appeal directly to his master with "a well-founded complaint against an overseer, though he may be repulsed" and even beaten for his temerity,

will "generally" be "vindicated by the relaxed rigor of the overseer's treatment" (83–84). This is an illustration of the way in which even the least favored slave in the plantation hierarchy might, in Genovese's terms, turn the doctrine of "paternalistic dependency" into an informal "doctrine of reciprocity." Genovese, *Roll, Jordan, Roll*, pp. 89–91, 146–47.

18. For the role of patriarchal honor in master-slave relationships, see Bertram Wyatt-Brown, *Southern Honor* (New York: Oxford University Press, 1982), pp. 362–65. See also Genovese, *Roll, Jordan, Roll*, p. 91.

19. Genovese comments on the idea among some slaves of God as "de Big Massa" in *Roll, Jordan, Roll*, p. 167. For an outline of the slavocracy's interpretations of the slaves' religious obligations to their masters and to God, see William Sumner Jenkins, *Pro-Slavery Thought in the Old South* (Chapel Hill: University of North Carolina Press, 1935), pp. 13–22, 207–15; and Donald G. Mathews, *Religion in the Old South* (Chicago: University of Chicago Press, 1977), pp. 142–45. In *My Bondage and My Freedom*, p. 159, Douglass states, "I have met many religious colored people, at the south, who are under the delusion that God requires them to submit to slavery, and to wear their chains with meekness and humility."

20. Auld's piety, according to Douglass, was consistent with Edward Covey's in the sense that for both, "religion was a thing altogether apart from . . . worldly concerns." But as Howard Thurman has noted in *Negro Slave Songs in the United States* (Ithaca: Cornell University Press, 1953), pp. 71–72, a rigid cleavage between the sacred and the secular was unacceptable to the slaves' religious conception.

21. For characterization of the Satan principle in Christian thought, see Christopher Nugent, *Masks of Satan* (London: Sheed and Ward, 1983), pp. 4–7, 184–87. See also Jeffrey Burton Russell, *The Devil and Perceptions of Evil from Antiquity to Primitive Christianity* (Ithaca: Cornell University Press, 1977), pp. 32–35, especially on the etymology of the word *devil*.

22. See the quotation from *My Bondage and My Freedom* in note 61.

23. The first half of *Blake; or the Huts of America* was published serially in the *Anglo-African Magazine*, beginning in January 1859; the entirety of the novel appeared serially in the *Weekly Anglo-African*, from Nov. 26, 1861, to late May 1862. The vagueness of the latter date is due to the fact that the final chapters of the novel have not been recovered. See Floyd J. Miller's edition of *Blake* (Boston: Beacon, 1970).

24. Shelley pays tribute to Prometheus and notes his reservations about Satan in the preface to *Prometheus Unbound* (1820). My quotation from *Prometheus Bound* is taken from *The Complete Greek Tragedies*, ed. David Grene and Richmond Lattimore, trans. David Grene (Chicago: University of Chicago Press, 1959), p. 347.

25. Harold Bloom, *The Ringers in the Tower* (Chicago: University of Chicago Press, 1971), p. 120.

26. In this interpretation Sandy Jenkins parallels Judas as betrayer of the Savior. It is also interesting to read in the context of the Prometheus myth Jenkins's foreboding dream of Douglass "in the claws of a huge bird" surrounded by other birds all pecking at him and threatening his eyes, since in this dream the tragic

outcome of Douglass's rebellious act earns him a punishment reminiscent of Prometheus's.

27. Genovese, *Roll, Jordan, Roll*, pp. 252–55.

28. Joseph Campbell reminds us that both the devil and Prometheus as light-stealer and defier of Zeus represent sublimations of the trickster, "the chief mythological character of the paleolithic world of story." *The Masks of God: Primitive Mythology* (New York: Penguin, 1978), pp. 273–81.

29. For Douglass's role in the A.M.E. Zion Church, see William J. Walls, *The African Methodist Episcopal Zion Church* (Charlotte, N.C.: A.M.E. Zion Publishing House, 1974), pp. 149–53; see also, William L. Andrews, "Frederick Douglass, Preacher," *American Literature* 54 (Dec. 1982), 592–97. Still unclear are the grounds on which Douglass charged the black Zion Methodists of New Bedford with "consent[ing] to the same spirit which held my brethren in chains."

30. Douglass to Sumner, Sept. 2, 1852, in Foner, ed., *Life and Writings of Frederick Douglass*, 2:210.

31. Stepto applies the concepts of *genius loci* and "symbolic geography" to W. E. B. Du Bois's *The Souls of Black Folk* in *From behind the Veil*, pp. 67–71.

32. Garrison defended the purchase of Douglass's freedom in his editorial in the *Liberator*, Mar. 19, 1847.

33. "Farewell Speech of Mr. Frederick Douglass," in John W. Blassingame, ed., *The Frederick Douglass Papers. Series I* (New Haven: Yale University Press, 1982), 2:48–50.

34. In addition to his farewell speech to his British supporters, Douglass also espoused an identity with and a spokesmanship for his enslaved brethren in the "Reply of Frederick Douglass to Dr. Cox," first published in the *National Anti-slavery Standard*, Oct. 15, 1846, and reprinted in Carter G. Woodson, ed., *The Mind of the Negro as Reflected in Letters Written during the Crisis 1800–1860* (Washington, D.C.: Association for the Study of Negro Life and History, 1926), pp. 432–33.

35. "Reply of Frederick Douglass to Dr. Cox," Woodson, ed., *Mind of the Negro*, p. 432. Douglass exemplifies the paternalism of white reformers other than Garrison in a series of anecdotes in *My Bondage and My Freedom*, pp. 398–402. For a thorough discussion of the prejudices and paternalism of white abolitionists toward their black co-workers, see Jane H. and William H. Pease, "Ends, Means, and Attitudes: Black-White Conflict in the Antislavery Movement," *Civil War History* 18 (June 1972), 117–28. For the attitudes of white abolitionists toward the plight of northern Negroes, see Leon F. Litwack, *North of Slavery: The Negro in the Free States, 1790–1860* (Chicago: University of Chicago Press, 1961), pp. 227–30; and Pease and Pease, *They Who Would Be Free*, pp. 281–85.

36. Stepto, *From behind the Veil*, p. 167.

37. *Incidents in the Life of a Slave Girl*, ed. L. Maria Child (Boston: the Author, 1861), was first published anonymously, introducing its author's name in its preface as "Linda Brent." Further references to *Incidents* will be taken from the first American edition. The best sources of information about Harriet Jacobs, the woman behind the pseudonym, are Jean Fagan Yellin's "*Written By Herself*: Harriet Jacobs' Slave Narrative," *American Literature* 53 (Nov. 1981), 478–86;

and Dorothy Sterling, ed., *We Are Your Sisters: Black Women in the Nineteenth Century* (New York: Norton, 1984), pp. 73–84, 245–48, 402–3. An expanded version of Yellin's essay under the title "Texts and Contexts of Harriet Jacobs' *Incidents in the Life of a Slave Girl: Written by Herself*" appears in Charles T. Davis and Henry Louis Gates, Jr., eds., *The Slave's Narrative: Texts and Contexts* (New York: Oxford University Press, 1985), pp. 262–82.

38. Alice Walker, "In Search of Our Mothers' Gardens," in her *In Search of Our Mothers' Gardens* (San Diego: Harcourt, Brace, and Jovanovitch, 1983), pp. 235–36.

39. A number of biographies of enslaved women in the United States appeared before Jacobs's landmark autobiography. See, for instance, Frances Whipple Greene, *Memoirs of Elleanor Eldridge* (Providence, R.I.: B. T. Albro, 1838); "A Lady of Boston," *Memoir of Mrs. Chloe Spear, a Native of Africa* (Boston: J. Loring, 1832); Margaretta M. Oddell, *Memoir and Poems of Phillis Wheatley* (Boston: G. W. Light, 1834); Benjamin Bussy Thatcher, *Memoir of Phillis Wheatley, a Native African and a Slave* (Boston: George W. Light, 1834); Mrs. T. C. Upham, *Narrative of Phebe Ann Jacobs* (London: W. & F. G. Cash, 1850); Olive Gilbert, *Narrative of Sojourner Truth, a Northern Slave* (Boston: the Author, 1850); and Isaac Williams, *Aunt Sally: or, The Cross the Way of Freedom* (Cincinnati: American Reform Tract and Book Society, 1858).

40. Frances Foster, "'In Respect to Females. . .': Differences in the Portrayals of Women by Male and Female Narrators," *Black American Literature Forum* 15 (Summer 1981), 66–67.

41. See Brown's *Narrative* (Boston: American Anti-slavery Society, 1847), pp. 49–50; Sue Eakin and Joseph Logsdon, eds., *Twelve Years a Slave* (Baton Rouge: Louisiana State University Press, 1968), pp. 142–43; Craft, *Running a Thousand Miles for Freedom*, pp. 17–22; and *Narrative of the Life of Frederick Douglass*, ed. Houston Baker (New York: Viking Penguin, 1982), pp. 51–52, 104–5. See also *My Bondage and My Freedom*, pp. 92–95, for the tribute to Nelly, the indomitable slave woman; and *The Life of John Thompson, a Fugitive Slave* (Worcester, Mass.: the Author, 1856), pp. 31–34; and *Narratives of the Sufferings of Lewis and Milton Clarke*, ed. J. C. Lovejoy (Boston: Bela Marsh, 1846), pp. 74–75, for similar tributes of these fugitive slaves to their sisters who managed to gain their freedom despite the sexual power their masters exerted over them.

42. Barbara Welter, *Dimity Convictions: The American Woman in the Nineteenth Century* (Athens: Ohio University Press, 1976), pp. 21–28. Welter points out that because the true woman was characterized by submissiveness, it was assumed that she required a protector to support her in her dependence.

43. Harriet Beecher Stowe, *The Key to Uncle Tom's Cabin* (Boston: J. P. Jewett, 1853), p. 333; L. Maria Child, *An Appeal in Favor of That Class of Americans Called Africans* (New York: John S. Taylor, 1836), p. 23. See also Ronald G. Walters's comments on women's antislavery fiction in his *The Antislavery Appeal* (Baltimore: Johns Hopkins University Press, 1976), pp. 106–8.

44. "Speech of James A. Thome, of Kentucky," in Henry B. Stanton, *Debate at the Lane Seminary* (Boston: Garrison and Knapp, 1834), p. 8; C. G. Memminger, *Lecture before the Young Men's Library Association of Augusta, April 10th,*

1851 (Augusta, Ga.: W. S. Jones, 1851), p. 14; Willie Lee Rose, "The Domestication of Domestic Slavery," in her *Slavery and Freedom*, ed. William W. Freehling (New York: Oxford University Press, 1982), pp. 20–21, 28; John Rankin, "Letter XI," in his *Letters on American Slavery* (Boston: Isaac Knapp, 1838), pp. 76–79; and James G. Birney, William Lloyd Garrison, and Angelina and Sarah Grimké as quoted in Walters, *Antislavery Appeal*, pp. 71, 74, 93, 105. The term *Erotic South* is Walters's invention. See his "The Erotic South: Civilization and Sexuality in American Abolitionism," *American Quarterly* 25 (May 1973), 177–201.

45. Robin Winks, ed., *Four Fugitive Slave Narratives* (Reading, Mass.: Addison-Wesley, 1969), p. vi. See *A Narrative of the Adventures and Escape of Moses Roper* (London: Darton, Harvey and Darton, 1838), p. 23; and Baker's edition of Douglass's *Narrative*, p. 105, for these representative reactions of male slaves to the sexual abuse of female slaves.

46. *Louisa Picquet, the Octoroon*, ed. Hiram Mattison (New York: H. Mattison, 1861), pp. 50–51. All further references to *Louisa Picquet* are taken from this edition. Excerpts from this narrative, including the four letters from Elizabeth Ramsey to Louisa Picquet, are reprinted in Bert James Loewenberg and Ruth Bogin, eds., *Black Women in Nineteenth-Century American Life* (University Park: Pennsylvania State University Press, 1976), pp. 54–69. Levi Coffin corroborates the facts of Mattison's account of Picquet's life and adds a few details of his own in his *Reminiscences* (Cincinnati: Robert Blake, 1898), pp. 419–28.

47. For information on the stereotype of the slave woman, see Winthrop D. Jordan, *The White Man's Burden* (New York: Oxford University Press, 1974), pp. 69–79; Erlene Stetson, "Studying Slavery: Some Literary and Pedagogical Considerations on the Black Female Slave," in Gloria T. Hull, Patricia Bell Scott, and Barbara Smith, eds., *But Some of Us Are Brave* (Old Westbury, N.Y.: Feminist Press, 1982), pp. 73–75; Bell Hooks, *Ain't I a Woman: Black Women and Feminism* (Boston: South End Press, 1981), pp. 15–49.

48. Jacobs spoke warmly of Post and Child as "whole-souled" friends in her letter to Post, Oct. 8, [1860?], as quoted in Yellin, "*Written by Herself*," p. 483. My information on the Jacobs-Post-Child relationship is taken from Yellin's article. For further biographical information, see Helene G. Baer, *The Heart Is Like Heaven: The Life of Lydia Maria Child* (Philadelphia: University of Pennsylvania Press, 1964), and Lucy N. Colman, "Amy Post," in her *Reminiscences* (Buffalo, N.Y.: H. L. Green, 1891), pp. 83–86.

49. See Yellin, "*Written by Herself*," pp. 482–86. The most recent scholar to doubt the veracity of Jacobs and Child is Blassingame in *Slave Community*, p. 234.

50. For the feminists' linkage of woman and slave, see Blanche Glassman Hersh, *The Slavery of Sex* (Urbana: University of Illinois Press, 1978), pp. 196–200.

51. Nina Baym discusses the role of the servant in *Woman's Fiction* (Ithaca: Cornell University Press, 1978), pp. 69–70. In his discussion of evasion as a major characteristic of *The Victorian Frame of Mind* (New Haven: Yale University Press, 1957), Walter E. Houghton notes that "for the Victorians, the disagreeable facts" that did not bear public airing "were primarily those of sex. . . . But there

were other facts . . . like the suffering of the poor and the ugliness of human nature, which called for veils and decorative lies, not so much from fear—though that enters in—as from a shallow and insistent optimism" (pp. 413–14). These were certainly the kinds of facts in which Jacobs specialized in *Incidents*.

52. I speak of understanding here according to Paul Ricoeur's sense of the word as a transference of the reader into the psychic life of the narrator. See p. 65 herein.

53. See Annette Niemtzow, "The Problematic of Self in Autobiography: The Example of the Slave Narrative," in Sekora and Turner, eds., *Art of Slave Narrative*, p. 106. Niemtzow analogizes *Incidents* to the domestic novel, a linkage that I will also comment on in the conclusion to this book. However, she confuses the domestic novel and the novel of seduction (with which, I would argue, *Incidents* has few similarities), two genres that, as Baym's *Woman's Fiction* points out (pp. 22–26), did not overlap in American literature. Dr. Flint is not a seducer, nor is the feminist thesis of *Incidents* "lost in the intensity of a seduction romance" (Niemtzow, "Problematic of Self," p. 106).

54. For further information on the "angel-woman" in nineteenth-century American fiction, see Nina Baym, "Portrayal of Women in American Literature, 1790–1870," in Marlene Springer, ed., *What Manner of Woman* (New York: New York University Press, 1977), pp. 228–30.

55. I use *directive* in the same sense as I introduce it on p. 83 herein.

56. Carroll Smith-Rosenberg, "The Female World of Love and Ritual: Relations between Women in Nineteenth-Century America," *Signs* 1 (Autumn 1975), 1–29.

57. Elaine Showalter, "Feminist Criticism in the Wilderness," in Elizabeth Abel, ed., *Writing and Sexual Difference* (Chicago: University of Chicago Press, 1982), pp. 21–22; Nina Auerbach, *Communities of Women: An Idea in Fiction* (Cambridge, Mass.: Harvard University Press, 1978), p. 9. The idea of women as a "muted group" in society is drawn from the work of three social anthropologists, Shirley Ardener, Edwin Ardener, and Judith Okely, all of whom are represented in Shirley Ardener, ed., *Perceiving Women* (London: Malaby, 1975). See Shirley Ardener's introduction, pp. xi–xv; Edwin Ardener's "The 'Problem' Revisited," pp. 19–27; and Okely, "Gypsy Women: Models in Conflict," pp. 58–59, 68–70. Adrienne Rich's axioms appear in her *On Lies, Secrets, and Silence* (New York: Norton, 1979), p. 189.

58. Discreet and discrete stem from Latin *discretus*, past participle of *discernere* (to separate); discretion from *discretio* (separation); and secret from *secretus*, past participle of *secernere* (to put apart or separate).

59. Ellen Moers, *Literary Women* (New York: Doubleday, 1976), pp. 90–112, and Sandra M. Gilbert and Susan Gubar, *The Madwoman in the Attic* (New Haven: Yale University Press, 1979), pp. 84–85.

60. White working-class women employed as nurses and domestics do not feel solidarity with Jacobs, it should be noted, as she points out in chap. XXXV.

61. Sterling points out that in the spring of 1862 Jacobs left Mrs. Bruce to investigate the condition of the black refugees gathering in Washington, D.C. See

Jacobs to William Lloyd Garrison, Aug., 1862, in Sterling, ed., *We Are Your Sisters*, pp. 245–47.

Conclusion, "Free at Last"

1. A survey of the scholarship and criticism devoted to the trickster reveals a consistent theme—the trickster's use of deception to mete out justice on a foolish, stupid, or hypocritical master. The trick is a "metaphor of mastery" for the slave, as Lucinda H. MacKethan has demonstrated in "Metaphors of Mastery in the Slave Narratives," in John Sekora and Darwin T. Turner, eds., *The Art of Slave Narrative* (Macomb: Western Illinois University Press, 1982), pp. 55–69. But mastery through deceit "carries with it no moral opprobrium" because we see it presented over and over in the slave narrative "as a means to a self-determined and culturally-valued end." See Keith Byerman, "Deceit as Theme and Style in Slave Narratives," in ibid., p. 74. Unquestionably Gilbert Osofsky was correct when he wrote in *Puttin' on Ole Massa* (New York: Harper & Row, 1969), p. 24: "For many slaves deception was a socially useful weapon of survival." But what did it mean when the deceptions one employed to survive did not serve a socially useful function? As Lawrence W. Levine has suggested, the human trickster in slave folktales provided a sense of "vicarious triumph" for his oppressed celebrators by engaging in guileful behavior "largely free of ambiguity or tensions" with the slave community's code of values. Critical comparison of tricky slave narrators to such unambiguous folk tricksters is inviting and usually appropriate, but J. D. Green's case demands that we consider what ambiguities and tensions may have been repressed in slave narratives in order to produce the trickster as a simple "rationale for the actions slaves found themselves resorting to." Levine, *Black Culture and Black Consciousness* (New York: Oxford University Press, 1977), pp. 131–32.

2. James Matlack, "The Autobiographies of Frederick Douglass," *Phylon* 40 (Mar. 1979), 15, 24–25. J. Saunders Redding, *To Make a Poet Black* (Chapel Hill: University of North Carolina Press, 1939), p. 38.

3. Stephen Butterfield, *Black Autobiography in America* (Amherst: University of Massachusetts Press, 1974), p. 70; Frances Smith Foster, *Witnessing Slavery: The Development of Ante-bellum Slave Narratives* (Westport, Conn.: Greenwood, 1979), pp. 147–48; and Kenny J. Williams, *They Also Spoke* (Nashville, Tenn.: Townsend, 1970), pp. 97–98, accord a paragraph to *My Bondage and My Freedom*. Philip S. Foner's introduction to the Dover reprint edition of *My Bondage and My Freedom* (1969) is brief and historical in its orientation. Only in William W. Nichols's essay, "Individualism and Autobiographical Art: Frederick Douglass and Henry Thoreau," *CLA Journal* 16 (Dec. 1972), 145–58, is *My Bondage and My Freedom* given anything like a sustained analytic discussion, in this case, by way of comparison to *Walden*.

4. Vernon Loggins, *The Negro Author: His Development in America to 1900* (New York: Columbia University Press, 1931), p. 228; Charles H. Nichols, *Many Thousand Gone* (Leiden: E. J. Brill, 1963), p. xiii.

5. Annette Niemtzow, "The Problematic of Self in Autobiography: The Example of Slave Narrative," in Sekora and Turner, eds., *Art of Slave Narrative*, pp. 104–7; H. Bruce Franklin, *Prison Literature in America* (Westport, Conn.: Lawrence Hill, 1978), p. 26; John W. Blassingame, *The Slave Community* (New York: Oxford University Press, 1972), p. 234; Bert James Loewenberg and Ruth Bogin, eds., *Black Women in Nineteenth-Century American Life* (University Park: Pennsylvania State University Press, 1976); Sharon Harley and Rosalyn Terborg-Penn, eds., *The Afro-American Woman* (Port Washington, N.Y.: Kennikat, 1978); Roseann P. Bell, Bettye J. Parker, and Beverly Guy-Sheftall, eds., *Sturdy Black Bridges* (Garden City, N.Y.: Anchor, 1979), p. 110. Jacobs is also not mentioned in Butterfield's *Black Autobiography*.

6. The quoted terms are Jacques Derrida's and are taken from his discussion of the supplement in *Of Grammatology*, trans. Gayatri Spivak (Baltimore: Johns Hopkins University Press, 1976), pp. 144–45.

7. Marion Wilson Starling, *The Slave Narrative: Its Place in American History* (Boston: G. K. Hall, 1981), p. 209; Foster, *Witnessing Slavery*, p. 148; Jean Fagan Yellin, *The Intricate Knot: Black Figures in American Literature, 1776–1863* (New York: New York University Press, 1972), p. 166; Matlack, "Autobiographies of Douglass," pp. 24–25.

8. Nichols, *Many Thousand Gone*, p. xii.

9. Blassingame's "Critical Essay on Sources" in *Slave Community*, pp. 227–38, outlines and applies these criteria.

10. Foster, *Witnessing Slavery*, pp. 58–59; Erlene Stetson, "Studying Slavery: Some Literary and Pedagogical Considerations on the Black Female Slave," in Gloria T. Hull, Patricia Bell Scott, and Barbara Smith, eds., *But Some of Us Are Brave* (Old Westbury, N.Y.: Feminist Press, 1982), p. 83.

11. M. M. Bakhtin, *The Dialogic Imagination*, trans. Caryl Emerson and Michael Holquist and ed. Michael Holquist (Austin: University of Texas Press, 1981), p. 7.

12. Ibid., pp. 262–63.

13. Ibid., pp. 293–94; 276–77.

14. *Narrative of William W. Brown* (Boston: American Anti-slavery Society, 1847), pp. 64–65.

15. See Claudia Mitchell-Kernan's discussion of signifying as a verbal duel that extends language "to cover a range of meanings and events" outside standard usage. "Signifying," in Alan Dundes, ed., *Mother Wit from the Laughing Barrel* (Englewood Cliffs, N.J.: Prentice-Hall, 1973), pp. 311–14. For an illuminating discussion of the applicability of the act of signifying to the interpretation of Afro-American literature, see Henry Louis Gates, Jr., *The Signifying Monkey* (New York: Oxford University Press, 1985), especially ch. 2, "The Signifying Monkey and the Language of Signifyin(g): Rhetorical Difference and the Orders of Meaning."

16. An excellent example of joking in this form can be found in the verbal trick played by a slave named Pompey on his master in Peter Randolph's *Sketches of Slave Life*, 2d ed. (Boston: the Author, 1855), pp. 64–65. A dialogue of defiance is recorded in *My Bondage and My Freedom* during Douglass's rendition of the af-

termath of his betrayed plot to escape. See the interchange between Henry Harris and the St. Michael's constables, pp. 292–93.

17. *Narrative of the Life of J. D. Green* (Huddersfield, England: Henry Fielding, 1864), pp. 34–35.

18. *Narrative of the Life of Frederick Douglass*, ed. Benjamin Quarles (Cambridge, Mass.: Belknap Press of Harvard University, 1960), p. xvi.

19. Harriet Jacobs, *Incidents in the Life of a Slave Girl*, ed. L. Maria Child (Boston: the Author, 1861), p. 61.

20. On Sept. 3, 1849, Douglass sent a letter to Thomas Auld, which he reprinted in the *North Star* on Sept. 7 under the title "To Captain Thomas Auld, Formerly My Master." In this letter Douglass congratulates Auld for having "ceased to be a slaveholder." Having learned from an undisclosed source that Auld had emancipated his slaves and had taken the infirm Betsey Baily into his home, Douglass stated, "I shall no longer regard you as an enemy of freedom, nor of myself—but shall hail you as a friend of both." Despite this promise, Douglass did not greatly soften his attack on Auld when he wrote *My Bondage and My Freedom*, nor did he mention in that book that his former master had "ceased to be a slaveholder." He did, however, truncate the passage from the *Narrative* that forecasts his grandmother's death so that *My Bondage and My Freedom* does not claim, as the *Narrative* had: "She [Betsey Baily] stands—she sits—she staggers— she falls—she groans—she dies—and there are none of her children or grandchildren present, to wipe from her wrinkled brow the cold sweat of death, or to place beneath the sod her fallen remains." Compare the *Narrative*, ed. Houston Baker (New York: Viking Penguin, 1982), pp. 91–93, to *My Bondage and My Freedom*, pp. 179–81. See also Dickson J. Preston, *Young Frederick Douglass: The Maryland Years* (Baltimore: Johns Hopkins University Press, 1980), pp. 166– 68, for further information about the Douglass-Auld relationship after the slave's escape to the North.

21. Douglass's *Narrative*, pp. 112–13.

22. I use the term *assertive* as descriptive of a certain class of speech acts on p. 82 herein.

23. The following discussion of *My Bondage and My Freedom* will be based on passages in the 1855 edition, pp. 242–46.

24. Richard Bridgman, *The Colloquial Style in America* (New York: Oxford University Press, 1966), pp. 22–23.

25. Bakhtin, *Dialogic Imagination*, p. 39. In "Individualism and Autobiographical Art," William W. Nichols is also struck by a "comic element" in the Covey episode in *My Bondage and My Freedom*, although he finds the source of the humor in a theme of the episode—"the radical alteration of reality which occurs when a slave forcefully asserts his humanity" (p. 153)—not, as I do, in the dialogic retelling of this event.

26. Northrop Frye, *Anatomy of Criticism* (Princeton: Princeton University Press, 1957), pp. 34, 43–45.

27. Bakhtin, *Dialogic Imagination*, pp. 299–300.

28. Bridgman, *Colloquial Style*, p. 9.

29. Henry Nash Smith, *Mark Twain: The Development of a Writer* (New York: Atheneum, 1967), pp. 20–21; Bridgman, *Colloquial Style*, pp. 9–12.

30. George W. Harris collected his antebellum comic dialect sketches in *Sut Lovingood. Yarns Spun by a "Nat'ral Born Durn'd Fool"* (New York: Dick and Fitzgerald, 1867). Johnson Jones Hooper's most important book was *Some Adventures of Captain Simon Suggs, Late of the Tallapoosa Volunteers* (Philadelphia: Carey and Hart, 1845). William T. Porter edited the racy *Spirit of the Times,* a "Chronicle of the Turf, Agriculture, Field, Sports, Literature, and the Stage," from 1831 to 1861. Among its contributors were T. B. Thorpe, W. T. Thompson, Solomon Smith, and Johnson Jones Hooper. For a study of one possible link between Mark Twain and the antebellum black autobiographical tradition, see William L. Andrews's "Mark Twain and James W. C. Pennington: Huckleberry Finn's Smallpox Lie," *Studies in American Fiction* 9 (Spring 1981), 102–12.

31. John Marrant, *The Journal of the Rev. John Marrant* (London: the Author, 1790), p. 66; *My Bondage and My Freedom*, p. 362; *Incidents in the Life of a Slave Girl*, p. 263.

Annotated Bibliography of
Afro-American Autobiography,
1760–1865

The following bibliography is intended to be of service to readers of this book and students of black autobiography in the United States. The former group can find here more complete bibliographical information on texts examined in this book as well as references to the autobiographies that are within the historical purview of this book but were not individually discussed. For the latter group, this bibliography is designed to provide as complete an enumeration as possible of the autobiographical books in English produced by black Americans from the mid-eighteenth century to the time of Emancipation. In speaking of autobiographical books, I do not mean to imply that this bibliography includes only book-length works, but rather that it is limited to separately published items—works that stand alone between their covers. Thus one may find in this bibliography individual autobiographical works of varying length, from one-page broadsides to multivolume memoirs, but no autobiographical writings published only as introductions or appendices to books, no collections of letters, and no reminiscences or interviews published in periodicals, except for the lengthy and historically important "The Freedman's Story," which appeared in the *Atlantic Monthly* in February and March 1866.

Some titles that regularly appear in bibliographies of slave narratives will not be found in this list because many texts traditionally listed as slave autobiographies are not first-person accounts but are instead biographies, often authored by white people. The "Annotated Bibliography of Afro-American Biography, 1760–1865," which follows this bibliography lists over fifty biographies of black people published during the antebellum and Civil War era. In an attempt to promote greater scholarly discrimination between these two important genres of Afro-American narrative, I have tried to distinguish one type of text from the other and in the first bibliography to present only those texts that are autobiographical.

The conditions under which a number of early black autobiographies were written make the goal of distinguishing between first- and third-person genres especially problematic. The first chapter of this book notes the large number of "dictated," "edited," "corrected," or outright ghostwritten narratives of either unlettered slaves or free black people who, for one reason or another, felt obliged to enter into collaborative relationships with white writers. The arrangement of information in the citations for this bibliography is designed to distinguish between two kinds of editorial roles in the publication of black autobiography. If an editor's name appears first in an entry, this indicates that his or her role was virtually that of ghostwriter. Charles Stearns may have written the *Narrative of Henry Box Brown* from a statement of facts given him by Brown, but there is little in the style or structure of the text to suggest that Stearns tried to communicate Brown's manner of autobiographical narration, only the matter of his recall. Unlike biographies, narratives like Stearns's are written in the first person and often claim, in addition to authenticity, the direct endorsement of the black subject who has not only heard the text read back but has had the opportunity to call for corrections. In sum, there is a special intimacy suggested between the authors and subjects of such ghostwritten texts that invites their listing among the autobiographies in this list, albeit coded for the reader's immediate recognition in the way I have just stated.

A second role that an editor might play in the creation of an antebellum black autobiography was much less intrusive than that of ghostwriter. Editors like Joseph Lovejoy or George Thompson acted as amanuenses for black narrators whose words, the editors stressed in their prefaces, they transcribed as accurately as they could in the autobiographies that came from their pens. Other editors functioned in traditional editorial roles: reading, criticizing, suggesting ways of stylistic or organizational improvement of manuscripts that black narrators had already written. When an editor served in either of these two capacities, I have denoted that supportive relationship to the text of the black narrator's own words by placing the editor's name after the title of the autobiography itself.

Each entry in this bibliography is annotated with the length, in pages, of the narrative portion of the text itself. This can be an aid to readers who desire to examine only works of a certain length; it can also help readers see at a glance which texts may be comparable in terms of length. In those cases in which a text underwent substantive revision from one edition to another, without a change in the title of the text itself, my annotations indicate each edition that marks a substantive revision. In the case of *The Experience of Thomas H. Jones*, for instance, each successive edition of the autobiography before 1865 incorporates substantive revisions. By listing the "2d ed., New York, 1854; 3d ed., Boston, 1862; 4th ed., New Bedford, Mass., 1865" in the annotation for the Jones citation, I indicate this fact. Very popular works, like John Marrant's *Narrative*, that went through numerous reprint editions without substantive revisions are annotated simply with the phrase "numerous reprint editions." Because the fourth edition of Marrant's *Narrative* was enlarged slightly with the addition of several of Marrant's notes, that edition along with its place and date of publication is mentioned in the annotation to the Marrant entry. The place and date of the first foreign editions of a given autobiography are also given, as are the known foreign language translations.

Aaron. *The light and truth of slavery. Aaron's history.* Worcester, Mass.: the Author, 1846 (?). [48 pp.]

Allen, Richard (1760–1831). *The life, experience and gospel labors of the Rt. Rev. Richard Allen to which is annexed the rise and progress of the African Methodist Church in the United States of America.* Philadelphia: Martin and Boden, 1833. [60 pp.]

Allen, William G. *The American prejudice against color. An authentic narrative, showing how easily the nation got into an uproar.* London: W. and F. G. Cash, 1853. [107 pp.]

———. *A short personal narrative, by William G. Allen (colored American).* Dublin: William Curry, 1860. [34 pp.]

Anderson, Osborne P. (1830–71). *A voice from Harper's Ferry.* Ed. Mary Ann Shadd Cary. Boston: the Author, 1861. [72 pp.]

Anderson, Thomas (b. 1785). *Interesting account of Thomas Anderson, a slave, taken from his own lips.* Ed. J. P. Clark. Virginia: n.p., 1854. [12 pp.]

Anderson, William J. (b. 1811). *Life and narrative of William J. Anderson, twenty-four years a slave . . . or, The dark deeds of American slavery revealed. Written by himself.* Chicago: Daily Tribune, 1857. [81 pp.]

Anecdotes and memoirs of William Boen, a coloured man, who lived and died near Mount Holly, New Jersey. To which is added, the testimony of Friends of Mount Holly Monthly Meeting concerning him. Philadelphia: J. Richards, 1834. [18 pp.]

Arthur (1747–68). *The life, and dying speech of Arthur, a Negro man; who was executed at Worcester, October 20th 1768. For a rape committed on the body of one Deborah Metca.* Boston, 1768. [broadside]

Asher, Jeremiah (b. 1812). *Incidents in the life of the Rev. J. Asher, pastor of Shiloh (coloured) Baptist Church, Philadelphia, U.S.* London: C. Gilpin, 1850. [80 pp.]

———. *An autobiography, with details of a visit to England, and some account of the history of the Meeting Street Baptist Church, Providence, R.I., and of the Shiloh Baptist Church, Philadelphia, Pa.* Philadelphia: the Author, 1862. [227 pp.]

Bayley, Solomon. *A narrative of some remarkable incidents, in the life of Solomon Bayley, formerly a slave, in the state of Delaware, North America: written by himself.* 2d ed. London: Harvey and Darton, 1825. [48 pp.]

Bonner, T. D., ed. *The life and adventures of James P. Beckwourth, mountaineer, scout, and pioneer, and chief of the Crow nation of Indians . . . Written from his own dictation.* London: S. Low and Son; New York: Harper, 1856. [537 pp.]

Bibb, Henry (1815–54). *Narrative of the life and adventures of Henry Bibb, an American slave, written by himself.* New York: the Author, 1849. [204 pp.]

Black, Leonard. *The life and sufferings of Leonard Black, a fugitive from slavery. Written by himself.* New Bedford: Benjamin Lindsey, 1847. [61 pp.]

Bristol. *The dying speech of Bristol.* Boston: Edes and Gill, 1763. [Lost item]

Brown, Henry Box (b. 1815). *Narrative of the life of Henry Box Brown, written by himself.* Manchester, [England]: Lee and Glynn, 1851. [61 pp.; 2d ed., Bilston, 1852]

Brown, William Wells (1814–84). *The American fugitive in Europe. Sketches of places and people abroad.* Boston: J. P. Jewett, 1855. [315 pp.]

———. *Narrative of William W. Brown, a fugitive slave. Written by himself.* Boston: American Anti-slavery Society, 1847. [110 pp.; 2d ed., Boston, 1848; 4th ed., Boston, 1849; 1st British ed., London, 1849; Dutch trans., 1850.]

———. *Three years in Europe: or, places I have seen and people I have met.* London: C. Gilpin, 1852. [312 pp.]

Campbell, Israel. *Bond and free: or, yearnings for freedom, from my green briar house. Being the story of my life in bondage, and my life in freedom.* Philadelphia: the Author, 1861. [325 pp.]

Campbell, Robert. *A pilgrimage to my motherland. An account of a journey among the Egbas and Yorubas of Central Africa, in 1859–60.* New York: T. Hamilton; Philadelphia: the Author, 1861. [145 pp.; British ed., London, 1861.]

Chamerovzow, L. A., ed. *Slave life in Georgia: a narrative of the life, sufferings, and escape of John Brown, a fugitive slave, now in England.* London: W. M. Watts, 1855. [250 pp.; German and Dutch trans., 1855.]

Clarke, Lewis Garrard (1815–97). *Narrative of the sufferings of Lewis Clarke, during a captivity of more than twenty-five years, among the Algerines of Kentucky; one of the so called Christian states of North America. Dictated by himself.* Ed. Joseph C. Lovejoy. Boston: D. H. Ela, 1845. [108 pp.]

Clarke, Lewis Garrard, and Milton (1817?-1901). *Narratives of the sufferings of Lewis and Milton Clarke, sons of a soldier of the revolution, during a captivity of more than twenty years among the slaveholders of Kentucky, one of the so called Christian states of North America. Dictated by themselves.* Ed. Joseph C. Lovejoy. Boston: B. Marsh, 1846. [144 pp.; British ed., London, 1846]

Coker, Daniel (1780–1846). *Journal of Daniel Coker, a descendant of Africa, from the time of leaving New York, in the ship Elizabeth, Capt. Sebor, on a voyage for Sherbro, in Africa, in company with three agents, and about ninety persons of colour.* Baltimore: Edward J. Coale, 1820. [52 pp.]

Craft, William. *Running a thousand miles for freedom; or, The escape of William and Ellen Craft from slavery.* London: William Tweedie, 1860. [111 pp.]

Cuffe, Paul. *Narrative of the life and adventures of Paul Cuffe, a Pequot Indian: during thirty years at sea, and in travelling in foreign lands.* Vernon, Conn.: Horace N. Bill, 1839. [21 pp.]

Daggett, David, ed. *Sketches of the life of Joseph Mountain, a Negro who was executed at New-Haven, on the 20th day of October, 1790, for a rape, committed on the 26th day of May last.* New Haven: T. and S. Green, 1790. [19 pp.]

Davis, Noah (b. 1804). *A narrative of the life of Rev. Noah Davis, a coloured man. Written by himself.* Baltimore: J. F. Weishampel, Jr., 1859. [82 pp.; 2d ed., Baltimore, 1866.]

Deane, Joseph (b. 1829). *Sketch of the life and travels of Joseph Deane. Written by himself.* Lancaster, Pa.: Pearsol and Geist, 1857. [35 pp.]

[Dorr, David F.]. *A colored man round the world. By a quadroon.* [Cleveland, Ohio?]: the Author, 1858. [192 pp.]

Douglass, Frederick (1818–95). *Narrative of the life of Frederick Douglass, an American slave. Written by himself.* Boston: American Anti-slavery Society, 1845. [125 pp.; 1st British ed., London, 1845; 1st Irish ed., Dublin, 1845; numerous reprint editions; French trans., 1848.]

————. *My bondage and my freedom.* New York and Auburn: Miller, Orton & Mulligan, 1855. [464 pp.; German trans., 1860.]

Elaw, Zilpha (b. 1790). *Memoirs of the life, religious experience, ministerial travels and labours of Mrs. Zilpha Elaw, an American female of colour. . . . Written by herself.* London: the Author, 1846. [172 pp.]

Elizabeth. *Memoir of Old Elizabeth, a coloured woman.* Philadelphia: David Heston, 1866. [26 pp.]

Equiano, Olaudah (1745?–97). *The interesting narrative of the life of Olaudah Equiano, or Gustavus Vassa, the African. Written by himself.* 2 vols. London: the Author, 1789. [3d ed., London, 1790; 1st U.S. ed., New York, 1791; 1st Irish ed., Dublin, 1792; numerous reprint editions; Dutch trans., 1790; German trans., 1792; Russian trans., 1794.]

Fedric, Francis. *Slave life in Virginia and Kentucky; or, Fifty years of slavery in the southern states of America.* Ed. Rev. Charles Lee. London: Wertheim, Macintosh, and Hunt, 1863. [115 pp.]

Fields, [Cook?]. "Observations" [1847], in Mary J. Bratton, ed., "Fields' Observations: The Slave Narrative of a Nineteenth-Century Virginian." *Virginia Magazine of History and Biography* 88 (Jan. 1980), 79–93.

Fisher, Isaac, ed. *Slavery in the United States: a narrative of the life and adventures of Charles Ball, a black man, who lived forty years in Maryland, South Carolina and Georgia as a slave.* Lewistown, Pa.: J. W. Shugert, 1836. [400 pp.; numerous reprint editions.]

———— *Fifty years in chains; or, The life of an American slave.* New York: H. Dayton, 1858. [430 pp.; 2d ed., Indianapolis, 1859.]

Fortis, Edmund. *Last words and dying speech of Edmund Fortis, a Negro man.* Exeter, Me.: n.p., 1796. [8 pp.]

Fortune. *The dying confession and declaration of Fortune, a Negro man.* Boston: Fowle and Draper, 1762. [only title page survives]

Grandy, Moses (b. 1786?). *Narrative of the life of Moses Grandy; late a slave in the United States of America.* Ed. George Thompson. Boston: O. Johnson, 1844. [45 pp.; 1st British ed., London, 1843.]

Green, Jacob D. (b. 1813). *Narrative of the life of J. D. Green, a runaway slave, from Kentucky, containing an account of his three escapes, in 1839, 1846, and 1848.* Huddersfield, [England]: Henry Fielding, 1864. [43 pp.]

Green, Johnson (1757–86). *The life and confession of Johnson Green, who is to be executed this day, August 17th, 1786, for the atrocious crime of burglary; together with his last and dying words.* Worcester, Mass.: Isaiah Thomas, 1786. [broadside]

Green, William. *Narrative of events in the life of William Green (formerly a slave), written by himself.* Springfield, Mass: L. M. Guernsey, 1853. [23 pp.]

Grimes, William (b. 1784). *Life of William Grimes, the runaway slave. Written by himself.* New York: the Author, 1825. [68 pp.]

———. *Life of William Grimes, the runaway slave, brought down to the present time. Written by himself.* New Haven: the Author, 1855. [93 pp.]

Gronniosaw, James Albert Ukawsaw (b. 1710?). *A narrative of the most remarkable particulars in the life of James Albert Ukawsaw Gronniosaw, an African prince.* Ed. W. Shirley. Bath: S. Hazzard, 1770. [1st U.S. ed., Newport, R.I., 1774, 48 pp.; 1st Irish ed., Dublin, 1790; numerous reprint editions; Celtic trans., 1779.]

Hammon, Briton. *A narrative of the uncommon sufferings, and surprising deliverance of Briton Hammon, a Negro man,—servant to General Winslow, of Marshfield, in New-England; who returned to Boston, after having been absent almost thirteen years.* Boston: Green and Russell, 1760. [14 pp.]

Harris, J. Dennis. *A summer on the borders of the Caribbean Sea.* New York: A. B. Burdick, 1860. [179 pp.]

Hayden, William (b. 1785). *Narrative of William Hayden, containing a faithful account of his travels for a number of years, whilst a slave, in the South. Written by himself.* Cincinnati: the Author, 1846. [156 pp.]

Henson, Josiah (1789–1883). *The life of Josiah Henson, formerly a slave, now an inhabitant of Canada, as narrated by himself.* Ed. Samuel A. Eliot. Boston: A. D. Phelps, 1849. [76 pp.; 1st British ed., London, 1851.]

———. *Truth stranger than fiction. Father Henson's story of his own life.* Ed. Samuel A. Eliot. Boston: J. P. Jewett, 1858. [212 pp.; 1st British ed., London, 1859.]

Jackson, Andrew (b. 1814). *Narrative and writings of Andrew Jackson, of Kentucky; containing an account of his birth, and twenty-six years of his life while a slave; his escape; five years of freedom, together with anecdotes relating to slavery; journal of one year's travels; sketches, etc. Narrated by himself; written by a friend.* Syracuse: Daily and Star Office, 1847. [120 pp.]

Jackson, Mattie J. *The story of Mattie J. Jackson; her parentage—experience of eighteen years in slavery—incidents during the war—her escape from slavery.* Ed. L. S. Thompson. Lawrence, Mass.: Sentinel, 1866. [31 pp.]

Jacobs, Harriet (1815?–97). *Incidents in the life of a slave girl. Written by herself.* Ed. L. Maria Child. Boston: the Author, 1861. [306 pp.]

———. *The deeper wrong: or, Incidents in the life of a slave girl. Written by herself.* Ed. L. Maria Child. London: W. Tweedie, 1862. [306 pp.]

Jea, John. *The life, history, and unparalleled sufferings of John Jea, the African preacher.* Portsea, [England]: the Author, 1811(?). [96 pp.]

Jefferson, Isaac. *Memoirs of a Monticello slave, as dictated to Charles Campbell in the 1840's by Isaac, one of Thomas Jefferson's slaves.* Ed. Rayford W. Logan. Charlottesville: University of Virginia Press, 1951. [36 pp.]

Jeffrey. *Declaration and confession of Jeffrey, a Negro.* Boston: T. Fleet, 1745. [lost item]

Johnstone, Abraham (d. 1797). *The address of Abraham Johnstone, a black man, who was hanged at Woodbury, in the county of Glocester, and state of New Jersey. To which is added his dying confession or declaration, also a copy of a letter to his wife, written the day previous to his execution.* Philadelphia, 1797. [47 pp.]

Jones, Thomas H. *The experience of Thomas H. Jones, who was a slave for forty-three years. Written by a friend, as given to him by Brother Jones.* Boston: Daniel Laing, Jr., 1850. [47 pp.; 2d ed., New York, 1854; 3d ed., Boston, 1862; 4th ed., New Bedford, Mass., 1865.]

Joseph, John. *The life and sufferings of John Joseph, a native of Ashantee, in West Africa: who was stolen from his parents at the age of 3 years, and sold to Mr. Johnstone, a cotton planter in New Orleans, South America.* Wellington, [New Zealand]: the Author, 1848. [8 pp.]

Joyce, John. *Confessions of John Joyce, alias Davis, who was executed on Monday, the 14th of March, 1808. For the murder of Mrs. Sarah Cross; with an address to the public, and people of colour.* Ed. Richard Allen. Philadelphia: Bethel Church, 1808. [18 pp.]

Kelley, Edmond. *A family redeemed from bondage; being Rev. Edmond Kelley, (the author,) his wife, and four children.* New Bedford: the Author, 1851. [72 pp.]

Lane, Lunsford (b. 1803). *The narrative of Lunsford Lane, formerly of Raleigh, N.C., embracing an account of his early life, the redemption by purchase of himself and family from slavery, and his banishment from the place of his birth for the crime of wearing a colored skin.* Boston: J. G. Torrey, 1842. [52 pp.]

Lee, Jarena (b. 1783). *The life and religious experience of Jarena Lee, a coloured lady, giving an account of her call to preach the gospel. Revised and corrected from the original manuscript, written by herself.* Philadelphia: the Author, 1836. [24 pp.]

——. *Religious experience and journal of Mrs. Jarena Lee, giving an account of her call to preach the gospel.* Philadelphia: the Author, 1849. [97 pp.]

McPherson, Christopher (1763?–1817). *A short history of the life of Christopher McPherson, alias Pherson, son of Christ, King of Kings and Lord of Lords.* Richmond, Va.: the Author, 1811. [2d ed., Lynchburg, Va., 1855, 40 pp.]

Marrant, John (1755–91). *A journal of the Rev. John Marrant, from August the 18th, 1785 to the 16th of March 1790. To which are added, two sermons.* London: the Author, 1790. [127 pp.]

——. *A narrative of the Lord's wonderful dealings with John Marrant, a black (now going to preach the gospel in Nova-Scotia) born in New-York, in North-America.* Ed. Rev. W. Aldridge. London: Gilbert and Plummer, 1785. [38 pp.; numerous reprint editions; 4th ed., London, 1785; 1st Irish ed., Dublin, 1790; 1st Canadian ed., Halifax, 1812; Welsh trans., 1818.]

Mars, James (b. 1790). *Life of James Mars, a slave born and sold in Connecticut. Written by himself.* Hartford: Case, Lockwood, 1864. [35 pp.]

Matthias, Peter. *Confession of Peter Matthias, alias Mathews, who was executed*

on *Monday, the 14th of March, 1808. For the murder of Mrs. Sarah Cross.*
Ed. Richard Allen. Philadelphia: Bethel Church, 1818 [18 pp.]

Offley, Greensbury Washington (1808–59). *A narrative of the life and labors of Rev. G. W. Offley, a colored man, and local preacher. Written by himself.* Concord, Conn.: n.p., 1860. [21 pp.]

Parker, Henry. *Autobiography of Henry Parker.* N.p., 186-?. [8 pp.]

Parker, William. "The Freedman's Story. In Two Parts." *Atlantic* 17 (Feb. 1866), 152–66; (Mar. 1866), 276–95.

Pennington, James W. C. (1807–70). *The fugitive blacksmith; or, Events in the history of James W. C. Pennington, pastor of a Presbyterian church, New York, formerly a slave in the state of Maryland, United States.* London: Charles Gilpin, 1849. [87 pp.]

Peterson, Daniel H. (b. 1805?). *The looking glass: being a true report and narrative of the life, travels and labors of the Rev. Daniel H. Peterson, a colored clergyman.* New York: the Author, 1854. [150 pp.]

Piquet, Louisa. *Louisa Picquet, the octoroon: a tale of southern slave life.* Ed. Hiram Mattison. New York: H. Mattison, 1861. [60 pp.]

Plummer, Jonathan, ed. *Dying confession of Pomp, a Negro man who was executed at Ipswich, on the 6th, August 1791 . . . taken from the mouth of the prisoner, by Jonathan Plummer, Jun.* Newburyport, Mass.: Jonathan Plummer, 1795. [broadside]

Potter, Richard J. (b. 1843). *A narrative of the experience, adventures, and escape of Richard J. Potter.* Philadelphia: Collins, 1866. [27 pp.]

Powers, Thomas (1776–96). *The narrative and confession of Thomas Powers, a Negro, formerly of Norwich in Connecticut, who was . . . executed at Haverhill, in the state of New-Hampshire, on the 28th July, 1796, for committing a rape.* Norwich, Conn.: John Trumbull, 1796. [12 pp.]

Prince, Mary. *The history of Mary Prince, a West Indian slave. Related by herself . . . To which is added, the narrative of Asa-Asa, a captured African.* London: F. Westley and A. H. Davis, 1831. [44 pp.]

Prince, Nancy Gardener (b. 1799). *A narrative of the life and travels of Mrs. Nancy Prince.* Boston: the Author, 1850. [87 pp.]

Randolph, Peter. *Sketches of slave life: or, illustrations of the 'peculiar institution.'* Boston: the Author, 1855. [35 pp.; 2d ed., Boston, 1855.]

Roberts, James (b. 1753). *The narrative of James Roberts, soldier in the revolutionary war and at the battle of New Orleans.* Chicago: the Author, 1858. [32 pp.]

Roper, Moses. *A narrative of the adventures and escape of Moses Roper, from American slavery.* London: Darton, Harvey and Darton, 1838. [72 pp.; 1st U.S. ed., Philadelphia, 1838; numerous reprint editions; Celtic trans., 1841.]

Smallwood, Thomas. *A narrative of Thomas Smallwood (coloured man:) giving an account of his birth—the period he was held in slavery—his release—and removal to Canada, etc. Together with an account of the underground railroad. Written by himself.* Toronto: James Stephens, 1851. [63 pp.]

Smith, Stephen (1769?–97). *The life, last words and dying speech of Stephen*

Smith. A black man, who was executed at Boston . . . October 12, 1797 for burglary. Boston, 1797. [broadside]

Smith, Venture (1729–1805). *A narrative of the life and adventures of Venture, a native of Africa: but resident above sixty years in the United States of America. Related by himself.* New London, Conn.: C. Holt, 1798. [32 pp.]

Stearns, Charles, ed. *Narrative of Henry Box Brown, who escaped from slavery enclosed in a box 3 feet long and 2 wide. Written from a statement of facts made by himself.* Boston: Brown and Stearns, 1849. [90 pp.]

Steward, Austin (1793–1860). *Twenty-two years a slave, and forty years a freeman; embracing a correspondence of several years, while president of Wilberforce Colony, London, Canada West.* Rochester, N.Y.: William Alling, 1857. [360 pp.]

Strickland, Simon, ed. *Negro slavery described by a Negro: being the narrative of Ashton Warner, a native of St. Vincent's.* London: S. Maunder, 1831. [50 pp.]

Thompson, John (b. 1812). *The life of John Thompson, a fugitive slave; containing his history of 25 years in bondage, and his providential escape. Written by himself.* Worcester, Mass.: the Author, 1856. [143 pp.]

A thrilling narrative from the lips of the sufferers of the late Detroit riot, March 6, 1863. Detroit: the Author, 1863. [24 pp.]

Tilmon, Levin (1807–63). *A brief miscellaneous narrative of the more early part of the life of L. Tilmon, pastor of a colored Methodist congregational church in the city of New York. Written by himself.* Jersey City: W. W. and L. A. Pratt, 1853. [97 pp.]

Trials and confessions of Madison Henderson, alias Blanchard, Alfred Amos Warrick, James W. Seward, and Charles Brown, murderers of Jesse Baker and Jacob Weaver, as given by themselves. St. Louis: Chambers and Knapp, 1841. [76 pp.]

Trumbull, Henry, ed. *Life and adventures of Robert, the hermit of Massachusetts, who has lived 14 years in a cave, secluded from human society. Comprising, an account of his birth, parentage, sufferings, and providential escape from unjust and cruel bondage in early life—and his reasons for becoming a recluse. Taken from his own mouth.* Providence, R.I.: H. Trumbull, 1829. [36 pp.]

Turner, Nat (1800–1831). *The confessions of Nat Turner, the leader of the late insurrection in Southampton, Va. as fully and voluntarily made to Thomas R. Gray, in the prison where he was confined, and acknowledged by him to be such when read before the court of Southampton.* Ed. Thomas R. Gray. Baltimore: T. R. Gray, 1831. [23 pp.]

Ward, Samuel Ringgold (1817–66?). *Autobiography of a fugitive negro: his anti-slavery labours in the United States, Canada, and England.* London: John Snow, 1855. [412 pp.]

Watkins, James (b. 1823). *Narrative of the life of James Watkins, formerly a "chattel" in Maryland, U.S.* Bolton: Kenyon and Abbatt, 1852. [48 pp.]

———. *Struggles for freedom: or the life of James Watkins, formerly a slave in the U.S.* Manchester, [England]: the Author, 1860. [104 pp.]

Watson, Henry (b. 1813). *Narrative of Henry Watson, a fugitive slave. Written by himself.* Boston: Bela Marsh, 1848. [48 pp.]

Wheeler, Peter (b. 1789). *Chains and freedom: or, The life and adventures of Peter Wheeler, a colored man yet living. A slave in chains, a sailor on the deep, and a sinner at the cross.* Ed. Charles E. Lester. New York: E. S. Arnold, 1838. [260 pp.]

White, George (b. 1764). *A brief account of the life, experiences, travels, and gospel labours of George White, an African: written by himself, and revised by a friend.* New York: John C. Totten, 1810. [60 pp.]

Wilkerson, James. *Wilkerson's history of his travels and labors, in the United States, as a missionary, in particular, that of the Union Seminary, located in Franklin Co., Ohio, since he purchased his liberty in New Orleans, La.* Columbus, Ohio: the Author, 1861. [43 pp.]

Williams, James (b. 1805). *Narrative of James Williams. An American slave; who was for several years a driver on a cotton plantation in Alabama.* Ed. John Greenleaf Whittier. New York: American Anti-slavery Society, 1838. [108 pp.]

Williams, James. *Narrative of the cruel treatment of James Williams, a Negro apprentice in Jamaica.* Ed. Thomas Price. London: John Hadden, 1837. [23 pp.]

Williams, Samuel (b. 1813). *Four years in Liberia. A sketch of the life of the Rev. Samuel Williams.* Philadelphia: King and Baird, 1857. [66 pp.]

Wilson, David, ed. *Twelve years a slave. Narrative of Solomon Northup, a citizen of New-York, kidnapped in Washington City in 1841, and rescued in 1853, from a cotton plantation near the Red River, in Louisiana.* Auburn, N.Y.: Derby and Miller, 1853. [336 pp.; 1st British ed., London, 1853.]

Annotated Bibliography of Afro-American Biography, 1760–1865

Included in this bibliography are individual biographical monographs and pamphlets, books of biographical sketches, historical volumes that contain a significant proportion of biographical narratives, and substantial biographical introductions to editions of authors' works. Eulogies are not listed here because they belong more to the sermonic than to the biographical narrative tradition. Also excluded from this bibliography are various other non-narrative forms, e.g., the commemorative speech, the newspaper, magazine, or journal article, and the obituary, even though they are sometimes used for biographical purposes. My hope is that this bibliography will promote the integration of biography into other studies of the Afro-American prose narrative tradition.

When speaking of the tradition of black American biography, it is important to distinguish among the genre's three subgroups: (1) works by black authors about black subjects, (2) works by whites about blacks, and (3) works by blacks about whites. While I have not always been able to identify the race of the authors of the biographies listed here, I have annotated works from subgroups (2) and (3) to distinguish them from those biographies by and about blacks. Thus white-authored biographies of black people are annotated "WA," and black-authored biographies of white people are annotated "BA." In some cases lengthy book titles have been shortened; only the first editions of works that went through several reprintings are listed. For a listing of Afro-American biography from its beginnings to the Depression, see William L. Andrews, "Annotated Bibliography of Afro-American Biography, 1760–1930," *Resources for American Literary Study*, 12 (Autumn 1982), 119–33.

Adams, H. G., ed. *God's image in ebony: being a series of biographical sketches, facts, anecdotes, etc.* London: Partridge & Oakey, 1854. [WA]

Alexander, William. *Memoir of captain Paul Cuffee, a man of colour*. York,

[England]: W. Alexander, 1811. [WA; life of a black sea captain and coloni-
zationist]

Allen, William G. *Wheatley, Banneker, and Horton.* Boston: Daniel Laing, Jr.,
1849. [edition with biographical introductions]

Allinson, William J. *Memoir of Quamino Buccau, a pious Methodist.* Philadelphia: Henry Longstreth, 1851. [WA; life of a pre-Revolutionary War slave]

Anecdotes, memoirs of William Boen, a coloured man. Philadelphia: Mount
Holly New Jersey Friends Monthly Meeting, 1834.

Armistead, Wilson. *Memoir of Paul Cuffee, a man of colour.* London: E. Fry,
1840. (WA)

————. *A tribute for the Negro.* Manchester and London: W. Irwin, 1848. [bio-
graphical sketches]

Barber, John Warner. *A history of the Amistad captives: being a circumstantial
account of the capture of the Spanish schooner Amistad, by the Africans on
board . . . with biographical sketches of each of the surviving Africans.*
New Haven: E. L. & J. W. Barber, 1840. [WA]

Barrett, Philip. *Gilbert Hunt, the city blacksmith.* Richmond, Va: James Wood-
house, 1859. [WA]

Beard, John R. *Toussaint L'Ouverture.* Boston: J. Redpath, 1863. [WA; life of a
Haitian slave revolutionary]

*Biography of London Ferrill, pastor of the First Baptist Church of Colored Per-
sons, Lexington, Ky.* Lexington, Ky.: A. W. Elder, 1854. [WA; subject was a
former slave from Virginia]

*The black prince, a true story; being an account of the life and death of Nai-
meanna, an African king's son.* Philadelphia: B. & J. Johnson, 1800. [WA]

Bluett, Thomas. *Some memoirs of the life of Job, the son of Solomon the high
priest of Boonda in Africa.* London: Richard Ford, 1734. [WA; life of a kidnapped Muslim merchant, enslaved in Maryland]

Brown, Josephine. *Biography of an American bondman, by his daughter.* Boston: Robert F. Wallcut, 1856. [life of William Wells Brown]

Brown, William Wells. *The black man: his antecedents, his genius, and his
achievements.* New York: T. Hamilton; Boston: R. F. Wallcut, 1863. [biograph-
ical sketches]

"Captain Stuart" [pseud.?]. *Reuben Maddison: a true story.* Birmingham,
[England]: B. Hudson, 1835. [life of an ex-slave]

Cooley, Timothy M. *Sketches of the life and character of the Rev. Lemuel Haynes.*
New York: Harper, 1837. [WA; subject was a black Congregationalist leader]

Cox, Susan H., & Mary L. *Narrative of Dimmock Charlton, a British subject,
taken from the brig "Peacock" by the U.S. sloop "Hornet," enslaved while a
prisoner of war, and retained forty-five years in bondage.* Philadelphia: the
Editors, 1859. [WA]

Dungy, J. A. *A narrative of the Rev. John Dungy, who was born a slave.* Rochester, N.Y.: the Author, 1866. [daughter's tribute to her father]

Edwards, J. Passmore. *Uncle Tom's companions: or, facts stranger than fiction
. . . being startling incidents in the lives of celebrated fugitive slaves.* London: Edwards, 1852. [WA; subjects are Frederick Douglass, Josiah Henson,

Moses Roper, Henry Bibb, William Wells Brown, Henry Highland Garnet, and Peter Wheeler]

Foster, Gustavus L. *Uncle Johnson, the pilgrim of six score years*. Philadelphia: Presbyterian Publication Committee, 186-?. [WA]

Gilbert, Olive. *Narrative of Sojourner Truth, a northern slave*. Boston: the Author, 1850. [WA; subject was an important female abolitionist]

Glorying in tribulation: a brief memoir of Hannah Carson, for thirteen years deprived of the use of all her limbs. Philadelphia: Protestant Episcopal Book Society, 1864.

Green, Augustus R. *The life of the Rev. Dandridge F. Davis of the African Methodist E. Church . . . Also a brief sketch of the life of the Rev. David Conyou of the A.M.E.C., and his ministerial labors*. Pittsburgh: Ohio A.M.E. Conference, 1853.

Greene, Frances Whipple. *Memoirs of Elleanor Eldridge*. Providence, R.I.: B. T. Albro, 1838. [WA; life of a former slave]

Gregoire, Henri. *An enquiry concerning the intellectual and moral faculties, and literature of Negroes; followed with an account of the life and works of fifteen Negroes and mulattoes*. Trans. D. B. Warden. Brooklyn, N.Y.: Thomas Kirk, 1810. [WA]

Gurley, Ralph Randolph. *Life of Jehudi Ashmun, late colonial agent in Liberia . . . With a brief sketch of the life of the Rev. Lott Cary*. Washington: J. C. Dunn, 1835. [WA]

Hawkins, William G. *Lunsford Lane: or, another helper from North Carolina*. Boston: Crosby and Nichols, 1863. [WA; life of a former slave]

The history of Prince Lee Boo, to which is added, the life of Paul Cuffee, a man of colour, also, some account of John Sackhouse, the esquimaux. Dublin: J. Jones, 1822. [Cuffee section, pp. 147–68]

Hopper, Isaac T. *Narrative of the life of Thomas Cooper*. New York: Isaac T. Hopper, 1832. [WA; life of a fugitive slave]

Jennings, Paul. *A colored man's reminiscences of James Madison*. Brooklyn, N.Y.: G. C. Beadle, 1865. [BA]

"A Lady of Boston." *Memoir of Mrs. Chloe Spear, a native of Africa*. Boston: J. Loring, 1832. [WA; life of a former slave]

Latrobe, John H. B. *Memoir of Benjamin Banneker*. Baltimore: John D. Toy, 1845. [WA]

Lee, Hannah, *Memoir of Pierre Toussaint, born a slave in St. Domingo*. Boston: Crosby, Nichols, 1853.

Lewis, John W. *The life, labors and travels of Elder Charles Bowles, of the Free Will Baptist denomination*. Watertown, Mass.: Ingals's and Stowell's, 1852.

Lewis, Robert B. *Light and truth, collected from the Bible and ancient and modern history, containing the universal history of the colored and Indian races*. Boston: B. F. Roberts, 1844. [biographical sketches]

The life of Joice Heth, the nurse of Gen. George Washington. (New York: the Authors, 1835). [WA; subject was a former slave claimed to be 161 years of age]

Lockwood, Lewis C. *Mary S. Peake, the colored teacher at Fortress Monroe*. Boston: American Tract Society, 1863. [WA]

Annotated Bibliography of Afro-American Biography

Mitchell, Joseph. *The missionary pioneer, or, a brief memoir of the life, labours, and death of John Steward, (man of colour) founder, under God, of the mission among the Wyandotts at Upper Sandusky, Ohio.* New York: the Author, 1827.

Moore, Samuel. *Biography of Mahommah G. Baquaqua, a native of Zoogoo, in the interior of Africa.* Detroit: George E. Pomeroy, 1854. [WA]

Mott, Abigail, comp. *Biographical sketches and interesting anecdotes of persons of colour.* New York: M. Day, 1826. [WA]

A narrative of "Griswold," the African youth, from the mission school at Cape Palmas. (Boston: the Author, 1845). [WA]

Nell, William Cooper. *The colored patriots of the American revolution.* Boston: Robert F. Wallcut, 1855. [BA; biographical sketches]

Norris, J. Saurin. *A sketch of the life of Benjamin Banneker.* Baltimore: John D. Toy, 1854.

Norris, Robert. *Memoirs of the reign of Bossa Ahadee, King of Dahomy.* London: W. Lowndes, 1789. [WA]

Oddell, Margaretta Matilda. *Memoir and poems of Phillis Wheatley.* Boston: G. W. Light, 1834. [WA]

Offley, G. W. *Sketch of Jane Brown and her two children.* Hartford, Conn.: n.p., 1860. (pp. 22–32 in *Narrative of the life and labors of the Rev. G. W. Offley, a colored man*)

Paul, Susan. *Memoir of James Jackson, the attentive and obedient scholar.* Boston: James Loring, 1835. [WA]

Pennington, James W. C. *A narrative of events of the life of J. H. Banks, an escaped slave.* Liverpool, [England]: M. Rouke, 1861.

Pickard, Kate E. R. *The kidnapped and the ransomed. Being the personal recollections of Peter Still and his wife "Vina," after forty years of slavery.* Syracuse: William T. Hamilton; New York and Auburn: Miller, Orton & Mulligan, 1856. [WA; fictionalized account of a celebrated case]

Purvis, Robert. *Remarks on the life and character of James Forten.* Philadelphia: Merrihew and Thompson, 1842. [life of an early black civil-rights activist]

The Rev. J. W. Loguen as a slave and as a freeman. Syracuse, N. Y.: J. G. K. Truair, 1859.*

Richmond, Legh. *The Negro servant; an authentic and interesting narrative.* Chelsea: Tilling and Hughes, 18—?. [WA]

Simpson, John Hawkins. *Horrors of the Virginia slave trade and of the slave-rearing plantations. The true story of Dinah, an escaped Virginian slave, now in London.* London: A. W. Bennett, 1863. [WA]

Sketch of the life of Thomas Green Bethune (Blind Tom.) Philadelphia: Ledger Book and Job, 1865. [WA; subject was an untaught musical virtuoso]

Smith, James McCune. "Sketch of the Life and Labors of Rev. Henry Highland Garnet," in Henry Highland Garnet, *A memorial discourse . . . delivered in the hall of the House of Representatives, Washington, D.C., on Sabbath, February 12, 1865.* Philadelphia: J. M. Wilson, 1865. [subject was a black abolitionist]

Stevens, Charles Emery. *Anthony Burns: a history*. Boston: John P. Jewett, 1856. [WA; life of a fugitive slave]

Taylor, James B. *Biography of the Elder Lott Carey*. Baltimore: Armstrong & Berry, 1837. [subject was the first American Baptist missionary to Africa]

Thompson, Mary W. *Sketches of the history, character and dying testimony of beneficiaries of the Colored Home in the city of New York*. New York: J. F. Trow, 1851.

Troy, William. *Hair-breadth escapes from slavery to freedom*. Manchester: Guardian, 1861. [BA; biographical sketches]

Twelvetrees, Harper. *The story of the life of John Anderson, the fugitive slave*. London: W. Tweedie, 1863. [WA]

Upham, Mrs. T. C. *Narrative of Phebe Ann Jacobs*. London: W. & F. G. Cash, 1850(?). [WA; tribute to a former slave]

Vale, Gilbert. *Fanaticism: its source and influences, illustrated by the simple narrative of Isabella*. New York: the Author, 1835. [WA; subject is in part the early religious activities of Sojourner Truth]

White, William S. *The African preacher*. Philadelphia: Presbyterian Board of Publication, 1849. [WA; life of "Uncle Jack," an African-born slave preacher in Virginia]

Williams, Isaac. *Aunt Sally: or, the cross the way of freedom*. Cincinnati: American Reform Tract and Book Society, 1858. [author's tribute to his slave-born mother, for young readers]

---

* *The Rev. J. W. Loguen as a Slave and a Freeman* (1859) has been a perplexing and controversial title for bibliographers of Afro-American writing. In her pioneering study *The Slave Narrative*, Marion Wilson Starling calls the book a biography of Loguen. In his equally important edition of *Slave Testimony*, John W. Blassingame argues that the book is Loguen's autobiography. The issue, no doubt, will be impossible to settle authoritatively. There is reason to conclude that while the book represents a reliable account of Loguen's life as a slave and his early years of freedom, Loguen himself did not write it. The book is prefaced by a statement from an anonymous "Editor" who states that he is writing "the Biography" of Loguen. Loguen's role is central, the biographer insists, for "we took the features from him and filled up the picture." But the biographer has not limited himself to Loguen's story; he has supplied "facts, circumstances, and discourse" that were "not connected with Mr. Loguen's experiences with slavery" in order "to connect the real facts of his life" and to "furnish variety for the reader."

Index

Index

Note on the Author

William L. Andrews is professor of English at the University of Wisconsin-Madison. A graduate of Davidson College, he received his M.A. and Ph.D. from the University of North Carolina at Chapel Hill. He is the author of *The Literary Career of Charles W. Chesnutt* and the editor of *Literary Romanticism in America*, *Critical Essays on W. E. B. Du Bois*, and *Sisters of the Spirit: Three Black Women's Autobiographies of the Nineteenth Century.*